I pray that these devotions will motivate more people to be *Ablaze!* and share the Gospel so others may know Jesus as Lord and Savior and inherit the gift of eternal life.

—Dr. Gerald B. Kieschnick
President, The Lutheran Church – Missouri Synod

Steve Carter's heart for mission is apparent in these daily devotions, which are written in a style familiar to readers of the ever-popular *Portals of Prayer.* Each day, these devotions will give a positive reminder that every witness to Jesus is important. And so it will be a positive contribution to *Ablaze!*, the worldwide movement to reach 100 million people with the Gospel by the 500th anniversary of the Reformation in 2017.

—Rev. Dr. Robert M. Roegner
Executive Director, LCMS World Mission

These daily devotions by Dr. Stephen Carter are 365 pilot lights for the *Ablaze!* campaign. Each is a gem in itself: a graphic illustration followed by an application of the biblical text to the lives we live today. Not a word is wasted, not a lesson overlooked as each day is brightened with the light of the Gospel.

—Dr. Paul L. Maier
Professor, Western Michigan University

Ablaze! ©

# Witness to the Light

To my wife, Gail, my son Mark, my daughter Amy who helped type the manuscript, and my daughter Becky whose witness to her Savior in her life and death in 1993 inspired me to write these *Ablaze!* devotions as a *Witness to the Light*.

Inspiring Daily Devotions

# Witness to the Light

Stephen J. Carter

Concordia Publishing House · Saint Louis

Published by Concordia Publishing House
3558 S. Jefferson Avenue
St. Louis, MO 63118-3968
1-800-325-3040 • www.cph.org

Copyright © 2006 Stephen J. Carter

All rights reserved. No part of this publication may be reproduced, stored in a retrieval system, or transmitted, in any form or by any means, electronic, mechanical, photocopying, recording, or otherwise, without the prior written permission of Concordia Publishing House.

Scripture quotations, unless otherwise indicated, are taken from The Holy Bible, English Standard Version, copyright © 2001 by Crossway Bibles, a division of Good News Publishers. Used by permission. All rights reserved.

Scripture quotations marked KJV are from the King James or Authorized Version of the Bible.

Scripture quotations marked NIV are from the HOLY BIBLE, NEW INTERNATIONAL VERSION®. NIV®. Copyright © 1973, 1978, 1984 by International Bible Society. Used by permission of Zondervan Publishing House. All rights reserved.

Hymn texts with the abbreviation *SP* are from *Sing Peace, Sing Gift of Peace: The Comprehensive Hymnary of Jaroslav J. Vajda*, copyright © 2003 by Concordia Publishing House. All rights reserved.

Hymn texts with the abbreviation *LW* are from *Lutheran Worship*, copyright © 1982 by Concordia Publishing House. All rights reserved.

Hymn texts with the abbreviation *HS 98* are from *Hymnal Supplement 98*, copyright © 1998 by Concordia Publishing House. All rights reserved.

Hymn texts with the abbreviation *TLH* are from *The Lutheran Hymnal*, copyright © 1941 by Concordia Publishing House. All rights reserved.

Scripture commentary from *Concordia Self-Study Bible*. Copyright © 1986 Concordia Publishing House.

Portions of this book were taken from *Luther's Small Catechism with Explanation*. Copyright © 1991 Concordia Publishing House. All rights reserved.

This publication may be available in braille, in large print, or on cassette tape for the visually impaired. Please allow 8 to 12 weeks for delivery. Write to the Library for the Blind, 7550 Watson Rd., St. Louis, MO 63119-4409; call 1-866-215-6852; or e-mail to blind.mission@blind-mission.org.

Manufactured in the United States of America

Library of Congress Cataloging-in-Publication Data

Carter, Stephen J., 1941-
Witness to the light : inspiring daily devotions / Stephen J. Carter.
p. cm.
ISBN 0-7586-1101-3
1. Devotional calendars. I. Title.
BV4811.C365 2006
242'.2–dc22

2006014383

1 2 3 4 5 6 7 8 9 10 15 14 13 12 11 10 09 08 07 06

## Author's Preface

I have been captured by the *Ablaze!* initiative in our church body to reach 100 million people with the Gospel of Jesus Christ by 2017, the 500th anniversary of the Lutheran Reformation. I am hopeful that this devotional book will contribute one small ingredient for that noble effort by God's grace.

My eyes have been opened to the outreach heartbeat of the Scriptures, summarized in Jesus' words to His disciples in the upper room on Easter Sunday evening, "as the Father has sent Me, even so I am sending you" (John 20:21). I was challenged to include an outreach message in every one of these daily devotions. By the end of my writing, I realized that I had barely scratched the surface of God's inexhaustible love for us in the death and resurrection of His Son, Jesus Christ, expressed through His continual sending of His Church to set the world ablaze with Christ until the Gospel is "proclaimed throughout the whole world as a testimony to all nations, and then the end will come" (Matthew 24:14).

The world around me came alive with the message of sharing Christ crucified: Seabiscuit, the felling of three oaks in our front yard, Busch Stadium in St. Louis, a tsunami and Hurricane Katrina, missionary stories from many countries, the ruins of ancient Corinth and Ephesus, and television series like *Everybody Loves Raymond* and *Town Haul*. But always the Word of Christ speaks to our hearts to bring us to daily repentance and to receive forgiveness at the cross as God's baptized children.

Following the pattern of *My Daily Devotion* (Concordia Publishing House), which I wrote in 1988, this devotional book is guided by the rhythms of the Church Year and often uses as prayers verses from the rich heritage of Christian hymnody. The hymns also remind us that personal and family devotions belong in the context of God's people gathered together around Word and Sacrament. I pray that these daily devotions will point you again to your Savior, Jesus Christ, and fill you with a joyful desire to help set the world ablaze with the Good News of salvation through Him alone.

# Ablaze in the New Year

## *Reading:* John 1:1–8

*Text:* In Him was life, and that life was the light of men. John 1:4

Happy New Year! On this day we begin a year of daily devotions, which we title *Ablaze*. *Ablaze* is a movement within the Lutheran Church to reach 100 million people worldwide with the Gospel of Jesus Christ by 2017, the 500th anniversary of the Lutheran Reformation. *Ablaze* is God at work in our hearts to lead us daily in repentance to the foot of the cross so we may rise with Christ to a life of witness and service. *Ablaze* is God's Church gathered around Word and Sacraments to bear witness to the Light and scattered to share the Light with a world in need of salvation. *Ablaze* is each of us, confessing our sins in the darkness, coming into the light of His forgiveness, and letting our light shine each day so others may believe in Jesus Christ, our Life and our Light.

Simply, John begins his Gospel, "In Him was life, and the life was the light of men." "The Word became flesh and made His dwelling among us. We have seen His glory, the glory of the One and Only, who came from the Father, full of grace and truth" (John 1:14). On this New Year's Day, we recognize that Jesus, through His life, death, and resurrection, brought us from death to life and from darkness to light. He is our Life and our Light. He calls us like John the Baptist to bear witness to that Light so many may believe in Him as their Savior.

On New Year's Day we also observe the circumcision and naming of our Lord as Jesus "because He will save His people from their sins" (Matthew 1:21). That name will set the world ablaze through our witness. Will you lift up His name? Happy New Year!

*Prayer:* Jesus! Name of wondrous love,
Name all other names above,
Unto which must ev'ry knee
Bow in deep humility.

Jesus! Name of priceless worth
To the fallen sons of earth
For the promise that it gave,
"Jesus shall his people save."
*LW* 182:1, 3

January 2

# What a World

## *Reading:* John 1:6–14

*Text:* He was in the world, and though the world was made through Him, the world did not recognize Him. John 1:10

How do we understand this world in which we live—full of bounty and beauty along with the marvels of modern technology on one hand or full of terror, degradation, and unspeakable evil on the other hand? For our own eternal salvation and for our daily witness to the world, we must know.

The next several devotions will focus on the meaning of the word "world" in the Gospel of John to help answer this profound question of our heart so that God can use us on One Mission Ablaze. John seems to use the word "world" in four ways and moves without explanation from one meaning to another. Altogether "world" appears 78 times in John's Gospel and 24 times in his letters. All four meanings are present or implied in John 1:10.

First, "world" refers to the created universe . . . "the world was made through Him." Jesus was there and participated in creation. No wonder our hearts sing for joy at the beauty of this world. Second, "world" describes the human system opposed to God's purposes, led by Satan, the prince of this world. "The world did not recognize Him." No wonder our hearts feel the burden and pain of a sinful world.

Third, "world" includes all people on earth for whom Christ came to give His life on the cross. "He was in the world." "I am the light of the world" (John 8:12). No wonder our hearts find eternal comfort in His redemption. Finally, "world" sometimes separates out from all people those who are opposed to God . . . again "the world did not recognize Him." In His famous high priestly prayer in John 17, Jesus includes the words, "so that the world may believe that You have sent Me" (John 17:21). No wonder our hearts burn within us to share Jesus with those who do not recognize Him as Savior and Lord. What a world indeed!

*Prayer:* Lord, help me to understand the world in which I live so I may believe in You and bear witness. Amen.

# My Father's World

## *Reading:* John 1:1–5

*Text:* And now, Father, glorify Me in Your presence with the glory I had with You before the world began. John 17:5

What do you have in common with every person on the face of the globe—red, yellow, black and white, Asian, African, European, North and South American, Muslim, Hindu, Buddhist, Jew, Christian, and Atheist? You live in the Father's world, created by the one true God, Father, Son, and Holy Spirit.

That's what John communicates when he uses the word "world" in today's text to describe the whole universe as God's creation. "In the beginning was the Word, and the Word was with God, and the Word was God. . . . Through Him all things were made" (John 1:1, 3). Jesus identifies His role in the creation of His Father's world when He prays in John 17, "And now Father, glorify Me in Your presence with the glory I had with You before the world began." Then He heads for Calvary to glorify the Father in His death.

As you seek to carry out One Mission Ablaze worldwide, you can start with a common appreciation of the wonders of creation. Although many, with a false religion or no religion at all, will not recognize or understand the Father's world as you do through faith in Jesus the Savior, you live together with them in the same universe as God's created children. Together with them you see the sunrise and sunset, feel the gentle rain, gather the golden grain, fish the streams, and live in families with shelter and daily bread.

When darkness comes, storms rage, famine spreads, and evil destroys, you reach out to bring light, restore calm, provide shelter and food, and help restore order. You also respect the culture, language, and created gifts of others in the Father's world. And you receive thankfully their hospitality and help.

Admitting our own prejudice, divisiveness, and selfishness, we look to Jesus and seek to let His light of salvation shine in the darkness through us.

*Prayer:* All people that on earth do dwell,
Sing to the Lord with cheerful voice;
Him serve with mirth, his praise forthtell;
Come ye before him and rejoice.
*LW* 435:1

January 4

# Midst Flaming Worlds

***Reading:*** **John 16:7–11**

*Text:* I have given them Your word, and the world has hated them, for they are not of the world any more than I am of the world. John 17:14

Recently my wife, Gail, and I visited the Roman ruins of Pompeii. Through careful reconstruction, the city almost seemed alive again, displaying both its luxury and its sinful lifestyle. But we were also reminded of its fiery destruction as we viewed plaster casts of a man covering his mouth from the ashes, a pregnant woman hiding, and a dog trying to escape the fiery molten lava of the Mt. Vesuvius volcanic eruption in AD 79.

The Father's beautiful world, created to serve and praise Him, has been shattered by the ugliness of sin. Satan, the prince of this world, conspires to destroy God's created world by sowing seeds of disobedience and rebellion. John uses that meaning of "world" to describe the human system opposed to God's purposes. Before we can even hope to set the world ablaze with the Gospel of Jesus Christ, we must come to grips with the reality of a sinful world that hates us as it hates Jesus. Those who reject God's love in Jesus face an eternity in the fires of hell.

We are born into a sinful world. By nature we are the children of wrath even as others. The Holy Spirit, the Counselor, convicts the world of guilt in regard to sin and condemns the prince of the world (John 16:7–11). There is absolutely no room for compromise with the sinful world. Only the death of Jesus on the cross atones for the sins of the world. As His baptized children through faith in His saving Word, we are set free from this sinful world system, led by Satan . . . set free to warn unbelievers of the consequences of their disobedience and to point them to Jesus' blood and righteousness. We are not of the world any more than Jesus is of the world.

*Prayer:* Jesus your blood and righteousness
My beauty are my glorious dress;
Mid flaming worlds in these arrayed
With joy shall I lift up my head.
*LW* 362:1

# A Son for the World

## *Reading:* John 3:16–21

*Text:* May they be brought to complete unity to let the world know that You sent Me and have loved them even as You have loved Me. John 17:23

The Father's beautiful world was created to serve and praise the one true God, Father, Son, and Holy Spirit. Flaming worlds are the result of Satan's rebellion, the fall into sin, and a human world system at enmity with God and His creation. Is there any hope for us in this twenty-first century where we see the effects of the devil, the world, and our sinful flesh upon the nations of the world?

John's simple but powerful words resound through the centuries to bring hope and purpose for life: "For God so loved the world that He gave His only Son, that whoever believes in Him should not perish but have eternal life" (John 3:16). And Jesus adds in His famous prayer, "May they be brought to complete unity to let the world know that You sent Me and have loved them even as You have loved Me."

Jesus came to live a perfect life in our stead and to die on the cross to pay the full punishment for the sins of the whole world. John applies the word "world" to all people on earth . . . including those who are opposed to God and do not now "recognize Him" (John 1:10). And He forms us believers into His Church for the purpose of showing unity so the world will know and believe in Jesus as the One sent by the Father to bring salvation.

What a privilege to help the world know Jesus as Savior! We go on one mission *Ablaze* just because the stakes are so high–life or death, salvation or damnation, light or darkness. We unite in love to lift up God's Son for the world!

*Prayer:* God loved the world so that he gave
His only Son the lost to save
That all who would in him believe
Should everlasting life receive.

Christ Jesus is the ground of faith,
Who was made flesh and suffered death;
All who confide in Christ alone
Are built on this chief cornerstone.
*LW* 352:1–2

# Arise, Shine!

## *Reading:* Isaiah 60:1–12

*Text:* "Arise, shine, for your light has come, and the glory of the LORD rises upon you." Isaiah 60:1

I'll never forget the closing candle ceremony in the Cotton Bowl during Expo '72 in Dallas. Following a stirring message to take the evangelism zeal back home, each of the 85,000 youth and adult counselors in the audience lit a candle. The flames grew until the Texas night was aglow with the light. It was certainly symbolic of the Epiphany message of God to Zion through the prophet Isaiah: What does God want us to do? "Arise, shine!" The words were spoken to Israel in exile, ready to return home.

In Matthew's gospel the Wise Men from the East saw the light of a special star and journeyed to Bethlehem to see the infant King. And the words speak to our hearts as well: "Arise, shine!" Hold up Jesus as the Light of the world for everyone to see.

Why are we to arise and shine? The world lies in darkness. Isaiah goes on: "See, darkness covers the earth, and thick darkness is over the people" (Isaiah 60:2). Israel had lived in the darkness of rebellion and ended up in the darkness of heathen Babylon. Today our world suffers from an energy crisis called sin, which extinguishes all lights.

How can we arise and shine? God has shined in our dark world with the light of His Son Jesus Christ. He brought Israel home to Jerusalem and sent the Messiah in the fullness of time. In the darkness of Good Friday, Jesus, the Light of the world, could not be extinguished. Victorious and risen, He shines brightly as Savior and Lord. His Word illumines us. Drawing upon that unfailing light each day, we let God shine through us with the light of His Son.

*Prayer:* Arise and shine in splendor,
Let night to day surrender:
Your light is drawing near.
Above, the day is beaming,
In matchless beauty gleaming;
The glory of the Lord is here.
*LW* 85:1

# Hearts Ablaze

## *Reading:* Romans 10:8–13

*Text:* Brothers, my heart's desire and prayer to God for the Israelites is that they may be saved. Romans 10:1

A former missionary in West Africa and a member of our congregation recently returned from a trip to Kenya representing the East Africa Mission Society, our partnership with two other local congregations. His moving report to our Sunday morning Bible class revealed a heart ablaze for reaching his brothers and sisters in Africa with the saving Gospel of Jesus Christ. His simple words stirred our hearts. He would love to return to Africa with his family if that were possible.

His passion reminded me of the words of St. Paul to the Christians in Rome: "Brothers, my heart's desire and prayer to God for the Israelites is that they may be saved." He cared deeply about his countrymen although many of them had persecuted him and rejected Jesus as the Messiah. His heart for their salvation even led him to write, "I could wish that I myself were cursed and cut off from Christ for the sake of my brothers, those of my own race" (Romans 9:3).

As the apostle to the Gentiles, he adds, "For there is no distinction between Jew and Gentile–the same Lord is Lord of all and richly blesses all who call on him, for 'Everyone who calls on the name of the Lord will be saved'" (Romans 10:12–13).

My missionary friend with a heart for Africa and Paul with a heart ablaze for Jews and Gentiles alike have something in common with you and me. God's Spirit has set our hearts ablaze through the Gospel of Christ. Heartless and rebellious on our own, as was Paul who persecuted Christians before his conversion on the Damascus road, we receive God's life-changing grace through Word and Sacraments: 'The word is near you; it is in your mouth and in your heart,' that is, the word of faith we are proclaiming: That if you confess with your mouth, 'Jesus is Lord,' and believe in your heart that God raised Him from the dead, you will be saved'" (Romans 10:8–9).

*Prayer:* Lord Jesus, set our hearts ablaze to reach the lost. Amen.

January 8

# Benediction for Outreach

## *Reading:* Psalm 67

*Text:* That Your ways may be known on earth, Your salvation among all nations. Psalm 67:2

What happens when you hear the benediction at the end of the church service each week? Are you relieved that the service is finally coming to a close? Are you mentally plotting your way out to avoid congested traffic and get quickly to your car? Has the service been meaningful to you? Do you hear the benediction as God's blessing of peace for your life? Do you keep those words for yourself and lock them in your heart to help you survive the next week? Are they familiar and comforting only for your peace of mind? Or do you hear that familiar benediction as a divine call from God for outreach to the world?

The psalmist begins Psalm 67 with words of benediction: "May God be gracious to us and bless us and make His face shine upon us" (Psalm 67:1). Familiar words of comfort and peace. Ritual words of worship for God's Old Testament people. Words sometimes taken for granted. Words of God's grace. Words of forgiveness through the promised Messiah. Words of hope for sinful hearts, living for themselves, preoccupied with daily survival, but repentant and longing to see the face of the crucified and risen Savior shining upon them.

But then unexpectedly to our ears, the psalmist adds these words, "that Your ways may be known on earth, Your salvation among all nations." Electrifying words of God's purpose for His church in our world. Salvation among all nations through His people. Words of outreach for you and for me, each week as we leave God's house, as we go home, live in the neighborhood, mingle with friends, spend opportune hours at work, and return to worship. Benediction for outreach.

Alerted to our calling from God to help "the nations be glad and sing for joy" (v. 4) as "all the ends of the earth will fear Him" (v. 7), we listen with rapt attention each week to the familiar words of the benediction: "May God be gracious to us and bless us and make His face shine upon us. . . ." Empowering words of benediction for outreach to the world.

*Prayer:* May God be gracious to us and bless us. Amen.

# In the Catacombs: Declaring His Praises

## *Reading:* 1 Peter 2:9–12

*Text:* But you are a chosen people . . . that you may declare the praises of Him who called you out of darkness into His wonderful light. 1 Peter 2:9

On a recent trip to Italy we visited the Catacombs of Saint Sebastian just outside the walls of ancient Rome. Our tour led us deep into the darkness and narrow passages of the catacombs where many early Christians lie buried, some individually and some in family groupings. At one location, we were told that Christians gathered there for worship. There on the wall we saw rough drawings of Jesus and His disciples celebrating the Last Supper and stick figures of sheep and the Good Shepherd.

As we emerged into the light, my heart was stirred by the silent witness of that early community of believers, persecuted for their faith, forced to bury their dead outside the city walls, but by their words and actions "declare the praises of Him who called [them] out of darkness into His wonderful light." In their Baptism they were connected with "the living Stone–rejected by men chosen by God and precious to Him" (1 Peter 2:4), formed as "a chosen people, a royal priesthood, a holy nation, a people belonging to God." "As aliens and strangers in the world" (1 Peter 2:11), they were enabled by God's grace, fortified at the Lord's table, to "live such good lives among the pagans" that their enemies might "see your good deeds and glorify God on the day He visits us" (1 Peter 2:12).

In today's twenty-first century world with its pagan beliefs and lifestyle, we have the privilege of "declare[ing] the praises of Him who called you out of darkness into His wonderful light." As aliens and strangers in the world, sometimes persecuted, often rejected, we are, by virtue of our Baptism into Jesus' death and resurrection, a chosen people belonging to God. By our lives lived in Christian community and our daily witness we can carry out one mission ablaze to the glory of God.

*Prayer:* Dear Father, open our eyes to see the bold witness of the early Christians, and move us to declare Your praises with our daily witness in a pagan world for Jesus' sake. Amen.

January 10

# Out of This World

## *Reading:* Ephesians 1:3–14

*Text:* In Him we were also chosen, having been predestined according to the plan of Him who works out everything in conformity with the purpose of His will, an order that we, who were the first to hope in Christ, might be for the praise of His glory. Ephesians 1:11–12

At a church leaders conference in Houston, we were privileged to visit the Houston Space Center and hear an astronaut describe with pictures his thrilling visit to outer space. As he relived his breathtaking views of earth from that vantage point, he also gave a clear witness of his faith in Jesus Christ as Savior and his firm belief in God's purpose for his life. His space experience was truly out of this world.

When St. Paul opens his letter to the Ephesians, he presents a panoramic view of God's plan for the created world and for us as individuals. "Praise be to the God and Father of our Lord Jesus Christ, who has blessed us in Him in the heavenly realms with every spiritual blessing in Christ" (Ephesians 1:3). Before the creation of the world, we were chosen and predestined to be adopted as His sons, redeemed through Christ's blood, and sealed by the promised Holy Spirit. We participate in His purpose "to bring all things in heaven and on earth together under one head, even Christ" (Ephesians 1:10). We do so by living for "the praise of His glory." Our place in God's plan is truly out of this world.

How will you respond to your breathtaking trip out of this world into the mystery of God's will? You see God's world as He intended it. You see the reality of sin in a fallen world and in your own heart. You see into the very heart of God choosing you, adopting you, redeeming you through the blood of His Son, forgiving your sins, lavishing you with His grace, setting you apart as holy and blameless for His purpose. Like the astronaut, you are changed forever by your new perspective–to witness of His salvation and to live for others according to His purpose with every breath you breathe.

*Prayer:* All glory to our Lord and God
For love so deep, so high, so broad;
The Trinity whom we adore
Forever and forevermore. Amen.
*LW* 275:7

# Bearing Witness to the Lamb

***Reading:* John 1:29–34**

*Text:* "Look, the Lamb of God, who takes away the sin of the world!" John 1:29b

All of us treasure events we have personally witnessed—a presidential inauguration, a World Series, or a Super Bowl game. We freely tell about our experience.

John's gospel records a dramatic moment in history. John the Baptist watches a man walk among the crowds of Israel. It is the long-awaited moment when the Messiah begins His public ministry. John, aware of this decisive moment, bears joyful witness: "Look, the Lamb of God, who takes away the sin of the world!" The phrase "Lamb of God" may have sprung from a recollection of Isaiah 53, where the Messiah is described as a lamb led to the slaughter. Clearly John labels Jesus as the Savior of the world.

We also need to bear witness. Each of us has seen the Lamb of God, crucified and risen, in the pages of Holy Scripture. By our lives of service and our words of witness we can say to others, "Look, the Lamb of God!" Yet we often fail. Our witness fades when the going gets rough. Sometimes it loses steam. Or we fall into the trap of witnessing to ourselves—our faithfulness, our commitment—instead of to the Lamb of God.

John could have experienced the same witness problems. But God chose John, empowered him through the Word, and disciplined his life so his witness to the Lamb never faded. He would not bend, nor would he permit the crowds to give him the honor that was due Jesus. He focused steadfastly on the Lamb of God.

The same God who sent the Lamb to be sacrificed on our behalf also makes us His strong, unwavering disciples through a disciplined life of Word and prayer. Refusing honor for ourselves, we steadfastly bear witness to the Lamb of God who takes away the sin of the world!

*Prayer:* See, the Lamb, so long expected,
Comes with pardon down from heav'n.
Let us haste, with tears of sorrow,
One and all, to be forgiv'n.
*LW* 18:3

January 12

# Encounters with Jesus: Andrew

***Reading:* John 1:35–42**

*Text:* The first thing Andrew did was to find his own brother Simon and tell him, "We have found the Messiah." John 1:41

Andrew—the story of his encounter with Jesus is a simple, powerful one that can help us as we seek to share the faith.

Andrews are needed to hear about Jesus. A little-known disciple of John the Baptizer sees the man from Nazareth and hears Him identified as the Lamb of God. He believes and rejoices. Before going out to witness, we need to see Jesus as the Lamb of God. By His grace we believe and rejoice. Again and again we hear His Word.

Andrews are needed to follow Jesus. Andrew, having seen Jesus, asked where He was staying and followed Him to learn more. He obeyed and became one of Jesus' disciples. We also need to follow Jesus. Believing, we want to hear Him again and again. We hear and obey and hear and obey. He makes us His disciples. We regularly grow through Word and Sacrament. We study the Word personally and in groups. We serve as Jesus leads.

Andrews are needed to bring others to Jesus. The minute Andrew left Jesus, he hurried to tell his brother, "We have found the Messiah." Then he brought Simon to Jesus. And Simon Peter became a powerful spokesman for the early church. Andrew: a quiet witness, a relatively unknown follower of Jesus, an important instrument of God's love.

God needs us also to bring a brother or sister to Jesus. He brought us to faith in our Baptism. We see Jesus, crucified and risen for us. We follow Him by hearing and obeying.

He provides us with power to witness. Very simply and quietly we go to the family member, the neighbor, the co-worker, the friend and say, "We have found the Messiah." And we bring that person to Jesus through His Church. Yes, Andrews—that means you and me—are needed today.

*Prayer:* Lord Jesus, use me like Andrew to bring someone to You. Amen.

# Encounters with Jesus: Philip and Nathanael

## *Reading:* John 1:43–51

*Text:* Philip found Nathaniel and told him, "We have found the one Moses wrote about in the Law, and about whom the prophets also wrote–Jesus of Nazareth, the son of Joseph." John 1:45

How do you witness of Jesus one on one? Do you consider the unique needs and personality of your friend or co-worker? In what ways do you pray for that person before speaking of Jesus' love? John the Baptist, familiar through his priest father, Zechariah, with the sacrificial system, points his disciples to Jesus as the Lamb of God who takes away the sin of the world. Andrew, moved by the Spirit to follow Jesus, witnesses to his brother, Simon Peter, by saying, "We have found the Messiah." Simon would understand that.

Now we observe Philip, recently asked by Jesus to follow Him, approaching his friend Nathanael with a unique testimony. Knowing he is a "true Israelite" devoted to prayer and the study of the Law and the Prophets, Philip tells Nathanael, "'We have found the one Moses wrote about in the Law, and about whom the prophets also wrote.'" That would register with this faithful Israelite believer. When Philip connects that promised Messiah with Jesus of Nazareth, the son of Joseph, Nathanael's skepticism emerges, "Nazareth! Can anything good come from there?" (John 1:26). But Philip's "come and see" brings him to Jesus where His prophetic knowledge leads Nathanael to confess, "Rabbi, You are the Son of God; You are the King of Israel" (John 1:49), a very informed Jewish identification of Jesus as Messiah. You see, Philip knew Nathanael well and Jesus knew him even better.

What a joy to believe in Jesus in ways we can understand and ask God's Spirit to guide our witness to the ones we know and love in words they can grasp so they join Nathanael in a Spirit-given confession of faith in Jesus as Savior.

*Prayer:* So much to sing about: all I have seen and heard,
Your glory in my talents' use my best reward:
that others see what I have seen
and sing with me: "It is the Lord!"
*SP* 210:4

Copyright © 1989 Concordia Publishing House

January 14

# Jesus, Song of My Heart

## *Reading:* Ephesians 5:19–20

*Text:* Sing and make music in your heart to the Lord. Ephesians 5:19b

I love to sing . . . at home, in the car, in church, in the choir, even at the ballpark. When my wife chose "Jesus, Song of my Heart" as the theme for some women's retreats she will be leading, my heart rejoiced. Singing can be a form of witness. Whether I am singing classical music, popular songs, barbershop, Broadway musicals, or church hymns, the melody or harmony for those songs comes from the reality that Jesus is the song of my heart.

St. Paul turns to music in his marvelous letter to the Ephesians: "Speak to one another with psalms, hymns, and spiritual songs. Sing and make music in your heart to the Lord, always giving thanks to God the Father for everything in the name of our Lord Jesus Christ" (Ephesians 5:19–20). Jesus is the song of Paul's heart. Less than the least of all God's people, Paul knows that God's grace has been given to him—redemption through the blood of Christ—to preach to the Gentiles the unsearchable riches of Christ. He sings the song of Jesus Christ in his life and witness.

Whether or not you enjoy singing, Jesus is the song of your heart, filling you with thankfulness for His saving love and moving you to overflow with psalms, hymns, and spiritual songs in your life and witness. Together in the darkness of this world, we lift up a song of praise to our Savior so others can join in the heavenly chorus.

*Prayer:* My song is love unknown, My Savior's love to me,
Love to the loveless shown That they might lovely be.
Oh, who am I That for my sake
My Lord should take frail flesh and die?

Here might I stay and sin, No story so divine!
Never was love, dear King, Never was grief like thine.
This is my friend, In whose sweet praise
I all my days Could gladly spend!
*LW* 91:1, 7

# How Can I Keep from Singing?

## *Reading:* Acts 16:25–34

*Text:* About midnight Paul and Silas were praying and singing hymns to God, and the other prisoners were listening to them. Acts 16:25

Jesus was the song of Paul's heart. Otherwise he would not have been able to sing hymns to God in the prison at midnight. Paul and Silas visited Philippi to proclaim the Gospel of Jesus Christ. When Paul cast out an evil spirit from a fortune-telling slave girl, the two of them were severely flogged and thrown into prison in the inner cell with their feet in stocks. Their prospects were dismal.

Yet at midnight they prayed and sang songs from their heart in earshot of the other prisoners. Their song expressed their confident faith in Jesus and a bold witness to the prison under dire circumstances. Had Paul been asked, "Why are you singing?" I believe he would have answered in the words of a well-known hymn, "How Can I Keep from Singing?"

Suddenly an earthquake shook the prison. All chains were broken. The jailer nearly committed suicide, thinking the prisoners had escaped. Paul had opportunity to spare his life and more important to answer his desperate question—"Sirs, what must I do to be saved?"—with the song of his heart, "Believe in the Lord Jesus Christ and you will be saved—you and your household" (Acts 16:30–31). Songs in the night heard, God's Spirit working through Paul's clear Gospel witness, the jailer and his family believed and were baptized.

When dire circumstances come into your life, when your faith is sorely tested, sometimes because of your faithful witness to Jesus, God's Spirit will work through His Word so you hear again Jesus as the song of your heart. Your witness in improbable circumstances may well bring others to faith in the Savior. With Paul you quietly ask, "How Can I Keep from Singing?"

*Prayer:* I will sing my Maker's praises<br>
And in him most joyful be,<br>
For in all things I see traces<br>
Of his tender love to me.<br>
Nothing else than love could move him<br>
With such deep and tender care<br>
Evermore to raise and bear<br>
All who try to serve and love him.<br>
*LW* 439:1

January 16

# Enlarge My Heart

## *Reading:* Proverbs 4:20–23

*Text:* I will run in the way of Your commandments when You enlarge my heart. Psalm 119:32 (ESV)

How many times have you heard someone who lives with courage, vision, and generosity described with these words: "He has a big heart!"? In these devotions we hopefully have enlarged your vision to help reach 100 million people with the Gospel of Jesus by 2017 as God sets the world ablaze through you. But where does it start? Within your heart!

The psalmist puts it simply: "I will run in the way of Your commandments when You enlarge my heart." "In Biblical language the heart is the center of the human spirit from which spring emotions, thought, motivation, courage, and action" *(Concordia Self-Study Bible,* note on Psalm 4:7, p. 790). Proverbs 4 counsels that when we are attentive to God's words and keep them within our heart, we receive life and healing. He adds, "Guard your heart for it is the wellspring of life" (Proverbs 4:20–23). We will never run to witness until God enlarges our heart. By nature our hearts are empty and desperately wicked (Jeremiah 17:9). Out of the heart proceeds all sorts of evil thoughts—murder, adultery, false witness, and blasphemy (Matthew 15:19). With a repentant David, we cry out, "Create in me a clean heart, O God, and renew a right spirit within me" (Psalm 51:10).

Where does it really start? Within God's heart! From the very heart of God comes His desire for all to be saved and to come to the knowledge of the truth. Therefore, He sent His own Son, Jesus, with a pure heart to pay for the world's sin by dying on the cross. In our Baptism, Christ dwells in our hearts through faith (Ephesians 3:17). Through Christ, our hearts are set free or literally "enlarged" because they "swell with joy" (Isaiah 60:5). Forgiven, restored, filled with the joy of our salvation, we "run in the way of [God's] commandments" to set the world ablaze with Christ. Our simple prayer today: "Lord, enlarge my heart!"

*Prayer:* Your Word it is that heals my heart,
That makes me whole in ev'ry part;
Your Word of joy within me sings,
True peace and blessedness it brings.
*LW* 197:2

# Personal Mission Statement

## *Reading:* Ephesians 3:7–13

*Text:* The purpose in a man's heart is like deep water, but a man of understanding will draw it out. Proverbs 20:5 (ESV)

With the church's vision to set the world ablaze before us and with hearts enlarged by the joy of our salvation, we ask our Lord to help us develop a personal mission statement to focus our energies day by day. After prayerful deliberation, I have written my own personal mission statement in these words: "To motivate others to join me in living with passion for the Word of Christ so many people are saved and discover the joy of Christian witness and service."

Proverbs 20 provides several verses that might help you develop and implement a personal mission statement. The next few devotions will highlight these verses. First, we read in verse 5, "The purpose in a man's heart is like deep water, but a man of understanding will draw it out." No shallow or casual approach will suffice. As saints and sinners, our heart's purpose is mixed and fuzzy. God's purpose for our lives is deep, honors our created gifts, personality, godly passions, and connects with His purpose of salvation for the world through Christ's atoning sacrifice and the Word and Sacrament ministry of His Church. Our fleshly purpose often clouds God's purpose with selfish motivation for personal gain, recognition, and comfort. God's Spirit can help you "draw it out" through His Word and the counsel of other Christians. Sinful purposes exposed. Forgiveness received. God's unique purpose for us uncovered. Strength for carrying out that purpose bestowed.

St. Paul, completely aware of the saint/sinner tension in his life, provides a powerful example of a personal mission statement: "Of this gospel I was made a minister according to the gift of God's grace, which was given to me by the working of His power. To me, though I am the very least of all the saints, this grace was given to preach to the Gentiles the unsearchable riches of Christ. . . . This was according to the eternal purpose that He has realized in Christ Jesus our Lord" (Ephesians 3:7–8, 11). And Paul single-mindedly lived out that mission.

*Prayer:* Let what you will be my desire,
And with new life my soul inspire.
*LW* 373:3

January 18

# Based on Honest Confession

***Reading:* 1 Timothy 1:12–17**

*Text:* Who can say, "I have made my heart pure; I am clean from my sin"? Proverbs 20:11 (ESV)

Letting God go deep into the purpose of our hearts to "draw out" His purpose for our lives begins with honest confession. Proverbs 20 raises the issue: "Who can say, 'I have made my heart pure; I am clean from my sin'?" The obvious answer is no one. "If we say we have no sin, we deceive ourselves and the truth is not in us" (1 John 1:8).

As we seek to develop a personal mission statement in tune with God's purpose for our lives, that same level of honesty is needed. Again St. Paul provides a helpful example when he writes to the young pastor, Timothy: "I thank Him who has given me strength, Christ Jesus our Lord, because He judged me faithful, appointing me to His service, though formerly I was a blasphemer, persecutor, and insolent opponent" (1 Timothy 1:12–13a). He adds, "The saying is trustworthy and deserving of full acceptance, that Christ Jesus came into the world to save sinners, of whom I am the foremost" (1 Timothy 1:15). Honest confession of past sins and of ongoing sin! Paul opens his own heart to receive God's daily forgiveness and a renewed sense of purpose for his personal mission.

He then proceeds to reveal how the very fact of his sinful nature can be used by God to point to Christ alone for salvation. "But I received mercy for this reason, that in me, as the foremost (sinner), Jesus Christ might display His perfect patience as an example to those who were to believe in Him for eternal life" (1 Timothy 1:16).

May God bless your honest confession as a first step for identifying your personal mission, shower you with His mercy and forgiveness in Christ, and use you, a forgiven sinner, as an example of Christ's patience for those in need of eternal salvation!

*Prayer:* Lord Jesus, think on me
And purge away my sin;
From selfish passions set me free
And make me pure within.
*LW* 231:1

# Put into Practice

## *Reading:* Proverbs 21:11–13

*Text:* Even a child makes himself known by his acts, by whether his conduct is pure and upright. Proverbs 20:11 (ESV)

Developing a personal mission statement is a process, not a finished product. Seeking God's unique purpose for your life and honestly confessing your sin help provide a focus for daily life. But you also gain clarity and passion for mission by putting into practice what you are learning.

Proverbs 20 demonstrates the practical nature of wisdom by describing the conduct of a child as a way of revealing the child's heart. The chapter further references the hearing ear and the seeing eye as gifts of God (20:12). Later it refers to "the lips of knowledge" as a "precious jewel" (20:15b). In other words, we discover and unfold God's purpose in our lives by how we listen, what we see, what we speak, and what we do—putting into practice God's love and forgiveness in our lives.

Test your preliminary mission statement in your life this week. Who do you see in need of the good news about salvation through Jesus? What do you hear from people in your life, revealing opportunities for personal caring and witness? How well do you really listen to them? What words come out of your mouth? How well do you speak the timely and encouraging word? How do your actions or inactions bear witness to Jesus in your life? Your giving, your serving, your sharing? What are you learning about your unique personal mission as you put your faith into action?

The searchlight of God's Word exposes our sins as we put into practice His purpose for our life. It also brings us to Jesus, the Light of the world, who paid for those sins on the cross and offers us daily forgiveness. Finally, the Word illumines our purpose and path to bring others to faith in Christ in a practical, consistent, and compassionate way.

*Prayer:* Your living Word shine in our heart
And to a new life win us.
With seed of light implant the start
Of Christ-like deeds within us.
Help us uproot what is impure,
And while faith's fruits in us mature,
Prepare us for your harvest.
*LW* 336:2

January 20

# Counsel for Our Mission

## *Reading:* Proverbs 20:24–27

*Text:* Plans are established by counsel; by wise guidance wage war. Proverbs 20:18 (ESV)

Our personal mission emerges as we ask the Lord's purpose for our life, honestly confess our sins, and put into practice this mission as a test. A final step involves gaining the counsel of the Christian community. Our pastor, trusted Christian friends, our family, and other Christian leaders can provide important insights to guide our mission. Some know us intimately, including our strengths and weaknesses, our talents, our passion, our level of maturity, our Christian faith, and our heart. Others with a sense of the Church and its mission in today's world can offer more objective counsel in keeping with God's Word and purpose for the world.

Proverbs 20:18 says, "Plans are established by counsel; by wise guidance wage war." Certainly these words apply to kings considering a building project or going forth to war. But they also describe counsel or guidance we need as we live in the daily callings of our lives whether we are young with strength or old with the gray hair of wisdom (Proverbs 20:29). Involving trusted advisors helps to hold us accountable for both the prayerful development of our personal mission and its ongoing implementation.

Ultimately, our seeking counsel helps us to lay our personal mission before the Lord. Through God's Word and His Church, we are led to confess sin, receive forgiveness, and confidently embark, by God's grace in Christ, on God's mission to bring Jesus as Savior to the world. What a privilege and a joy to serve as His unique instruments of the saving Gospel! Consider developing your own personal mission statement as part of God's Church, alongside trusted Christian friends, relying on God's forgiveness and strength through Christ. You will help set the world ablaze with Christ!

*Prayer:* Now carry out at any cost
A rescue mission to the lost
Before this time of grace runs out:
This is what life is all about.
God's loving plan is there for all
Who heed the Savior's urgent call.
*SP* 248:3

Copyright © 2001 Concordia Publishing House

# "Bridge of Faith"

## *Reading:* 1 Peter 1:18–21

*Text:* Jesus answered, "I am the way and the truth and the life. No one comes to the Father except through Me." John 14:6

A large framed picture hangs over our fireplace mantel: "Bridge of Faith" by Thomas Kinkade. An arched stone bridge spans a flowing stream and connects with a path leading into a mist. Beautiful flowering trees and shrubs fill the foreground but some lie in the dark shadows. For us the painting provides a constant reminder of God's marvelous creation and our fall into sin with all the resulting shadows of problems, temptations, and suffering. Most important, we focus again and again on that rock solid bridge of faith in Jesus Christ as the only way to salvation. Although the future is shrouded in mist, we are confident that because of Jesus' atoning death on the cross and victorious resurrection from the dead God will lead us safely on His path to heaven.

Thomas asks his Master, "Lord, we don't know where You are going, so how can we know the way?" Jesus replies, "I am the way and the truth and the life. No one comes to the Father except through Me" (John 14:5–6). Peter adds in his first letter: "For you know that is was not with perishable things such as silver or gold that you were redeemed from the empty way of life handed down to you from your forefathers, but with the precious blood of Christ, a lamb without blemish or defect. . . . Through Him you believe in God, who raised Him from the dead and glorified Him, and so your faith and hope are in God" (1 Peter 1:18–19, 21).

We love to show "Bridge of Faith" to our house guests as a witness to Jesus as the way, the truth, and the life. In a confusing world with many conflicting religious views, will you invite your family and friends to join you on that arched stone bridge of faith in Jesus Christ as the only Savior from sin?

*Prayer:* You are the way, the truth, the life;
Grant us that way to know,
That truth to keep, that life to win,
Whose joys eternal flow.
*LW* 283:4

January 22

# "Paris: City of Lights"

*Reading:* Proverbs 1:20–33

*Text:* Wisdom calls aloud in the street, she raises her voice in the public squares. Proverbs 1:20

Another Thomas Kinkade picture hangs in our dining room: "Paris: City of Lights." Your eyes are drawn to a busy Paris street scene at dusk. Cars with headlights and pedestrians crowd the street. In the foreground people sit under umbrellas at sidewalk cafes and observe the bustle of activity.

We treasure the painting because of a special time we spent together in Paris. But the street full of people also reminds us of our calling to share Jesus as Savior with people in cities everywhere. The serene painting "Bridge of Faith" set in the beauty of God's creation stands in sharp contrast to this picture of life in a big city. Jesus Christ as the only "Bridge of Faith" is needed here too.

Proverbs in the very first chapter contrasts wisdom and foolishness: "Wisdom calls aloud in the street . . . at the head of the noisy streets she cries out: 'How long will mockers delight in mockery and fools hate knowledge?" (Proverbs 1:20–22).

God loves all people, including city dwellers. He challenges us to recognize the foolishness and mockery of our selfish and sinful ways. He says, "If you had responded to My rebuke, I would have poured out My heart to you and made My thoughts known to you" (Proverbs 1:23). His heart reveals the promised sending of His Son as the Messiah to pay for our sins on the cross. He adds, "Whoever listens to Me will live in safety and be at ease, without fear of harm" (Proverbs 1:33).

As we view people's faces, whether smiling or impassive on crowded city streets, we know that many are experiencing distress and trouble and headed for disaster and calamity. How can God use us to relate to them, care for them, and bring them Jesus, their Wisdom and Salvation?

*Prayer:* And not alone to nations In faraway retreats,
But ev'rywhere I broadcast His love through crowded streets:
The lives that my life touches, However great or small—
Let them through me see Jesus, Who served and saved us all.
*LW* 320:4

# God's Surprises

## *Reading:* Ephesians 5:15–20

*Text:* Making the most of every opportunity, because the days are evil. Ephesians 5:16

A longtime friend in Denver, struggling with a serious form of cancer in an advanced stage, wrote me an e-mail at the beginning of the new year in response to our expression of prayers and concern. Instead of dwelling on his condition and prognosis, he wished us a year filled with "God's surprises." He was witnessing powerfully to his faith in the Lord Jesus by that expression, "God's surprises." I pictured him dealing with many uncertainties by awaiting opportunities for service in the middle of a dreaded disease. What surprises did God have in store for his family this year? As a result, we have been looking for similar windows of opportunity in all circumstances–the good, the bad, and the ugly. Amazingly, we have already been discovering many of "God's surprises" for witness and service right before our eyes.

In Ephesians Paul writes, "Be very careful, then, how you live–not as unwise but as wise, making the most of every opportunity, because the days are evil." He goes on to contrast the foolish choice of getting drunk on wine, which leads to debauchery, with the wise choice of being filled with the Spirit. That wise choice expresses itself in the speaking to one another of psalms, hymns, and spiritual songs as we sing and make music from our hearts to the Lord. That wise choice also involves "giving thanks to God the Father for everything, in the name of our Lord Jesus Christ" (Ephesians 5:20).

Aware of our foolish choices to run away from our problems and sins, confessing our sins of missed opportunities to serve in these evil days, we join my friend and St. Paul in speaking God's Word of forgiveness through the atoning sacrifice of Jesus and embrace "God's surprises" as opportunities to connect people to Jesus with thanksgiving.

*Prayer:* Grant us grace to see thee, Lord, Present in thy holy Word;
Grace to imitate thee now And be pure, as pure art thou;
That we might become like thee, At thy great epiphany
And may praise thee, ever blest, God in flesh made manifest.
*LW* 88:4

January 24

# Celebrate?

***Reading:* Luke 15:11–32**

*Text:* But we had to celebrate and be glad. Luke 15:32a

A celebration in progress. New believers in Christ as guests of honor. They seem so happy and enthused about their faith. They are welcomed with open arms.

Do you really want your church to reach the lost? Our world is so evil. So many people have wasted their lives in the pursuit of selfish gain, riotous living, and gross sensuality. They seek spiritual experiences from idolatrous religions and embrace values totally alien to God's holy law. You, on the other hand, have remained faithful to Christ and His church through regular worship in God's house. How can you celebrate the invasion of your church by new believers from an irreverent past bringing their worldly music, lack of respect for church customs, and proper dress into your midst? Celebrate? Never.

The elder brother in the well-known story from Luke 15 doesn't feel like celebrating at all. Angry at the sounds of music and dancing for his dissolute brother, he refuses to join the festivities. After all, he has faithfully served his father, slaving in the fields and obeying his father's orders. No fattened calf or even a young goat prepared in his honor. Then his resentment explodes in these words: "But when this son of yours who has squandered your property with prostitutes comes home, you kill the fattened calf for him" (Luke 15:30). Celebrate? Never.

Enter the father who has welcomed the wayward son with lavish forgiveness. To this bitter older son, he says tenderly, "You are always with me, and everything I have is yours." Then pointedly he adds, "But we had to celebrate because this brother of yours was dead and is alive again; he was lost and is found." Celebrate? Always.

Confession time for us. Sinful like the younger son and the elder brother. Repentant. Unworthy recipients of the loving embrace of the forgiving Father. Washed clean in the blood of His only Son on Calvary. Invited to the celebration now and forever. Welcoming all the lost. Celebrate? Always.

*Prayer:* Father, help us to celebrate with You that the lost are found through Jesus. Amen.

# Twin Towers

### *Reading:* Luke 13:1–3

*Text:* "How is it that you don't know how to interpret this present time?" Luke 12:56b

Who in America will ever forget September 11, 2001? Radical Islamic terrorists intentionally forced commercial airlines to crash into the World Trade Center in New York City and the Pentagon in Washington, D.C., killing thousands of innocent civilians and rescue workers. This heinous act focused attention on a growing threat to the world with major political, military, diplomatic, and economic consequences. But how does one interpret this event from the perspective of God's kingdom at hand through Jesus' ministry?

Jesus challenged his audience, who always looked for signs in the sky, with this question: "How is it that you don't know how to interpret this present time?" Some told Jesus about a heinous act committed by Pilate's soldiers who rushed into the temple area while some Galilean Jews were offering sacrifices and mixed their own blood with the sacrifices. The crowd expected Jesus to condemn Pilate's action or the sin of the Galileans. Jesus refused to condemn the Galileans as worse sinners but turned it back on the crowd and us as well, "Unless you repent, you too will perish" (Luke 13:3).

In a similar fashion, senseless events like September 11 point beyond the tragedy to a sinful world where "all have sinned and fall short of the glory of God" (Romans 3:23). "God is not willing that any should perish but that all should come to repentance" (2 Peter 3:9). God's mercy sent Jesus to perish for our sins on the cross. Led to repentance, we place our trust in Jesus Christ alone for our salvation. And we respond to the terrorist tragedy by using this present time of God's judgment and mercy to bring others to Jesus for rescue from their sins.

*Prayer:* As surely as I live, God said, I would not see the sinner dead.
I want him turned from error's ways, Repentant, living endless days
To us therefore Christ gave command: "Go forth and preach in every land;
Bestow on all my pard'ning grace Who will repent and mend their ways."
*LW* 235:1–2

January 26

# Tsunami

## *Reading:* Luke 13:4–5

*Text:* "How is it that you don't know how to interpret the present time?" Luke 12:56b

The world was staggered in December 2004 when giant tsunami waves, triggered by an underwater earthquake in Southeast Asia, devastated coastal regions of the Indian Ocean. This tsunami took the lives of tens of thousands of people—fishermen, villagers, and tourists. Massive humanitarian aid came in response to help in the rebuilding effort. Survivors continue to struggle with their loss and grief. Why? How does one interpret this event from the perspective of God's kingdom at hand through Jesus' ministry?

Jesus brings another example to bear on the question of how to interpret the present time. He refers to eighteen people who died in an accident when the tower in Siloam fell on them. Whereas Pilate's action to shed the blood of Galilean Jews as they offered sacrifices was a conscious and cruel act, the tower collapse was a senseless accident.

Again Jesus refuses to explain the accident by claiming that the victims were more guilty than any others living in Jerusalem. Again He challenges the crowd: "Unless you repent, you too will perish" (Luke 13:5).

The tsunami victims died from an act of nature, no more guilty than the rest of the world. But this tragedy underscores the urgency of a sinful world in danger of perishing eternally unless each individual repents of sin and turns to Jesus, who took our punishment on the cross that we might live eternally. God's judgment and mercy converge in Jesus and are proclaimed through us in this present world so many may "not perish but have eternal life" (John 3:16).

*Prayer:* "Come unto me, ye wand'rers, And I will give you light."
O loving voice of Jesus, which comes to cheer the night!
Our hearts were filled with sadness, And we had lost our way,
But thou hast brought us gladness And songs at break of day.

"And whoever cometh, I will not cast him out."
O patient love of Jesus, Which drives away our doubt.
Which, though we be unworthy Of love so great and free,
Invites us very sinners To come, dear Lord, to thee!
*LW* 345:2, 4

# Taking Care of Business

***Reading:* Luke 2:41–52**

*Text:* "Did you not know that I must be in My Father's house?" Luke 2:49 (ESV)

Frequently, conscientious mangers and workers place foremost the mission of their company to produce and deliver products, information, or services in a timely manner, with high quality, at the lowest possible price. They refer to this priority as "taking care of business." In its best sense, this commitment brings positive results for both the customer and the business. Today's devotion will address the problem of business becoming self-serving.

In the Christian Church, conscientious leaders and the community of believers place foremost the mission of setting the world ablaze with the Gospel of Jesus Christ with urgency, with a faithful Biblical proclamation, as God's free gift. We can refer to this priority as "taking care of business." In its best sense, this commitment results in God's Spirit bringing many to Christ and a revitalized, joyful Christian fellowship.

At age 12, Jesus stayed at the temple, sitting among the teachers, listening to them and asking them questions, resulting in their amazement at His understanding and answers. When His worried parents discovered His absence and returned to the temple to chide Him, He replied, "Did you not know that I must be in My Father's house?" A footnote in the English Standard Version says, "Or 'about My Father's business.' " You see, Jesus belonged in His Father's house to carry out His Father's business, which would cost Him His life on the cross. His journey from cradle to cross started in the temple as He perfectly fulfilled God's Law on our behalf before taking our burdens upon His shoulders to pay for the world's sin.

His Great Commission to the disciples (Matthew 28:19–20) engaged all of us in His saving mission, the Father's business. Forgiven, empowered, through Word and Sacraments, relying only on His grace, we simply and joyfully continue "taking care of business."

*Prayer:* Jesus, be with me and direct me;
Jesus, my plans and hopes inspire;
Jesus, from tempting thoughts protect me;
Jesus, be all my heart's Desire;
Jesus, be in my thoughts all day
Nor suffer me to fall away.
*TLH* 120:5

# When Business Interferes

## *Reading:* Acts 19:23–41

*Text:* "Men, you know we receive a good income from this business." Acts 19:25b

What stands in the way of setting the world ablaze? As Paul traveled from city to city on his missionary journey, he faced many obstacles to the spread of the Gospel. One such obstacle occurred in Ephesus, where he taught for more than two years. Many turned from idols, like Artemis of the Ephesians, to serve the living God. A silversmith named Demetrius became concerned about Paul's preaching because members of his trade made silver shrines of Artemis.

Demetrius called together the craftsmen and said, "Men, you know we receive a good income from this business." He went on to castigate Paul for ruining their business: "He says that man-made gods are no gods at all. There is danger not only that our trade will lose its good name, but also that the temple of the great goddess Artemis will be discredited . . ." (Acts 19:26b–27a). He made the tradesman furious and they started a riot in the whole city, which was finally quelled by the city clerk.

What happens when business interferes with the Gospel message? The silversmiths seemed more concerned about their livelihood than about the goddess Artemis, yet used the goddess to incite a riot. Their business caused them to attack the true God.

Can your business interfere with your relationship to God and your witness to Christ? Only if you make it an idol. Sometimes we compartmentalize our business goals from our faith in Jesus because we don't want to give up our financial gain. Sometimes others block our witness because business success means more to them than their relationship to the true God.

In either case, the Gospel will prevail because God would have all to be saved and come to the knowledge of the truth. Admitting our idolatry, we can join Paul as forgiven sinners on a mission to set the world ablaze with Christ. Our business can actually provide an arena for witness rather than an interference.

*Prayer:* Lord Jesus, think on me And purge away my sin;
From selfish passions set me free And make me pure within.
*LW* 231:1

# Multiplying Loaves for Witness

## *Reading:* John 6:25–40

*Text:* "Here is a boy with five barley loaves and two small fish, but how far will they go among so many?" John 6:8

During the Lenten season, our Sunday morning Bible class has been viewing the 2003 movie on *The Gospel of John.* This excellent film uses only the words of John's Gospel while dramatizing the action. Last Sunday we saw Jesus' miracle of feeding 5,000 people with only five barley loaves and two small fish. After Andrew's question—"How far will they go among so many?"—and Jesus' blessing of the boy's lunch, the screen was filled with basket after basket of loaves and fish being distributed to a joyful crowd. Astonishment shows on the faces of the disciples as they participate. Multiplying loaves.

The true meaning of the miracle becomes clear the next day on the other side of the lake when Jesus identifies Himself as follows: "I am the bread of life. He who comes to Me will never go hungry, and he who believes in Me will never be thirsty" (John 6:35). At the end of His discourse on bread from heaven, Jesus concludes, "For My Father's will is that everyone who looks to the Son and believes in Him shall have eternal life, and I will raise him up on the last day" (John 6:40).

As I watched those loaves multiply in the baskets so all were fed, I suddenly realized that I am privileged to join those disciples and my fellow believers in the miraculous process of multiplying loaves for witness. Jesus, the Bread of Life, by His death on the cross and resurrection from the dead, brings life to the world. He enlists me in sharing that bread with countless people. From His precious Word of Life, He offers an unlimited supply of spiritual bread to feed the hungry.

With a look of astonishment, I witness others receiving Jesus as their Savior and savoring the rich feast of Word and Sacraments to sustain their faith. They join me in multiplying loaves through their own witness to Jesus as the Bread of Life. Multiplying loaves for witness.

*Prayer:* Jesus, Bread of Life, feed Your children through our witness with the food that endures to eternal life. Amen.

January 30

# Salvation without Measure

## *Reading:* Ephesians 3:14–19

*Text:* My mouth will tell of Your righteousness, of Your salvation all day long, though I know not its measure. Psalm 71:15

As a teenager making an evangelism call with an adult near downtown Indianapolis, I felt very inadequate to speak of my faith in Jesus. We were inviting strangers to a special service at church. At a light supper afterward and then at the service, I marveled at God's salvation through His Son's death—a salvation without measure.

My mouth was dry and my heart beat a little faster as I led two other members of our church in knocking on a door in Peru, Indiana, to share Jesus with a person in need of salvation. Now a pastor, I marvel at how God's Spirit touched lives and brought many to believe in the Savior—a salvation without measure.

In a Seattle hospital where our 23-year-old daughter lay near death, on an airplane between St. Louis and Phoenix sitting next to a professed atheist from Israel, and on an elevator in Houston meeting a troubled young man, I found opportunities to share Jesus as Savior in words inadequate to describe His marvelous salvation without measure.

David's words in Psalm 71 near the end of his life speak to my heart. For all his depth of experience with God's saving acts in the midst of incredible challenges, problems, and suffering, he marvels at God's righteousness and admits that he "knows not its measure." Nevertheless, he exclaims, "My mouth will tell . . . of Your salvation all day long." St. Paul in Ephesians lifts up a marvelous prayer to the Father: "I pray that you . . . may have power to grasp how wide and long and high and deep is the love of Christ and to know this love that surpasses knowledge—that you may be filled to the measure of all the fullness of God" (Ephesians 3:17–19). Ongoing witness of a salvation without measure!

*Prayer:* Jesus, your boundless love so true
No thought can reach, no tongue declare;
Unite my thankless heart to you,
And reign without a rival there.
Yours wholly, yours alone I am;
Be you alone my sacred flame.
*LW* 280:1

# Refreshing Others

***Reading:*** **Acts 3:11–20**

*Text:* He who refreshes others will himself be refreshed. Proverbs 11:25b

So many people these days are drained and exhausted—time pressures, chaos and conflict at home, mountains of bills, a hectic commute, performance and relationship strains at work. Oh, the need for refreshment—quiet time, a cool drink, companionship, an oasis from the rat race, God's salvation.

Have you ever thought of Christian witness as refreshing others? Do you place demands on others or refresh them? Do you add to their exhaustion by your own hectic life or do you refresh them? Are you refreshed at the water of life flowing from God's love in Christ? Or do you yourself desperately need to be refreshed?

The writer of Proverbs simply states, "He who refreshes others will himself be refreshed." In the Ancient Near Eastern culture, a nomadic people would refresh by offering hospitality to a weary traveler, dusty and with parched throat. Shade, rest, water and food were generously provided. Similar refreshment would be received when the host became the traveler. The host would witness of faith in the God of Abraham, Isaac, and Jacob by refreshing others.

Peter and John, in the early days after Pentecost, refreshed by the outpouring of the Holy Spirit, heal a lame beggar who only expected a silver or gold coin and then proclaim salvation through faith in the crucified and risen Savior in whose name they have healed the crippled man. Peter concludes, "Repent, then, and turn to God so that your sins may be wiped out, that times of refreshing may come from the Lord" (Acts 3:19).

Refreshing others is witnessing. And witnessing to repentance and forgiveness through Jesus Christ does provide refreshment for others now and eternally. Refreshed by Word and Sacraments, we can refresh others in every way. Whom will you refresh this week?

*Prayer:* I heard the voice of Jesus say, "Behold I freely give
The living waters, thirsty one; Stoop down and drink and live.
I came to Jesus, and I drank Of that life-giving stream;
My thirst was quenched, my soul revived, And now I live in him.
*LW* 348:2

February 1

# Senior Saints in Mission

***Reading:* Psalm 71:1–9**

*Text:* My mouth is filled with Your praise, declaring Your splendor all day long! Psalm 71:8

This psalm may have been written by David in his old age. Threatened and attacked over the years by many enemies who challenged his position as the Lord's anointed, David remembers God's faithful protection since birth and gives bold witness to his Rock and Hope: "My mouth is filled with Your praise, declaring Your splendor all day long." His witness is more compelling because of his old age.

One senior saint whose lifelong mission stands out in my mind is my former colleague and mentor, Dr. Alvin W. Mueller who died in 2002 at the age of 97. A former district president and long time pastor at St. Paul Lutheran Church, Decatur, Illinois, Dr. Mueller continued in mission during his long years of retirement–preaching, teaching, and influencing children, grandchildren, and great-grandchildren in his 72 years of marriage. When I last saw him in a nursing home two months before his death, he was still interested in the mission efforts of the church at large and encouraging residents of his home for the elderly to attend worship services there. Like David, aware of his own sins and need for a Savior, his mouth was filled with God's praise, and he was declaring God's splendor all day long.

At his funeral, which I attended, his widow, other family members, former members, and many church leaders gave testimony to his faithful witness to Jesus Christ as the only way to salvation. Thank God for David and for Dr. Alvin Mueller, senior saints in mission. What senior saints inspire you to believe in the Savior and share His message with others?

*Prayer:* For all the saints, who from their labors rest,
All who by faith before the world confessed,
Your name, O Jesus, be forever blest. Alleluia!

You were their rock, their fortress and their might;
You, Lord, their captain in the well-fought fight;
You, in the darkness drear, their one true light. Alleluia!

Oh, may your soldiers, faithful, true, and bold,
Fight as the saints who nobly fought of old
And win with them the victors crown of gold. Alleluia!
*LW* 191:1–3

# A Senior Saint Named Minnie

***Reading:* Psalm 71:10–17**

*Text:* Since my youth, O God, You have taught me, and to this day I declare Your marvelous deeds. Psalm 71:17

When I served as pastor at St. John's Lutheran Church, Peru, Indiana, I was privileged to know a senior saint named Minnie Krieg and officiated at her funeral. Minnie lived alone in an apartment. A shut-in with one leg amputated, Minnie never complained but was alive in Christ and intent on the church's worldwide mission. She supported many international ministries and cared deeply about her local church. I kept her abreast of our outreach to the community, and she willingly served as a prayer warrior. I will always remember her intelligent eyes and her ready smile.

In Psalm 71, David goes on to look beyond his own problems and accusers to affirm his hope in God and his determination to tell of God's salvation all day long. Then he declares in his old age: "Since my youth, O God, You have taught me, and to this day I declare Your marvelous deeds." God had indeed taught David a great deal. He chose him as the Lord's anointed, gave him victory over the giant Goliath, protected him from Saul's efforts to take his life, preserved him from the Philistines and other enemy nations, made him king first of Judah and then of all Israel, convicted him of his adulterous relationship with Bathsheba and his murder of Uriah, and then forgave his sin through the prophet Nathan.

God also helped David deal with all of the family problems that resulted from his earlier sin, restored him as king after Absalom's rebellion, and fulfilled His promise to continue his reign through his son, Solomon, and ultimately through David's greater Son, Jesus, the Messiah. No wonder, David bears witness in old age to God's marvelous deeds!

In similar fashion, Minnie's mature witness to Jesus and powerful prayer life resulted from a lifetime of God's faithful teaching. Forgiven saints in their senior years like David and Minnie strengthen us for a lifelong mission in the Lord's service.

*Prayer:* O blest communion, fellowship divine,
We feebly struggle, they in glory shine;
Yet all are one within your great design. Alleluia!
*LW* 191:4

# My Own Gray Hair

## *Reading:* Psalm 71:18–24

*Text:* Even when I am old and gray, do not forsake me, O God, till I declare Your power to the next generation. Psalm 71:18

All during my life, I have learned from mentors who were older than I. Dr. Alvin W. Mueller and Minnie Krieg described in the last two devotions serve as examples. As I have continued to read Psalm 71 on a monthly basis over the past many years, I suddenly realize that David is talking about me, "even when I am old and gray" (or even white).

David in his old age has a compelling reason for not wanting God to forsake him—not just because he is surrounded by enemies or because he feels frail and infirm, but so he can declare God's power to the next generation. David is energized to pass on God's promises to his son, Solomon, and through Solomon to all the people of Israel for generations to come. He knows that God has promised to send a Messiah from his own descendants to save the world from their sin. God assures David that although he will not get to build a temple as a physical house, his house will endure forever through the promised Messiah.

I am thankful to be old and gray and ask God not to forsake me so I can pass on to the next generations, including my children and grandchildren, the good news of salvation through faith in Jesus Christ. Confessing my many sins of the past and rejoicing in God's forgiveness and restoration through Word and Sacraments, I desire to help the church faithfully carry the Gospel of Jesus to the ends of the earth. How about you? Young or old, learning from an older saint or teaching the next generation, we say with David, "My lips will shout for joy when I sing praise to You—I, whom you have redeemed" (Psalm 73:23).

*Prayer:* Father, thank You for providing older mature Christians to deepen my faith and encourage my witness. Use me now to declare Your glory in Christ to the next generation. Amen.

# A Tale of Three Oaks

***Reading:* Psalm 1**

*Text:* He is like a tree planted by streams of water, which yields its fruit in season and whose leaf does not wither. Psalm 1:3

In the next five devotions I tell a tale of three oaks to focus your attention on witnessing for Christ in your neighborhood. God's one mission ablaze starts close to home. Seven years ago we bought our dream home on the bluffs of the Mississippi River. We especially treasured all of the trees and shrubs on our property, a constant reminder of God's creation during all seasons of the year.

As we viewed the mighty oak trees, some over 100 years old, our heart's desire was to be like the blessed man described in Psalm 1, "a tree planted by streams of water which yields its fruit in season." We wanted our home to be a welcoming place for family and friends, new and old. We hoped that those visiting would also find and enjoy the peace and warmth of love which comes only from our Savior Jesus Christ. We counted on the beautiful trees as part of that welcoming atmosphere for our Christian witness.

To be sure, we also knew the reality of living in a world where temptations abound to "walk in the counsel of the wicked or stand in the way of sinners or sit in the seat of mockers" (Psalm 1:1). We knew the reality of sin in our own hearts. And we recognized the importance of caring for our home and property so people would feel welcome in our home. Only God can plant us by streams of water so we bear fruit in season. Only Christ, by His death on the tree of the cross, brings forgiveness of sin. Only God's Spirit can bring opportunities for witness. And our beautiful surroundings in nature were likewise the gift of our Creator. But we were not prepared for problems with three oak trees. More on that tomorrow. How is God blessing your witness in the neighborhood?

*Prayer:* Dear heavenly Father, thank You for sturdy trees and for planting us in a neighborhood with opportunity to be a witness to Your Son Jesus. Help us to bear daily fruit by the power of Your Spirit. Amen.

# A Note on Our Door

***Reading:* Luke 3:1–9**

*Text:* "The ax is already at the root of the trees, and every tree that does not produce good fruit will be cut down and thrown into the fire." Luke 3:9

Content in our tree-shaded home, we were shocked one day to find an envelope at our front door with a note from a certified arborist: "Your trees are hazardous to property and humans." He went on to tell us that oaks are very sensitive to construction and probably had been dying for the past 15 years. He added that when a tree is dead at the crown, the same degree of death exists below the soil. He recommended prompt action to have the oaks cut down.

Our desire was to bring a positive witness to Christ in our neighborhood. Instead we had a problem with our coveted oak trees that could cause harm to the neighbors, including their children. The oaks still bore leaves but fewer than before. The branches still lifted proudly in the sky but more dead branches had been falling each year. We had observed but refused to accept that the trees might be dying. Now we had received a definitive word from a tree expert.

John the Baptizer provided a similar definitive word to the crowds in the country around the Jordan as he preached a baptism of repentance for the forgiveness of sins: "You brood of vipers! Who warned you to flee from the coming wrath? . . . The ax is already at the root of the trees and every tree that does not produce good fruit will be cut down and thrown into the fire" (Luke 3:7–9).

In our hearts, our homes, and our neighborhoods we often observe the presence of evil, even sense a dying or rotting from within, yet go on living as usual and try to flee from the coming wrath, hoping things will work out on their own. But our Christian witness is tarnished, and we are not good neighbors. John's stark words: "Produce fruit in keeping with repentance" (Luke 3:8)–like the certified arborist's note at our front door, startle us into facing reality. What next?

*Prayer:* Lord, lead us to repentance and forgiveness through Your cross. Amen.

# Felling of the Oaks

***Reading:*** **Luke 3:10–18**

*Text:* "What should we do then?" the crowd asked. Luke 3:10

The tale of three oaks continues. That note from the certified arborist moved us to take immediate action. We got a recommendation for a reputable tree service company, an estimate, and arranged for not one but three oaks in our front yard to be cut down, including the grinding of their stumps. The next day, a crew of men and heavy equipment arrived to do the job competently, safely, and completely. Currently all that remains are three piles of sawdust.

When John the Baptizer spoke with authority to the crowds about the coming wrath and their need for repentance, they asked with a sense of urgency, "'What should we do then?'" John had a specific answer for each group–the man with two tunics to share with him who has none, tax collectors not to collect any more taxes than required, soldiers not to extort money or to accuse people falsely. Their question indicated a sincere repentance and an expectant waiting for the promised Messiah. John's answer helped them to understand how their forgiven lives of faith might bear fruit in actions of witness and service.

The felled trees symbolize sins confessed and forgiven through Christ's death on the tree of the cross. No excuses, no delay, prompt action to eliminate the dying and dangerous trees from our yard. We experienced pain at the loss of those once beautiful oaks, just as confession of sins can be painful, and losses are real. But God helps us to move on with our neighborhood witness and to bear fruit in words and deeds. What will the future hold with these three oaks felled?

*Prayer:* Lord, to you I make confession: I have sinned and gone astray,
I have multiplied transgression; Chosen for myself my way.
Led by you to see my errors, Lord, I tremble at your tenors.

Your Son came to suffer for me, Gave himself to rescue me,
Died to heal me and restore me, Reconciled and set me free.
Jesus' cross alone can vanquish These dark fears and soothe their anguish.
*LW* 233:1, 3

# A Shoot from the Stump

***Reading:* Isaiah 11:1–3a**

*Text:* A shoot will come up from the stump of Jesse; from his roots a Branch will bear fruit. Isaiah 11:1

The three oaks have been felled in our front yard. No damage done. Danger to neighborhood children avoided. Dead wood removed. But what does the future hold for our landscaping? Everything looks different now. A large empty space exists where once three beautiful trees stood. Our home does not seem as welcoming to family and friends for a witness to the neighborhood.

That's exactly how Israel must have felt at the time of Isaiah and beyond. The northern kingdom and later the southern kingdom would be destroyed because of their sin and rebellion against the true God. First Assyria wielded the mighty ax to chop down the dying tree of Israel, and then the Babylonians cut down Judah, including Jerusalem and the temple, dragging off a remnant into captivity. At that point, the necessary punishment had taken place. But what did the future hold? How would God's promises be fulfilled for the repentant and faithful remnant?

Isaiah prophesies, "A shoot will come up from the stump of Jesse; from his roots a Branch will bear fruit." From the dead stump of sinful Israel would come the living shoot of David's greater Son, Jesus the Messiah, who would bring new life to the world. The remnant would patiently wait for the time when a new tree would grow strong and tall from that shoot, welcoming Jews and Gentiles alike as a result of Jesus' death and resurrection.

As we look at our front yard without the trees, we await new life and growth which will once again welcome all to come and visit. Jesus Christ brings forgiveness, life, and salvation to our hearts, our home, and our neighborhood. During our Advent wait, what can we expect God to do with our lives of witness in this place?

*Prayer:*

Come, O long expected Jesus'
Born to set your people free,
From our fears and sins release us
By your death on Calvary.
Israel's strength and consolation;
Hope to all the earth impart,
Dear desire of ev'ry nation,
Joy of ev'ry longing heart.
*LW* 22:1

# Oaks of Righteousness

## *Reading:* Isaiah 61:1–4

*Text:* They will be called oaks of righteousness, a planting of the LORD for the display of His splendor. Isaiah 61:3d

The tale of three oaks ends with this devotion. The story helps you to focus on witnessing for Christ in your neighborhood. Our home intended as a welcoming place of Christ's love featured beautiful oak trees. A note at our door informed us that some of them were dying and posed a hazard. Prompt action brought a tree service company to fell three oaks in our front yard. The danger was removed but an empty space remained in need of new life.

On recommendation from the tree company, we selected a nursery to help us provide that new life that will make our property warm and welcoming again. We plan to plant a Japanese maple with red leaves, a fair-sized oak tree, and a new shrub. Over a period of time, God-willing, these new trees will grow and provide increasing shade. We also have made arrangements for deep-root feeding and anti-fungal sprays on a regular schedule to keep our other trees and shrubs healthy.

God's plan for new life far exceeds any landscape efforts in our yard. In chapter 6 Isaiah declares the coming Messiah who has been anointed "to preach good news to the poor, to bind up the brokenhearted, to proclaim freedom for the captives and release from darkness for the prisoners" (61:1). Jesus applies these words to Himself in the Nazareth synagogue (Luke 4:16–21). That's new life. Then the Messiah in Isaiah promises those who grieve in Zion—"They will be called oaks of righteousness, a planting of the LORD for the display of His splendor."

Through Jesus' death and resurrection, we are oaks of righteousness (strong healthy trees with roots deep in the soil of God's love). Our purpose in life is to be "a planting of the LORD for the display of His splendor." Through our witness in the neighborhood, others will see Christ as their Savior from sin.

*Prayer:* Dear Father, thank You for planting us in our neighborhood as "oaks of righteousness" for the display of Your splendor. Amen.

# An Unlikely Witness

***Reading:* 1 Corinthians 2:1–5**

*Text:* I came to You in weakness and fear, and with much trembling. 1 Corinthians 2:3

A teenager named Bob in one of the churches I served stands out as a great inspiration to me because he was such an unlikely witness. When we made plans to attend a national evangelism training event in Dallas, I was surprised that Bob volunteered to go as one of the 14 youth and adults. He was very shy, turned red when you looked at him, and stuttered nervously when talking. During the event I saw Bob come alive in his desire and confidence to share Jesus with others. The Spirit was powerfully at work. Upon returning, he made weekly calls on other youth. At an area-wide evangelism training seminar, Bob stood up at the banquet and gave a compelling testimony of his faith in Jesus Christ as Savior and his joy in telling others about Him. An unlikely witness indeed!

St. Paul writes to the Corinthians about his weakness and God's power: "I came to you in weakness and fear, and with much trembling." He adds that his message and preaching demonstrated the Spirit's power "so that your faith might not rest on men's wisdom, but on God's power" (1 Corinthians 2:5). He is quite clear on the content of his message and its importance for salvation: "For I resolved to know nothing while I was with you except Jesus Christ and Him crucified" (1 Corinthians 2:2).

Paul and my young friend Bob had in common a powerful message of Christ-crucified as the only way to salvation and an unlikely witness in their manner of speech. Both provide inspiration for us as we reach out to people in need of salvation, fully aware of our human weakness and limitations, but equally confident of the Spirit's power and the compelling message of Christ-crucified.

*Prayer:* His strength within my weakness Will make me bold to say
How his redeeming power Transforms my stubborn clay;
His touch of fire ignites me, With courage I am sent,
My tongue-tied silence broken, With grace made eloquent.
*LW* 320:3

# A Pocket Cross

## *Reading:* Galatians 3:26–29

*Text:* May I never boast except in the cross of our Lord Jesus Christ. Galatians 6:14a

God powerfully used a man named Carl to witness to his family and friends through a pocket cross. Father of a large family, for many years working with the railroad, Carl did not attend church often during his younger years. In retirement he became much more involved in serving as a church board leader, encouraging his family to attend church, and demonstrating a growing prayer life. One year the church distributed pocket crosses as part of the Lenten worship emphasis. Carl proudly carried that cross and showed it to many people as pointing to His Savior and theirs. When he died not long afterward, his family insisted that the pocket cross be placed in his casket as a witness to his faith in Jesus.

St. Paul writes pointedly about the importance of the cross in his letter to the Galatians. They had been returning to an emphasis on the law as contributing to their salvation instead of trusting in Christ alone. Paul concludes his letter, "May I never boast except in the cross of our Lord Jesus Christ." Earlier he reminds them, "You are all sons of God through faith in Christ Jesus, for all of you who were baptized into Christ have clothed yourself with Christ. There is neither Jew nor Greek, slave nor free, male nor female, for you are all one in Christ Jesus" (Galatians 3:26–28).

Carl gave testimony to the importance of his baptismal faith for his family and friends by holding dear that simple pocket cross. We can provide no better witness than joining Paul and Carl in "never boasting except in the cross of our Lord Jesus Christ."

*Prayer:*

When I survey the wondrous cross
On which the prince of glory died,
My richest gain I count but loss
And pour contempt on all my pride.

Forbid it Lord, that I should boast
Save in the death of Christ, my God;
All the vain things that charm me most,
I sacrifice them to his blood.
*LW* 114:1–2

February 11

# A Dacha Conversation

## *Reading:* Colossians 1:3–6

*Text:* So then, just as you received Christ Jesus as Lord, continue to live in Him, rooted and built up in Him, strengthened in the faith as you were taught, and overflowing with thankfulness. Colossians 2:6

St. Paul's words to the Colossians remind me of a recent visit to Russia where we were welcomed at the dacha, or county home, of Fyodor and Natasha, a few miles outside of Moscow. We had never met them before but were treated graciously with a tour of the surrounding countryside, including a small village church and museum, plus a hike through fields and a hilly wooded area near a river. Seated around their table, we ate delicious food from their garden and engaged in meaningful conversation.

To our joy, we learned that these highly educated scientists, at one time prominent in the Soviet nuclear program, shared our faith in the triune God. Their parents and grandparents had experienced persecution for their faith. The church is an integral part of their lives, and they arranged for their grandson to be baptized. Their faith in Christ Jesus as Lord with its deep roots expresses itself in their caring lives and thankfulness for God's gifts, including the wonders of His creation in the Russian countryside.

Paul's words to the Colossians in the first chapter describe our ongoing communication with Fyodor and Natasha: "All over the world this gospel is bearing fruit and growing, just as it had been doing among you since the day you heard it and understood God's grace in all its truth" (Colossians 1:6).

Our faith in Christ was strengthened as a result of our dacha visit. We shared God's saving grace at work in our lives in America and gave thanks with them for His saving presence in Russia. We need each other around the world to tell the story of Jesus and His love.

*Prayer:* Dear Father, thank You for moving in the hearts of our new Russian friends to believe in Your Son as Savior and to share that faith with us as encouragement for witness worldwide. Amen.

# Hosted in a Moscow Apartment

## *Reading:* Ephesians 4:1–6

*Text:* As a prisoner of the Lord, then, I urge you to live a life worthy of the calling you received. Ephesians 4:1

Our Russian trip also took us to the crowded streets and metro of Moscow. We saw many people struggling to make a living and evidence of a fast-paced life. Our host, Nick, a computer science professor and author, invited us for an evening dinner prepared by his wife Luci at their Moscow apartment. They displayed so many of the Christian qualities described by St. Paul in Ephesians: "a life worthy of the calling you received, ... humble, gentle, patient, bearing with one another in love" (Ephesians 4:1–2). They were true servants in their generous sharing of delicious food and conversation.

The couple traveling with us knew Nick from his time as visiting professor in California. They knew of his faith in Christ. He helped them translate Christian books into Russian for outreach purposes. He showed us many Russian Orthodox churches in Moscow and along the "Golden Ring." Months later, he phoned us on December 24 to wish us a blessed Christmas as he awaited January 6, Epiphany, for the Orthodox observance.

This rich evening together in that Moscow apartment gave us a broader understanding of Paul's words about "the unity of the Spirit through the bond of peace . . . one body and one Spirit–just as you were called to one hope when you were called–one Lord, one faith, one baptism; one God and Father of all, who is over all and through all and in all" (Ephesians 4:3–6).

So aware of different cultures, so far away from our home in America, conscious of significant differences between our Lutheran Church and Russian Orthodoxy, we nevertheless saw God at work in that tiny, well-lit apartment in Moscow where Nick and Luci's faith in Jesus as Savior radiated a warmth of hospitality to us that bonded us to them.

*Prayer:* We thank thee that thy Church, unsleeping
While earth rolls onward into light,
Through all the world her watch is keeping,
And never rests by day or night.
*HS 98* 904:2

# A Plea from North Carolina

## *Reading:* 2 Corinthians 1:3–11

*Text:* On Him we have set our hope that He will continue to deliver us, as you help us by your prayers. 2 Corinthians 1:10b–11a

Have you thought about the witness to Jesus that occurs when prayer is needed and requested? The next four devotions will focus on a plea for prayer from North Carolina and how many lives were impacted by the aftermath of that request. I am asking you to read St. Paul's words to the church in Corinth (2 Corinthians 1:3–11) each of the next three days.

About seven months ago, we received an e-mail request for prayer from our dear friends in Hickory, North Carolina. Their six-year-old grandson Stephen, had been diagnosed with Acute Myelogenous Leukemia (AML), and the prospects looked dim. They contacted hundreds of people for prayer support and, as a result, thousands joined them on Stephen's behalf before the throne of God. Those prayers continued over several months as he experienced increasingly severe symptoms, received several treatments, and finally was moved to Duke University Hospital for a bone marrow transplant with his younger brother Jacob as the donor.

St. Paul involves the Corinthians in prayer on his behalf. While in the Roman province of Asia, probably in Ephesus, Paul endured life-threatening hardships and suffering. Under extreme pressure, he writes, "Indeed, in our hearts we felt the sentence of death" (2 Corinthians 1:9a). Relying on God who raises the dead, Paul adds, "On Him we have set our hope that He will continue to deliver us, as you help us by your prayers."

Paul and our friends witnessed to their need for God's grace and mercy in Christ as they asked for help through the prayers of fellow believers. By joining countless other Christians in prayer for Stephen, we bore testimony to the same God who sent His Son to be our Savior.

*Prayer:* Before our Father's throne We pour our ardent prayers,
Our fears, our hopes, our sins are one, Our comforts and our cares.

We share our mutual woes, Our mutual burdens bear,
And often for each other flows The sympathizing tear.
*LW* 295:2–3

# Touched by a Family

***Reading:*** **2 Corinthians 1:3–11**

*Text:* Who comforts us in all our troubles, so that we can comfort those in any trouble with the comfort we ourselves have received from God. 2 Corinthians 1:4

In the eye of the storm raging in Stephen's medical struggle with Acute Myelogenous Leukemia (AML) is the Ludwig family—his parents Mike and Stephanie, his four-year-old brother, Jacob, the bone marrow donor, his grandparents, our close friends Dave and Kathy, and his uncles, aunts, and cousins. The months of medical treatments, hospitalization, and the bone marrow transplant took their toll physically, emotionally, and spiritually.

But God is sustaining that family by His grace alone and enabling them to bear testimony to their Savior Jesus Christ with hospital staff, other patients and their families, and all those around the world praying for them. They prepared a website for updates, sent e-mails, gave others an opportunity to write notes of encouragement to Stephen, and displayed a map with red dots indicating places in America and the world where specific prayers were being lifted up for Stephen. We are touched by the Ludwigs and pointed to God's love in Christ.

St. Paul, under duress and facing death, turned to the Corinthians for comfort but also comforted them in return—because he received comfort from God. In this great exchange, Paul gives all credit to God: "Praise be to the God and Father of our Lord Jesus Christ, the Father of compassion and the God of all comfort, who comforts us in our troubles, so that we can comfort those in any trouble with the comfort we ourselves have received from God" (2 Corinthians 1:3–4). Paul touched their lives and pointed them to God the source of his comfort.

God has been touching the Ludwig family in profound ways during this extended illness and through them our family as well. How is God touching your family with His love right now and how might He be touching the lives of others through you?

*Prayer:* Christians, while on earth abiding, Let us never cease to pray,
Firmly in the Lord confiding As our parents in their day.
Be the children's voices raised To the God their parents praised.
May his blessing, failing never, Rest upon his people ever.
*LW* 434:1

February 15

# An Outpouring of Thanks

## *Reading:* 2 Corinthians 1:3–11

*Text:* Then many will give thanks on our behalf for the gracious favor granted us in answer to the prayers of many. 2 Corinthians 1:11b

A few weeks ago we received an e-mail from the Ludwigs that Stephen's bone marrow transplant seemed successful and that, although his recovery would be very lengthy, he was able to return home as an outpatient. They thanked us for our prayers. We shared the good news with all of the groups at our church praying for his health. When Dave and Kathy visited us briefly a few days ago, we were able to see pictures of Stephen's physical condition at various stages and rejoiced with them at his improvement while continuing to pray for his ongoing healing.

St. Paul was delivered from the crisis he faced but continued to need help in his ministry. He writes regarding the Corinthian Christians' support: "Then many will give thanks on our behalf for the gracious favor granted us in answer to the prayers of many." First century Christians and twenty-first century Christians joined in an outpouring of thanks to the God and Father of our Lord Jesus Christ. That outpouring of thanks in the middle of ongoing troubles, hardships, and struggles serves as a powerful witness to our Savior. Paul writes, "For just as the sufferings of Christ flow over into our lives, so also through Christ our comfort overflows" (2 Corinthians 1:5).

Pray that your life will overflow with thanksgiving for God's gracious favor in your own circumstances and in the lives of those for whom you pray. His greatest gift is eternal life through faith in Jesus Christ crucified and risen.

*Prayer:* Now thank we all our God With heart and hand and voices,
Who wondrous things has done, In whom his world rejoices;
Who from our mother's arms Has blest us on our way
With countless gifts of love And still is ours today.

Oh may this bounteous God Through all our life be near us,
With ever joyful hearts And blessed peace to cheer us
And keep us in his grace And guide us when perplexed
And free us from all harm In this world and the next.
*LW* 443:1–2

# An Orange Bracelet

***Reading:*** **Deuteronomy 6:4–9**

*Text:* Impress them on your children. . . . Tie them as symbols on your hands. Deuteronomy 6:7a, 8

What a profound and far-reaching impact the serious illness of Stephen Ludwig has had on our family. When Dave and Kathy visited us from North Carolina earlier this week, they left us an orange bracelet with Stephen's name on it to be given to one of our grandchildren as a prayer reminder. We decided to give it to six-year-old Josiah, who is closest in age to Stephen. He was delighted to receive it and wears it proudly. Wednesday afternoon he walked up to the kitchen table where my wife was sitting, closed his eyes and said, "I'm praying for Stephen." At Lenten service he told his mother that he was praying for Stephen's "zucchinia." While he understands the vegetable, zucchini, better than the disease, leukemia, he is sincerely praying for his new friend to be healed. Our daughter wrote a note to his teacher explaining the bracelet and the name. Saturday, when we babysit our daughter's five sons, we will show Josiah Stephen's picture on our refrigerator.

That orange bracelet reminds me of Moses' instructions to Israel in Deuteronomy 6. After telling them, "Hear O Israel: The LORD our God, the LORD is one. Love the LORD your God with all your heart and with all your soul and with all your strength" (Deuteronomy 6:4–5), he describes how God's words are to penetrate their hearts and their homes: "Impress them on your children. . . . Tie them as symbols on your hands." Both God's commands and His promises, including a coming Messiah to save them from their sins, are to be a practical part of everyday life in words, symbols, and actions.

Josiah is learning at a young age to trust Jesus as his Savior, to pray to God for healing, and to care about a young boy his age who is sick. An orange bracelet with Stephen's name helps him remember God's love. In what ways does your home bear witness to your Lord?

*Prayer:* In Christian homes, Lord, let them be
Your blessing to their family;
Let Christian schools your work extend
In living truth as you intend.
*LW* 470:2

# Favorite Bible Verses As Witness

***Reading:*** **2 Timothy 3:14–17**

*Text:* From a child thou hast known the Holy Scriptures, which are able to make thee wise unto salvation through faith which is in Christ Jesus. 2 Timothy 3:15 (KJV)

What is your favorite Bible verse? How did it become meaningful to you? With whom have you shared it? Have you ever thought of that verse as a tool for witness of your faith in Jesus Christ as Savior? Perhaps, a simple first step to setting the world ablaze! During the next few devotions, I will be sharing some favorite Bible verses that have powerfully impacted our family.

In our text, we find Paul writing to his student, Timothy, now serving as a young pastor. He stresses the importance of Holy Scriptures in bringing Timothy to faith and in building up others to whom he will minister. "From a child thou hast known the Holy Scriptures." How many Bible verses did Timothy learn from his grandmother, Lois, and his mother, Eunice, as he grew up? (2 Timothy 1:5). What events in his home life made these verses especially vivid for him? In what settings did he repeat them to others? One thing we know: The Holy Scriptures were able to make Timothy "wise unto salvation through faith which is in Christ Jesus." And these words, "given by inspiration of God," would be "useful for teaching, rebuking, correcting and training in righteousness" (NIV). Others could receive eternal salvation and strength for daily living through these Holy Scriptures.

As you read the stories of favorite Bible verses, search your own memory for special Gospel texts and be open to new verses in your daily reading that might become favorites for sharing with others. You can count on God's Spirit to quicken these Bible verses for your faith and witness.

*Prayer:* Your living Word shine in our heart
And to a new life win us.
With seed of light implant the start
Of Christ-like deeds within us.
Help us uproot what is impure,
And while faith's fruits in us mature,
Prepare us for your harvest.
*LW* 336:2

# Becky and Jeremiah 29:11

*Reading:* Jeremiah 29:1–14

*Text:* For I know the plans I have for you, declares the LORD, plans to prosper you and not to harm you, plans to give you hope and a future. Jeremiah 29:11

This Bible verse requires two devotions because of its powerful impact upon our family and many others. Our youngest daughter, Becky, was diagnosed with aplastic anemia in 1989 and died 3 ½ years later at 23 years of age. In early 1992, she was receiving more frequent blood transfusions and preparing to graduate from college. On a March Monday I received a letter of encouragement from a fellow pastor in New York with a bookmark, containing the words of Jeremiah 29:11.

When I called Becky that day to hear the latest news on her blood counts, I decided to share the passage with her. She said, "I also have a verse to share with you. You go first." I shared Jeremiah 29:11 with her, and there was dead silence on the phone line. She simply said, "That's my verse too." The very same day she had received the same verse in the mail from her former high school journalism teacher. From that point on, Jeremiah 29:11 became our favorite Bible verse: "For I know the plans I have for you, declares the LORD, plans to prosper you and not to harm you, plans to give you hope and a future." We were praying that Becky's future would include healing from her aplastic anemia, but we knew that God loved her deeply and had won salvation for her through the death and resurrection of Jesus Christ.

Becky shared that verse with other students in a Bible study and wrote about it in the newspaper of her former high school. We got extra copies of the bookmark to remind us and share with others. In a Seattle hospital, we had occasion to use Jeremiah 29:11 in conversation with other family members whose loved ones were receiving bone marrow transplants—always pointing to Jesus as our Savior. More on this remarkable Bible verse tomorrow.

*Prayer:* So when the precious seed is sown,
Your quick'ning grace bestow
That all whose souls the truth receive
It's saving pow'r may know.
*LW* 342:4

# Jeremiah 29:11 Lives On

*Reading:* Jeremiah 29:1–14

*Text:* For I know the plans I have for you declares the LORD, plans to prosper you and not to harm you, plans to give you hope and a future. Jeremiah 29:11

Our daughter, Becky, died on January 9, 1993, from bone marrow transplant complications, but our favorite Bible verse, Jeremiah 29:11, lives on. At the funeral, the pastor used it as a text. Becky's fiancé and her former high school math teacher independently referred to it also. Invited to lead chapel at Concordia High School Fort Wayne, which had supported Becky with prayer and cards, I was asked to use Jeremiah 29:11 as a text. That spring the Concordia girl's track team sent us their special T-shirts with Jeremiah 29:11 on the back. We have in our home as gifts a framed picture with Jeremiah 29:11 in calligraphy and a folio page from the 1640 King James Version of that chapter. The gravestone with Becky's name and ours features Jeremiah 29:11.

Asked to speak and teach Bible studies on Jeremiah 29:11, I studied the passage carefully in its context. Judah, feeling hopeless in Babylonian exile because of the repeated sins of idolatry in their homeland, receives a letter from Jeremiah, urging them to prepare for a long stay in exile, remaining faithful in prayer and worship of the God of Israel. Then to these repentant believers, Jeremiah delivers the Lord's message of plans to give His people "hope and a future," in the short term, after 70 years, a return to Israel and in the long term, from the very heart of God, eternal salvation through the death and resurrection of Jesus, the promised Messiah.

Yes, Jeremiah 29:11 lifted up Becky and our family in critical times and continues to touch lives with the Good News of Jesus Christ. We call that verse "the gift that keeps on giving."

*Prayer:* Heavenly Father, we rejoice that Your Word of "hope and a future" brings comfort to our family and leads us to share this passage about salvation through Jesus Christ with others. Amen.

# Mark and Psalm 37:5

### *Reading:* Psalm 37:1–9

*Text:* Commit thy way unto the LORD, trust also in Him, and He shall bring it to pass. Psalm 37:5 (KJV)

When my son, Mark, was 13 years old, we traveled to Indianapolis to spend some quality time together as father and son at a time when my mother was hospitalized with cancer. While there, my mother died from a sudden stroke. At the funeral, Pastor Maas used Mom's confirmation verse as his text: "Commit thy way unto the LORD, trust also in Him, and He shall bring it to pass." During the service, Mark asked me if he could have that verse as his confirmation text. Obviously his grandma's faith in Jesus and lifelong walk with the Lord had moved him to make that request. As Mark's pastor in Peru, Indiana, I was able to grant his request at his confirmation several months later.

Twelve years later to the day of Mom's funeral, Mark was married in Rochester, Minnesota. In a brief message as his father, I quoted that favorite Bible passage, Psalm 37:5, as guidance for the newlyweds. Tears formed in Mark's eyes as he remembered. A few days ago my only brother, Stan, died in Indianapolis. Mark drove there for the funeral, joining his sister, Amy, in support of us. At the family burial plot, both of us looked down at the grave of my mother and saw those familiar words, "Commit thy way unto the LORD," engraved on her stone. God's Spirit had given faith in Jesus Christ as Savior to Mom, Mark, and me as His baptized children. Flowing from that trust comes a commitment to walk in His ways and witness His love to our family and friends.

In Psalm 37, David, attacked by foes and aware of his own sins, looks back over his life and sees the Lord as his stronghold and his hope for the future. Gladly he commits his way unto the Lord and trusts His saving promises. Another favorite Bible passage for life and witness! I will never forget Mark and Psalm 37:5.

*Prayer:* Oh, that the Lord would guide my ways
To keep his statutes still!
Oh, that my God would grant me grace
To know and do his will!
*LW* 392:1

# Stan and Revelation 3:11

## *Reading:* Revelation 3:7–13

*Text:* Hold on to what you have, so that no one will take your crown. Revelation 3:11b

My brother, Stan, died on April 10 at age 62 after a long struggle of eleven years, begun by a major disabling stroke. During that time he served productively in many ways, reached out to countless people where he lived, including his home near a small town, assisted living facilities, and nursing homes—and faithfully went to worship among God's people. As the end approached, his daughters asked about any Bible texts or hymns he would choose for his funeral. Without hesitation he selected Revelation 3:11, which the pastor then used at his funeral: "I am coming soon. Hold on to what you have, so that no one will take your crown."

In John's book of Revelation, these words are addressed to the church in Philadelphia. Although they have little strength, God promises to be with them in the hour of trial and give them the crown of life through faith in Jesus when He comes again. He urges them to remain faithful in difficult times.

I believe Stan wanted that Bible verse as a testimony to God's saving grace in his own life's struggles, but more important as a message to his daughters and other family members and friends to "hold on to what you have, so that no one will take your crown." Responsive to Stan's witness, his 2 ½ year old granddaughter was baptized in his room the day before he died. And the clear message of salvation was proclaimed at his funeral. Revelation 3:11—a favorite Bible verse for my brother, Stan, and a witness to many!

*Prayer:* Fight the good fight with all your might;
Christ is your strength and Christ your right.
Lay hold on life, and it shall be
Your joy and crown eternally.

Faint not nor fear, his arms are near;
He changes not who holds you dear;
Only believe, and you will see
That Christ is all eternally.
*LW* 299:1, 4

# Foot Washing in East Africa

## *Reading:* John 13:1–17

*Text:* "Now that I, your Lord and Teacher, have washed your feet, you should also wash one another's feet." John 13:14

The story of Jesus washing the feet of His disciples models His servant role as God in the flesh, carrying out a ministry of preaching and healing and, especially, giving himself obediently into death on a cross. That story also reveals our servant role in today's world, saved by God's grace. The following account from a missionary in East Africa makes that servant role very real for us:

"That verse of Scripture came vividly to my mind last month as I visited a small congregation of Lutheran Sudanese refugees in a village in Ethiopia. The people knew we were coming and had been waiting all morning for our arrival. When we finally approached the church site, we could hear the joyful singing and drumming. The singing continued as we arrived, and we were given places to sit. Unexpectedly, a woman with a basin of water appeared and knelt down in front of me and began to remove my shoes and socks and wash my feet with cool, clear water. Then she did the same for each of those who were traveling with me. In that hot, dusty place, we were refreshed and humbled by this loving Christian example of servanthood!

"I saw a demonstration of such servanthood again among the Sudanese Christians in Gambella, Ethiopia. When they heard there were more than 300 people waiting to be baptized in the Penyudo refugee camp in Sudan, they took up a collection and commissioned their own Pastor Matthew to go with the evangelist from Penyudo and baptize their brothers and sisters in Christ. They also collected enough money from their own meager resources to enable Rev. Matthew and Evangelist Jacob to stay for several days of teaching and to provide bread and wine in order that these new Christians could also receive the Lord's Supper. . . . I know the church there was truly refreshed by the love and servanthood of their fellow Lutheran believers who, out of their own poverty, provided for their needs."

*Prayer:* Lord Jesus, help us to follow the example of the Sudanese believers of Your servant death on Calvary. Amen.

# Temptations As Obstacles to Witness

## *Reading:* 1 Corinthians 10:1–13

*Text:* No temptation has seized you except what is common to man. 1 Corinthians 10:13a

After describing his Gospel ministry to the world as a demanding race like no other, Paul continues with a warning about temptations that can serve as obstacles to a Christian witness. In the next several devotions we will consider nine temptations that are Satan's tools to derail our witness to Jesus Christ as Savior.

Paul points to the example of Israel in the wilderness as a way of introducing the subject of dangerous temptations. First, he reaffirms God's grace and mercy to the forefathers. Their deliverance through the Red Sea was like Christian Baptism. Their constant provision of food and drink from a loving God was, in a spiritual sense, like the regular reception of Christ's body and blood in Holy Communion. And the rock that provided water was like Christ, the rock of our salvation.

Yet, Israel succumbed to many temptations that did not please God. They gave into idolatry. They engaged in sexual immorality. They grumbled and put God to the test because of their dissatisfaction. These temptations caused many to die in the wilderness and presented a negative witness about God's people to the neighboring nations.

Now Paul turns to the Corinthian Christians and to us with a warning of sin in the making and a promise of God's faithfulness: "So, if you think you are standing firm, be careful that you don't fall! No temptation has seized you except what is common to man. And God is faithful; He will not let you be tempted, He will also provide a way out so that you can stand up under it" (1 Corinthians 10:12–13). Read carefully about specific temptations in the following devotions. Trust your faithful God for forgiveness and strength. The witnessing race goes on by His grace until He comes again.

*Prayer:* O God forsake me not!
Lord, hear my supplication!
In every evil hour
Help me resist temptation;
And when the prince of hell
My conscience seeks to blot,
Be then not far from me
O God forsake me not!
*LW* 372:3

# Judgmental Attitude

***Reading:*** **Matthew 23:23–24**

*Text:* You blind guides! You strain out a gnat but swallow a camel. Matthew 23:24

The first temptation that presents an obstacle to our Christian witness is a judgmental attitude. We turn to Matthew 23 for those first three temptations. On His way to the cross, Jesus comes into sharp conflict with the teachers of the law and the Pharisees. They desired very much to bear witness to the Torah of God. Somehow they failed. Jesus exposes them: "You travel over land and sea to win a single convert, and when he becomes one, you make him twice as much a son of hell as you are" (Matthew 23:15).

One major obstacle to their witness was a judgmental attitude. They criticized even the smallest infractions of regulations on the part of others. They judged Jesus on several occasions for breaking the Sabbath law. Implicit in their judging was the sense that their own keeping of these regulations was beyond reproach. With this judgmental attitude, how could they possibly reach out with the love of God to bring sinners to their Savior? Therefore, Jesus says, "You blind guides! You strain out a gnat but swallow a camel." Their own attitudes, like swallowing a camel, stood under God's judgment while their judging others on minor infractions, like straining a gnat, only destroyed their witness.

Are you ever tempted to be judgmental? Do you look at the person without Christ as someone to be criticized for their behaviors? Does your attitude stand in the way of showing Jesus' compassion toward sinners? How does God view your own attitudes, even while you externally live a Christian life? God is faithful to reveal the sin in your heart. God is faithful to forgive your sin for Jesus' sake. God is faithful to give you "justice, mercy, and faithfulness" (Matthew 23:23) so you can see others as Jesus sees them—sheep without a shepherd needing forgiveness of sins, life, and salvation. A judgmental attitude poses an obstacle to our witness. God will provide a way out through Christ so our witness is life-changing.

*Prayer:* God, be merciful to me a sinner so I can see others as You do. Amen.

# Greed

## *Reading:* Matthew 23:25–26

*Text:* "But inside they are full of greed and self-absorption." Matthew 23:25c

Jesus exposes greed as a second temptation that impedes our witness. Continuing to address the teachers of the law and the Pharisees, He accuses them of cleaning the outside of the cup as a ritual observance without cleaning the inside—"but inside they are full of greed and self-absorption." He notes their having more interest in the gold of the temple than the temple. They are greedy for more and more wealth, rich garments, and favorable attention from the people in places of honor at banquets and in the synagogue. What an obstacle to their witness!

Does greed tempt you? Do we find ourselves seeking more material blessings and then taking them for granted? Does having friends and even fellow church members of higher social standing affect our witness to others with little wealth to commend them? Does our greed cause us to fill our time with work and efforts to advance our standing, so we lose sight of the race to set the world ablaze with Christ? Confessing our sin of greed that blunts our witness, we turn to the One who paid the price on Calvary for forgiveness.

Paul writes, "For you know the grace of our Lord Jesus Christ, that though He was rich, yet for your sakes He became poor, so that you through His poverty might become rich" (2 Corinthians 8:9). And he describes the powerful witness of the Macedonian churches: "Out of the most severe trial, their overflowing joy and their extreme poverty welled up in rich generosity . . . they gave themselves first to the Lord and then to us in keeping with God's will" (2 Corinthians 8:2, 5b). God is faithful to forgive our sin of greed and provide a way out through Christ so our witness is life-changing.

*Prayer:* Grant us hearts, dear Lord, to give you
Gladly, freely of your own.
With the sunshine of your goodness
Melt our thankless hearts of stone
Till our cold and selfish natures,
Warmed by you, at length believe
That more happy and more blessed
'Tis to give than to receive
*LW* 402:2

# Hypocrisy

***Reading:* Matthew 23:27–28**

*Text:* "You are like whitewashed tombs." Matthew 23:27b

The third temptation that serves as an obstacle to our witnessing is hypocrisy. Jesus introduces each of His seven woes with the words: "Woe to you, teachers of the law and Pharisees, you hypocrites!" (Matthew 23:13). Then He makes the same point with a powerful image, "You are like whitewashed tombs, which look beautiful on the outside but on the inside are full of dead men's bones and everything unclean" (Matthew 23:27). Hypocrisy! They pretend to be righteous in every way and take great pains to maintain appearances, but inside are full of hypocrisy and wickedness. Their witness turns out to be phony and pious.

Are you tempted to be hypocritical? You want to be seen as decent and upright, capable and intelligent, civic-minded and generous. The list goes on. You work to protect and enhance your image. The problem comes when we hide our true motives and pretend to be something we are not. When we fail to be honest and admit our shortcomings, others see right through us. How many unbelievers say, "I'm not the best person in the world, but I would never want to go to a church with all those hypocrites."

We come to our knees, unlike the Pharisees, and with the publican cry out, "God, have mercy on me, a sinner" (Luke 18:13). And the Son of Man who came to seek and to save that which was lost places His hand of forgiveness on us and frees us to live authentically as His witnesses. We point not to ourselves or our righteousness but to Jesus and His righteousness. We let Him live through us as His baptized children so His love shines through us to others. The obstacle of hypocrisy is removed. Our witness to the Savior continues by His grace.

*Prayer:* All this for my transgression,
My wayward soul to win;
This torment of your Passion,
To set me free from sin.
I cast myself before you,
Your wrath my rightful lot;
Have mercy, I implore you,
O Lord, condemn me not!
*LW* 113:3

February 27

# Sloth

## *Reading:* Proverbs 6:6–11

*Text:* How long will you lie there, you sluggard? When will you get up from your sleep? Proverbs 6:9

The fourth temptation impeding our witness is sloth. We are tempted to take it easy, spend a little extra time in bed or in front of the television. Maximize the break at work. Slow down your motions as you work. Daydream about your next vacation. Spend your retirement relaxing. Yes, telling others about Jesus is important when you get around to it. Before we know it, the day, week, month, year, lifetime is over, and little has been accomplished.

The writer of Proverbs warns against sloth: "How long will you lie there, you sluggard? When will you get up from your sleep?" He recommends that we consider the ways of the industrious ant who, with no overseer to crack the whip, stores its provisions in summer and gathers its food at harvest. He suggests that, with a slothful attitude, poverty will come on us like a bandit and scarcity like an armed man as we idle the hours away.

Meanwhile, the race is on to reach people with the saving Gospel before Christ comes again. Each day counts. Each opportunity needs to be seized. It is a life or death matter. Paul writes in Ephesians, "Wake up, O sleeper, rise from the dead, and Christ will shine on you. Be very careful, then, how you live–not as unwise but as wise, making the most of every opportunity, because the days are evil" (Ephesians 5:14–16).

Confessing the sin of sloth, we look to the One who stayed awake in the Garden of Gethsemane to pray and went sleepless to the cross where He made the most of the once for all opportunity to pay for the world's sin. Forgiven, we pray for spiritual energy to seek and find the lost. God's Spirit will fill our days and deeds with a compassion for reaching others with the Gospel of Jesus.

*Prayer:* The Bridegroom soon will call us,
"Come to the wedding feast."
May slumber not befall us
Nor watchfulness decrease.
But may our lamps be burning
With oil enough and more
That with our Lord returning,
We find an open door.
*LW* 176:1

# Compromise

### *Reading:* 2 Timothy 4:1–5

*Text:* Demas, because he loved the world, has deserted me and has gone to Thessalonica. 2 Timothy 4:10a

A fifth temptation blocking our witness to Christ is compromise. Satan tempts us in the middle of our life and witness to listen to the voice of the world. Just give a little. You can still represent Christ. Avoid conflict and disagreement. Join in with the world's agenda and lifestyle. You will be more accepted, so you can witness. How very seductive is the temptation to compromise!

St. Paul, in one short sentence, conveys to Timothy the end result of such compromise, however alluring. The same brother in the faith, once greeted by Paul in his letter to the Colossians (Colossians 4:14), now has deserted not only Paul but his Lord.

In this same letter, Paul urges Timothy to an uncompromising proclamation of the Christian faith: "Preach the Word; be prepared in season and out of season; correct, rebuke and encourage–with great patience and careful instruction. For the time will come when men will not put up with sound doctrine. Instead, to suit their own desires, they will gather around them a great number of teachers to say what their itching ears want to hear. They will turn their ears away from the truth and turn aside to myths. But you, keep your head in all situations, endure hardship, do the work of an evangelist. Discharge all the duties of your ministry" (2 Timothy 4:2–5).

That time has come. Confessing our willingness to compromise, we embrace the truth of God's forgiveness through the death and resurrection of Jesus. And we accept Paul's admonition to Timothy for our own daily witness: Clear, bold, truthful proclamation of salvation through Christ alone.

*Prayer:* Cast afar this world's vain pleasure
And boldly strive for heavenly treasure.
Be steadfast in the Savior's might.
Trust the Lord, who stands beside you,
For Jesus from all harm will hide you.
By faith you conquer in the fight.
Take courage, weary soul! Look forward to the goal!
Joy awaits you.
The race well run, Your long war won,
Your crown shines splendid as the run.
*LW* 303:2

# Cynicism

## *Reading:* Ecclesiastes 1:1–18

*Text:* "Meaningless! Meaningless!" says the Teacher. "Utterly meaningless! Everything is meaningless." Ecclesiastes 1:2

A sixth temptation blocking our witness is cynicism. We live in a cold, cruel world. Terrorist acts occur at random with horrible death and destruction the result. People manipulate others for their own ends in governments, corporations, and even churches. Unborn babies are slaughtered through abortion; and innocent victims of all ages are killed in the city streets and even rural areas of our country. Famous people in every arena often attract respect and hero-worship, only to be exposed for sexual immorality, lying, or embezzlement. We are tempted to cynicism. We believe nothing, suspect everybody, and steel ourselves against love, hope, and compassion. No wonder our witness suffers.

In Ecclesiastes, the Teacher writes with the voice of experience. Having lived a long time, he cries out, "Everything is meaningless." In the book, he traces the futility of hard work, wealth, pleasures, wisdom, and prestige. Does he not sound cynical? Apart from God nothing makes sense, and you may as well die. But he concludes with a reference to the one Shepherd, whom we know as giving us life in all its fullness (John 10:10).

When our cynicism depresses us and we live without hope, God leads us to acknowledge our sin in an evil world as a reality. Confessing that sin, we look to Jesus, our Good Shepherd who came to rescue us and give us abundant life. He brings us victory over evil by His crucifixion and hope through His Resurrection. Just because of an evil world, we see the need to bring God's hope to others and witness realistically but positively of salvation through Christ.

*Prayer:* Judge not the Lord by feeble sense,
But trust him for his grace;
Behind a frowning providence
Faith sees a smiling face.

Blind unbelief is sure to err
And scan his work in vain;
God is his own interpreter,
And he will make it plain.
*LW* 426:2–3

# Discouragement

## *Reading:* Psalm 102:1–11

*Text:* For my days vanish like smoke; my bones burn like glowing embers. My heart is blighted and withered like grass; I forget to eat my food. Psalm 102:3–4

A seventh temptation blocking our witness is discouragement. We get excited about our faith as we witness God's faithfulness at work in our lives. We reach out to tell others, starting close to home. Then Satan brings us discouragement. The jeering response or deathly quiet throws a wet blanket on our witness. We start to struggle with our own doubts. Things deteriorate in our own lives—sickness, strife at home, financial problems, troubles at church. Before we know it discouragement renders us ineffective in our witness of the Savior.

The psalmist has clearly become discouraged as a result of his affliction, perhaps physical illness: "For my days vanish like smoke; my bones burn like glowing embers. My heart is blighted and withered like grass." He feels lonely, taunted by his enemies, physically and emotionally drained. His discouragement dampens his praise to God and his witness of God's salvation. Therefore, he cries out, "Hear my prayer, O LORD . . . Turn Your ear to me; when I call, answer me quickly" (Psalm 102:1–2). Later he is able to look to God's rule and trust His deliverance of Zion. He then bears witness: "Let this be written for a future generation that a people not yet created may praise the LORD" (Psalm 102:18).

Admitting our discouragement as experienced by the psalmist, we turn to the Lord for forgiveness, healing, and encouragement. He helps us remember His covenant promises, the sending of His Son as the crucified Messiah, and the Spirit's presence in the Church at the eucharistic altar. Encouraged, we respond with a joyful witness to our Savior so future generations may praise the Lord.

*Prayer:* Take heart, have hope, my spirit,
And do not be afraid.
From any low depression,
Where agonies are made,
God's grace will lift you upward
On arms of saving might
Until the sun you hoped for
Delights your eager sight.
*LW* 427:3

# Distraction

*Reading:* Luke 9:57–62

*Text:* "No one who puts his hand to the plow and looks back is fit for service in the kingdom of God." Luke 9:62

The eighth temptation in our series that sees temptations as obstacles to Christian witness is distraction. How many times do you decide to share your faith then get distracted by more pressing matters? The phone call is never made, the e-mail not sent, the name never added to your prayer list, the breakfast conversation never held. You have been mightily tempted by Satan and distracted from your witness goal.

In Luke's Gospel, Jesus stresses the destructive nature of giving in to distractions: "No one who puts his hand to the plow and looks back is fit for service in the kingdom of God." Can you imagine what happens when a farmer plows a field with plow or tractor and takes his eye off of the goal (some distant point straight ahead)? When he looks back or down or sideways or up, the row is ruined. Jesus suggests that earthly concerns can often distract a disciple from following Him. One man wanted to first bury his father, another to first go back and say good-bye to his family. Jesus answers with the plowman who looks back and is unworthy of service.

We confess giving in to distractions, many of which seem legitimate, and impeding our mission to the lost. Thank God, we have a Savior who refused to be distracted. In this same chapter, Luke tells us, "As the time approached for Him to be taken up to heaven, Jesus resolutely set out for Jerusalem" (Luke 9:51). Because He went to the cross for us, our sins are forgiven, the world has a Savior, and we are witnesses of His salvation. In our Baptism, we have been pressed into His service with His Gospel.

*Prayer:* "I teach you how to shun and flee
What harms your soul's salvation;
Your heart from every guile to free,
From sin and its temptation.
I am the refuge of the soul
And lead you to your heavenly goal."
*LW* 379:4

---

# Self-absorption

## *Reading:* Colossians 3:1–5

*Text:* But for those who are self-seeking and who reject the truth and follow evil, there will be wrath and anger. Romans 2:8

We come to the end of our list of temptations Satan uses to thwart our Christian witness. The final temptation is self-absorption. In a way, this temptation lies behind most of the others. Our culture glorifies the self, psychoanalyzes the self, develops the limitless potential of the self, and pampers the self with every product imaginable. If that cultural emphasis isn't a temptation to self-absorption, then I don't know what is. Our Christian witness to declare the great things God has done is often blunted by our self-absorption with our problems, our struggles, our discoveries, our insights, our desires, our satisfactions.

Paul nails self-absorption in his catalogue of sins in Romans 1 and 2, demonstrating that all have sinned and fall short of the glory of God. He writes, "But for those who are self-seeking . . . there will be wrath and anger." Indeed we stand condemned before the wrath of God on the basis of our self-absorption and feeble efforts to justify ourselves before God. We confess our self-absorption as a serious roadblock to any Christian witness on our part.

In Colossians, though, Christ puts our self in perspective, based on Christ's death and resurrection. "Since then you have been raised with Christ, set your hearts on things above. . . . Set your minds on things above not on earthly things. For you did and your life is now hidden with Christ in God. ... You have taken off your old self with its practices and have put on the new self, which is being renewed in knowledge in the image of the Creator" (Colossians 3:1–2, 9–10). Christ for us on Calvary. Christ in us through Baptism. New selves absorbed in the new creation, ready and empowered to witness of Christ to the world.

*Prayer:* Lord Jesus, think on me
By anxious thoughts oppressed;
Let me your loving servant be
And taste your promised rest.
*LW* 231:2

# The Witness of Courageous Confession

## *Reading:* Matthew 10:17–20

*Text:* The governor asked Him, "Are you the king of the Jews?" "Yes, it is as you say," Jesus replied. Matthew 27:11

How often do you fear knowing what to say or having the courage to speak out for your Savior, especially in hostile situations? In some ways, our increasingly anti-Christian culture may add fuel to those fears: *What if others laugh at me or harshly criticize my expression of faith in Jesus?*

Jesus helped to prepare His disciples for such a courageous confession of faith when He sent them on a mission in Matthew 10. He predicted that they would be handed over to local councils, flogged in their synagogues, and brought before governors and kings as witnesses to them and to the Gentiles. Then he added, "But when they arrest you, do not worry about what to say or how to say it. At that time you will be given what to say, for it will not be you speaking, but the Spirit of your Father speaking through you" (Matthew 10:19–20).

More important, Jesus demonstrated during His own trial before Pontius Pilate, the Roman governor, what courageous confession means. To the question, "Are You the king of the Jews?" Jesus simply answers, "Yes, it is as you say." Jesus courageously bears testimony that He is king of the Jews, no matter what the consequences. And His answer continues His journey to Golgotha.

Because Jesus made a courageous confession of His kingship and submitted to suffering and death on our behalf, His forgiven disciples were empowered by the Spirit to stand before religious leaders and secular rulers with a faithful witness. That same Spirit empowers us to overcome our fears and bear courageous witness to Jesus as Savior at home, work, and even before modern people of influence and power in our communities and world.

*Prayer:* Ashamed of Jesus? Yes, I may
When I've no guilt to wash away,
No tear to wipe, no good to crave,
No fear to quell, no soul to save.

Till then—nor is my boasting vain—
Till then I boast a Savior slain,
And oh, may this my glory be,
That Christ is not ashamed of me!
*LW* 393:5–6

# The Witness of Startling Silence

***Reading:* James 3:1–12**

*Text:* But Jesus made no reply, not even to a single charge–to the great amazement of the governor. Matthew 27:14

"The Witness of Courageous Confession" is both difficult and important as a tool of God's Spirit. But at times, "The Witness of Startling Silence" is equally crucial. How often our wagging tongues stand in the way of our witness to the Savior. James exposes the sins of the tongue, comparing them to a great forest set on fire by a small spark. We know the devastating effects of fire upon thousands of acres of timber in the western part of the United States.

So often we talk too much and as a result diminish our Christian witness. Especially when others criticize our job performance, our family life, or our volunteer service, we feel compelled to justify our actions or our character with a torrent of words in our defense.

Jesus' silence at a crucial time of His life and ministry stands in sharp contrast to our endless words. Appearing before Pilate and accused falsely by the obvious lies of the chief priests and elders of the Jews, Jesus amazes the governor by His silence: "But Jesus made no reply, not even to a single charge." By this Jesus bears powerful and dignified witness. Centuries before Jesus' trial, Isaiah describes His actions so well: "He was oppressed and afflicted, yet He did not open His mouth; He was led like a lamb to the slaughter, and as a sheep before her shearers is silent, so He did not open His mouth" (Isaiah 53:7). Jesus' silent and obedient humbling himself unto death on a cross won for us salvation.

Justified before God through Christ's death, we need not justify ourselves before others with many words but, forgiven, can bear silent testimony when needed so others might ask about the hope that is in us through the silent Lamb of God, who takes away the sins of the world. Startling silence indeed!

*Prayer:* O Christ, Thou Lamb of God, that takest away the sin of the world, have mercy upon us and grant us Thy peace. Amen.

# A Funeral Witness

## *Reading:* 1 Thessalonians 4:13–18

*Text:* Brothers, we do not want you to be ignorant about those who fall asleep, or to grieve like the rest of men, who have no hope. 1 Thessalonians 4:13

We attended a funeral last night at our church that moved many people deeply. That funeral was a powerful witness, not only to salvation through faith in Jesus Christ, but also to the urgency of sharing Jesus with those who do not believe in Him. Indeed, that funeral led me to reflections for the next four daily devotions.

A relatively young man, Rev. Mark D. Spitz, age 45, died after a four-year struggle with A.L.S., a debilitating neuro-muscular condition also known as Lou Gehrig's disease. Surrounded by family and friends, church leaders, and members of the congregation, Mark's casket was draped with a white funeral pall, reminding us of the white robe of his Baptism and the white robe of Christ's righteousness, ushering him into the presence of God's heavenly throne. All of us grieved his loss as a vibrant witness to the saving Gospel of Jesus Christ, but rejoiced in his deliverance from a dread disease into the Father's waiting arms of eternal love.

St. Paul's words to the Thessalonians also witness to my heart: "We do not want you to be ignorant about those who fall asleep, or to grieve like the rest of men, who have no hope." He further assures his readers: "We believe that Jesus died and rose again and so we believe that God will bring with Jesus those who have fallen asleep in Him" (1 Thessalonians 4:14). Clearly Mark lives with Jesus because of his Spirit-worked faith. We claim that same sure hope because of God's unfailing promise. But Mark's lifelong passion for reaching the lost also caused me to reflect on how to reach "the rest of men who have no hope." More on that tomorrow.

*Prayer:* When life's brief course on earth is run
And I this world am leaving,
Grant me to say, 'Your will be done,'
Your faithful Word believing.
My dearest friend, I now commend
My soul into your keeping,
From sin and hell, And death as well,
By you the victory reaping.
*LW* 425:4

# The Witness of Mark's Journey

## *Reading:* 2 Corinthians 12:7–10

*Text:* "My grace is sufficient for you, for My power is made perfect in weakness." 2 Corinthians 12:9

Mark Spitz was on a mission to proclaim Jesus as pastor, Christian radio program manager, and director of media production for Lutheran Hour Ministries. But perhaps his most profound witness to his Savior came through his four-year journey with A.L.S. Like St. Paul, he had a thorn in the flesh. With his once powerful body and rich voice deteriorating day by day, his passion for reaching the lost, and his clear witness to Jesus as Savior continued.

Unable to speak, he communicated on his computer by using his head to stroke the keys. Many received a message of encouragement. With refreshing honesty, he described how God was using his disease to help him recognize and confess his sins and lean more heavily on God's grace. Particularly moving was an e-mail message of thanks to those who had befriended him through a special benefit on his behalf a few months before his death. His simple words: "Now I know you have gathered as friends of Mark, but I hope we also gather hereafter as friends of Jesus."

St. Paul in his second letter to the Corinthians refers to God's humbling through an unnamed "thorn in the flesh." After praying fervently for healing, he received God's answer: "My grace is sufficient for you, for My power is made perfect in weakness." Like Mark, Paul decided to boast all the more gladly about his weaknesses. He concludes: "For when I am weak, then I am strong" (2 Corinthians 12:10b). Weak in body, Mark Spitz was strong in witness to Jesus.

*Prayer:* Rely on God your Savior And find your life secure.
Make his work your foundation That your work may endure.
No anxious thought, no worry, No self-tormenting care
Can win your Father's favor; His heart is moved by prayer.

Take heart, have hope, my spirit, And do not be afraid.
From my low depression, Where agonies are made,
God's grace will lift you upward On arms of saving might
Until the sun you hoped for Delights your eager sight.
*LW* 427:2–3

# The Witness of Caregivers

***Reading:* 1 Thessalonians 1:1–10**

*Text:* We continually remember before our God and Father your work produced by faith, your labor prompted by love, and your endurance inspired by hope in our Lord Jesus Christ. 1 Thessalonians 1:3

That funeral also prompted me to consider the witness of caregivers. In Mark's case, his wife, family members, and friends joined him in that four-year journey with A.L.S. Giving, encouraging, vigilant to his growing physical need for minute-by-minute help, they cared, often to the point of physical, emotional, and spiritual exhaustion. But by God's grace, these caregivers just kept giving. At the funeral they gave silent witness to Jesus as their Savior also. I know that in their weakness they were probably unaware of their witness. But others noticed and marveled. Jesus shines through caregivers with His saving love demonstrated in Calvary's cross.

St. Paul writes to the Thessalonian Christians words of thanks and encouragement. In the midst of their trials, temptations, and persecution, God's Spirit brought them faith, love, and hope to live as caregivers. A clear witness to Jesus Christ as Savior shone through their daily actions. Therefore, Paul commends their "work produced by faith," their "labor prompted by love," and their "endurance inspired by hope" in their Lord Jesus Christ. The Thessalonians, painfully aware of their sins and weakness, probably didn't realize how they were witnessing to their Savior. But Paul noticed and gave them public thanks.

What can we learn from these caregivers? How is God preparing our hearts to serve as caregivers? What sins should we confess as we give care? Do you know someone without a saving faith in Jesus who might be marveling at the silent witness of faithful caregivers right now? How might you witness to them?

*Prayer:* Oh, from our sins hide not your face;
Absolve us through your boundless grace!
Be with us in our anguish still!
Free us at last from ev'ry ill!

So we with all our hearts each day
To you our glad thanksgiving pay,
Then walk obedient to your Word,
And now and ever praise you, Lord.
*LW* 428:5–6

# The Witness of Changed Lives

## *Reading:* 1 Peter 1:3–9

*Text:* So that your faith—of greater worth than gold, which perishes even though refined by fire—may be proved genuine and may result in praise, glory, and honor when Jesus Christ is revealed. 1 Peter 1:7

A funeral. A journey through illness. Caregivers. In this devotion, I reflect on the witness of changed lives. Twelve years ago our 23-year-old daughter, Becky, died in Seattle after a 3 1/2 year struggle with a disease called aplastic anemia. Attending Mark's funeral caused me to relive her journey and its impact on the lives of two friends. Becky had no awareness of how God changed these two lives through her witness to Jesus.

As chaplain of her college sorority, Becky, during her time of weekly blood counts and frequent blood transfusions, stayed up one night to support a sorority sister who was contemplating suicide because of breaking up with a boyfriend. Some two years after Becky's death, her friend, now in her final year of medical school, called me to ask my permission for access to Becky's medical records so she could do a senior paper on the disease that had taken Becky's life.

Becky witnessed to another new friend who had many questions about the Christian faith and who was dating a future pastor. A few years after Becky's death, I learned from the girl's husband, now a pastor and theological professor, that the two of them had attended Becky's funeral. On the 300 mile drive home, her friend indicated her desire to be baptized as a believer in Jesus Christ.

St. Peter writes to believers facing persecution for their faith. He describes these trials as a refining process to strengthen their faith in Jesus Christ so their resulting witness "may result in praise, glory, and honor when Jesus Christ is revealed." Two changed lives bear eloquent witness to God's love in Jesus Christ through Becky's trial of faith.

*Prayer:* Sing, pray, and keep his ways unswerving,
Offer your service faithfully,
And trust his word; though undeserving,
You'll find his promise true to be.
God never will forsake in need
The soul that trusts in him indeed.
*LW* 420:4

# Seabiscuit

***Reading:* 1 Peter 2:20–25**

*Text:* He himself bore our sins in His body on the tree, so that we might die to sins and live for righteousness; by His wounds you have been healed. 1 Peter 2:24

Do you ever get discouraged when you try to set the world ablaze with your witness to Jesus as Savior, only to meet rejection and even suffering for your efforts?

Not too long ago, the movie *Seabiscuit* was released in theaters and then on DVD. The story moved me to tears as I watched a depression era nation rise up to cheer this small racehorse with a big heart conquer obstacle after obstacle to win the big races—a match race win over the sleek powerful thoroughbred War Admiral and a year later, after serious injury, the Santa Anita, when he was almost seven years old. Seabiscuit's plucky victories also lifted up Charles Howard, the owner who had lost his only child in a tragic accident; Tom Smith, the trainer who was a loner struggling to make ends meet; and Johnny "Red" Pollard, the Canada-born jockey who overcame hard luck, serious injury, and an on-going alcohol problem to ride the winner.

*Seabiscuit* presents life in its reality—tragedy and triumph, suffering and joy. St. Peter writes to Christian people undergoing suffering and persecution as the struggle to witness in both word and action. He points them to the One who against all odds lived a sinless life and endured suffering, rejection, and death for us. "He himself bore our sins in His body on the tree, so that we might die to sin and live for righteousness; by His wounds you have been healed."

Far more uplifting than the story of Seabiscuit is the once for all victory of our Lord Jesus Christ. Lifted up by Jesus' death and resurrection, we find courage, determination, and zeal to bear witness to His saving name in a suffering world that desperately needs His healing wounds.

*Prayer:* Sing, pray, and keep his ways unswerving
Offer your service faithfully
And trust his word though undeserving,
You'll find his promise true to be.
God never will forsake in need
The soul that trusts in him indeed.
*LW* 420:4

# Praying the Lord's Prayer As Witness

***Reading:* Matthew 6:1–8**

*Text:* "After this manner, therefore, pray ye: Our Father who art in heaven." Matthew 6:9 (KJV)

My pastor encourages us to pray the Lord's Prayer thoughtfully every week by reflecting on one petition each day, entitled the Sunday prayer, the Monday prayer, etc. Although I have prayed the Lord's Prayer frequently since childhood in our home and at church, I have found this simple approach very powerful in my personal devotional life.

In the next several devotions, we will look at each petition of the Lord's Prayer, not only to strengthen our prayer life, but also to view the Lord's Prayer as a powerful tool for our witness. Think how many believers worldwide pray the Lord's Prayer on a regular basis, individually and as part of the gathering of God's people around Word and Sacrament. What a witness to the triune God–Father, Son, and Holy Spirit!

I know that my faith is strengthened when Gail and I are privileged to be with our daughter's five sons, ages 1, 3, 4, 7, and 10 who pray the Lord's Prayer with their father and mother either at the supper table or right before bedtime. The same is true of our son and daughter-in-law praying with their son, 9, and daughter, 5. They learn, they pray, and they witness.

Jesus, in His sermon on the mount, addresses prayer with His disciples. After criticizing the prayers of hypocrites who seem to pray so they will be seen by others and commended for their religiosity, Jesus encourages prayer in secret with concern only for praying as dear children trusting their dear heavenly Father. Instead of endless babbling like the pagans, Jesus encourages praying the prayer He gives them, which we now call "The Lord's Prayer."

"After this manner, therefore, pray ye: Our Father who art in heaven." We go to the heavenly Father in prayer, confident that He knows our needs and has made us His children through the suffering, death, and resurrection of His only Son, Jesus Christ. What a witness when we simply pray, teach our children to pray, and join with others to pray, "Our Father who art in heaven"!

*Prayer:* Our Father who art in heaven.

March 12

# The Sunday Prayer

***Reading:*** **Philippians 2:9–11**

*Text:* "Hallowed be Thy name." Matthew 6:9b (KJV)

The Sunday prayer is the first petition of the Lord's Prayer, "Hallowed be Thy name." The key word is "reverence." How appropriate that we pray this petition on the first day of the week, the day upon which Christ rose from the dead, they day when we gather with the people of God around Word and Sacraments to sing the praises of His holy name. Reverence indeed in His holy presence, receiving forgiveness of sins, life, and salvation in the Word read and preached and at the Lord's Table.

The words of that early Christian hymn, recorded by St. Paul in Philippians 2, ring in our ears in our personal and home devotions as well as in church: "Therefore God exalted Him to the highest place and gave Him the name that is above every name, that at the name of Jesus every knee should bow in heaven and on earth and under earth, and every tongue confess that Jesus Christ is Lord, to the glory of God the Father" (Philippians 2:9–11).

Can you see the clear witness in those exalted words? Our prayer, "Hallowed be Thy name," recognizes that God's name is already holy, even without our prayers, but implores God to make His name holy in our worship, in our witness, in our daily lives so many others will be led by God's grace to bend the knee and confess with their mouths that Jesus Christ, who humbled Himself and became obedient to death on a cross for the world, is Lord, to the glory of God, the Father.

In other words, our regular Sunday prayer shows reverence for and dependence upon the mighty name of God to reach an unbelieving world through us with the saving Gospel. What a privilege and a responsibility for us to pray, "Hallowed be Thy name" Sunday after Sunday!

*Prayer:* Our heav'nly Father, hear
The prayer we offer now.
Thy name be hallowed far and near;
To Thee all nations bow.
*TLH* 455:1

# The Monday Prayer, Part One

***Reading:* Matthew 6:5–15**

*Text:* "Thy kingdom come." Matthew 6:10a

My pastor has taught me to pray one of the petitions of the Lord's Prayer each day of the week. The Monday prayer is always "Thy kingdom come." In the first place, I pray for God's kingdom of grace to come, which leads me to pray for those who don't know Jesus as Savior. On my list week after week–a longtime friend who lives in California, a self-professed atheist from Israel who works as an engineer in Arizona, and some neighbors whom I have not yet been able to know very well. Who is on your list? A worldwide mission to connect people to Jesus begins in prayer one person at a time.

Thankful that God has brought me to a saving faith in Jesus as Savior because my parents brought me to the baptismal font many years ago and taught me the Word of God, I also confess that I often fail to share that saving faith with others in my life who need to hear the story of Jesus and His love.

In His sermon on the mount, Jesus includes an important teaching on prayer. Renouncing the showy, wordy prayers of hypocrites and pagans, He counsels heartfelt prayer in the words we now know as the Lord's Prayer. Approaching God as our loving Father with reverence according to His will, depending on Him for daily bread, forgiveness, spiritual protection, and deliverance, we simply pray, "Thy kingdom come," believing that He will use us to bring others into a saving relationship with His Son.

Will you join millions of other Christians worldwide in praying that Monday prayer (no matter what day or time), believing that your prayer will lead to the bringing of many into God's kingdom of grace, beginning with your list and mine?

*Prayer:* Our Father, who from heav'n above
Has turned toward us the face of love,
Bless us, your children, with your name!
Its holy wonders now proclaim;
Your kingdom and your will alone
Through us and in us here make known. Amen.
*LW* 430:1

# The Monday Prayer, Part Two

***Reading:*** **Luke 12:22–34**

*Text:* "Do not be afraid, little flock, for your Father has been pleased to give you the kingdom." Luke 12:32

That Monday prayer, "Thy Kingdom come," leads me to pray secondly for God's kingdom of glory to come. My pastor has taught me to focus on those facing death and the reality of my own death. The simple weekly prayer points me again and again to the importance of eternal life in heaven through the death and resurrection of Jesus Christ.

In January 1993, our 23-year-old daughter Becky died in a Seattle hospital after a 3½ year struggle with a disease called aplastic anemia. During the weeks in Seattle for Becky's bone marrow transplant, we were surrounded by the reality of death, even while praying for her healing through a team of competent doctors in one of the finest hospitals in the world. All of the cares of the world and the normal busy activities of family and career were put on hold for Becky's life and death struggle with her illness.

By God's grace, Becky trusted in Jesus Christ alone for her salvation. During the 3½ year period, she had many opportunities to witness of her faith in Jesus, as did we during her hospitalization. As God's child through Baptism, she had no fear of death, although she wanted to get well physically. In her death, she was ushered into God's kingdom of glory, prepared for her from eternity. We look forward to joining her someday in that kingdom of Glory.

Jesus' words in Luke point out the futility of worrying about material possessions and commend the much more important "treasure in heaven that will not be exhausted" (Luke 12:33). Then He speaks the words of today's text: "Do not be afraid, little flock, for your Father has been pleased to give you the kingdom." Jesus ushered in the kingdom of God through His life, death, and resurrection from the dead. Through Jesus, the Father is pleased to give us the kingdom here on earth and in the glory of heaven. The Monday prayer prepares us for our own death and leads us to share Jesus with those facing death.

*Prayer:* Thy kingdom come. Amen.

# The Tuesday Prayer

***Reading:* 1 Timothy 2:1–6**

*Text:* "Thy will be done on earth as it is in heaven." Matthew 6:10b (KJV)

The Tuesday prayer is the third petition of the Lord's Prayer, "Thy will be done on earth as it is in heaven." The key word is "submission." God's good and gracious will is done indeed, without our prayer, but we pray that it may be done among us also. We observe how the angels in heaven carry out God's will without question, praising Him, obeying His commands, and protecting His little ones.

As sinners, we realize that every day we face the will of the devil, the world, and our sinful flesh. These three enemies seek to prevent us from hallowing God's name or letting His kingdom come. Often we give in to their rebellious wills and sin against God. Confessing our own willfulness and rebellion, we pray to our Father who forgives us for Jesus' sake: "Thy will be done." Then God, out of His mercy, breaks and hinders Satan's will on the basis of His Son's once for all atoning sacrifice on the cross and strengthens and preserves us steadfast in His Word through His Holy Spirit, bestowed upon us in our Baptism.

The result is that God's will is done among us. Paul counsels Timothy and us, as we lift up "requests, prayers, intercessions and thanksgiving for everyone. ...This is good and pleases God our Savior, who wants all men to be saved and to come to a knowledge of the truth. For there is one God and one mediator between God and men, the man Christ Jesus, who gave himself as a ransom for all—the testimony given in its proper time" (1 Timothy 2:1, 3–6).

You see, submission to God's will by the Spirit's power leads to our testimony or witness of the one God and one mediator who gave Himself as a ransom for all. The Lord's Prayer as witness to the saving will of God!

*Prayer:* Your gracious will on earth be done
As it is done before your throne,
That patiently we may obey
In good or bad time all you say.
Curb flesh and blood and ev'ry will
That sets itself against your will.
*LW* 431:4

March 16

# The Wednesday Prayer

***Reading:* Psalm 145**

*Text:* "Give us this day our daily bread." Matthew 6:11 (KJV)

The Wednesday prayer is the fourth petition of the Lord's Prayer, "Give us this day our daily bread." The key word is "thanksgiving." The second petition, "Thy kingdom come," describes both God's kingdom of grace and kingdom of glory. This fourth petition describes God's kingdom of power. As the Creator of the universe, God establishes order through families and governments. He showers material blessings on believers and unbelievers alike, including food, drink, clothing, shoes, home, gainful employment, strong families, friends and neighbors, good rulers, and good weather.

The whole thrust of this petition moves us to recognize these material blessings as God's gifts and to receive them with daily thanksgiving. That attitude of praise and thanksgiving provides a powerful witness to those around us, including unbelievers. By God's grace and because of our faith in Jesus as our Savior, we thank God by being content with what we have and by sharing our blessings with those in need.

The psalmist in Psalm 145 exalts God as King and praises His name forever and ever. Thankful for all of God's mighty acts from generation to generation and for His faithfulness to all His promises, including His loving kindness for those who are bowed down, he joyfully proclaims: "The eyes of all look to You, and You give them Your food at the proper time. You open Your hand and satisfy the desires of every living thing" (Psalm 145:15–16).

We confess our sins of grumbling and complaining or holding tightly to earthly wealth. That witness is negative. But we claim God's forgiveness in Christ and pray for thankful hearts as He gives us this day our daily bread. That positive witness points many to the only true God and Jesus Christ whom He has sent as Savior of the world.

*Prayer:* As your prosp'ring hand has blest,
May we give you of the best
And by deeds of kindly love
For your mercies grateful prove,
Singing thus through all our days:
Lord, to you immortal praise.
*LW* 496:4

# The Thursday Prayer

**_Reading:_ Matthew 6:14–15**

*Text:* “Forgive us our trespasses as we forgive those who trespass against us.” Matthew 6:12 (KJV)

The Thursday prayer is the fifth petition, “Forgive us our trespasses as we forgive those who trespass against us.” The key word is “forgiveness.” Every petition bears witness to God. The fifth petition perhaps provides the most powerful witness.

We witness first by confessing our sins every day, “Forgive us our trespasses.” By doing so, as Luther writes in his Small Catechism, “We pray in this petition that our Father in heaven would not look upon our sins, nor on their account deny our prayer, for we are worthy of none of the things for which we pray, neither have we deserved them, but that He would grant them all to us by grace; for we daily sin much and indeed deserve nothing but punishment” (Explanation to the Fifth Petition, Lord’s Prayer). Our honest and regular confession of sins points us and others to God’s plan of salvation worked out through Jesus Christ, who bore our sins on the cross. Only His forgiveness enables us to pray and to forgive the sins of others.

Second, we witness by forgiving others, “as we forgive those who trespass against us.” Jesus adds in Matthew 6, “For if you forgive men when they sin against you, your heavenly Father will also forgive you.” Difficult as it is, forgiving others bears convincing witness to our Savior who forgave His enemies on the cross. We often fall short of forgiving others because we cannot do so on our own power. But forgiven again by our Lord, we can let His forgiveness flow through us to others. And the world takes note of that forgiveness. What a witness to Christ as individual believers and within the Christian community!

*Prayer:* Forgive our sins, let grace outpour
That they may trouble us no more;
We too will gladly those forgive
Who harm us by the way they live.
Help us in each community
To serve with love and unity.
*LW* 431:6

March 18

# The Friday Prayer

***Reading:* James 1:12–15**

*Text:* "And lead us not into temptation." Matthew 6:13 (KJV)

The Friday prayer is the sixth petition, "And lead us not into temptation." The key word is "strength." God indeed tempts no one, but we ask Him to protect us so we do not give in to the temptations of the devil, the world, and our sinful flesh. We also ask God to temper us like steel when He puts us to the test and when He leads us safely through Satan's temptations.

James writes to believers, facing various trials that test their faith: "Blessed is the man who perseveres under trial, because when he has stood the test, he will receive the crown of life that God has promised to those who love Him. When tempted, no one should say, 'God is tempting me!' For God cannot be tempted by evil, nor does He tempt anyone; but each one is tempted when, by his own evil desire, he is dragged away and enticed. Then, after desire has conceived, it gives birth to sin; and sin when it is full grown, gives birth to death" (James 1:12–15).

How vital this prayer is for our Christian witness, "And lead us not into temptation"! When we succumb to sin, we bring negative witness about our God, for we bear His name in our Baptism. How often the sinful conduct of believers has brought shame to Christ's Church and to God's salvation through Christ.

But positively, the repentant believer, clinging to Christ's forgiveness and growing to spiritual maturity through trials and temptations, brings life-changing testimony to God's free gift of eternal life through Jesus Christ. In this petition, we pray, in Luther's words, that God would guard and keep us that, "though we be assailed by them, still we may finally overcome and obtain the victory"—for us and for those to whom we witness.

*Prayer:* Lead not into temptation, Lord,  
Where our grim foe and all his horde  
Would vex our souls on ev'ry hand.  
Help us resist, help us to stand  
Firm in the faith, armed with your might;  
Your Spirit gives your children light.  
*LW* 431:7

# The Saturday Prayer

***Reading:* 2 Timothy 4:16–18**

*Text:* "But deliver us from evil." Matthew 6:13b (KJV)

The Saturday prayer is the seventh petition, "But deliver us from evil." The key concept is "courageous faith." Luther views this petition as a summary prayer, "that our Father in heaven would deliver us from every evil of body and soul, property and honor, and finally when our last hour has come, a blessed end" (explanation to the Seventh Petition, Lord's Prayer). In this sense, evil is anything, even what might otherwise be considered good, that can separate us from God—material possessions, love of family, commitment to vocational success, etc.

St. Paul describes God's deliverance in his life that he might fully proclaim the Gospel. He writes, "At my first defense, no one came to my support, but everyone deserted me. May it not be held against them. But the Lord stood at my side and gave me strength, so that through me the message might be fully proclaimed and all the Gentiles might hear it. And I was delivered from the lion's mouth. The Lord will rescue me from every evil attack and will bring me safely to His heavenly kingdom. To Him be glory for ever and ever. Amen" (2 Timothy 4:16–18). Paul is living the Lord's Prayer and thanking Him for His answer to the petition, "Deliver us from evil."

How about adding to your spiritual discipline, praying the Lord's Prayer one petition a day, in the service of your helping to set the world ablaze through your Christian witness? Keep a list of people in front of you who need your witness. Come humbly to your dear heavenly Father each day, confessing your sin and thanking Him for both spiritual and material blessings. Pray for His strength against temptation and deliverance from evil. And trust Him to place your witness squarely in the center of His advancing kingdom according to His will for the praise of His holy name.

*Prayer:* Amen, that is, it shall be so.
Make our faith strong that we may know
We need not doubt but shall receive
All that we ask, as we believe.
On your great promise we lay claim
Our faith says amen in your name.
*LW* 431:9

# Our Crime, His Crime

***Reading:*** **Matthew 27:15–26**

*Text:* "Why? What crime has He committed?" asked Pilate. Matthew 27:23

Great attention is given these days to DNA evidence when criminal cases, particularly murders, are brought to trial so the innocent are not condemned and the guilty pay for their crimes. Solid DNA evidence is compelling and has helped to bring justice in many cases.

What strange justice in the trial of Jesus before Pilate! Pilate offers the people a choice that he considers obvious: "Which one do you want me to release to you?" Barabbas, a notorious criminal, or Jesus, whom he deems innocent. He expects Barabbas to continue paying for his crime and Jesus to be set free by the crowd. Instead the crowd roars for the criminal, Barabbas, to be set free and the innocent victim, Jesus, to be crucified. Would DNA evidence have helped?

Symbolically, this judicial decision describes God's great plan for our salvation. We are the true criminals because of our sin from birth. Like Barabbas, our spiritual DNA condemns us to death. Jesus, true God and true man, is not a sinner and has committed no crime. But He has willingly taken upon himself our sin and is therefore guilty and condemned to death on the cross. He dies so we can live, freed from the burden of our sin. Our crime becomes His crime.

Legally set free, we have a message for the whole human race: "Don't hide from the law. Admit your crimes. Your spiritual DNA condemns you. Place your sins at the foot of the cross. Jesus has paid for your sins. Your crimes are His crimes. Justice has been done. You are set free."

*Prayer:* O dearest Jesus, what law have you broken
That such sharp sentence should on you be spoken?
Of what great crime have you to make confession,
What dark transgression?

What is the source of all your mortal anguish?
It is my sins for which you, Lord, must languish;
Yes, all the wrath, the woe that you inherit,
This I do merit.
*LW* 119:1, 3

# March Madness

***Reading:*** **Acts 26:19–28**

*Text:* "You are out of your mind, Paul!" Acts 26:24

Yesterday with great fanfare the pairings for the NCAA Basketball Tournament were announced on network television. March Madness they call it. Many talk freely and enthusiastically about their favorite team. During the next three weeks, millions of loyal basketball fans and the curious will follow the media frenzy to see who is crowned national champion. March Madness, indeed!

In a quieter but no less intense setting, the apostle Paul makes a defense of his faith in Jesus Christ before King Herod Agrippa II at the request of Festus, the Roman governor. At stake is his life and whether he will face trial in Rome. Paul gives eloquent testimony of his conversion on the Damascus road, his unfair arrest in Jerusalem, and explains: "But I have had God's help to this very day, and so I stand here and testify to small and great alike . . . that the Christ would suffer and, as the first to rise from the dead, would proclaim light to His own people and to the Gentiles" (Acts 26:22–23).

At this point Festus interrupts Paul's defense and shouts, "You are out of your mind, Paul!" "Madness" in his zeal for Christ crucified and risen. Paul continues his remarks to King Agrippa. Agrippa responds, "Do you think that in such a short time you can persuade me to be a Christian?" (Acts 26:28). Paul's "madness" for connecting people to Jesus follows the example of his Savior who was accused of being "raving mad" when He predicted His death and resurrection (John 10:17–21).

As God's special people through Christ, we have a dramatic story to tell that far exceeds the March Madness of cheering for a favorite basketball team. Every day God's Spirit provides us opportunities to share Jesus with loyal believers and curious onlookers alike. Our enthusiasm may be called "madness" by some, but others will be led to place their trust in Jesus as Savior for the crown of eternal life.

*Prayer:* Dear Lord, give me courage and zeal to tell others about Your salvation. Amen.

# The Road to Betrayal

***Reading:*** **Luke 22:21–27**

*Text:* Also a dispute arose among them as to which of them was considered to be greatest. Luke 22:24

In Luke's Gospel the upper room discussion takes a strange twist. Jesus has just instituted the sacramental meal by giving them His body and blood. Shockingly He then asserts, "But the hand of him who is going to betray Me is with Mine on the table" (Luke 22:21). Understandably they question one another as to who might be the guilty party. Up to this point, we are in familiar territory. We know Judas is the one on "the road to betrayal." He will join the crowd from the high priest to betray Jesus with a kiss. What a terrible deed! What a tragic suicidal end!

Now comes the strange twist. Luke continues, "Also a dispute arose among them as to which of them was considered to be greatest." What a switch–from who is the betrayer to who is the greatest. That discussion hits closer to home. We would love to be considered important, if not great, in our Christian witness and role in the church. Betrayal is the farthest subject from our minds.

Jesus' answer brings us to our knees–literally. Worldly greatness, lording it over others, just might lead us on "the road to betrayal" of our Lord. Jesus chides the disciples and us: "But you are not to be like that. Instead the greatest among you should be like the youngest." He adds, "But I am among you as one who serves" (Luke 22:27b). The other disciples are no better than Judas. He betrays Jesus openly. They flee in the darkness and abandon their Master. An attitude of worldly greatness leads to betrayal every time.

On our knees in repentance, we find Jesus on His knees to serve by washing feet and on the cross to serve by shedding His life blood to pay for the world's sins. The true meaning of the sacramental meal of His body and blood comes home to our hearts. Rescued from "the road to betrayal" we walk "the road of humble service and witness."

*Prayer:* Lord, forgive our betrayal and place our feet on the road of humble service. Amen.

# In the Hour of Trial: Prediction

***Reading:* Luke 22:31–34**

*Text:* "But I have prayed for you, Simon, that your faith may not fail. And when you have turned back, strengthen your brothers." Luke 22:32

A well-known hymn, "In the Hour of Trial," is often sung during the Lenten season. The next four devotions will focus on Peter's hour of trial set in the context of our Lord's trial on the way to Calvary. First, St. Luke describes our Lord's prediction to Peter of his approaching test of faith. Yes, when Peter boldly asserts that he is ready to go with Jesus to prison and to death, Jesus predicts, "I tell you, Peter, before the rooster crows today, you will deny three times that you know Me" (Luke 22:34). He confronts him sharply.

But today's text provides a much more comprehensive and caring prediction of Peter's "Hour of Trial." Informing Peter urgently with the words "Simon, Simon" of Satan's intent to "sift the disciples like wheat," Jesus speaks with compassion: "But I have prayed for you, Simon, that your faith may not fail. And when you have turned back, strengthen your brothers." Jesus has prayed. What a powerful assurance for Peter—"that your faith may not fail." Aware that Peter will deny his Lord, Jesus is praying for Peter's repentance and restoration. *When* you have turned back. Not *if.* Jesus tells Peter that His forgiveness to be won on Calvary is sure and that His grace will turn Peter back. Strengthen your brethren. Jesus predicts Peter's significant leadership role in the church after Pentecost. What a comprehensive prediction for Peter!

As we face the hour of trial in our lives, Jesus prepares us by warning of Satan's intent, by mediating for us before the throne, by offering His forgiveness won on the cross, by assuring us of God's grace, and by calling us to strengthen others with our witness. What a comprehensive prediction for us!

*Prayer:* In the hour of trial, Jesus plead for me
Lest by base denial I depart from thee
When thou see'st me waver, With a look recall
Nor for fear or favor Suffer me to fall.
*LW* 511:1

# In the Hour of Trial: Fall

***Reading:* Luke 22:54–62**

*Text:* But he denied it. "Woman, I don't know Him," he said. Luke 22:57

The sad story of Peter's denial is very well-known to us and to him in later years. The rapid and tumultuous events in the garden led Jesus to the house of the high priest. Peter follows at a distance with heart thumping and desperation clutching his frenzied mind. Warming himself at a fire in the middle of the courtyard, Peter observes a servant girl examining him closely and asserting, "This man was with Him" (Luke 22:56). Confronted and fearful, Peter adamantly denies the accusation. "I don't know Him." A little later someone else confronted him. An hour later he is challenged again, this time as a Galilean. In each case, he openly denies any connection with Jesus, the accused. St. Luke records during the third denial, "Just as he was speaking, the rooster crowed" (Luke 22:60). Peter falls in his hour of trial. A negative witness.

How many times do we fail in our witness to the Savior? Opportunities abound as we mingle with people who may not believe in Jesus–in our family, our neighborhood, our place of work, our social contacts, our travels. Sometimes the setting may be actually hostile with others ridiculing God or belittling His Church. How do we respond to these challenges to the faith? Silence? Outright denial? Or clear testimony that we believe in Jesus as Savior? Often we fall in our hour of trial. A negative witness.

Even when we fall, Jesus is still there on our behalf. While Peter denied his Lord, Jesus faced his accusers in silence and moved on to the cross as the Lamb of God who takes away the sin of the world. He is the Lamb of God for us too.

*Prayer:* With forbidden pleasures Should this vain world charm
Or its tempting treasures Spread to work me harm,
Bring to my remembrance Sad Gethsemane
Or, in darker semblance, Cross-crowned Calvary.
*LW* 511:2

# In the Hour of Trial: Repentance

***Reading:*** **Luke 22:60–62**

*Text:* The Lord turned and looked straight at Peter. Then Peter remembered the word the Lord had spoken to him. Luke 22:61

Jesus predicted Peter's hour of trial. Faced with the pressure to deny his Lord, Peter falls three times. The rooster crows. Jesus turns and looks straight at Peter. As a result, Peter remembers the words the Lord spoke to him: "Before the rooster crows today, you will disown Me three times" (Luke 22:61). Then St. Luke simply records, "And he went outside and wept bitterly" (Luke 22:62). In Peter's hour of trial repentance has occurred.

Without any attempt to rationalize his actions, Peter remembers Jesus' prediction, confesses his sin of threefold denial, and gives evidence of his repentance by weeping bitterly. God's Spirit is also working in Peter's heart the assurance that his sin is forgiven. Unlike Judas, whose betrayal leads him to recognition of sin, despair, and suicide, Peter takes time to reflect on the Lord's forgiveness and love. He may have also remembered Jesus' words, "I have prayed for you that your faith may not fail. And when you have turned back, strengthen your brothers" (Luke 22:32). Jesus' look in the hour of trial may have also communicated that forgiveness. Certainly post-resurrection, Peter discovers that all of his sins have been forgiven at the cross.

We fall also when our witness is tested. Denial of our relationship to Jesus results. Remembering Jesus' prediction to Peter, we confess our sins without excuse, cling to His forgiveness won at the cost of His shed blood, and reflect on our ongoing need for His grace as we experience the hours of trial in our lives. Forgiven, we face problems and perils with a desire to proclaim Christ. Repentance for witness to His forgiveness.

*Prayer:* Should thy mercy send me Sorrow, toil, and woe,
Or should pain attend me On my path below,
Grant that I may never Fail thy hand to see;
Grant that I may ever Cast my care on thee.
*LW* 511:3

# In the Hour of Trial: Bold Witness

***Reading:*** **Acts 4:1–12**

*Text:* Salvation is found in no one else, for there is no other name under heaven given to men by which we must be saved. Acts 4:12

Our story of Peter's hour of trial concludes in a different arena with a different result. Jesus predicted Peter's denial on the night He was betrayed but also looked ahead to Peter strengthening the brothers after he turned back. Peter fell hard in the courtyard of the high priest when he denied Jesus three times. But the Spirit led him to repentance as he wept bitterly for his cowardly witness.

Now the scene shifts to a different hour of trial before the Jewish Sanhedrin where Peter and John, arrested, face the rulers, elders, and teachers of the law in Jerusalem. Christ, crucified, has risen from the dead and ascended into heaven. The Holy Spirit has been poured out on the apostles at Pentecost. Peter and John have healed a beggar crippled from birth. Now they must answer a question with their lives on the line: "By what power or what name did you do this?" (Acts 4:7).

Peter, filled with the Holy Spirit, does not cower in the shadows or vociferously deny his Lord. Instead he boldly witnesses that "it is by the name of Jesus Christ of Nazareth, whom you crucified but whom God raised from the dead, that this man stands before you healed" (Acts 4:10). Without fear of death, Peter adds, "Salvation is found in no one else." Bold witness!

In our hours of trial God's Spirit stands ready to empower us for a similar bold witness. Whether we face a hostile crowd, a hospital bed, or our dying hour, the words of Peter ring in our ears and sound from our lips: "Salvation is found in no one else, for there is no other name under heaven given to men by which we must be saved."

*Prayer:* When my last hour cometh, Fraught with strife and pain,
When my dust returneth to the dust again,
On thy truth relying, Through that mortal strife,
Jesus, take me dying to eternal life.
*LW* 511:4

# Astonishing Courage

***Reading:*** Acts 4:13–22

*Text:* When they saw the courage of Peter and John and realized that they were unschooled, ordinary men, they were astonished and took note that these men had been with Jesus. Acts 4:13

Yesterday we heard the bold witness of Peter and John with their lives on the line, testifying that Jesus Christ crucified and risen was the only way to salvation. How was their testimony received by their enemies? Although they did not believe in Jesus, they were astonished at the courage of these men to speak so boldly. Their astonishment increased because Peter and John were "unschooled and ordinary" from their lofty perspective as learned teachers of the law. And they took special note that these men had been with Jesus. Peter and John knew Him, followed Him, forsook Him, but now believed in His death and resurrection and were willing to die for Him. Astonishing courage, the grudging assessment of Jesus' opponents!

How would your Christian witness be assessed by friends and enemies alike? Could being "unschooled and ordinary" give you a witnessing advantage rather than a handicap or excuse? Would others who know you take special note or even be aware that you "have been with Jesus"? Rather brutal questions to be sure, but worth asking.

Is there any reason our witness to Jesus could not be characterized as displaying astonishing courage? We have a Lord who never wavered on the road to Calvary. His resistance to Satan, compassionate ministry, willing suffering, and agonizing death could all be described as courageous. He promises that He will be with us to the end of the age and possesses all power in heaven and on earth. His promised Spirit is the Comforter, who makes us strong to speak boldly. His daily forgiveness in Baptism and His Holy Meal restores our courage to witness. His armor equips us for battle against Satan himself. Why not astonishing courage—Christ's courage—as an assessment of our witness?

*Prayer:* His strength within my weakness Will make me bold to say
How his redeeming power Transforms my stubborn clay;
His touch of fire ignites me, With courage I am sent,
My tongue-tied silence broken, With grace made eloquent.
*LW* 320:3

March 28

# Holy Week Cleaning

## *Reading:* John 15:1–8

*Text:* "You are already clean because of the word I have spoken to you." John 15:3

I am writing this devotion during Holy Week. This morning a carpet cleaning company came to our home. We had noticed that our carpet was showing dirt with some especially troublesome spots. To prepare for the carpet cleaners, we needed to move some plants and furniture. Now we need to wait a few days for the drying process to be complete. But the cost and the preparations are well worth the result: a clean carpet to welcome visitors in our home.

On the night before His trial and crucifixion, Jesus taught His disciples in the upper room. He used the imagery of the vine and branches and described how His Father, the gardener, cuts off the branches that bear no fruit and prunes the branches that do so they will be more fruitful. Then He adds, "You are already clean because of the word I have spoken to you." Unclean because of their sin, the disciples are attached to Jesus the true vine, who will shed His blood for them on the cross. On this very night, He also institutes the Holy Meal of His true body and blood for the forgiveness of sins.

During Holy Week, we likewise recognize our need for cleaning because of our sins. We receive Jesus' body and blood in Holy Communion for the forgiveness of sins, based on His once-for-all death on the cross. Attached to the true vine, we accept the Father's pruning so we can bear much fruit of witness and service. Like the clean carpet in our home, we stand ready to welcome guests so they also can become part of the Father's vineyard and experience Jesus' cleansing blood.

*Prayer:* Fountain of goodness, Jesus, Lord and God:
Cleanse us, unclean, with Thy most cleansing blood
Increase our faith and love, that we may know
The hope and peace which from Thy presence flow.
*HS 98* 849:4

# Sent Forth from the Meal

## *Reading:* Matthew 26:17–30

*Text:* "This is My blood of the covenant which is poured out for many for the forgiveness of sins." Matthew 26:28

What a pivotal night for Jesus and the disciples! They gather in the upper room to celebrate a final Passover together. Jesus uses this occasion to take the unleavened bread and the wine of the Passover in order to institute the Sacrament of Holy Communion. He offers them His true body and blood for the forgiveness of sins.

But the Holy Meal is not the ending but the beginning. Jesus, after they sing a hymn, is sent forth by the Father to Gethsemane, the judgment hall, and Calvary where He will sacrifice His body and shed His blood to atone for the world's sin. He sends forth the disciples to follow Him and after His resurrection to go and make disciples of all nations, baptizing them in the name of the Father, the Son, and the Holy Spirit. Every time they celebrate His Holy Meal in remembrance of Him, they will be sent forth again as His witnesses.

As we again receive that Holy Meal on Maundy Thursday, our sins are forgiven, and we are sent forth to witness of His salvation to the world. Yes, we come with His people to hear His Word and receive the Sacrament as sinners in need of forgiveness. But our meal together is not an ending but a beginning. We are sent forth to bring others back with us to the table until we gather at the heavenly feast forever.

*Prayer:* Heirs together of the grace of life,
All baptized into the death of Christ
Born again, in love maturing,
From the altar free and cheerful,
Caring, winsome family of God.
Catch the vision! Share the glory!
Show the captives, tell them Christ is here!
*SP* 58:3

Copyright © 1986 Concordia Publishing House

# An Inscription for all Time

*Reading:* John 19:17–22

*Text:* And the sign was written in Aramaic, Latin and Greek. John 19:20b

The chief priests of the Jews got what they wanted–almost. They wanted Jesus crucified as a common criminal. John records, "Finally Pilate handed Him over to them to be crucified" (John 19:16). But then Pilate had an inscription prepared and fastened to the cross which read: "Jesus of Nazareth, The King of the Jews" (John 19:19). The chief priests protested that the sign should read "this man claimed to be king of the Jews" (John 19:21). With finality Pilate answered, "What I have written, I have written" (John 19:22).

That simple inscription seen by many at the time has been read by many more through the centuries. It is an inscription for all time. Jesus was and is the King of the Jews, the promised Messiah, who came to pay for the sins of the whole world, Jews and Gentiles alike. It was written in Aramaic, the common language of the Jewish people and the Middle East; Latin, the official language of Rome, which ruled the world; and Greek, the common language throughout the empire that would be used as the language of the New Testament.

An inscription for all time! For you. For me. For your neighbors and friends. For those in your community from other groups, speaking different languages. For the people of every nation in the world. For then. For now. For future generations until the crucified, risen, and ascended Christ comes again as King of kings and Lord of lords.

*Prayer:* Sing my tongue, the glorious battle;
Sing the ending of the fray
Now above the cross, the trophy,
Sound the loud triumphant lay;
Tell how Christ, the world's redeemer,
As a victim won the day.
Faithful cross, true sign of triumph,
Be for all the noblest tree;
None in foliage, none in blossom,
None in fruit your equal be;
Symbol of the world's redemption,
For your burden makes us free.
*LW* 117:1

# Passing by Calvary

*Reading:* Matthew 27:32–44

*Text:* Those who passed by hurled insults at Him, shaking their heads. Matthew 27:39

Picture the procession to Golgotha, the Place of the Skull–from Pilate's judgment hall outside the city walls to Calvary where they crucified Jesus–the Roman soldiers, Simon of Cyrene, the chief priests and teachers of the law, some women and other supporters loyal to Him, and many others passing out of curiosity or spite. St. Matthew records: "Those who passed by hurled insults at Him, shaking their heads." Some recalled His promise to destroy the temple and rebuild it in three days, and challenged that if He was the Son of God, to come down from the cross. The chief priests and crucified robbers added their insults.

How do you and others in your life pass by Jesus' cross? What words describe the reactions–ignorance? indifference? hostility? mockery? Or grief? guilt? repentance? wonder? trust? thankfulness? Everything depends on the answers to these questions. We stand at a crossroads at Jesus' cross. At stake, life or death, forgiveness or damnation. Your answer comes first by God's grace. But the response of others for whom Christ died becomes very important to His forgiven people, showing forth the praises of Him who has called us out of darkness into His marvelous light. Passing by Calvary!

*Prayer:* Do we pass that cross unheeding,
Breathing no repentant vow,
Though we see you wounded, bleeding,
See your thorn encircled brow?
Yet your sinless death has brought us
Life eternal, peace, and rest;
Only what your grace has taught us
Calms the sinners deep distress

Jesus, may our hearts be burning
With more fervent love for you;
May our eyes be ever turning
To behold your cross anew
Till in glory, parted never
From the blessed Savior's side,
Graven in our hearts forever,
Dwell the cross, the Crucified.
*LW* 90:2–3

# Stationed at Calvary

## *Reading:* Mark 15:33–39

*Text:* And when the centurion, who stood there in front of Jesus, heard His cry and saw how He died, he said, "Surely this man was the Son of God." Mark 15:39

The centurion had no choice but to witness the crucifixion of Jesus. He was stationed there at Calvary to see that his soldiers properly carried out the execution of three convicted criminals. Initially, there was little reason to consider this event as anything more than a grim day's work. Yet, remarkably, the centurion is deeply moved by the death of the man on the center cross.

Mark records this reaction: "When the centurion . . . heard His cry and saw how He died, he said, 'Surely this man was the Son of God.'" While many from Jesus' own people passed by Calvary mocking and insulting Him, this hardened soldier, a Gentile, makes a reverent confession of faith in the crucified Christ as the Son of God. His dignity in suffering. His forgiving love–the way He died touches this centurion to believe.

Wherever you find yourself in life–your calling at home, at work, in the community, God has stationed you at Calvary to bear witness that the crucified Jesus is the Son of God and Savior of the world. Although others around you mock, scorn, or ignore the Redeemer, you are in just the right position to bear testimony to Him. He died for your sins as the sinless Son of God and rose victorious from the grave. Bearing the sign of His cross through Holy Baptism, you can lift high the cross for all to see. Stationed at Calvary!

*Prayer:* Come to Calvary's holy mountain
Sinners ruined by the fall;
Here a pure and healing fountain
Flows for you, for me, for all,
In a full perpetual tide,
Opened when our Savior died.

Take the life that lasts forever,
Trust the soul renewing flood.
God is faithful: God will never
Break his covenant of blood,
Signed when our Redeemer died,
Sealed when he was glorified.
*LW* 96:1, 4

# Tasting Death for Everyone

## *Reading:* Psalm 34:1–8

*Text:* So that by the grace of God He might taste death for everyone. Hebrews 2:9b

Many producers of food and drink talk about the "taste test" as a way of convincing consumers to buy their product. They suggest that if you sample their soft drink, beer, or wine or the flavor of their sauce or pastry, you will be convinced of its superiority. David in Psalm 34 applies this principle to the far more important matter of deliverance for the afflicted in this life and eternally: "Taste and see that the LORD is good; blessed is the man who takes refuge in Him" (Psalm 34:8).

The writer to the Hebrews describes Jesus' salvation as passing the ultimate taste test by His death on the cross for us. "But we see Jesus, who was made a little lower than the angels, now crowned with glory and honor because He suffered death, so that by the grace of God He might taste death for everyone." But Jesus tasted death for everyone that through faith in Him, we might taste life here on earth and eternally in heaven.

Every time we come to the Lord's Table to receive His body and blood in, with, and under the bread and wine, we taste the goodness of the Lord as forgiven sinners. And our regular reception of the Sacrament brings witness to the world of salvation through Jesus Christ alone. By our actions of worship with God's people at the Lord's table we invite others to taste and see that the Lord is good.

As we live our daily lives in the world, forgiven and strengthened at the table, we have opportunity to encourage others to take the taste test and, by the Spirit's power, discover that Jesus tasted death for everyone so they might live also.

*Prayer:* Lord Jesus, thank You for tasting death that we might live. Strengthened by Your body and blood, help us to invite others to taste and see Your salvation, won for us on the cross. Amen.

April 3

# Perfect through Suffering

## *Reading:* Hebrews 2:10–18

*Text:* It was fitting that God . . . should make the author of their salvation perfect through suffering. Hebrews 2:10

The writer to the Hebrews further explains what it meant for Jesus to "taste death for everyone" (Hebrews 2:9). Addressing Jewish Christians, perhaps in Rome, under pressure from Nero to hide their belief in Jesus as Savior and tempted to relapse into Judaism to avoid persecution, the writer clearly points them to the author of their salvation, Jesus Christ, who was made "perfect through suffering."

He makes it clear that only by becoming a flesh and blood human being could Jesus win our salvation: "Since the children have flesh and blood, He too shared in their humanity so that by His death He might destroy him who holds the power of death–that is, the devil–and free those who all their lives were held in slavery by their fear of death" (Hebrews 2:14–15). As a sinless human being, Jesus could "become a merciful and faithful high priest in service to God" and "make atonement for the sins of the people" (Hebrews 2:17). In other words, Jesus was made "perfect through suffering."

Our own assurance of salvation is based on Jesus "tasting death for everyone" and being made "perfect through suffering." And our witness to those who do not believe in Jesus as their Savior is based on the same scriptural truths. The comforting words of Hebrews 2:18 apply to us and also to the people we reach in our daily callings: "Because He Himself suffered when He was tempted, He is able to help those who are being tempted."

God, then, gives us boldness to face persecution or rejection in the world with an unwavering confession of our Savior Jesus: perfect through suffering!

*Prayer:* Paschal Lamb, by God appointed,
All our sins on you were laid;
By almighty love anointed,
You have full atonement made.
Ev'ry sin has been forgiven
Through the virtue of your blood;
Open is the gate of heaven,
Peace between mankind and God.
*LW* 284:2

# Lasting Impact

## *Reading:* Romans 16:1–16

*Text:* A certain man from Cyrene, Simon, the father of Alexander and Rufus, was passing by on his way in from the country, and they forced him to carry the cross. Mark 15:21

What contacts with others have made a lasting impact on your life regarding faith in Jesus as Savior? How might God be using you to make a lasting impact on someone else through even a single contact?

A front page article in last Wednesday's newspaper made me consider the above questions. Pictured in the hospital was a two-year-old boy named Bryson, the son of a Navy petty officer. Bryson, attending a Cardinals baseball game with his parents, had been struck in the head by a foul ball from the bat of slugger, Albert Pujols. Albert visited the hospital the next day to visit little Bryson. He brought him an autographed baseball bat with the words, "God bless you," inscribed. A very strong believer in Christ, Pujols no doubt intended those words as a witness. As Bryson grows up, the foul ball incident and the visit of the famous player will probably make a lasting impact on his life.

Simon of Cyrene, a devout Jew, probably on his way to Jerusalem for the Passover, was not expecting a personal contact that would make a lasting impact on his life. Yet he was forced to carry the cross of a man named Jesus of Nazareth on the way to Calvary. In those brief moments, he came face to face with the Savior of the world, who would absorb all of the cruel blows of death by crucifixion to pay for the sins of the world, including Simon's. The fact that Mark identifies Simon as the father of Alexander and Rufus may suggest that the Rufus mentioned in Paul's personal greetings in Romans 16:13 is part of God's family as a result of Simon's encounter with Jesus! A lasting impact indeed!

Whether you receive a contact like Bryson or make a contact like Albert Pujols, consider how God might be using others and you to make a lasting impact with the Gospel of Jesus Christ!

*Prayer:* Lord use my daily contacts to bring others to You. Amen.

# Anatomy of the Wicked: Heart

***Reading:* Psalm 38:1–8**

*Text:* Transgression speaks to the wicked deep in his heart. Psalm 36:1a (ESV)

When we desire to reach the lost with the saving Gospel of Christ, we need to understand clearly the nature of those we care about deeply. The next several devotions will focus on Psalm 36, where God supplies an anatomy of the wicked–those separated from God. Rather than separating ourselves from the wicked, we seek opportunities for witness. And in the process, we rediscover our own wickedness apart from Christ.

First, the psalmist references the heart of the wicked. "Transgression speaks to the wicked deep in his heart." The *Concordia Self-Study Bible* commenting in its notes on Psalm 4:7 describes the heart: "In biblical language the center of the human spirit, from which spring emotions, thought, motivations, courage and action–'the wellspring of life'" (p. 790). Apart from God's grace, the wicked hear only transgression deep in their inner being, their heart. They may look normal, sound pious, and act altruistic, but disobedience and rebellion control their emotions, form their thoughts, shape their motivations, and guide their actions. In short, they live in slavery to sin and desperately need true freedom.

Psalm 38 tells us that we can understand the plight of the wicked far better than we might think. The believing but despairing David writes, "There is no health in my bones because of my sin. For my iniquities have gone over my head; like a heavy burden, they are too heavy for me" (Psalm 38:3b–4). Like David, we confess our sin and cry out, "But for You, O LORD, do I wait; it is You, O LORD my God who will answer" (Psalm 38:15).

Trusting in Christ alone, the bearer of our transgressions on Calvary, we understand the wickedness of our own hearts and the magnitude of His all-sufficient sacrifice for the sins of the world. God's Spirit impels us to reach the wicked with their only hope for salvation, Jesus Christ for them and deep within their hearts.

*Prayer:* As surely as I live, God said,
I would not see the sinner dead.
I want him turned from error's ways,
Repentant, living endless days.
*LW* 235:1

# Eyes

## *Reading:* Psalm 38:9–12

*Text:* There is no fear of God before his eyes. For he flatters himself in his own eyes that his iniquity cannot be found and hated. Psalm 36:1b–2 (ESV)

What do you see in the eyes of another person? Do they look away from you? Are they shifty? Do they stare right through you? Do they flatter you with intent to manipulate? Or do they reveal a sincerity of truth and compassion? As the saying goes, the eyes are a window to the soul.

Psalm 36, in its anatomy of the wicked, references second the eyes of the wicked: "There is no fear of God before his eyes. For he flatters himself in his own eyes that his iniquity cannot be found and hated." As you seek to share Christ with those separated from Him by their sin, what do you see in their eyes? The psalmist tells us that whatever their intent at the moment, there is no fear of God before their eyes and they are blind to the reality of their own sin. They flatter themselves as good people, fully able to handle any moral problems, unaware of sin as spiritual death and bondage.

David in Psalm 38 sees with different eyes. Physically ill, abandoned by friends, attacked by his enemies, aware of his own burdensome iniquity, he cries, ". . . even the light has gone from my eyes" (Psalm 38:10b). While he is describing his physical weakness, David clearly knows "the fear of God" and does not "flatter himself in his own eyes." Therefore, he says, "I confess my iniquity; I am troubled by my sin" (Psalm 38:18). With confidence, he writes, "Come quickly to help me, O LORD my Savior" (Psalm 38:22).

Knowing the times when we flatter ourselves in our own eyes and need "the fear of God" before our eyes, we confess our sin with David and turn to our Savior, Jesus Christ, who alone can restore light to our eyes physically and spiritually. Then we can pray for the compassionate eyes of Jesus to see others as He sees them, sinners in need of repentance.

*Prayer:* For this time and place have we been born,
Gifted by the Spirit, trained and sent:
With the eyes of Jesus seeing. . .
*SP* 58:4

Copyright © 1986 Concordia Publishing House

April 7

# Mouth

## *Reading:* Psalm 39:1–9

*Text:* The words of his mouth are trouble and deceit; he has ceased to act wisely and do good. Psalm 36:3 (ESV)

Psalm 36, in its anatomy of the wicked, references third the mouth of the wicked: "The words of his mouth are trouble and deceit; he has ceased to act wisely and do good." What stands in the way of our witness to the wicked? Often we have been hurt by the words of their mouths. They have caused us trouble by slandering us or harshly criticizing us. They have spoken deceitful words that we took in good faith, only to discover later their sinister intent. The hostile words of their mouths flow from hearts of iniquity and eyes that fail to see their wickedness. No wonder we see them as enemies instead of lost souls in need of Christ.

In Psalm 39 David has been seriously wounded by his enemies and therefore guards his mouth: "I will guard my mouth with a muzzle, so long as the wicked are in my presence" (Psalm 39:1b). Despite his attempt to avoid sinning with his tongue, he ends up with such great distress and a heart so hot within him that he speaks with his tongue. Confessing his sins of the mouth, he becomes mute before God: "And now, O Lord, for what do I wait? My hope is in You" (Psalm 39:7).

The mouth of the wicked often turns us against them and leads us to sins of the tongue for which we need forgiveness. The One who, although oppressed and afflicted, "opened not His mouth" (Isaiah 53:7a) speaks to us and the world a word of pardon, "Father, forgive them, for they know not what they do" (Luke 23:34). His blood-bought forgiveness enables us to keep silent when attacked and speak words of forgiveness to our enemies from our hearts cleansed through Baptism and our compassionate eyes enlightened by God's Spirit. What a witness!

*Prayer:* Give us lips to sing thy glory,
Tongues thy mercy to proclaim,
Throats that shout the hope that fills us,
Mouths to speak thy holy name.
Alleluia, alleluia!
May the light which thou dost send
Fill our songs with alleluias,
Alleluias without end!
*LW* 328:5

# Mind

## *Reading:* Psalm 39:10–13

*Text:* He plots trouble while on his bed; he sets himself in a way that is not good; he does not reject evil. Psalm 36:4 (ESV)

Psalm 36, in its anatomy of the wicked, references last the mind of the wicked: "He plots trouble while on his bed." When Satan takes over the mind, the sinful flesh causes people in their thoughts to operate totally out of self-interest, day and night. The psalmist describes the wicked as plotting trouble while on his bed, forsaking the good for the evil. The devious mind then drives the wicked to words and actions that oppose God and harm His creation. How can we witness to those with minds bent on evil?

David is more concerned about his own sinful mind, triggered by the scheming minds of the wicked: "When you discipline a man with rebukes for sin, you consume like a moth what is dear to him; surely all mankind is a mere breath!" (Psalm 39:11). Forgiven, David has learned the futility of a mind bent on self-gratification and evil, and recognizes himself as "a sojourner with You, a guest like all my fathers" (Psalm 39:12b). As we examine our own thought world at night and during the day, we see clearly our selfishness and evil, separating us from God and clouding our witness.

Repentant, we turn to Christ whose mind was yielded to the Father as He set His face like flint toward Jerusalem (Luke 9:51) and the saving cross. We respond to Paul's words as preface to his great hymn of Christ's humiliation and exaltation: "Have this mind among yourselves, which is yours in Christ Jesus . . ." (Philippians 2:5). Our witness is clear to the wicked with clouded minds in the final verses of that hymn to Christ—"so that at the name of Jesus every knee should bow in heaven and on earth and under the earth, and every tongue confess that Jesus Christ is Lord, to the glory of God, the Father" (Philippians 2:10–11).

Heart, eyes, mouth, mind—the whole anatomy, by God's grace in Christ, yielded to Him now and forever!

*Prayer:* Fill with the radiance of your grace
The wand'rers lost in error's maze.
Enlighten those whose secret minds
Some deep delusion haunts and blinds.
*LW* 314:2

# Forgiven to Rescue

***Reading:* Psalm 51**

*Text:* Then I will teach transgressors Your ways, and sinners will turn back to You. Psalm 51:13

Psalm 51 is famous as David's honest confession of sin after his adultery with Bathsheba and his murder of her husband Uriah. Each verse cries out his deep sorrow over his transgressions. David throws himself on the mercies of God for forgiveness described as washing, blotting out, and cleansing from iniquity. So many of these verses are incorporated in the liturgy of the church including, "Create in me a pure heart, O God, and renew a steadfast spirit within me" (Psalm 51:10). We regularly join David in confession of our sins and receiving God's forgiveness through the cross of Jesus Christ.

Perhaps less famous is the missionary dimension of Psalm 51 in verse 13: "Then I will teach transgressors Your ways, and sinners will turn back to You." Forgiven and restored to the joy of his salvation, David desires to rescue other sinners from unrepentant destruction. He has seen and confessed his own terrible sin: "I know my transgressions, and my sin is always before me" (Psalm 51:3). He wants wayward sinners like him to see and confess their sin so their crushing burdens may be lifted and a full cleansing received from God through His promised Messiah, the great Burden-bearer. David's purpose might well be described as "forgiven to rescue."

How about you? Could our desire to help set the world ablaze with the Gospel of Christ be labeled "forgiven to rescue"? Because we know our daily sin and the burden it brings, because we know the daily forgiveness received through our Baptism, flowing from Christ's once-for-all atoning death on Calvary, we want to teach transgressors God's ways so, as sinners, they will turn back to their Savior. Yes, both our purpose and strength for daily witness come from God alone: forgiven to rescue!

*Prayer:* Come, O sinners, one and all,
Come accept his invitation;
Come and take his free salvation!
Firmly in these words believe:
Jesus, sinners will receive.
*LW* 229:4

# Teaching from a Painful Lesson

***Reading:* Psalm 32**

*Text:* I will instruct you and teach you the way you should go. Psalm 32:8a

Who are our best teachers? Whether they teach in the classroom, guide us at home, serve as our boss at work, or mentor as a valued friend, our best teachers often share wisdom with us based on personal experience, both positive and painful.

In Psalm 32, David teaches others about sin and forgiveness, based on his own very painful lesson. He writes, "Blessed is he whose transgressions are forgiven, whose sins are covered" (Psalm 32:1). He then goes on in this psalm to reveal his terrible experience with unconfessed sin, using descriptive words like "bones wasted away," "strength sapped as in the heat of summer," "Your hand heavy upon me" (Psalm 32:3, 4). He also describes the wonderful assurance received from God after his honest confession: "Then I acknowledged my sin to You and did not cover up my iniquity. I said, 'I will confess my transgression to the LORD'–and You forgave the guilt of my sin" (Psalm 32:5).

Now, David reaches out to others from his painful lesson to point them to God's forgiveness: "I will instruct you and teach you in the way you should go." Don't be as stubborn as a horse or mule as I was. Avoid the woes of the wicked by honest confession. Trust in the Lord's unfailing love and forgiveness through the promised Messiah. Then, you will rejoice in the Lord. Teaching from a painful lesson.

We help set the world ablaze with Christ by teaching others, based on painful lessons we have learned. God's faithfulness in our lives–exposing our sins, leading us to repentance, providing full and free forgiveness through Christ's death–will shine through our teaching to others in need of that same forgiveness. Whom does God want you to teach based on your experience? May God bless your teaching from a painful lesson!

*Prayer:* For by your Word we clearly see
That we have sinned continually;
But show us too, forgiving Lord,
Your saving Gospel's great reward.

That all of us, your children dear,
By Christ redeemed, may Christ revere;
Lead us in joy that all we do
Will witness to our love for you.
*LW* 470:4–5

# Mona's Confession

## *Reading:* John 14:1–6

*Text:* Jesus answered, "I am the way and the truth and the life. No one comes to the Father except through Me." John 14:6

I will never forget hearing Mona's confession of faith in her Savior. We were gathered around a campfire at Camp Halekipa on the Island of Oahu in the Hawaiian Islands for evening devotions. As a Walther League Caravaner from Indiana and staff member for this youth camp, I had already been exposed to many cultures and religions in Hawaii far beyond my experience: Japanese, Chinese, Hawaiian, Buddhist, Mormon, Shinto.

Mona stood and simply said: "My whole family is Buddhist. I have come to believe that Jesus Christ died on the cross for my sins. In the Bible, Jesus says, 'I am the way and the truth and the life. No one comes to the Father except through Me.' I believe that even though my family is not happy with me. I am so glad to be with you at this camp as Christian friends."

What a courageous confession of faith! Jesus, on His way to the cross, left no doubt that He was the only way to salvation. God's Spirit has worked that faith in my heart as He did in Mona's heart.

In our pluralistic world today, we have reason to make bold confession of our faith in Jesus and stand shoulder to shoulder with those from every nation, language, and people who are making the same confession by the Spirit's power. Is He not setting the world ablaze through us as He did through Mona at that campfire in 1959?

*Prayer:* You are the way; to you alone From sin and death we flee;
And he who would the Father, seek Your follower must be.

You are the truth; your Word alone True wisdom can impart;
You only can inform the mind And purify the heart.

You are the life; the rending tomb Proclaims your conquering arm;
And those who put their trust in you Not death nor hell shall harm

You are the way, the truth, the life, Grant us that way to know,
That truth to keep, that life to win, Whose joys eternal flow.
*LW* 283:1–4

# My Delight—His Desires

***Reading:* Psalm 37:1–20**

*Text:* Delight yourself in the LORD and He will give you the desires of your heart. Psalm 37:4

Do you delight in the Lord or do you live according to the sinful desires of your heart? Any thought of bearing witness to the world of a Savior from sin depends on your answer to that question. Psalm 37 makes a sharp contrast between the wicked who persecute the righteous and the righteous who trust in the Lord and walk in His ways. The wicked seem to prosper, but their success will be brief before they perish. The righteous face disaster from the wicked, but their inheritance will endure forever.

Do you delight in the Lord or live according to the sinful desires of your heart? The answer is yes. As sinful human beings, we often give way to sinful desires that result in sinful words and deeds. But God sent His only Son to die for our sins. He not only delighted in His heavenly Father but also desired in His heart only to do the Father's will. His perfect life and sacrificial death on the cross made satisfaction for our sins. We are declared righteous for Christ's sake and receive that righteousness through faith.

Therefore, we are counted among the righteous, not the wicked. Trusting in the Lord by God's grace, we delight in the Lord. Living daily in our Baptism, we also desire in our hearts to serve Him. As St. Paul writes, "Those who belong to Christ Jesus have crucified the sinful nature with its passions and desires" (Galatians 6:24).

That is what the psalmist means when he says, "Delight yourself in the LORD and He will give you the desires of your heart." Our delight in the Lord through faith places His desires in our heart to obey, serve, and witness to others of salvation through Christ. Admitting daily my wickedness, clinging daily to Christ's righteousness, I rejoice that my delight in the Lord results in His desires in my heart.

*Prayer:* Create in me a new heart, Lord,
That gladly I obey your Word.
Let what you will be my desire,
And with new life my soul inspire.
*LW* 373:3

April 13

# His Delight—My Steps

*Reading:* Psalm 37:21–40

*Text:* If the LORD delights in a man's way, He makes his steps firm. Psalm 37:23

Does the Lord delight in your ways as you walk each day in steps of service and witness? This is another very important question in your mission to set the world ablaze with Christ. The psalmist in Psalm 37 continues to contrast the wicked and the righteous, vowing destruction for the wicked and promising "a future for the man of peace" (Psalm 37:37b).

We learned yesterday that only Christ's righteousness rescues us from wickedness and through faith counts us among the righteous. Therefore, we delight in the Lord and conform the desires of our heart to His desires. But does the Lord delight in our ways so our steps are firm? The answer is yes. Why? Not because of our righteousness but because of His. The psalmist makes it very clear: "The salvation of the righteous comes from the LORD; He is their stronghold in time of trouble. The LORD helps them and delivers them; He delivers them from the wicked and saves them, because they take refuge in Him" (Psalm 37:39–40).

And so we walk in His steps by faith. We dare to walk daily in the world in our calling, obeying God's will, working faithfully and joyfully, using every opportunity to share the hope that is in us through Christ, looking for ways to serve our neighbor. Never denying our sinful nature or our dependence on Christ's forgiveness, we walk with a firm step.

Yes, the Lord delights in our way because of Christ. Although we stumble, we will not fall for the Lord upholds us with His hand. As the psalmist puts it, "For the LORD loves the just and will not forsake His faithful ones" (Psalm 37:28). His delight—my steps!

*Prayer:* I walk with Jesus all the way,
His guidance never fails me;
Within his wounds I find a stay
When Satan's pow'r assails me;
And by his footsteps led,
My path I safely tread.
No evil leads my soul astray;
I walk with Jesus all the way.
*LW* 391:5

# Remember and Tell

***Reading:* Luke 24:1–9**

*Text:* "He is not here; He has risen! Remember how He told you, while He was still with you in Galilee." Luke 24:6

What a morning for the women! Grieving Jesus' death, they make their way to the tomb with spices. Shocked, they find the stone rolled away from the tomb and no body inside. Dazzled and terrified, they see two men in clothes gleaming like lightning. What could possibly turn them into believing witnesses of Jesus' physical resurrection from the dead?

First, a question and an announcement: "Why do you look for the living among the dead? He is not here; He has risen!" The question gets their attention. The announcement startles them to consider that Jesus might actually be alive. Then comes the evidence in a single word–*remember*. "Remember how He told you, while He was still with you in Galilee: The Son of Man must be delivered into the hands of sinful men, be crucified and on the third day be raised again" (Luke 24:6–7). God's Holy Spirit had done His work in their minds and hearts because Luke simply records: "Then they remembered His words" (Luke 24:8).

And the word "remember" triggered another key word, "tell," because Luke describes their transformation into believing witnesses to Christ's resurrection with these words: "When they came back from the tomb, they told all these things to the eleven and to all the others" (Luke 24:9).

In this Easter season we join the women at the tomb in a world of grieving, shock, and doubt. The messengers question our folly for being in a graveyard and announcing Jesus' physical resurrection from the dead. The key words for us are also remember what Christ clearly tells us in His Word about His death to pay for our sins and His resurrection on the third day, and tell everyone that He is alive to give them the sure hope of eternal life in heaven.

*Prayer:* Risen Lord, help us to remember all that You have told us about Your death and resurrection. Move us to tell others the great good news about salvation through faith in You. Amen.

# A Telling Response

***Reading:*** **Luke 24:10–12**

*Text:* But they did not believe the women, because their words seemed to them like nonsense. Luke 24:11

Often we need courage to tell others the story of the crucified and risen Christ. We stumble for the right words and fear their reaction. What if they reject us and our story?

That is exactly what happened to the women at the tomb who heard the angels' message, remembered the words of Jesus in Galilee, and then ran breathlessly to tell the disciples that Jesus had risen bodily from the dead. Luke records the disciples' reaction: "But they did not believe the women, because their words seemed to them like nonsense." What a telling response! At last Peter ran to the tomb to see for himself. He observed the empty tomb and went away wondering what had happened, not believing but wondering.

A long time ago I learned a simple scriptural principle for witnessing: Success in witnessing is sharing Christ in the power of the Holy Spirit and leaving the results to God. St. Paul writes, "No one can say, 'Jesus is Lord,' except by the Holy Spirit" (1 Corinthians 12:3). The women faithfully told the resurrection story. At this point, the disciples did not believe because their words seemed like nonsense, but the Spirit was at work, especially moving Peter to visit the empty tomb.

In our weakness we fear the response of others. We may or may not tell the story in the best way possible. But whenever God's unfailing Word is spoken, His Spirit is at work. Nonsense words can become words of life, light, and joy. We know from reading Luke's Gospel that wonderful events lie ahead for the disciples. More on that tomorrow.

*Prayer:* Let hearts be purged of evil That we may see aright
The Lord in rays eternal Of resurrection light
And, listening to his accents, May hear so calm and plain,
His own "All hail!" and, hearing, May raise the victor strain.
*LW* 133:2

# Told to Touch

***Reading:* Luke 24:36–43**

*Text:* "Touch Me and see; a ghost does not have flesh and bones, as you see I have." Luke 24:39b

The women have told the disciples the message that Christ is risen, although the disciples did not believe their words. Simon Peter visited the tomb and found it empty. The risen Christ then appeared to Peter (Luke 24:34). The two disciples on the road to Emmaus have just returned to Jerusalem to tell how they recognized Jesus in the breaking of the bread (Luke 24:35). But now on that Easter Sunday evening, Jesus, the Risen One, appears to the eleven and all those with them.

Despite His words, "Peace be with you," they are startled and frightened, thinking they are seeing a ghost. They are troubled, according to Jesus, with doubts rising in their minds. Consequently, they are told to touch Jesus, to see His nail-pierced hands and feet and to touch His flesh, the very body that died on the cross to pay for all their sins, the very body laid in the brand-new tomb of Joseph of Arimathea, the very glorified body now physically risen from the dead. And to make absolutely clear to them that He is alive in the flesh, He eats a piece of broiled fish in their presence. Those words said by the women no longer seem like nonsense. Told to touch by Jesus Himself, they now believe.

We are also told to touch Jesus. Not only do we read and hear His precious Word, but we have been touched and made His own children in the waters of Baptism, and we regularly touch and taste His body and blood in, with, and under the bread and the wine of Holy Communion. Told to touch, we believe and desire to touch others with the story of salvation through faith in the crucified and risen Savior.

*Prayer:* Praise we him, whose love divine
Gives his sacred blood for wine,
Gives his body for the feast,
Christ the victim, Christ the priest. Alleluia!

Easter triumph, Easter joy!
This alone can sin destroy!
From sin's pow'r, Lord, set us free,
Newborn souls in you to be. Alleluia!
*LW* 126:2, 7

# Told to Tell

***Reading:*** **Luke 24:44–49**

*Text:* "You are witnesses of these things." Luke 24:48

Easter is a day to celebrate Christ's resurrection from the grave. Trumpets, full organ, Easter lilies, and overflowing churches singing hymns loudly. But what does God want us to take home from our Easter worship?

Having touched the risen Christ, the disciples now understand what Jesus told them while He was still with them and what He wants them to tell all nations as "witnesses of these things." Jesus says, "Everything must be fulfilled that is written about Me in the Law of Moses, the Prophets and the Psalms" (Luke 24:44). Jesus makes it clear that the Old Testament Scriptures testify that He is the promised Messiah.

Just as the women remembered Jesus' words in Galilee and the Emmaus disciples' hearts burned within them when Jesus talked with them on the road and opened the Scriptures to them, so the disciples in the upper room now understand. "Then He opened their minds so they could understand the Scriptures" (Luke 24:45). "This is what is written: The Christ will suffer and rise from the dead on the third day, and repentance and forgiveness of sins will be preached in His name to all nations, beginning at Jerusalem. You are witnesses of these things" (Luke 24:46–48).

Clearly the disciples are told to tell! And so are we. That is God's Easter message to us. Jesus was crucified for the sins of the world, including ours. He rose from the dead to declare His victory over sin, death, and the devil. We repent and proclaim repentance as part of Christ's Church. We are forgiven and proclaim forgiveness of sins in His name to all nations. We are witnesses of Good Friday and Easter Sunday. Told to tell! What a privilege!

*Prayer:* Gracious God, fill us with Easter joy as we celebrate the triumphant resurrection of Your Son Jesus Christ from the dead as proof of His victory over sin, death, and the devil. As witnesses of those things, lead us to tell others about the crucified and risen Lord so that they too may believe in Him. Amen.

# Hearts Burning Within?

## *Reading:* Luke 24:13–35

*Text:* "Were not our hearts burning within us while He talked with us on the road and opened the Scriptures to us?" Luke 24:32

What impact does Easter have on your life? Is it a once-a-year festive celebration with brightly colored spring clothing and Easter lilies or a life-changing reality that motivates you all year long?

The excited declaration of the Emmaus disciples describes a lasting Easter effect: "Were not our hearts burning within us?" But on Easter Sunday afternoon they were walking home from Jerusalem to Emmaus with heavy hearts. No fire burned within. They were downcast. A stranger, whom they did not recognize as the risen Christ, joined them. They were sad because they thought Jesus was still dead. They told the stranger about the visit of the women and the message of the angels that Jesus was alive. They even knew about the visit of the disciples who found an empty tomb. Still, they hadn't seen Jesus personally and thus doubted His resurrection.

We know the story of Easter and may even accept Jesus' resurrection as a historical fact. But we don't always believe He is alive today in our lives and for our problems. Like the Emmaus disciples, our hearts are cold.

Jesus makes the difference. He opens the Old Testament Scriptures to them about the Messiah's saving mission. While breaking bread with them in their home, Jesus reveals Himself. Now they joyfully speak the words of our text. They believe in the risen Christ and hurry to the city to bear witness.

Jesus kindles a flame also in our hearts. Sins exposed and confessed, we see Jesus as Savior, alive from the dead. The Scriptures come alive for us. Our hearts burn within and we hurry to bear witness. Easter all year long. Burning hearts aglow with the risen Christ present in Word and Sacraments!

*Prayer:* Risen Lord, kindle the fire of Your Word in our hearts. Amen.

# Easter Family in Japan

## *Reading:* Luke 24:28–35

*Text:* Let us not give up meeting together, as some are in the habit of doing, but let us encourage one another—and all the more as you see the Day approaching. Hebrews 10:25

Easter and the family of God. Images from Scripture and Japan. Two weary, disheartened disciples inviting a stranger to their table, only to discover the risen Christ in the breaking of the bread. Their rush to join the eleven and celebrate the good news. Strong encouragement from Hebrews to worship regularly (not just on Easter) as the Day of the Lord approaches. Now these words from Bethany Paulus in Japan:

"Easter was a special celebration for me. The service included Easter banners, singing by the choir, and the Baptism of the pastor's granddaughter! Afterward, the church members gathered together for a special lunch and time together. . . . As we ate lunch, I visited with one of the older high school girls. The day before, she had come to the church, and it had been her first time to dye Easter eggs! I usually dye Easter eggs with my family, and she was surprised to hear that I don't usually dye them with the congregation. But then, she began to explain that she is the only Christian in her family. She told me it would be strange for her to do something like that with her family.

"That's when it occurred to me that this church *is* her family. Like many Christians in Japan, she is the only member of her family who is a believer in Jesus. No wonder these believers linger together, celebrating a day and a reason that many others, including their families, are unaware of. They gather to support and encourage one another. This year, Easter has reminded me not only of Christ's death and resurrection, but of the gift of the family of God. My prayer is that God will continue to teach me how to build up and encourage others in His family, especially those in His family here."

*Prayer:* Blest be the tie that binds
Our hearts in Christian love;
The unity of heart and mind
Is like to that above.
*LW* 295:1

# First Watch

## *Reading:* John 21:1–14

*Text:* Early in the morning, Jesus stood on the shore, but the disciples did not realize that it was Jesus. John 21:4

Right across the street from our church is a restaurant named First Watch. We eat there often for meetings and visits with friends from church. It is a place for Christian witness. Conversation abounds while waiting for a table and during the meal.

At first watch, Jesus' disciples needed encouragement because they had fished all night and had caught nothing. At first watch, "Jesus stood on the shore, but the disciples did not realize that it was Jesus." Shortly thereafter, He got their day started out right by instructing them to cast their nets on the right side of the boat. With an unexpected and overwhelming catch of fish, they realized, "It is the Lord" (John 21:7a). When they landed, a fire was burning with fish on the coals–a first watch breakfast if you will. "Come and have breakfast," said Jesus. They saw Him again as their risen Lord!

When you sit at the table for breakfast, lunch, or dinner with business associates, family, old friends, or new acquaintances, do you see the Christian witness opportunity? They may be discouraged, weary, distracted, preoccupied, or hurting. They may not recognize or know Jesus as their Lord and Savior. You may be God's appointed representative to introduce them to Jesus as you eat together. What a joy when they discover, "It is the Lord," their crucified and risen Savior, at their side with forgiveness for every first watch.

*Prayer:* Awake, my soul and with the sun
Your daily stage of duty run;
Shake off dull sloth and joyful rise
To pay your morning sacrifice.

All praise to you, who safe have kept
And have refreshed me while I slept,
Grant, Lord, when I from death shall wake,
I may of endless light partake.

Lord, I my vows to you renew.
Disperse my sins as morning dew;
Guard my first springs of thought and will,
And with yourself, my spirit fill.
*LW* 478:1–3

April 21

# A Chariot Witness

*Reading:* Acts 8:26–40

*Text:* Then Philip ran up to the chariot and heard the man reading Isaiah the prophet. Acts 8:30a

The award-winning film *Chariots of Fire* describes the 1924 Olympic success of the United Kingdom track team. They ran with the intensity of fiery chariots. Eric Liddell, a Church of Scotland believer, anchored that track team and shocked the press by refusing to run on Sunday at the Olympics because of his religious convictions. One year after winning an Olympic gold medal, Liddell journeyed to China as a missionary with the London Missionary Society. He now ran for the Lord as a Christian witness. In addition to teaching science at an Anglo-Chinese college, he served as a rural evangelist, traveling many miles on foot and bicycle. During World War II he spent two years in a Japanese prison camp as an "enemy national," dying there of a brain tumor in 1945. Throughout his career he served as a tremendous inspiration to those around him—a chariot of fire in his witness to Jesus Christ.

In Acts we read about the evangelist Philip, who was asked to seek out a foreign dignitary from Ethiopia traveling home by chariot. "Then Philip ran up to the chariot and heard the man reading Isaiah the prophet." Philip, like Eric Liddell, ran in order to witness to Christ. The Ethiopian eunuch believed and was baptized through Philip's witness. No doubt the Gospel came to Ethiopia as the man's chariot reached his home.

We can also be "chariots of fire" for the Lord. God sent His Son to run the race for us and win the victory on the cross. He endured persecution, suffering, and death to pay for our sins. He chooses us as His own forgiven children. By His power we can run like Philip and Eric Liddell to tell others about Jesus the Savior. What chariot witness does God have in store for you?

*Prayer:* Give me a faithful heart, Likeness to thee,
That each departing day Henceforth may see
Some work of love begun, Some deed of kindness done,
Some wand'rer sought and won, Something for thee.
*LW* 374:3

# Authentic Witness: David

***Reading:* Psalm 32**

*Text:* Then I acknowledged my sin to You and did not cover up my iniquity. I said, "I will confess my transgression to the LORD," and You forgave the guilt of my sin. Psalm 32:5

How can we bring the good news of salvation through Jesus to others with a personal touch? The next several devotions will examine the authentic personal witness of biblical characters. We begin with King David in the Old Testament.

David is a towering and heroic figure in Israel, from humble shepherd boy to slayer of the giant, Goliath, to fugitive pursued relentlessly by jealous King Saul to courageous king, first of Judah and then of all Israel. Conquering warrior, wise king, empire builder, and temple musician, David commands attention and respect. However, his authentic witness comes from his human fallibility, honest confession of sin, and total dependence on God for forgiveness and strength for daily life. His adulterous relationship with Bathsheba and consequent murder of Uriah is well-known and his confession is chronicled in Psalm 51. But his entire life featured problems, attacks, suffering, and illnesses beyond his human ability to cope, and he regularly confessed his sin and need for salvation.

In Psalm 32, David describes a period of difficulty because of unconfessed sin and then honestly writes, "Then I acknowledged my sin to You and did not cover up my iniquity . . . and You forgave the guilt of my sin." Authentic witness about his own failures and his only source of forgiveness and strength–the one true God, who would send the Messiah as David's Son and David's Lord.

That authentic witness of David points us to Jesus as the One who saves His people from their sin and provides an example for our own authentic witness to those around us.

*Prayer:* Jesus sinners will receive; May they all this saying ponder
Who in sin's delusions live And from God and heaven wander!
Here is hope for all who grieve: Jesus sinners will receive.

We deserve but grief and shame, Yet his words, rich grace revealing,
Pardon, peace, and life proclaim. Here our ills have perfect healing;
We with humble hearts believe Jesus sinners will receive.
*LW* 229:1–2

# Authentic Witness: Jeremiah

***Reading:* Jeremiah 1:4–10**

*Text:* "Ah, Sovereign LORD," I said, "I do not know how to speak; I am only a child." Jeremiah 1:6

Elsewhere in the Old Testament, the prophet Jeremiah brings the authentic witness of bold words proclaimed to a rebellious nation and a life of suffering lived without renouncing his call as God's prophet of judgment and mercy. His example stands tall in a permissive and politically correct world where God's prophetic message needs to be proclaimed.

Jeremiah's obedient life as servant of Jahweh, peppered with rejection, beatings, imprisonment, and time in a cistern, and his courageous, sometimes radical, messages from God in word and symbol provoked the political and religious establishment of his day and jar our modern ears. Yet his authentic witness began already when God called him as a youth.

The word of the Lord came to him saying, "Before I formed you in the womb I knew you, before you were born I set you apart; I appointed you as a prophet to the nations" (Jeremiah 1:5). In Jeremiah's words, the story continues, "Ah, Sovereign LORD,… I do not know how to speak; I am only a child." The Lord then pressed that call as prophet upon Jeremiah but with a wonderful promise: "You must go to everyone I send you to and say whatsoever I command you. Do not be afraid of them for I am with you and will rescue you" (Jeremiah 1:7–8).

God has called each of us in our Baptism to be His child and witness to Jesus as Savior. The sign of the cross upon our lives impels us to authentic witness and carries with it the promise of daily forgiveness and His presence in our lives. In what ways will your life of obedience and words of Law and Gospel bring others to a saving relationship with Jesus Christ?

*Prayer:* Speak, O Lord, your servant listens,
Let your Word to me come near;
Newborn life and spirit give me,
Let each promise still my fear.
Death's dread pow'r, its inward strife,
Wars against your Word of life;
Fill me, Lord, with love's strong fervor
That I cling to you forever!
*LW* 339:1

# Authentic Witness: Peter

## *Reading:* 2 Peter 1:12–21

*Text:* We ourselves heard this voice that came from heaven when we were with Him on the sacred mountain. 2 Peter 1:18

Simon Peter, the rock, strides through the pages of the New Testament as an authentic witness of Jesus: "You are the Christ, the Son of the living God" (Matthew 16:16). For that confession of faith, Peter was commended by his Lord, "You are Peter, and on this rock I will build My church" (Matthew 16:18). Peter in many ways is larger than life—a simple fisherman called as one of the first disciples, loud spokesman for the disciples, often putting his foot in his mouth (trying to stop Jesus from suffering and rebuked as a tool of Satan; rushing to walk on water and needing rescue when he sank; boasting he would never deny Jesus then denying Him with an oath). At the same time, Peter makes bold confessions of faith, preached powerful sermons after Pentecost, obediently brought the Gospel to the Gentile Cornelius, and testified to this worldwide outreach at the Jerusalem Council. Tradition tells us that he was martyred for his faith by being crucified upside down.

That Peter provides an eyewitness testimony to his readers of his experience with Jesus on the Mount of Transfiguration where he saw Jesus in all His glory and heard God's voice from heaven, "This is My Son whom I love; with Him I am pleased" (2 Peter 1:16–18). Peter's authentic witness points us to the even greater light of the sacred Scriptures written by holy men of God moved by the Holy Spirit (2 Peter 1:19–21). He is very believable.

We can bear authentic witness to Jesus as Savior, revealed in Holy Scripture. Through the power of the Holy Spirit we believe in the Savior, know His forgiving presence in our daily lives, and can tell others about His love for them.

*Prayer:* Then let your Word within me
Shine as the fairest star,
Your reign of love revealing
How wonderful you are.
Help me confess you truly
And with your Christendom
Here own you King and Savior
With all the world to come.
*LW* 79:6

# Authentic Witness: Paul

***Reading:* Ephesians 3:7–13**

*Text:* Although I am less than the least of all God's people, this grace was given to me: to preach to the Gentiles the unsearchable riches of Christ. Ephesians 3:8

St. Paul's witness is unimpeachable. His proclamation of Jesus Christ and Him crucified was consistent day in and day out. His life characterized his commitment to suffer all things for the Gospel—beatings, imprisonment, shipwrecks, and many attempts on his life.

But part of his authentic witness comes from his previous life as a Pharisee persecuting Christians. When the Lord spoke to him on the Damascus road, his whole life was turned around. Converted to faith in Jesus by God's grace, baptized, and called to be an apostle to the Gentiles, Paul never forgot that he was "less than the least of all God's people." He knew his own sinful nature and need for daily forgiveness. He knew his own hardness of heart as a persecutor that only made him desire even more the salvation of his own people, the Jews. And because he knew firsthand the grace of God in the death and resurrection of Jesus that brought justification through faith, he was impelled "to preach to the Gentiles the unsearchable riches of Christ." Unashamedly he told the story of his conversion time after time as a witness to God's grace.

Does Paul's authentic witness move you to thank God for His grace in Christ? Does his humility help you realize how we are all "less than the least of all God's people"? Does his story focus your daily attention on Jesus Christ and Him crucified? Does his zeal motivate you to proclaim the unsearchable riches of Christ to those near to you and beyond your immediate circle of family and friends? Because of Paul, God's Spirit engages each of us to help set the world ablaze with Christ!

*Prayer:* If you cannot speak like angels,
If you cannot preach like Paul,
You can tell the love of Jesus;
You can say he died for all.
If you cannot rouse the wicked
With the judgments dread alarms,
You can lead the little children
To the Savior's waiting arms.
*LW* 318:2

# Authentic Witness: John

## *Reading:* 1 John 1:1–10

*Text:* That which was from the beginning, which we have heard, which we have seen with our eyes, which we have looked at and our hands have touched—this we proclaim concerning the Word of life. 1 John 1:1

Picture the apostle John in the twilight of his life. Jesus had called him from his fishnets as a disciple, along with his brother, James. Chosen to witness Jesus' transfiguration, he was known as "the disciple whom Jesus loved" (John 21:20). Jesus, while dying on the cross, entrusted His mother, Mary, to John's care. John visited the empty tomb, saw the risen Lord, and proclaimed Him after Pentecost. Tradition places his ministry in Ephesus among the churches of Asia Minor (modern Turkey). He wrote the fourth Gospel, three letters, and the book of Revelation. Here is an authentic witness of the Gospel!

John's words are palpable: "That which was from the beginning, which we have heard, which we have seen with our eyes, which we have looked at and our hands have touched—this we proclaim concerning the Word of life." John proclaims Jesus as the Word made flesh (John 1:14), the Lamb of God, who takes away the sin of the world (John 1:29), and the Light of the world (John 8:12). Now, in this letter, his personal witness to Jesus leads his hearers to recognize that they walk in darkness, need to confess their sin and receive God's forgiveness because "the blood of Jesus, His Son, cleanses us from all sin" (1 John 1:7). John: an authentic witness!

Have not our eyes seen, our ears heard, and our hands touched the crucified and risen Christ? His Word, read and heard, transforms us. The water of Baptism has touched us, and we have held in our hands the bread that is His body and tasted the wine that is His blood. Confessing our sins, we receive His forgiveness won by His shed blood and walk as authentic witnesses of Jesus!

*Prayer:* For your beloved disciple
Exiled to Patmos' shore,
And for his faithful record,
We praise you evermore.
Praise for the mystic vision
His words to us unfold.
Instill in us the longing
Your glory to behold.
*LW* 193:8

# A Word from the "Amen Corner"

## *Reading:* Revelation 7:9–17

*Text:* Amen! Blessing and glory and wisdom and thanksgiving and honor and power and might be to our God forever and ever. Amen. Revelation 7:12

Today I attended a memorial service for Dr. Oswald C.J. Hoffmann. The former radio speaker for the Lutheran Hour from 1955–1988, classical linguist, and influential churchman worldwide, touched the lives of countless thousands with his clear proclamation of faith in Jesus Christ as the only way to salvation. After preaching at length from Scripture about the wonders of God's plan of salvation for sinful human beings, he would often conclude, "What more is there to say but 'Amen!'? At his funeral, Pastor Vern Gundermann used as his theme: "A Word from the 'Amen Corner.'"

At Dr. Hoffmann's Baptism in 1913, his confirmation, his marriage, his ordination, and the many aspects of his worldwide ministry, believers in the "Amen Corner" were constantly saying, "Amen!" to God's grace, mercy, and forgiveness through the death and resurrection of Jesus Christ. Now, at this memorial service with organ, brass, and the Bach Society Choir, in Scripture readings and proclamation, we were lifting our voices to say once again, "Amen!" Yes, it shall be so! And our eyes were lifted to that scene described in Revelation 7—a great multitude from every nation, tribe, people, and language standing before the throne and in front of the Lamb, wearing white robes and holding palm branches. What will they say? "Salvation belongs to our God, who sits on the throne and to the Lamb" (Revelation 7:10), followed by angelic praise from the Amen Corner: "Amen! Blessing and glory and wisdom and thanksgiving and honor and power and might be to our God forever and ever. Amen."

I don't know about you, but I am moved by the life and proclamation of Dr. Hoffmann to keep the Amen going while I have breath so many may join those multitudes at the throne singing Amens forever.

*Prayer:* "For thine is the kingdom and the power and the glory forever and ever. Amen. What does this mean? This means that I should be certain that these petitions are pleasing to our Father in heaven and are heard by Him. . . . Amen, amen means 'yes, yes, it shall be so.'"
*Luther's Small Catechism*

# Galatians 2:20

## *Reading:* Galatians 2:15–21

*Text:* I have been crucified with Christ. It is no longer I who live, but Christ, who lives in me. And the life I now live in the flesh I live by faith in the Son of God who loved me and gave Himself for me. Galatians 2:20 (ESV)

When Dr. Hoffmann's autobiography, *What More Is There to Say but Amen*, was published by Concordia Publishing House in 1996, he wrote a message in my copy and, below his signature, referenced Galatians 2:20. That passage characterized his life and ministry: "I have been crucified with Christ. It is no longer I who live, but Christ who lives in me. And the life I now live in the flesh I live by faith in the Son of God who loved me and gave Himself for me."

St. Paul has been forcefully chiding the Galatians for departing from faith in Jesus to rely again on the works of the law for their salvation. He repeats the truth, "We know that a person is not justified by works of the law but through faith in Jesus Christ" (Galatians 2:16a). Christ *for* us on Calvary. Christ *in* us through our Baptism, where we daily die to sin and live unto righteousness. All by faith. All by God's grace for Christ's sake.

That message was Dr. Hoffmann's theme every week on the Lutheran Hour and in every one-on-one and group encounter. In his first broadcast he said, "I want you to know that our only purpose in these broadcasts is to share—and to share—and again to share—Jesus Christ with you."

Galatians 2:20 gives us all the power we need to help set the world ablaze with Christ and provides the message as well: "faith in the Son of God who loved me and gave Himself for me." Thank God for the singular focus of Oswald Hoffmann on the Gospel of Jesus Christ for today's world!

*Prayer:* Faith clings to Jesus' cross alone
And rests in him unceasing;
And by its fruits true faith is known,
With love and hope unceasing.
For faith alone can justify;
Works serve our neighbor and supply
The proof that faith is living.
*LW* 355:5

# Tribute to Marcia

***Reading:*** **Proverbs 31:25–31**

*Text:* He who finds a wife finds what is good and receives favor from the LORD. Proverbs 18:22

When Dr. Hoffmann wrote his 1996 autobiography, he paid tribute to his wife, Marcia. In 2000, she preceded him in death after 60 years of marriage. His stirring words reveal how God uses each of us to testify to Jesus Christ in our lives: "To Marcia, with love–art student in Minneapolis and promising dress designer who married a struggling preacher; mother of four strapping children, and their educator in the perennial absence of the same struggling preacher; anonymous contributor to one good cause after another; discerner of the spirits with a clear eye focused on the Gospel; bearer of the burning torch of Christ the Savior to anyone who has ever met her."

How tenderly the book of Proverbs describes a godly wife: "He who finds a wife finds what is good and receives favor from the LORD." In Proverbs 31, the wife of a noble character has these traits, "She speaks with wisdom. . . . Her children arise and call her blessed; her husband also, and he praises her. . . . A woman who fears the Lord is to be praised" (v. 25–31). Marcia Hoffmann obviously was a godly person for her husband, her family, and the many people she met worldwide as she traveled with him and supported his ministry. God's favor in Jesus' death and resurrection came through Marcia to many.

How do you bear "the burning torch of Christ the Savior" to everyone you meet? What special and creative gifts has God given you for service and witness? What opportunities is God presenting you in your home and through your home to many others? How does God's favor, first freely bestowed on you as an undeserving sinner, pass through you to others? Thanks be to God for Oswald and Marcia Hoffmann.

*Prayer:* Love be our banner, forgiveness our theme,
Compassion our nature, your vision our dream;
Who knows what the Spirit of God yet can do,
What joy may be tasted, or what promise come true?
*SP* 82:3

Copyright © 1983 Concordia Publishing House

# A Blazing Sense of Humor

## *Reading:* Proverbs 15:13, 23, 30

*Text:* The cheerful heart has a continual feast. Proverbs 15:15b

Dr. Paul Maier, son of the first Lutheran Hour speaker, writes comments about Oswald Hoffmann in the front part of *What More Is There to Say but Amen*: "He always had–and has–a blazing sense of humor that is only augmented when his own laughter takes on a 'second wind' and a merely funny joke becomes hilarious." Dr. Hoffmann, free in Christ, enthused about the Gospel, loving to relate with people, displayed a "blazing sense of humor." His hearty laughter was contagious.

How well the words of Proverbs describe his life, ". . . the cheerful heart has a continual feast." In the same chapter, "A happy heart makes the face cheerful" (v. 13). "A man finds joy in giving an apt reply–and how good is a timely word" (v. 23). "A cheerful look brings joy to the heart and good news gives health to the bones" (v. 30).

To be sure, Oswald Hoffmann knew the depth of human depravity, including his own sin. He knew the reality of war and the pain of human suffering. But he also knew the joyful good news of God's salvation through Jesus Christ, who shouldered our sins on the cross and won the victory over Satan. He knew God's grace, which brings us to faith in Christ, and His sure promise of abundant life now and life forever in heaven.

That gave him reason for joy and laughter–"the cheerful heart has a continual feast." He laughed at Lutheran Hour rallies, pastoral conferences, private homes, on fishing trips, and at the annual Schlachtfest in Frankenmuth, Michigan, where sausage is made. All because of the Gospel of Jesus Christ! The Gospel is contagious. Let that "blazing sense of humor" spread.

*Prayer:* Light the candle of JOY today,
The Giver of joy is here!
Welcome the joy we crave and pray for,
But only Christ can give.
Flicker and flame and glow with joy,
Light up the world around you.
Flicker and flame and glow with joy,
Light up the world around you.
*SP* 156:3

Copyright © 1987 Concordia Publishing House

# Ablaze Worldwide

## *Reading:* John 17:13–19

*Text:* "As You sent Me into the world, I have sent them into the world." John 17:18

The funeral of Dr. Oswald Hoffmann gave us opportunity to reflect on the impact of his life and ministry worldwide. His joy and zeal for the Gospel of Jesus Christ led him to travel extensively to Europe, Africa, and the Far East and visit with presidents and kings—Dwight Eisenhower, John F. Kennedy, Lyndon Johnson, Richard Nixon, Norway's King Olaf, Haile Selassie of Ethiopia, and the King of Tonga. He also visited the troops in Vietnam. He served as honorary president of the United Bible Societies and participated in national and international evangelism congresses as well as Vatican 2. His joyful faith and consistent focus on Christ as Savior as revealed in the Scripture helped set the world ablaze with Christ.

In His high priestly prayer, Jesus prays for His disciples, "As You sent Me into the world, I have sent them into the world." He wants them to have "the full measure of [His] joy within them" and the truth of God's Word so they will be able to witness powerfully and effectively (John 17:13). His prayer is answered after Pentecost when they are set ablaze in their bold testimony and courageous actions in the face of persecution, imprisonment, and death.

Recognizing your own fearfulness and flagging zeal, receiving Christ's forgiveness and the full measure of His joy, are you inspired by Dr. Hoffmann's "amen" to God's love in Christ to let God set you ablaze? "As You sent Me into the world, I have sent them into the world." We thank God for the joyful witness of Dr. Oswald C.J. Hoffmann—ablaze worldwide!

*Prayer:* Cast afar this world's vain pleasure
And boldly strive for heav'nly treasure.
Be steadfast in the Savior's might.
Trust the Lord, who stands beside you,
For Jesus from all harm will hide you.
By faith you conquer in the fight.
Take courage, weary soul! Look forward to the goal!
Joy awaits you. The race well run,
Your long war won,
Your crown shines splendid as the sun.
*LW* 303:2

# Tarrying the Good News

***Reading:* Luke 24:44–53**

*Text:* "Tarry ye in the city of Jerusalem, until ye be endued with power from on high." Luke 24:49 (KJV)

I was driving down main street one day and noticed the following sermon title on the bulletin board of a local church: "Tarrying the Good News." I thought it rather unusual.

Turning to Luke 24 in the King James Version, I began to get the message. Jesus was preparing to ascend into heaven. He had personally made possible the Good News by coming to earth, announcing the kingdom of God, living the Gospel life, dying on the cross in full payment of sins, and rising from the dead. Yes, Jesus wanted the disciples to carry the Good News of His death and resurrection to the ends of the world.

But first He wanted them to "tarry" the Good News. He asked them to wait with prayer and the Scriptures until the Holy Spirit empowered them. During the 10-day period of waiting, they reflected on all Jesus had done for them. They had been confused and afraid. Now "tarrying" the Good News for 10 days, they see that the Old Testament Scriptures explain Jesus as the crucified and risen Messiah. The Holy Spirit enables them to speak what they are learning and carry the Good News boldly to a world in need.

Have you been "tarrying" the Good News? Sometimes we fall short in carrying the Good News through our daily witness because we fail to spend adequate time in the Scriptures. Rather, through worship and group and individual Bible study, we can reflect on all Christ has done for us in His life, death, and resurrection. As His followers, we tarry over that Good News, relish and savor it, discuss it with one another, and prayerfully praise God for it.

Then, empowered by the Holy Spirit, we faithfully carry the Good News to a world hungering and thirsting for it. We don't limit ourselves to 10 days of tarrying but, like the disciples, develop an ongoing rhythm of tarrying and carrying the Good News.

*Prayer:* Father, help us to tarry for the Good News of Jesus Christ so we may carry it to others. Amen.

# A Thirst for the Living God

***Reading:* Psalm 42:1–4**

*Text:* My soul thirsts for God, for the living God. Psalm 42:2

Any thought of mission to the world begins with our own need for the saving Gospel of Jesus Christ. Scripture sometimes describes that need as a thirst, an unquenchable thirst for water.

In Psalm 42:1, the psalmist describes himself as a deer that is pursued by hunters and needs water to continue the flight: "As the deer pants for streams of water, so my soul pants for You, O God." Then the psalmist, oppressed by enemies and denied access to worship in God's temple, cries out, "My soul thirsts for God, for the living God." As these words were incorporated into liturgical worship at the temple, that very thirst for the living God makes powerful witness to Israel and those outside that the only hope for salvation now and eternally lies in the God who will send His only Son as the Messiah.

Living in a world determined to oppress those who trust in Christ alone for salvation, do you thirst for the living God? Living as a sinner desperately weak in your own flesh against this oppression, do you thirst for the living God? Remembering your wonderful moments spent in God's presence through Word and Sacrament worship among God's people, do you thirst for the living God? Aware that your very need for forgiveness and salvation and your quenching that thirst in the worship assembly of God's people provide a mighty testimony to the world, do you thirst for the living God?

God's Spirit can use your thirst and the quenching of that thirst in Jesus Christ's living water to create in countless others worldwide a genuine thirst for the living God that will lead them to the waters of salvation.

*Prayer:* I heard the voice of Jesus say,
"Behold, I freely give
The living water, thirsty one;
Stoop down and drink and live."
I came to Jesus, and I drank
Of that life-giving stream;
My thirst was quenched, my soul revived,
And now I live in him.
*LW* 348:2

# A Thirst for Your Word

***Reading:* Revelation 21:6–7**

*Text:* Come, all you who are thirsty, come to the waters. Isaiah 55:1a

A number of years ago, as a young pastor, I was learning to carry out all of my responsibilities for preaching, leading worship, teaching Bible studies, and providing pastoral care. When a group of young people came to work with our youth for a week, I discovered that their passion for the Word of God, their regular and specific prayer, and their desire to share Christ with others brought a fresh and powerful witness to our congregation and to me. As a result, I was led to pray a simple prayer that has transformed my ministry over the years: "Lord, give me a thirst for Your Word. Amen."

Isaiah states an invitation to Israel with similar simplicity and power, "Come, all you who are thirsty, come to the waters." Describing salvation as God's free gift "without money and without cost" based on His everlasting covenant promised to David (Isaiah 55:1), he goes on to describe God's Word, which goes out from His mouth and will not return empty but will achieve the purpose for which He sent it as the rain and snow that water the earth and make it bud and flourish (Isaiah 55:10–11).

In Revelation 21, Jesus says, "I am the Alpha and the Omega, the Beginning and the End. To him who is thirsty I will give to drink without cost from the spring of the water of life" (Revelation 21:6).

The more I thirst for the Word of God as a sinner in need of repentance, the more that Word brings me Jesus as Savior, crucified and risen. He enables me to drink from the water of life. The more I thirst for the Word of God, the more He works in me a desire to share the Word of Christ with others who are thirsty for salvation. I invite you to join me in that simple prayer: "Lord, give me a thirst for Your Word. Amen."

*Prayer:* Here springs of sacred pleasure rise
To ease your ev'ry pain,
Immortal fountain, full supplies;
Nor shall you thirst in vain.
*LW* 350:3

# Bringing Water to the Thirsty

***Reading:* John 4:7–15**

*Text:* "Whoever drinks the water I give him will never thirst. Indeed the water I give him will become in him a spring of water welling up to eternal life." John 4:14

When our Boy Scout troop camped for a week each year at Lake Ridinger in northern Indiana, there was a marvelous source of clear cold spring water flowing from a pipe near the small general store. We passed the word to others and always stopped to fill our canteens before embarking on a hike. The news spread. In the same way, a thirst for the living God and a thirst for the Word of Christ will lead us to drink deeply and to spread the good news to the thirsty everywhere.

Jesus meets the Samaritan woman at Jacob's well where He stopped to quench His physical thirst. The news of this famous well had spread far and wide. But far more important, Jesus uses the well to bring living water to this sinful and hopeless woman who is desperately thirsty. As she places her trust in Jesus as the Messiah, she discovers a "spring of water welling up to eternal life." Now she brings water to the thirsty as she witnesses to all in her village. They find their thirst quenched by Jesus.

That's our task of setting the world ablaze with Christ: bringing water to the thirsty! First, we thirst because of our sin and hopeless situation. Then we are led through the waters of our Baptism to Jesus Christ and the well of salvation. Refreshed, we return again and again to the Lord's table to drink and be filled. And God's Spirit produces in us a spring of water welling up to eternal life. We look for those who are thirsty and bring to them the life-giving water of the crucified and risen Savior, Jesus Christ.

*Prayer:* See the streams of living waters,
Springing from eternal love,
Well supply your sons and daughters
And all fear of want remove.
Who can faint while such a river
Ever will their thirst assuage–
Grace which, like the Lord, the giver,
Never fails from age to age.
*LW* 295:2

# Bell of Hope in New York

***Reading:* Psalm 103**

*Text:* He remembers that we are dust. Psalm 103:14b

In St. Paul's Chapel near ground zero in New York City sits a 5-foot, 650-pound bell known as the Bell of Hope. Cast by London's Whitechapel Bell Foundry, which also cast the Liberty Bell and the bell at London's Big Ben, this bell was a gift to New York from the people of London after the terror attack on the World Trade Center, September 11, 2001. Londoners expressed their sadness and solidarity with New Yorkers as they presented this bell on the first anniversary "to the greater glory of God and in recognition of the enduring links between the city of London and the city of New York." Gratefully, New Yorkers see the gift as a Bell of Hope for the future.

In Psalm 103, David describes God as one who "remembers that we are dust." Because of our fall into sin, evil explodes in our twenty-first century world, leading fanatical terrorists to murder thousands of innocent civilians, destroying commercial buildings, and crippling the economy. That evil brings grief and despair to all of us. But at the same time, David praises God for forgiving our sins, healing our diseases, redeeming our life from the pit, and working righteousness and justice for all the oppressed. Through the death of His Son Jesus on Calvary, the Father removes our transgressions from us and shows compassion from everlasting to everlasting.

That Bell of Hope symbolizes the compassion of one city for another, but more powerfully, Jesus' triumph over evil on the cross. From the ashes of the Twin Towers rises hope for the future in New York. From the ashes of fallen humanity rises hope for all who believe in Jesus Christ as Savior. Ring His bell of hope that all might live eternally at the Father's throne.

*Prayer:* Let praises ring; Give thanks, and bring
To Christ our Lord adoration.
His honor speed By word and deed
To ev'ry land, every nation.
So shall his love Give us above,
From misery And death set free,
All joy and full consolation.
*LW* 134:3

# For Whom the Bell Tolls

***Reading:* Psalm 111**

*Text:* He remembers His covenant forever. Psalm 111:5b

On Thursday, July 7, 2005, the terrorists struck London with death and injury-causing explosions in three separate subway cars and a double-decker bus. Remembering London's shared grief after the Twin Towers destruction in New York, New Yorkers solemnly rang the Bell of Hope in St. Paul's Chapel the following day–four times, once for each explosion in London, then tolled steadily for one minute in memory of the victims. That gift bell to New York was tolling now for London.

All of us stand as sinners under the wrath of God. Unspeakable evil is perpetrated on unsuspecting people worldwide. Not only murder on our doorsteps but murder anywhere in the world unites us in human suffering and despair.

The psalmist remembers something more powerful than evil: he extols the Lord for His works, deeds, righteousness, and redemption for His people. Summarizing the Lord's saving compassion the psalmist writes, "He remembers His covenant forever." Yes, God is faithful. Into this sin-filled world, He sent His Son to die that we might live. He is there with His grace and forgiveness for the people of London as He was and is for the people of New York.

The Bell of Hope tolls death, but it also rings with life–eternal life through faith in the crucified and risen Christ. We identify with a fallen world and share its grief. But we identify through our Baptism with the Christ who carries our God's covenant promises through us. The resurrection bell rings for us and the world.

*Prayer:* Christ is arisen
From the grave's dark prison.
So let our song exulting rise:
Christ with comfort lights our eyes. Alleluia!
All our hopes were ended
Had Jesus not ascended
From the grave triumphantly
Our neverending life to be. Alleluia!
So let our song exulting rise:
Christ, our comfort, fills the skies. Alleluia!
*LW* 124

Copyright ©1982 Concordia Publishing House

# A Wedding in Three Languages

***Reading:* John 2:1–11**

*Text:* Jesus and His disciples had also been invited to the wedding. John 2:2

Jesus performed the first of His miraculous signs at a wedding in Cana of Galilee. He blessed the wedding by changing water into abundant high quality wine as the Lord of creation, and revealed His glory that would ultimately lead Him to the cross. We are told, "His disciples put their faith in Him" (John 2:11b).

The glory of Christ revealed itself at a recent wedding in three languages. *The Doorstop*, a publication of International Student Ministry, gives this account: "Two students from different parts of Asia venture to the University of Wisconsin in Stevens Point to study. They meet on campus, fall in love, and become husband and wife. Xian Wang and Sun Joo Oh are not an ordinary couple. They both are committed Christians but from different cultures. Xing came from China and Sun Joo's home is South Korea. Their common language is English. For their August 6 wedding, they decided to have their ceremony in three languages. Throughout the entire celebration, translators were used and English, Mandarin and Korean were spoken. Sun Joo asked Paula Sallach, her American conversation partner for two years, to be her maid of honor.

As the couple prepared the wedding service, they wanted it to be a Christian witness to the many guests and intentionally chose Scripture and music that reflected God's love for them. Campus pastor Carl Selle reflects, "Working with Xing and Sun Joo has been a wonderful experience since they both understand living out God's love in their daily lives." For the wedding, the couple wore traditional American wedding clothes. Their reception was held in a local Chinese restaurant, but there they wore traditional Korean wedding clothes. Jesus at a wedding in Cana. Jesus at a Wisconsin wedding in three languages. Signs of a world ablaze with the Savior!

*Prayer:* Oh, blessed home where man and wife
Together lead a godly life,
By death their faith confessing!
There many happy days are spent,
There Jesus gladly will consent
To tarry with his blessing.
*LW* 466:1

# Does Everybody Love Raymond?

***Reading:* Ephesians 4:17–32**

*Text:* Be kind and compassionate to one another, forgiving each other, just as in Christ God forgave you. Ephesians 4:32

Recently, my wife and I viewed the final episode of the hit comedy sitcom, *Everybody Loves Raymond.* Does everybody love Raymond? Few series achieve the prominence of *I Love Lucy* in the 1950s. But clearly *Everybody Loves Raymond,* in its nine-year run with over 200 episodes, captured the hearts of many Americans. Why?

The well-written and brilliantly acted show succeeds in touching the realities of family life today with a touch of humor. The relationships between Ray Barone and family provide abundant opportunities to reveal our own problems, dysfunctions, thoughtless and angry words, and ongoing hurts. We laugh to relieve our own tensions and to let someone else's family suffer the consequences.

In Ephesians, Paul captures the realities of living in the darkness of sin—"futility of their thinking," "separated from the life of God," "having lost all sensitivity," "falsehood," "unwholesome talk," "bitterness, rage and anger, brawling and slander, along with every form of malice" (Ephesians 4:17–31). Every one of these characteristics rears its ugly head in this long-running sitcom, in today's world and in our own family experience.

Our Christian witness comes with a sense of humor, not taking ourselves too seriously, in St. Paul's words: "Be kind and compassionate to one another, forgiving each other." Then, he offers the only, but all-sufficient strength for bearing that witness, "just as in Christ God forgave you" (Ephesians 4:32). *Everybody Loves Raymond* leads us to recognize our own struggles and sin in a comedy setting and ultimately points us to a forgiving Christ as power for forgiving others.

*Prayer:* Oh, blest the house, whate'er befall,
Where Jesus Christ is all in all!
For if he were not dwelling there,
How dark and poor and void it were!

Oh, blest the house where faith is found
And all in charity abound
To trust their God and serve him still
And do in all his holy will!
*LW* 467:1–2

# Does Everybody Love Raymond? Part 2

## *Reading:* Genesis 27:1–45

*Text:* Jacob said to his father, "I am Esau your firstborn. I have done as you told me." Genesis 27:19a

This second devotion on the hit television sitcom focuses on the main character within the drama, Ray Barone. Does everybody love Raymond? His mother, Marie, clearly loves him best, which troubles Debra because of her interference in their marriage and enrages Robert, the "other brother" who always feels second-class and rejected. Raymond, caught in the middle, tries to please everyone even when that means telling a lie or at least concealing the truth. As a result, he usually pleases no one and finds himself attacked from all sides. Perhaps no one loves Raymond. How very close to real life in our homes! Do we bear witness to our faith in Christ when we try to please everyone, even to the point of deception?

A well-known biblical story in Genesis comes to mind. Isaac and Rebekah have twin sons, Esau, the elder, and Jacob. As different in their physical characteristics and interests as they can be, a rivalry develops. As Isaac nears death, he determines to give the coveted birthright blessing to Esau. Rebekah, who loves Jacob more than Esau, conspires to help Jacob deceive his father through a disguise and tasty meal. Jacob approaches Isaac with a clear lie, "I am Esau your firstborn. I have done as you told me." Successful in his ruse, Jacob receives the blessing, but he creates great pain for Isaac when he finds out and a murderous rage in Esau, forcing Jacob to flee from home.

Before we can witness to Jesus as Savior through our home life, we need to confess our sins of lying and deception. Turning to Christ, the obedient Son of the Father (blood descendant of Abraham, Isaac, and Jacob), sinless in life, the Sin-bearer for the world in His death on the cross, we receive forgiveness. Does everybody love Raymond? It does not matter. The life-changing question is Does Jesus love everybody? "This is love: not that we loved God, but that He loved us and sent His Son as an atoning sacrifice for our sins" (1 John 4:10).

*Prayer:* Feed your children, God most holy,
Comfort sinners poor and lowly.
*LW* 468

May 11

# Thirty Seconds of Death

## *Reading:* 1 Samuel 20:1–42

*Text:* Jonathan said to David "Whatever you want me to do, I'll do for you." 1 Samuel 20:4

In the final episode of *Everybody Loves Raymond*, Ray reluctantly has surgery scheduled to remove his infected adenoids. Debra encourages him, but his mother, Marie, opposes the idea. As the family gathers nervously in the waiting room, a nurse tells them that the doctors are having trouble waking Ray up after the surgery. For about thirty seconds, they face the possibility of his death and fall apart. Even Robert wants him to live. A doctor quickly appears to say that all is well. The rest of the story line deals with how that thirty seconds affected family relationships.

In 1 Samuel, the relationship between David and Jonathan, Saul's son, is described. More and more, Saul desires to kill his rival, David. David says to Jonathan, "There is only a step between me and death" (1 Samuel 20:3). Although Jonathan can't believe that his father has such murderous intentions, he agrees to find out whether it is safe for David to return to King Saul's court. Soon Jonathan learns the truth when Saul hurls his spear at him and realizes that David is only a step from death. Their tearful farewell reveals the depth of their friendship and their close relationship with the God of Israel.

What difference would the possible death of a family member make in your relationship with each other and with the Lord? What witness opportunities might present themselves when friends or acquaintances face "thirty seconds of death"? The God of David and Jonathan loved them and fulfilled His promise to send Jesus as the Messiah. Those moments of near death, or death itself, can bring us to confession of our sins, assure us of forgiveness through our Savior's death for us, strengthen our relationships with family, and provide openings to share Jesus with others.

*Prayer:* Lord, till we see the ending
Of all this life's distress,
Faith's hand, love's sinews strengthen,
With joy our spirits bless.
As yours, we have committed
Ourselves into your care
On ways made sure to bring us
To heav'n to praise you there.
*LW* 427:6

# A Mother's Day Witness

### *Reading:* Colossians 3:18–21; 4:5–6

*Text:* Let your conversation be always full of grace, seasoned with salt, so that you may know how to answer everyone. Colossians 4:6

Starring as Debra in *Everybody Loves Raymond* gave Patricia Heaton an opportunity for Christian witness. On Mothers' Day weekend, *Life*, America's Weekend Magazine, featured her on the cover with her own four boys. The interview asked her about the challenge of caring for her own family while working for nine years on the television sitcom. Then she was asked, "Has faith always been a part of your life?" She answered, "I was raised Catholic and I'm Presbyterian now, but I've always been a Christian, regardless of denomination. I believe that Jesus is the way. So, of course, I pass that on to my kids."

In response to the question, "How does your faith influence your dreams for your kids?" she replied, "My goal is not . . . that they should achieve a certain amount of fame or financial success or even worldly success. . . . Whatever they end up choosing to do, my goal for them is that they know God in their life. The only way to know who you are is to know the One who made you. That's my hope."

Her powerful witness to Jesus reminds me of Paul's words in Colossians, "Let your conversation be always full of grace, seasoned with salt, so that you may know how to answer everyone." In the previous verse, Paul wrote, "Be wise in the way you act toward outsiders; make the most of every opportunity" (Colossians 4:5).

What an inspiration for us, knowing our salvation through Christ's death, to let our conversation about home and work be always full of God's grace and seasoned with salt so we may seize opportunities to point to our Savior and the importance of regular worship in His name around Word and Sacraments.

*Prayer:* Oh, blest that house; it prospers well!
In peace and joy the parents dwell,
And in their children's lives is shown
How richly God can bless his own

Then here will I and mine today
A solemn cov'nant make and say:
Though all the world forsake his Word,
My house and I will serve the Lord.
*LW* 467:3–4

# Loving Raymond in Rerun

## *Reading:* Deuteronomy 5:1–22

*Text:* It was not with our fathers that the LORD made this covenant, but with us, with all of us who are alive today. Deuteronomy 5:3

Although the final episode of *Everybody Loves Raymond* was viewed with appropriate fanfare, the series will continue for years on many television channels in rerun and will be available on DVD. Some of the situations may not be as humorous or effective with the passing of time, but the basic family foibles will continue to touch a nerve in our daily lives. And as is often the case with reruns, the comedy of this dysfunctional extended family may even reach a generation of viewers who never saw the original series.

In our reading today, Moses addresses a new generation of Israelites as they prepare to enter the Promised Land. Forty years have passed since the giving of the Law at Mount Sinai. Most people have perished in the wilderness. Yet Moses repeats God's covenant of mercy and His Law. Amazingly, he tells them this is much more than a rerun: "It was not with our fathers that the Lord made this covenant, but with us, with all of us who are alive here today." God's unchanging Word—His Law exposing our sin and His Gospel revealing salvation through the Messiah, Jesus Christ crucified and risen—speaks freshly to each generation including our own. Our Spirit-empowered response of faith to His invitation not only saves us, but also provides a powerful witness of God's saving power to succeeding generations.

Whether it's a rerun or it's the first time we've heard the words, through us God intends "that at the name of Jesus every knee should bow . . . and every tongue confess that Jesus Christ is Lord, to the glory of God the Father" (Philippians 2:10–11).

*Prayer:* God's Word is our great heritage
And shall be ours forever;
To spread its light from age to age
Shall be our chief endeavor.
Through life it guides our way,
In death it is our stay.
Lord, grant, while worlds endure,
We keep its teachings pure
Throughout all generations.
*LW* 333

# Tell Your Family

***Reading:* Mark 5:1–20**

*Text:* Go home to your family and tell them how much the Lord has done for you, and how He has had mercy on you. Mark 5:19

A great miracle has occurred. A demon-possessed man, a maniac, has been healed by Jesus.

Now the grateful man pleads to go with Jesus and tell the world about God's great miracle. He wants to be an itinerant evangelist. But Jesus has other plans for him: "Go home to your family and tell them. . . ." What a challenge. This is probably more difficult than going with Jesus, and certainly a more effective form of witnessing. His family must have felt totally estranged by his madness. Would they now be able to accept him as a new person in Christ? Would they forget his past behavior? Would his new peace and sanity continue? The man obeyed Jesus and returned home. Apparently the miracle of readjustment to family and friends also worked because we are told that the whole region was amazed at what Jesus had done.

Jesus Christ has also worked a great miracle within you. By nature estranged from God and controlled by selfish lusts, you have been cleansed by the blood Jesus Christ shed on the cross. In Baptism you have become a special child of God. Clothed in His righteousness, you are in your right mind, a mind new in Christ Jesus.

Grateful, you want to tell the world about Christ, but He has other plans for you: "Go home to your family and tell them. . . ." What a challenge! Your family knows you, your shortcomings, your bad habits, your thoughtless, selfish words and actions. Will they accept your witness? Will they see Christ in you and rejoice at God's mercy? Jesus gives you the power to obey and return home. Just think how great a miracle would occur throughout our land if families everywhere would experience the healing of God and join in telling other families about God's mercy to them in Jesus Christ!

*Prayer:* Lord, make me a witness of Your love at home. Amen.

# A Baptismal Testimony

***Reading:*** **Acts 2:36–41**

*Text:* Repent and be baptized, every one of you, in the name of Jesus Christ for the forgiveness of your sins." Acts 2:38

The testimony of Ran Xu, a PhD student at the University of Nebraska, on the day of her Baptism makes Acts 2 come alive in our hearts for witness to the world:

"Back in mainland China, I didn't have many opportunities to know who Jesus really was. After I came to the U.S., in order to make friends and to improve my English, I went to University Lutheran Chapel. Just like a kid in school, I was curious about the Bible, but I didn't pay much attention to it.

"As I became more involved in activities and met more Christians, I began to wonder, 'What drives the Christians to cook for those homeless people, to give money to the Chinese baby who needed eye surgery, and to help build houses destroyed by a storm?' Eventually, I attended more Bible studies and had more conversations with other Christians. I began to realize it is not human ability, but the power of God's Word that guides the Christians to give their lives to others.

"According to the Bible, we are all sinners and the wages of sin is death. We all need repentance and forgiveness. We are saved from our own death because Jesus died in our place. God not only gave us His Son. He also gave us the Holy Spirit. We know what it means to be loved by God, so we can return love and serve others.

"My Baptism is a result of two very happy years of learning God's Word, sharing love from other Christians, examining my own life, and repenting of my own sin. As a new Christian, I really need others to help me strengthen my faith. I am also more excited to share my faith with non-Christians. I will let God's Word guide my life, no matter what happens."

*Prayer:* Today your gate is open, And all who enter in
Shall find a Father's welcome And pardon for their sin.
The past shall be forgotten, A present joy be given,
A future grace be promised, A glorious crown in heaven.
*LW* 347:2

# Sounds of Pentecost

***Reading:*** **Acts 2:1–13**

*Text:* Suddenly a sound like the blowing of a violent wind came from heaven and filled the whole house where they were sitting. Acts 2:2

What does Pentecost have to do with setting the world ablaze with the Gospel of Jesus Christ? Everything! On this birthday of the Christian Church, God's promised Holy Spirit comes in power to the assembled crowd, Jewish believers from many parts of the world. That day, 3,000 believed in Jesus as the crucified and risen Savior and were baptized. From Jerusalem, the Gospel spread to the ends of the earth. The next few devotions will describe the Spirit's role in world mission through the apostolic church by asking you to listen to the sounds of Pentecost.

Luke writes in Acts about the Jewish festival of Pentecost, also known as the Feast of Weeks, the Feast of Harvest, and the day of firstfruits. On this 50th day after the Sabbath of Passover week, many Jews were gathered in one place from many language groups around the world. The first event described involves a sound: "Suddenly a sound like the blowing of a violent wind came from heaven and filled the whole house where they were sitting." What does this dramatic sound mean to the listeners? A threat to their safety as when a tornado comes? A warning of coming judgment? A sign of God's powerful Spirit at work? At the very least, an attention getter. No ordinary festival day. Listen, listen, God is calling!

In the next few devotions, we will listen to sounds of God's Spirit at work, some dramatic, some ordinary but powerful. All sounds of Pentecost. All empowering believers in Christ, saved by grace through faith, for the church's worldwide mission. Listen, listen, God is calling you!

*Prayer:* Speak, O Lord, your servant listens,
Let your Word to me come near;
Newborn life and spirit give me,
Let each promise still my fear,
Death's dread pow'r, its inward strife,
Wars against your Word of life;
Fill me, Lord, with love's strong fervor
That I cling to you forever!
*LW* 339:1

# Sounds of Confession

*Reading:* Acts 2:22–38

*Text:* When the people heard this; they were cut to the heart and said to Peter and the other apostles, "Brothers, what shall we do?" Acts 2:37

The sound of the violent wind certainly got the crowd's attention. Whether they experienced it as a threat, a warning, or a sign of the promised Spirit's outpouring, they were listening. When they heard the apostles speaking to them the wonders of God, each in their own language, they were amazed and led to exclaim, "What does this mean?" (Acts 2:12).

When Peter stood up to preach, they were all ears. He quoted the Old Testament prophet Joel to connect these Pentecost events with the promised pouring out of God's Spirit. Then he boldly proclaimed Jesus of Nazareth as accredited by God and by His purposes: handed over to His enemies with the help of wicked men for a cruel death by crucifixion. He then points to God raising Jesus from the dead in keeping with Old Testament prophecy and to himself and the other apostles as witnesses of the resurrected Christ. Then, he concludes with the clear words: "Therefore let all Israel be assured of this: God has made this Jesus, whom you crucified, both Lord and Christ" (Acts 2:36).

What we now hear from this Pentecost crowd are the sounds of confession! Cut to the heart, they cried out, "Brothers, what shall we do?" Those sounds of confession are our words too. Before any worldwide mission comes confession of sins from the heart. Before any worldwide mission comes also God's words of absolution spoken here by Peter and for us by our pastor: "Repent and be baptized every one of you, in the name of Jesus Christ for the forgiveness of your sins and you will receive the gift of the Holy Spirit" (Acts 2:38). Or simply from the pastor: "I forgive you all your sins in the name of the Father and of the Son and of the Holy Spirit. Amen."

*Prayer:* Lord, on you I cast my burden.
Sink it to the depths below.
Let me know your gracious pardon,
Wash me, make me white as snow.
Let your Spirit leave me never;
Make me only yours forever.
*LW* 233:4

# Sounds of Water

***Reading:*** **Acts 2:38–41**

*Text:* Those who accepted his message were baptized, and about three thousand were added to their number that day. Acts 2:41

Pentecost begins with the dramatic sound of a violent wind. It ends with an ordinary but no less powerful sound of splashing water. Three thousand people were baptized. The sounds of confession by people cut to the heart were followed by Peter's words of absolution: "In the name of Jesus Christ for the forgiveness of your sins" (Acts 2:38). He continued, "Repent and be baptized, every one of you." Three thousand received the "washing of rebirth and renewal by the Holy Spirit, whom He poured out on us generously through Jesus Christ our Savior, so that having been justified by His grace, we might become heirs having the hope of eternal life" (Titus 3:5–7).

The sounds of water precede setting the world ablaze with the Gospel of Christ. Every time a child, youth, or adult is brought to the waters of Baptism, the sounds of water announce grace, forgiveness, salvation, and a sending into the world. In a special sense, each person present in the fellowship of God's people remembers the power and meaning of Baptism and reaffirms God's sending: "Therefore go and make disciples of all nations, baptizing them in the name of the Father, and of the Son, and of the Holy Spirit" (Matthew 28:19).

When the sounds of baptismal water are heard worldwide, Pentecost is happening over and over again as God's Holy Spirit works through water and the Word proclaiming Jesus Christ as the crucified and risen Savior. Ordinary sounds with extraordinary, life-transforming power!

*Prayer:* All who believe and are baptized
Shall see the Lord's salvation;
Baptized into the death of Christ,
They are a new creation;
Through Christ's redemption they will stand
Among the glorious heav'nly band
Of every tribe and nation.
*LW* 225:1

# Sounds of Broken Bread and Poured Wine

## *Reading:* 1 Corinthians 11:23–26

*Text:* They devoted themselves to the apostles' teaching and to the fellowship, to the breaking of bread and to prayer. Acts 2:42

Other ordinary but powerful sounds of God's Holy Spirit at work are the sounds of bread breaking and wine pouring in Holy Communion. Immediately after Pentecost we discover that the new community of believers in the crucified and risen Jesus as Lord and Christ "devoted themselves to . . . the breaking of bread." As they gathered together on a daily basis in homes and the temple courts, as they shared everything in common, as they remained faithful to the apostles' teaching based on the Old Testament Scriptures and the words of Jesus, as they praised God, the celebration of the Sacraments of Christ's true body and blood was a regular and important part of their fellowship.

In a real sense, the sounds of the broken bread and poured wine signaled the Spirit's presence in their midst and also reminded them of their charge to share Christ with others. We are told: "And the Lord added to their number daily those who were being saved" (Acts 2:47b).

St. Paul writes to the Corinthians the true intended meaning of the Lord's Supper as he chides them for their selfish and unexamined use of the Holy Meal. Jesus intended His Supper to be eaten and drunk in remembrance of Him. Paul adds, "Whenever you eat this bread and drink this cup, you proclaim the Lord's death until He comes" (1 Corinthians 11:26).

When the Word is preached and the Sacrament is rightly administered according to the Gospel, God's faithful people proclaim the Lord's death worldwide until Jesus comes again. The breaking bread and poured wine–sounds of Pentecost–proclaim the urgency of reaching to the ends of the world with the saving message of Christ.

*Prayer:*

I eat this bread, I drink this cup,
Your promise firm believing;
In truth your body and your blood
My lips are here receiving.
Your word remains forever true;
All things are possible for you;
Your searching love has found me.
*LW* 246:3

# Sounds of Sending

***Reading:*** **Acts 1:6–11**

*Text:* "And you will be My witnesses in Jerusalem, and in all Judea and Samaria, and to the ends of the earth." Acts 1:8b

The sounds of Pentecost have filled the air—the sound of a violent wind, the sound of confession, the sound of water, and the sounds of breaking bread and poured wine. All of them, heard at the birth of the Christian Church, announce the outpouring of the Holy Spirit on all flesh and are sounds of sending into a world desperately needing the saving Gospel of Jesus Christ.

Already at the time of His ascension, Jesus announces the sending of His disciples: "But you will receive power when the Holy Spirit comes on you, and you will be My witnesses in Jerusalem, and in all Judea and Samaria, and to the ends of the earth." Sent to witness of the crucified and risen Christ. Sent to confess their own sins and to call for repentance. Sent to be baptized and to baptize all nations. Sent to receive Christ's true body and blood in the Sacrament and to offer forgiveness of sins in the broken bread and the poured wine. Sent to make disciples and to teach all that Jesus commanded them.

We hear the sounds of sending in Jerusalem, Judea, Samaria, and all cities from Antioch to Rome as the Holy Spirit reveals Jesus Christ through the Word in the book of Acts. Because they were sent to us, we hear the sounds of our sending—in the wind, the word of absolution, the water, the bread and wine. We gather to be sent again and again, drawing on the Spirit's power for our witness in the world. Pentecost has everything to do with setting the world ablaze with Christ! Listen to its sounds!

*Prayer:* Holy Spirit, gather us together around Word and Sacraments so that You might send us freely and joyfully to bring Christ to a world in need. Amen.

# Pentecost Movement

***Reading:* John 3:1–17**

*Text:* "The wind blows wherever it pleases." John 3:8a

On Pentecost this year, I sat in the balcony as a member of the choir and looked at the beautiful stained glass windows behind the altar. Those windows testify to the triune God bringing salvation through the Word and the Sacraments. Appropriate symbolism tells that story. But I noticed something different that Sunday. The stained glass seemed to be in motion. I concluded that wind was blowing outside and moving tree branches and leaves beyond the church walls to create this effect. A new insight occurred: Pentecost in motion!

When Jesus visited with a man of the Pharisees who came to Him at night, He challenged him with these words, "I tell you the truth, no one can see the kingdom of God unless he is born again" (John 3:3). Credulous, Nicodemus asked how it was physically possible for someone to be born again. Explaining that a person was born again only of water and the Spirit, Jesus uses analogy, "The wind blows wherever it pleases." Ultimately Jesus describes the Spirit's work in terms of God's plan for the world in the very familiar John 3:16, the Gospel in a nutshell: Whoever believes in God's Son, Jesus Christ, will have everlasting life.

On the first Pentecost there was a dramatic sign–the sound of a rushing, mighty wind. But the wind in the trees outside my church that caused movement in the stained glass windows tells again that God's Spirit is mightily at work today through water, bread and wine and through the inspired Word of God to bring rebirth, based on Christ's death and resurrection. And that Pentecost movement is not confined to stained glass on the walls of a church building but brings life to God's world so "whoever believes in Him shall not perish but have eternal life." I am part of that movement to set the world ablaze with Christ!

*Prayer:* Blessed Spirit, still renewing
All who dwell upon the earth,
When the evil one assails us
Help us prove our heav'nly birth;
Arm us with your mighty sword
In the legions of the Lord.
*LW* 115:3

# The Nations in South County

***Reading:*** **Acts 10:34–48**

*Text:* There before me was a great multitude . . . from every nation, tribe, people and language, standing before the throne and in front of the Lamb. Revelation 7:9a

We live in South County, St. Louis. My wife called to my attention the other day that a new shopping area nearby features an authentic Mexican restaurant, a Chinese restaurant, and a manicure shop operated by Vietnamese women. The three languages are freely spoken in these businesses. The nations have come to South County, America!

Any strategy to set the world ablaze with Christ starts at home. Any vision for outreach moves quickly to St. John's vision in Revelation, ". . . there before me was a great multitude . . . from every nation, tribe, people and language, standing before the throne and in front of the Lamb." They will stand there only because "they have washed their robes and made them white in the blood of the Lamb" (Revelation 7:14b). "For the Lamb at the center of the throne will be their shepherd; He will lead them to springs of living water" (Revelation 7:17).

In the book of Acts, Peter, his life changed by a vision of clean and unclean animals together, proclaims to Cornelius that "God does not show favoritism but accepts men from every nation who fear Him and do what is right" (Acts 10:35). Those Gentiles who believe in the crucified and risen Christ receive the Holy Spirit for saving faith through Baptism.

With eyes open to the multicultural reality in our city and county, we pray for opportunities to bear witness to Jesus among those of a different language and culture. Organizations like Christian Friends of New Americans hold promise for demonstrating practical love as an entry point for verbal witness. As we seek God's guidance and remember that vision in Revelation, we will be like the circumcised believers who came with Peter—"astonished that the gift of the Holy Spirit had been poured out even on the Gentiles" (Acts 10:45).

*Prayer:* Lord, gather all your children, Wherever they may be,
And lead them on to heaven To live eternally
With you, our loving Father, And Christ, our brother dear
Whose Spirit guards and gives us The joy to persevere.
*LW* 320:6

# God's People on the Move

***Reading:* Psalm 105**

*Text:* "As the Father has sent Me, I am sending you." John 10:21

In a recent issue of *Missio Apostolica,* Dr. Robert Kolb reflected on the readings for the Easter vigil and concluded that in Scripture, God's people are always on the move. Psalm 105 confirms this observation. God called Abraham to leave his home and trek from Ur of the Chaldees to a land He would show him. To prepare His people for the Promised Land, Joseph was taken as a slave to Egypt followed later by Jacob and the rest of the family. For them to escape Egypt, years later, God raised up Moses to lead the people across the Red Sea through the desert to that Promised Land. Later a rebellious nation, needing purification, would move into exile before a return home to rebuild and await the Messiah. From creation to Christ's Second Coming, God himself is always on the move in history.

No wonder, Jesus–on the move from birth and Baptism to crucifixion and resurrection–about to ascend and reign at the Father's right hand, says to His disciples gathered behind locked doors, "As the Father has sent Me, I am sending you." As part of God's people, Jesus sends us on the move to people hiding behind the locked doors of sin and unbelief.

Our comfort zone behind locked doors of self-centeredness will never reach our society imprisoned in sin. Kolb writes, "If North Americans in the early twenty-first century wish to experience the joy and pleasure of being the Lord's people, sent to forgive and retain sins, we must emerge from under the stifling, smothering shroud of our 'me-first' or 'me-alone' culture. The streets of a modern city are as scary as were the streets of Jerusalem . . . in our Lord's time." God on the move to save has incorporated us through Baptism into a people on the move, sent to proclaim Jesus as Savior to people lost in sin.

*Prayer:* Guide me ever, great Redeemer,<br>
Pilgrim through this barren land.<br>
I am weak, but you are mighty;<br>
Hold me with your pow'rful hand.<br>
Bread of heaven, feed me now and evermore.<br>
*LW* 221:1

# Village Church Planting in Central Asia

## *Reading:* Luke 9:1–6

*Text:* So they set out and went from village to village, preaching the gospel and healing people everywhere. Luke 9:6

When we consider how God might use us as missionaries in our neighborhoods and communities, it is helpful to learn from some of our missionaries in other parts of the world. They face language and cultural challenges far more difficult than ours. Where do they turn for help in their daunting tasks? The next several devotions will communicate how one of our missionaries in central Asia turned to the Gospel of Luke for insights from Jesus' ministry through His disciples.

This question was raised: "How does the missionary plant churches in the villages of central Asia?" Writing in the *Journal of the Lutheran Society for Missiology*, Missionary Tim Nickel comments, "We had no training to answer this specific question. So we used Luke 10:1–9 as a field guide. We learned anew that the Bible is timeless in practicality and application. The Bible does not give a strategy with steps to follow. But Jesus does provide guidelines and principles. We studied Luke 10 with local new believers. We did not make a plan to follow Jesus' strategy step by step, but in retrospect we see that the Holy Spirit led us through much of Luke 10."

This first devotion focuses on Jesus sending out His twelve disciples two by two in Luke 9 with instructions. "So they set out and went from village to village, preaching the Gospel and healing people everywhere." Subsequent devotions will focus on the sending out of the seventy-two and describe the principles taught and applied in central Asia. The twelve trusted Jesus as Savior and learned from Him as their master Teacher. When they set out, they modeled His example and spoke His life-giving words. God blessed their missionary work in the villages.

Are you ready for a similar adventure in your home "villages," trusting your Savior, following His teaching, and learning from the villages of central Asia?

*Prayer:* Send now, O Lord, to ev'ry place
Swift messengers before your face,
The heralds of your wondrous grace,
Where you yourself will come.
*LW* 316:1

# Send and Pray

***Reading:* Luke 10:1–2**

*Text:* After this the Lord appointed seventy-two others and sent them two by two ahead of Him to every town and place where He was about to go. Luke 10:1

Missionary Nickel shows God at work in Central Asia, learning from Jesus' sending of the seventy-two into the villages of Palestine: "I am not the Lord, but I sent twelve trained believers by twos ahead of me to the villages where I would later go. After observing the commitment and evangelistic desire of new believers in this village, we trained them for over six months. This is the meaning of 'sent.' They chose the villages in which they would minister. Four went to one village and teams of two to the others. Cell groups have been started in five villages, and all will eventually become new congregations. As the missionary who trained the evangelists, I visited these groups after about two months to baptize and teach. We still meet weekly with the 12 for debriefing, encouragement and prayer for the ministry."

Jesus says, "The harvest is plentiful, but the workers are few. Ask the Lord of the harvest, therefore, to send out workers into this harvest field" (Luke 10:2). Missionary Nickel emphasizes the importance of frequent and fervent prayer. They pray for the workers, their home village, neighboring villages, and the whole nation. Their prayer recognizes that Christ is the Lord of the harvest and that He will do the sending. Only by God's grace through faith in Christ have they been saved. Only by His grace will others come to faith in Jesus. Only by His grace will the workers have the strength and wisdom to reach the lost.

What can you learn from Luke 10 and the village story in central Asia? As a forgiven sinner saved by Christ's death and resurrection, do you hear His sending call in your Baptism to pray for workers in the harvest and then to go in His power and training through Word and Sacraments to "villages" He leads you to choose?

*Prayer:* Send men whose eyes have seen the King,
Men in whose ears his sweet words ring;
Send such your lost ones home to bring;
Send them where you will come.
*LW* 316:2

# Freely Give and Sacrifice

***Reading:* Luke 10:3–4**

*Text:* "Go! I am sending you out like lambs among wolves." Luke 10:3

No one ever said that witnessing is easy or that Satan will be no problem when you are sent to your "villages" to proclaim Christ. Jesus describes the mission of the seventy-two as "sending you out like lambs among wolves."

Missionary Nickel continues: "Part of the training involved spiritual warfare, settling conflicts, and overcoming the fear of witnessing in a hostile environment. . . . The Holy Spirit always knows how to teach Law and Gospel in the school of experience. However, the most important part of His curriculum is learning to be humble, to be lowly, and to serve, to give, to love, and to sacrifice. For then the lamb-like nature of the believer overcomes the threats of the wolves that always abound, especially in enemy territory where there are very few believers. Only God can teach people to be like lambs who will give their lives for others." He adds that in the process three of the twelve dropped out and three others stepped up to replace them. "Learning humility is always hard and usually painful."

Aware of the difficulty of our mission task, we look to the Lamb of God, who takes away the sin of the world. He freely gave Himself in a world filled with wolves bent on His destruction. But His perfect sacrifice won the victory over sin, death, and the devil. Daily confessing our sin, we rely on His forgiveness and strength to live as lambs among wolves, giving freely and sacrificing so others will see Him as the Lamb for time and for eternity.

Prayer: A lamb alone bears willingly
Sin's crushing weight for sinners;
He carries guilt's enormity,
Dies shorn of all his honors. . . .
His spotless life to offer.
He bears the stripes, the wrath, the lies,
The mockery, and yet replies,
"Willing all this I suffer."
This lamb is Christ, our soul's great friend,
The Lamb of God our Savior.
*LW* 111:1–2

Copyright ©1982 Concordia Publishing House

## Building Relationships and Look for Man of Peace

***Reading:* Luke 10:5–6**

*Text:* "When you enter a house, first say, 'Peace to this house!'" Luke 10:5

Luke 10:5–6 and its application in Central Asia offer much insight for our daily mission in the "villages" of our lives. Missionary Nickel continues: "First, we make friendly and winsome contact with local villagers. Then we develop relationships. This is not hard for those sent ones because they are also poor villagers who speak the same language. They are very much like the villagers they greet. It is easy to say 'Salaam Aleykum' (peace with you) and mean it. After 'Kondai' (how are you) the conversation moves to common concerns and then to spiritual matters and then to testimony about Jesus Christ. A relationship is developed and it does not take long to discern whether the person is open or closed to the message. Either way, a new acquaintance is made."

Jesus adds, "'If a man of peace is there, your peace will rest on him; if not, it will return to you'" (Luke 10:6). Nickel applies this instruction: "The first goal involves looking for this 'man of peace.' We define a 'man of peace' as a person, man or woman, who is open to the Gospel and the Gospel messenger. He may or may not be a believer, but he or she is willing to host a Bible study in his home and invite relatives and friends.

"This person is easy to recognize. One can almost see the peace of God resting on a person who welcomes the man of God into his home. The man of peace usually anticipates and welcomes the blessing that a 'God meeting' brings to his home and family. It is also obvious when a villager is hostile and does not receive your offer of peace. . . . The man of peace is vital, not only because he opens his home to meetings but also because he has a web of relationships, and people will respond to his invitation. If that person becomes a believer, his life changes, and he becomes a stronger witness. He and those with him begin to bear the testimony of Jesus Christ."

*Prayer:* The Lord look upon you with favor and give you peace. Amen.

# Stay and Love

### *Reading:* Luke 10:7–8

*Text:* "Stay in that house, eating and drinking whatever they give you." Luke 10:7a

Missionary Nickel, based on Jesus' words in Luke 10:7, emphasizes the importance of accepting the local culture and staying the course with God's love: "Asian hospitality is extremely warm. Even the poorest of people will share their tea and bread. Simply enjoy life and take the witness to one place. Make a stand in that house. It does not take long for village folks to see what is happening. Word spreads rapidly. We insist that the Bible study time and place be regular and weekly. Traditions about day and place develop very quickly. There is no need to go door to door as the cults do. If you have something to offer they will come. There is no need to intrude on others' lives. Prayer, care, and love are powerful magnets. The spirit of a group of believers is the only force necessary. Any kind of manipulations will never be fruitful."

Americans live in a vastly different culture from first century Judaism or central Asia in our day. Nevertheless, what might we learn from the words of Jesus and the approach of Missionary Nickel? Nothing replaces authentic and consistent love in relationships. The witness of our daily lives begins with those who share our culture–at home, in the neighborhood, at work. These relationships make possible a consistent caring with actions and words. When we form new relationships with people different from us in values, customs, and beliefs, the best approach involves staying and loving over a period of time so Christ's salvation might shine through our actions and words.

Jesus, God's only Son, took on flesh and lived in our midst. His life and ministry among people gave powerful and consistent witness to God's love, sealed with His suffering and death on Calvary's cross. He lives in His body, the Church, gathered together around Word and Sacraments and sent to bring His love into the cultural settings of our world.

*Prayer:* For all are kindred, far and wide,
Since Jesus Christ for all has died;
Grant us the will and grace provide
To love them all in you.
*LW* 397:4

# Heal and Tell

***Reading:* Luke 10:17–23**

*Text:* Heal the sick who are there and tell them, "The kingdom of God is near you!" Luke 10:9

Jesus' words to "heal" and "tell" find concrete application in central Asia villages: "We pray for every need that the people have, no matter how small, no matter how big. We expect God to heal the sick and answer our prayers. When they see that Jesus Christ is a real and present God, it is easy to say that the kingdom of God has come to this village. Praying for the sick and praying for jobs shows that you really care. Answers to these prayers show that God really cares. Jesus must be real. He must be power. He must be love. This is ministry. . . .

"We also understand that 'heal the sick' and 'kingdom of God' are closely related and cannot be effectively separated. We bring a mobile medical trailer, we offer a free eyeglass clinic, we distribute clothing, we teach English, and we offer community health education. These medical and humanitarian social ministries are not only hooks for the spiritual ministry, but they are also designed to offer free and unconditional help to those in need. The social and spiritual dimensions of faith must be related and connected. We cannot do without saying and we cannot say without doing."

Jesus' words to the seventy-two in Luke 10 not only apply to village church planting in central Asia but to us as well. Send and pray. Freely give and sacrifice. Build relationships and look for the man of peace. Stay and love. Heal and tell. Jesus, our Savior and Master, is the Lord of the harvest in our place and time.

To what "village" is Jesus sending us? We pray for His direction and discernment. How will we be trained to witness in word and deed? We trust His salvation, enlightening, and empowering through Word and Sacraments. "The seventy-two returned with joy" (Luke 10:17a) and so shall we because Jesus was "full of joy through the Holy Spirit" (Luke 10:21a)!

*Prayer:* Raise up, O Lord the Holy Ghost,
From this broad land a mighty host;
Their war cry, "We will seek the lost
Where you, O Christ, will come."
*LW* 316:6

# A Commons and a Crossing

***Reading:* Mark 1:21–34**

*Text:* The whole town gathered at the door. Mark 1:33a

We go to Concordia Lutheran Church, located in the village of Kirkwood, Missouri, just west of St. Louis. As I drive to church, I notice two newer shopping centers across Kirkwood Road from each other, one called Kirkwood Commons and the other Kirkwood Crossing. They house chain retail stores and specialty shops. Apparently they chose the names to indicate a common meeting place (commons) and a spot where people driving by from other areas might stop to shop (crossing). Might there be some ideas here for Christian witness in today's world?

Jesus in Mark's Gospel had preached in the Capernaum synagogue on the Sabbath and drove out an evil spirit to the people's amazement. Powerful things do happen in our churches through the ministry of Word and Sacraments. But much more was to happen in Capernaum that day. News about Jesus spread about the region even with people who had not attended the synagogue that day.

Jesus proceeded to the home of Simon where He healed Simon's mother-in-law of a fever. That evening after sunset, our text tells us, "The whole town gathered at the door of Simon's house" with their sick and demon-possessed. He healed many of their diseases. The Capernaum Commons that night was Simon's house because Jesus was there, and Capernaum Crossing may have been there too because the word had spread over the whole region of Galilee (Mark 1:28).

Where is the Commons and Crossing in your neighborhood, community, or town—the local public school, coffee shop, mall, post office, or your home? Or perhaps your church if you sponsor community events. Jesus is there if you are there because He died for you and lives in you through your Baptism. Is the news about Jesus spreading from your church through the whole region? Is He proclaimed in the common and crossing spots through your witness?

*Prayer:* Show us the common places, Lord, and the crossings where we can meet and bear testimony to Your salvation. Amen.

# The Walking Dead

## *Reading:* Ephesians 2:1–3

*Text:* As for you, you were dead in your transgressions and sins. Ephesians 2:1

How do you view the people in your life—that neighbor two doors down, the co-worker in your department, the doctor or nurse whom you visit for an appointment, the passenger next to you on an airline flight? Beyond the surface interaction, have you considered that they might be part of "the walking dead"?

In Ephesians 2, St. Paul writes to the Gentile believers in Christ, now part of the church: "As for you, you were dead in your transgressions and sins." He means that they were spiritually dead, cut off from God, disobedient to the point of being rebellious, following the ways of the world in their attitudes, values, and behaviors, led by Satan described as "the ruler of the kingdom of the air," gratifying the cravings of their sinful nature whether in sexual immorality or insatiable greed (Ephesians 2:2). They were blind, dead, and enemies of God. Only now in Christ could they see their precious situation. Although physically alive, they had been part of the walking dead, bound for physical death and eternal separation from God.

Redeemed by the precious blood of Christ, we know what it means to be spiritually alive although as sinners we daily struggle against the devil, the world, and our sinful flesh. We rejoice in God's forgiveness and new life each day. And we want those special people in our lives to also know Jesus, who alone can bring them from death to life.

How might God use you to bear testimony of the life that is in you by God's grace through faith in Christ? What questions might you ask? What interest might you take in their daily struggles? How might you invite them to come and see, to learn more from God's Word, to receive Christ as their life by the Spirit's power? No longer part of the walking dead but alive with Christ now and eternally.

*Prayer:* As by one man all mankind fell
And, born in sin, was doomed to hell,
So by one Man, who took our place,
We all received the gift of grace.
*LW* 363:5

# Alive and Soaring

## *Reading:* Ephesians 2:4–6

*Text:* God, who is rich in mercy, made us alive with Christ even when we were dead in transgressions. Ephesians 2:4–5a

What do we have to offer others who might be part of "the walking dead"? After all, we have feet of clay, express doubts, and are afraid. We sometimes lack patience, become angry, and act selfishly. In short, we daily sin much and indeed deserve nothing but punishment.

But St. Paul has an amazing word of Gospel for the Ephesian Christians and for us: "God, who is rich in mercy, made us alive with Christ even when we were dead in transgressions." He goes on to add, "God raised us up with Christ and seated us in the heavenly realms in Christ Jesus" (Ephesians 2:6). Christ lived a sinless life in our stead, died on the cross to pay for all of our sins, rose from the grave to conquer death, and ascended to heaven where He is seated at the right hand of God the Father. In our Baptism we died with Christ, rose from the dead with Him, and are seated in the heavenly realms with Him. Amazingly, in Christ we are alive and soaring.

Alive and soaring! By God's grace through faith in Christ, we have Christ to offer others. His love, His forgiveness, His life, His sure promise of eternal life in heaven. Humble before God, honest about our own shortcomings, we can point to Him as our source of joy and life. God's Spirit works through us so others see Christ in us and desire, by His grace, to be alive and soaring too.

*Prayer:* Oh, where is your sting, death? We fear you no more;
Christ rose, and now open is fair Eden's door.
For all our transgressions his blood does atone;
Redeemed and forgiven, we now are his own.

Then sing your hosannas and raise your glad voice;
Proclaim the blest tidings that all may rejoice.
Laud, honor, and praise to the Lamb that was slain;
In glory he reigns, yes, and ever shall reign.
*LW* 138:4–5

# In Order That

## *Reading:* Ephesians 2:6–10

*Text:* In order that in the coming ages He might show the incomparable riches of His grace, expressed in His kindness to us in Christ Jesus. Ephesians 2:7

For what purpose has God made us alive and soaring? Not for our own security and happiness, although He gives us eternal security and joy. But "in order that" for generations to come, through His Church "the walking dead" will come to know Jesus Christ as their life and salvation.

St. Paul follows up his startling statement that "God has raised us up with Christ and seated us with Him in the heavenly realms" (Ephesians 2:6) with the words, "in order that in the coming ages He might show the incomparable riches of His grace, expressed in His kindness to us in Christ Jesus."

He first tells the individual believers, saved by grace through faith–a gift of God not of works–that they are "God's workmanship created in Christ Jesus to do good works" (Ephesians 2:10). As a response to the gift of faith in Jesus Christ as Savior, each of us is to let God shine through us to "the walking dead" with His new life through our words and our deeds "in order that" they might believe in Christ.

Second, St. Paul describes how Christ Jesus through His death on the cross has broken down the wall of hostility between Gentiles and Jews "in order that" He might reconcile "the walking dead" to God through the Church, which is His body. As individuals, we along with the Ephesian Christians are "being built together to become a dwelling in which God lives by His Spirit" (Ephesians 2:22).

Alive and soaring for the purpose of God's plan from before creation "to bring all things in heaven and on earth together under one head, even Christ" (Ephesians 1:10). From death to life "in order that"!

*Prayer:* Give me a faithful heart, Likewise to thee,
That each departing day Henceforth may see
Some work of love begun, Some deeds of kindness done,
Some wandr'er sought and won Something for thee.
*LW* 374:3

# Half Time

### *Reading:* Psalm 90:10–12

*Text:* So teach us to number our days that we may get a heart of wisdom. Psalm 90:12 (ESV)

God uses us as individual Christians to help set the world ablaze with the Gospel of Jesus Christ. The question is where, when, and how do we participate as part of Christ's body, the Church, to reach the world. I discovered great insights from a book, *Half Time*, written a few years ago by a Christian businessman, named Bob Buford. His book challenges people in mid-life to reflect on their first half, like a sports team meeting together at half time, and seeking God's direction and strength for significant mission in the second half of life. The next several devotions will bring Scripture to bear on some of my discoveries from reading Bob's book and hopefully help you, whatever your chronological age, to rely on God's Spirit for your personal mission in God's world.

Psalm 90, a prayer of Moses, provides profound insight into our everlasting God and the fleeting moments of human life on earth. Reflecting on the short life span of 70 or 80 years, the psalmist concludes, "So teach us to number our days that we may get a heart of wisdom." Aware of our many sins, having experienced many difficult circumstances, thankful for God's purposeful creation and His redemption through Christ on the cross, we pause at "half time" to number our days and make ourselves available for His saving purpose in today's world. We pray for "a heart of wisdom" to discuss His plan for our lives and to rely on His grace and forgiveness in Christ each day.

Perhaps a key ingredient of our church body's *Ablaze!* movement to reach 100 million people for Christ by 2017 is half time, individual believers setting aside time for repentance and reflection so God may empower us through Word and Sacraments to discover our unique role in His worldwide mission.

*Prayer:* Our God, our help in ages past,
Our hope for years to come,
Still be our guard while troubles last
And our eternal home.
*LW* 180:6

# First Half

### *Reading:* Psalm 90:1–9

*Text:* You have set our iniquities before You, our secret sins in the light of Your presence. Psalm 90:8 (ESV)

In his book, *Half Time*, Bob Buford candidly describes the first half of his life. As participant and then CEO of a family television business, he achieved great financial success in his 20s, 30s, and early 40s. Although a Christian believer intent on serving the Lord in family, work, and church, he realized that he was mostly driven by a burning desire for success and in danger of addiction to success, a clear form of idolatry. This awareness led him to prayerful consideration of his future.

How do you view the first half of your life? Moses, who could well remember his first 40 years of rising success in Pharaoh's court and his 40 years of testing in the Sinai wilderness before the burning bush incident, exclaims in Psalm 90, "You have set our iniquities before You, our secret sins in the light of Your presence." No wonder he was reluctant to accept the challenging mission Yahweh had in store for him—to lead Israel out of Egypt to the Promised Land. He knew his sinful nature. He had been chastened. Yes, God was using all his education and experiences in those earlier years to prepare him for his leadership role. But Moses needed first to repent and receive God's forgiveness and then rely on God's power and guidance for the task before him. He focuses on the Lord: "LORD, You have been our dwelling place in all generations" (Psalm 90:1). Repentant and relying on God's steadfast love, Moses has learned from his first half.

How has God been preparing you in your first half to serve Him in mission? What sins and idolatries need confession and forgiveness? How is His steadfast love through Christ's death and resurrection lifting you up for your mission?

*Prayer:* Come with hurts and guilts and meanness,
Come, however soiled within;
From the most ingrained uncleanness,
Wash your robes and make them white;
You shall walk with God in light.
*LW* 96:3

# Turning Points

## *Reading:* Ecclesiastes 3:1–8

*Text:* There is a time for everything, and a reason for every activity under heaven. Ecclesiastes 3:1

Reflection on the "first half" leads us to examine the turning points in life. Bob Buford remembers a moment in the ninth-grade English class of Miss Mittie Marsh (*Half-Time*, p. 37) and the sudden death by drowning of his only son, Ross, at age 24 (*Half-Time*, chapter 6) as significant turning points in his life. What are the major turning points in your life that God may be using to shape your mission to set the world ablaze with Christ?

The writer of Ecclesiastes, fully aware of the futility of mortal life without God, describes a number of turning points, "There is a time for everything, and a reason for every activity under heaven." He lists among others—"a time to be born, and a time to die; a time to plant, and a time to pluck up what is planted; a time to break down, and a time to build up; a time to mourn, and a time to dance; a time to keep, and a time to cast away" (Ecclesiastes 3:2–8). Without God, all these turning points lead to vanity or despair, create cynicism or discouragement. With God, the believer can find comfort, encouragement, and purpose in these turning points: "I have seen the business that God has given to the children of man to be busy with. He has made everything beautiful in its time. Also He has put eternity into man's heart" (Ecclesiastes 3:10–11a).

Focusing on God's free gift of eternal life through His Son, Jesus Christ, consider turning points in your life: Baptism, confirmation, marriage, vocational or educational decisions, death of a loved one, tragedies in work or family, serious illness. How might God be working in your life of witness and service through these turning points? Because He has placed eternity into our hearts, our Lord "has made everything beautiful in its time."

*Prayer:* We were by God created In his own time and place
And by his Son persuaded To follow truth and grace.
The Spirit guides our ways And faithfully will lead us
That nothing can impede us. To God be all our praise!
*LW* 409:6

# Open to Change?

### *Reading:* Genesis 12:1–9

*Text:* "Leave your country, your people and your father's household and go to the land I will show you." Genesis 12:1

As you reflect on the first half of your life, a question emerges, "Am I open to change?" We often become stuck in our comfort zones. All is not well. We may be less than satisfied with our life's purpose, our work setting, or our place of residence. We may have identified sinful patterns of behavior in our lifestyles. Yet the thought of moving, changing jobs, or addressing family issues that need attention threatens our comfort zone. We are not open to change.

Abraham may have found a comfort zone in Haran with his extended family. But God called him to radical change: "Leave your country, your people and your father's household and go to the land I will show you." God's plan of salvation called for Abram to settle in Canaan, the Promised Land. From his seed would come the Messiah who would walk the dusty roads of that same land and be crucified outside the walls of its chief city.

But Abram needed first to be open to change for that plan to unfold. On his own, that radical change would have been impossible. But God supplied Abram with His promises, that He would bless him with land and descendants so that through him all peoples on earth would be blessed. God's grace opened Abram to change, and the result was salvation through Jesus Christ.

What areas in your life need change? How is God working within you and through others to make you open to His changes? How is God speaking to you through Word and Sacraments in the presence of His people? What other circumstances, ministries, or people in need are nudging you toward possible change? The real mission question: Am I open to God's change in my life?

*Prayer:* The God of Abr'am praise,
Whose all-sufficient grace
Shall guide me all my pilgrim days
In all my ways.
He deigns to call me friend;
He calls himself my God.
And he shall save me to the end
Through Jesus' blood.
*LW* 450:3

# The Mainspring

### *Reading:* Philippians 1:12–26

*Text:* For to me, to live is Christ and to die is gain. Philippians 1:21

Reflection on the first half of life ultimately leads to a basic question: "What is the mainspring of my life?" A fine Swiss watch depends on its principal mechanism or mainspring to make it run smoothly, reliably, and efficiently. We may be muddled in our thinking about motivations and directions in life until we face this basic question. What is your mainspring–money, career, family, freedom, or Jesus Christ?

Paul had many driving forces in his life prior to his Damascus road experience–Pharisee of the Pharisees, zealous persecutor of Christians, lover of learning. But to the Philippians he describes the mainspring of his life simply and powerfully, "For to me, to live is Christ and to die is gain." A prisoner with an uncertain fate but bathed in God's baptismal grace, Paul's mainspring is Christ for earthly life and beyond physical death for eternal life. That mainspring of Christ gives Paul a missionary boldness, a compassion for Jews and Gentiles alike, and a courageous endurance through trials and suffering.

As we gear up for the remainder of our days in service and witness, aware of our sinful nature, the uncertainty of our future, and God's overflowing grace in Christ, what better way could there be to describe our life's mainspring than the words of St. Paul, "For to me, to live is Christ and to die is gain." Everything else is the fine print. Christ for us on Calvary. Christ in us at Baptism. Christ through us in word and deed. Our mainspring, Christ, drives the mission, Christ, to the world for which Christ died. I can hardly wait for the second half! Missionary boldness. Genuine compassion for the lost. Courageous endurance through trials and suffering. All because of Christ, our mainspring!

*Prayer:* Therefore you alone, my Savior,
Shall be all in all to me;
Search my heart and my behavior,
Root out all hypocrisy.
Through all my life's pilgrimage,
Guard and uphold me,
In loving forgiveness, O Jesus, enfold me.
This one thing is needful, all others are vain;
I count all but loss that I Christ may obtain!
*LW* 277:6

June 8

# Called Or Driven?

### *Reading:* Romans 8:1–11

*Text:* I therefore, a prisoner for the Lord, urge you to walk in a manner worthy of the calling to which you have been called. Ephesians 4:1 (ESV)

What drives you? A dangerous question. We would like others to see us as balanced in our life between family and career, mind and emotions, others and self. We want our faith in Christ to be evident in our words and actions. Bob Buford finally considered the question, "Do you understand the difference between being called and being driven?" He concluded at half time that his business behavior evidenced "being driven" more than "being called."

In Ephesians, Paul admonishes the believers in Christ with these words: "I therefore, a prisoner for the Lord, urge you to walk in a manner worthy of the calling to which you have been called." Called in Baptism by God's choosing, through the blood of Christ, which bestows redemption and forgiveness of sins, sealed by the Holy Spirit. Called to a life of service and witness, characterized by humility, gentleness, patience, love, unity, maturity of faith, and bold confession of faith. Called, not driven.

Yet in Romans 7 and 8, Paul describes his daily struggle against his sinful flesh. "For those who live according to the flesh set their minds on the things of the flesh [driven], but those who live according to the Spirit set their minds on the things of the Spirit [called]" (Romans 8:5). He adds, ". . . but I see in my members another law waging war against the law of my mind and making me captive to the law of sin that dwells in my members. Wretched man that I am." (Romans 7:23–24a).

We confess our sinful drives that consume us—for power, success, wealth, self-gratification. Then, we rejoice in God's forgiveness and restoration of our calling. Paul writes, "Thanks be to God through Jesus Christ our Lord! . . . There is therefore now no condemnation for those who are in Christ Jesus" (Romans 7:25a–8:1). Although sinfully driven, God's call in Christ stands. We walk by faith in a manner worthy of that calling.

*Prayer:* Give me the strength to do
With ready heart and willing
Whatever you command,
My calling here fulfilling.
*LW* 371:2

# Taking Stock

## *Reading:* Psalm 139:1–12

*Text:* Search me, O God, and know my heart; test me and know my anxious thoughts. Psalm 139:23

Relying on Christ as our mainspring, confessing that we often live as driven rather than called, we see half time as a time for taking stock in preparation for the second half of our lives when God sets us ablaze with Christ for the world.

The psalmist turns to the Lord for help in taking stock of his life: "Search me, O God, and know my heart; test me and know my anxious thoughts. See if there is any offensive way in me, and lead me in the way everlasting" (Psalm 139:23–24). No pale self-analysis here. No self-righteous and rationalizing list of virtues and vices. No psychological and endless probing of the victimized ego leading to deeper depression. But God-analysis. Letting the Spirit of God like a surgeon focus laser-sharp attention on the very spot most in need of repentance. Not too much exposure, leading to despair. Not too little exposure, leading to self-righteousness. But just the right surgery, leading to confession and then full forgiveness and healing through the death and resurrection of Jesus Christ. "Search me, O God, and know my heart."

That kind of taking stock prepares us well to serve and witness, living daily in our Baptism. Step by step He leads us. He is the One who has searched us and known us, who knows when we sit and when we rise, whether we are in the heavens or in the depths, who brings our darkness into His light (Psalm 139:1–11). We can trust our Savior to know us, to discipline us, to heal us, to send us with His saving light into the world around us. Taking stock at half time. Nothing hidden. Sins forgiven. Darkness to light. Christ's light shining through us in a dark world!

*Prayer:* Your grace and love alone avail
To blot out sin with pardon.
In your gaze our best efforts pale,
Develop pride, and harden.
Before your throne no one can boast
That he escaped sin's deadly coast.
Our haven is your mercy.
*LW* 230:2

# Finding Your Uniqueness

## *Reading:* Psalm 139:13–18

*Text:* For You created my inmost being; You knit me together in my mother's womb. Psalm 139:13

Part of taking stock involves understanding God's creation of us in our mother's womb, or finding our uniqueness. God has gifted each of us with a mind, body, and spirit to praise Him and serve others. He has brought us into the world and placed us in a family, nurtured us, and developed our natural gifts in a unique environment which includes experiences, education, relationships, and challenges. Even in a sin-scarred world with its hurts, defeats, discouragements, and cruelty, our Creator God preserves us and shapes us for ongoing witness to His salvation through Jesus Christ. As His baptized children, we know Him as Creator and call Him Father.

The psalmist captures this uniqueness with the words in Psalm 139, "For You created my inmost being; You knit me together in my mother's womb." He affirms God's unique creation, "I praise You because I am fearfully and wonderfully made; Your works are wonderful, I know that full well" (Psalm 139:14). That is why we seek to protect the unborn and to affirm a culture of life in today's world. That is also why at half time, we turn to God for the purpose of understanding our unique contribution toward setting the world ablaze with the Gospel of Christ.

Bob Buford in *Half Time* suggests identifying your uniqueness through these questions: "What is your purpose? What makes you tick? What do you do so well that you would enjoy doing it without pay? What is your passion, the spark that needs only a little breeze to ignite into a raging fire (p. 81)?" Good questions for the child of God, saved through the blood of Christ, forgiven daily in the rhythm of the baptismal life, seeking to live out God's vocation or calling in daily life!

*Prayer:* Someone Special–God and man,
You were there when I began,
You'll be there when I depart,
For you live within my heart.
Someone Special, now I see,
That someone is really me.
*SP* 212:5

Copyright © 1978 Concordia Publishing House

# Balance

## *Reading:* Philippians 3:12–14, 4:11–13

*Text:* But I press on. Philippians 4:11b – for I have learned to be content whatever the circumstances. Philippians 3:12b

Part of our reflection on the first half of life may reveal a life out of balance. On one hand, we perhaps aggressively pursued challenging goals and achieved considerable success but at the cost of burning out, neglecting important relationships, and feeling physically, emotionally, and spiritually drained. On the other hand, we perhaps experienced quiet times of reflection, satisfying relationships, and personal enjoyment. But the cost of the relative leisure was a sense of little purpose in life, dull routine, and even boredom. What does it mean to have a balance between these two extremes?

St. Paul on a vigorous and costly mission to bring Christ to the Gentiles, seems to find balance with God's help in the paradoxical reality of living between the two extremes. On one hand, he writes to the Philippians, "Not that I have already obtained all this, or have already been made perfect, but I press on to take hold of that for which Christ Jesus took hold of me . . . forgetting what is behind and straining toward what is ahead, I press on toward the goal to win the prize for which God has called me heavenward in Christ Jesus" (Philippians 3:12–14).

On the other hand, he writes in chapter 4, "I have learned to be content whatever the circumstances. . . . I can do everything through Him who gives me strength" (Philippians 4:11, 13). When I was a college sophomore, the president of Concordia College, Milwaukee, articulated the following theme for the school year: Constantly challenged but continually content. That theme remains with me as God's strength for living as a Christian witness in a world of paradox.

Constantly challenged to set the world ablaze with Christ–making the most of every opportunity, pressing on no matter what the cost. Continually content in the arms of the Savior–saved, daily forgiven, waiting on Him, doing everything through Him who strengthens me. No easy answers for second half living, but a Savior who goes on before me! That's balance!

*Prayer:* For you I joyously employ
Whatever you in grace have given,
I run my course with even joy,
I closely walk with you to heav'n.
*LW* 380:5

# A Change of Heart

## *Reading:* Ezekiel 36:24–28

*Text:* "I will give you a new heart and put a new spirit in you; I will remove from you your heart of stone and give you a heart of flesh." Ezekiel 36:26

When you look at the first half of your life during half time reflection, you may jump to the conclusion that you are supposed to quit your job or totally change your career in the second half. While some people do just that with varying degrees of satisfaction, your time of reflection needs to start with a change of heart in the presence of God.

The prophet Ezekiel speaks to the nation of Israel, suffering the consequences of their idolatry and rebellion against God. They have profaned His name among the nations. What they need is not a new job in a new place but a change of heart. God, by His grace, promises them, "I will give you a new heart and put a new spirit in you; I will remove from you your heart of stone and give you a heart of flesh." He is talking about repentance–godly sorrow for their rebellious hearts of stone and Spirit-created new hearts of flesh, trusting in salvation and new life through God's promised Messiah, Jesus, the crucified and risen Savior. God's purpose for this change of heart: "Then the nations will know that I am the LORD . . . when I show myself holy through you before their eyes" (Ezekiel 36:23).

We thank God for our change of heart through Baptism in the name of the Trinity. We pray each day, and especially during our half time reflection, for the guidance that comes from a change of heart so the nations will know that He is the Lord through our witness to Jesus. New job? Same job? New location? Old location? Answers flow over time from God's change of our heart to His purposes!

*Prayer:* Grant us hearts, dear Lord, to give you
Gladly, freely of your own.
With the sunshine of your goodness
Melt our thankless hearts of stone
Till our cold and selfish natures,
Warmed by you, at length believe
That more happy and more blessed
'Tis to give than to receive.
*LW* 402:2

# A Change of Perspective

## *Reading:* Philippians 3:7–11

*Text:* But whatever was to my profit I now consider loss for the sake of Christ. Philippians 3:7

Right alongside a change of heart comes a change of perspective, all before a potential shift of direction as we enter the second half or the next phase in our lives. We often view the world from our selfish perspective and don't realize how far removed that is from God's perspective.

Paul lived an intense life as a Pharisee, thinking that his perspective was correct until Jesus met Him on the Damascus road. When the scales were removed from his eyes physically and spiritually after his Baptism, Saul became Paul with God's perspective to win the world for Christ. Paul writes the Philippian Christians, "But whatever was to my profit I now consider loss for the sake of Christ. What is more, I consider everything a loss compared to the surpassing greatness of knowing Christ Jesus my Lord, for whose sake I have lost all things. I consider them rubbish, that I may gain Christ and be found in Him, not having a righteousness of my own that comes form the law, but that which is through faith in Christ" (Philippians 3:7–10). God's perspective through Christ impelled Paul to press on with the saving Gospel.

God's new perspective of the world in Christ will transform our daily lives at home, work, and in our communities. His perspective will shape the directions of our service and witness in youth, middle age, and our later years. We pray for a godly change of heart and perspective as we explore new ways of setting the world ablaze with Christ. Bob Buford's simple steps for reflection from God's perspective: Make peace. Take time. Be deliberate. Share the journey. Be honest. Be patient. Listen and trust God (pp. 66–70).

*Prayer:* Wisdom's highest, noblest treasure,
Jesus, is revealed in you.
Let me find in you my pleasure,
Make my will and actions true,
Humility there and simplicity reigning,
In paths of true wisdom my steps ever training.
If I learn from Jesus this knowledge divine,
The blessing of heavenly wisdom is mine.
*LW* 272:5

# Releasing and Relinquishing

## *Reading:* Matthew 10:32–42

*Text:* "Whoever finds his life will lose it, and whoever loses his life for My sake will find it." Matthew 10:39

A final aspect of taking stock of ourselves and our life's mission at half time involves releasing and relinquishing those things that impede our future service and witness. We hold many things tightly. Not wrong in themselves, they may separate us from God or His mission through us to others. . . . A high standard of living, financial security, status in our job or community, a network of relationships. We fear releasing or relinquishing those things that we treasure.

Jesus describes the cost of discipleship as He sends out the twelve two by two on a mission: "Anyone who does not take up his cross and follow Me is not worthy of Me. Whoever finds his life will lose it, and whoever loses his life for My sake will find it" (Matthew 10:38–39). He hides nothing from them about the difficulty of their mission. He tells them that following Him may cause divisions within families, hostility from friends and neighbors, and persecution by rulers. He predicts that those who hold on tightly to their lives will lose them but those who release and relinquish their lives will find them.

But Jesus asks nothing that He does not graciously give. Jesus willingly released His own life first in humble service to others then by taking up His cross on the way to Calvary. By His death and resurrection, He saved our lives from sin, death, and the devil. As He calls us to follow Him and sends us on a mission to the world, He gives us abundant life. Releasing and relinquishing for His sake by His grace often leads us to marvel at His overwhelming blessings both physical and spiritual. With no need to fear, we step forward into the second half, confident of His presence and power for setting the world ablaze.

*Prayer:* "I teach you how to shun and flee
What harms your soul's salvation;
Your heart from ev'ry guile to free,
From sin and its temptation.
I am the refuge of the soul
And lead you to your heav'nly goal."
*LW* 379:4

# Second Half

## *Reading:* Psalm 90:13–17

*Text:* Make us glad for as many days as You have afflicted us, and for as many years as we have seen evil. Psalm 90:15 (ESV)

In the last several devotions you have been challenged to review the first half of your life at half time when we ask God to prepare us to help set the world ablaze for Christ in our second half. This taking stock is based on the book *Half Time* by Christian businessman Bob Buford. In his 40s, he carefully evaluated his life and business in the light of God's Word with the help of family, Christian friends, and a competent business consultant. As a result, Bob built on his organizational skills to create a Leadership Network for Christian leaders to "transform the latent energy in American Christianity into active energy" (p. 122). As we explore God's possibilities for our second half, let God direct you at your current stage of life, regardless of your chronological age.

Psalm 90 continues to guide us. Acutely aware of the many challenges in his life, some caused by his own grievous sin and some by overwhelming circumstances of fierce enemies like Egypt and the constant rebellion of his own people Israel, Moses looks ahead and prays, "Make us glad for as many days as You have afflicted us, and for us many years as we have seen evil." He means glad days of God's blessings, as a forgiven people pass on the message of salvation to the next generation (Psalm 90:16–17). Moses looks to the future with anticipation of ongoing service and witness: "Satisfy us in the morning with Your steadfast love, that we may rejoice and be glad all our days" (Psalm 90:14).

With the first half considered and sins forgiven, we approach God's second half of our lives in joyful anticipation of His daily steadfast love through Word and Sacraments. We dare to offer ourselves at God's bidding to proclaim His blessings in Christ to the next generation worldwide and await His guidance.

*Prayer:* Make theirs with ours a single voice
Uplifted ever to rejoice
With wond'ring gratitude and praise
To you, O Lord, for boundless grace.
*LW* 314:5

# Life Mission

*Reading:* Galatians 2:1–10

*Text:* On the contrary, they saw that I had been entrusted with the task of preaching the Gospel to the Gentiles. Galatians 2:7

Bob Buford, in his book *Half Time,* insists on the importance of a personal mission statement or a "life mission" as the foundation for second half living. This simple statement, based on prayer, reflection on God's Word, and the counsel of Christian friends, can be developed as the answer to some important questions: "What is my passion? What have I done uncommonly well? Where do I belong?" (p. 120). These questions will help lead you to discover the task for which you were especially made.

St. Paul, by God's grace with Jesus Christ as his "mainspring," had a clear life mission. He stated it many times. In his letter to the Galatians, Paul describes his 14 years of seasoning before beginning his apostolic ministry. Then he goes to Jerusalem to seek the counsel of the early church's "pillars"–James, the brother of our Lord and head of the Jerusalem church; Peter, known as apostle to the Jews; and John. When Paul explained to them the Gospel he was preaching and the focus of his preaching, the Gentiles, they confirmed his life mission. Not adding anything to his message or mission, "on the contrary they saw that I had been entrusted with the task of preaching the Gospel to the Gentiles." Paul then acted on his personal mission statement and, with the blessing and sending of the Antioch church (Acts 13:1–3), embarked on his missionary journeys that would lead at last to Rome. Paul's passion, his competence as a bridge between the Jewish and the Gentile worlds, and his powerful Spirit-inspired proclamation of Christ-crucified made his life mission fruitful and life-changing throughout the first century world.

What is your life mission? Can you describe it in a personal mission statement? In the supportive context of fellow believers, are you receiving counsel, affirmation, and opportunities to live out that mission in your daily calling? What an adventure for second half living as a forgiven, baptized child of God!

*Prayer:* Raise up, O Lord the Holy Ghost,
From this broad land a mighty host;
Their war cry, "We will seek the lost
Where you, O Christ, will come."
*LW* 316:6

# Life Commitments

## *Reading:* 1 Samuel 7:2–13

*Text:* Commit yourselves to the LORD and serve Him only. 1 Samuel 7:3b

Bob Buford connects his personal mission statement with his life commitments. He writes, "One of the consequences of my transition into the second half is that I no longer organize my life in terms of goals. Instead, I now make commitments. These commitments also help me stay focused on my mission" (p. 122).

Based on your life mission, what might be your life commitments? They will come very close to your vocations in life or daily callings: home, school, work, church, government. Luther in his catechism section on confession simply writes, "Consider your place in life according to the Ten Commandments: Are you a father, mother, son, daughter, husband, wife, or worker?" *(Luther's Small Catechism).* In short, bringing Christ to others in the areas of your life commitments.

Samuel, the judge of Israel, assembles God's people at Mizpah where he leads them to repentance over their idolatry. They confess, "We have sinned against the LORD" (1 Samuel 7:6b). Faced with a military threat from the Philistines, they beseech Samuel to pray for deliverance. The Lord answers by throwing the Philistines into a panic and giving Israel the victory. Samuel creates a stone memorial, Ebenezer, which simply means, "Till now the LORD has helped us" (1 Samuel 7:12). Based on God's salvation, Samuel challenges a repentant and forgiven Israel to "commit yourselves to the LORD and serve Him only." The people respond with their life commitments, according to God's Commandments.

What life commitments do you make based on the Ten Commandments of God in the light of His life mission for you? How will they lead you to daily repentance as part of your baptismal life? How will they guide you to fulfill your personal mission statement to share your faith in Christ with others? How will your crucified and risen Savior, who has helped you until now, empower you with His steadfast love and forgiveness to carry out those life commitments each day?

*Prayer:* Give me a faithful heart, Likeness to thee,
That each departing day Henceforth may see
Some work of love begun, Some deed of kindness done,
Some wand'rer sought and own, Something for thee.
*LW* 374:3

# Your Cup of Life

## *Reading:* Psalm 23:5b; Psalm 116:13

*Text:* "Father, if You are willing, take this cup from Me, yet not My will, but Yours be done." Luke 22:42

With life mission in mind, Buford suggests reviewing your current schedule and daily events to see if there is room in your "cup of life" for anything new. What might you need to change or eliminate to gain time for your new priorities? That imagery of your life as a cup stimulates some interesting scriptural reflections. What a blessing God's cup of life has given to us! How sad the way we often fill our cup with sinful behaviors and frivolous, self-serving activities! With what does God want us to fill our cup of life in His service?

In Psalm 23, the king who once tended flocks rejoices in God's abundant blessings, "My cup overflows" (Psalm 23:5b). Grateful for God's salvation in his time of trouble and sorrow, another psalmist responds, "I will lift up the cup of salvation and call on the name of the LORD" (Psalm 116:13). The greatest evidence of God's cup of blessing comes in the prayer of Jesus in Gethsemane, who faces suffering and death to pay for all of our sins which pollute our cup of life: "Father, if You are willing, take this cup from Me; yet not My will, but Yours be done." Because Jesus obediently filled His cup of life with the cup of suffering on our behalf, our cup of life is filled to overflowing with forgiveness and salvation so we can generously share with others. Did not Jesus say in the upper room, "This cup is the new covenant in My blood which is poured out for you" (Luke 22:20)?

How do you fill your cup of life? First, with Christ's forgiveness through Word and Sacrament in the presence of God's people. Then, with precious opportunities to share His cup of salvation with others in our daily life. Making room for those opportunities, we let God help us eliminate unnecessary, time-consuming activities that clog the flow of God's abundant blessings through us to others.

*Prayer:* Dear Father, my cup runneth over. Help me to share Your love in Jesus with others. Amen.

# Saying No

### *Reading:* 2 Corinthians 1:12–23

*Text:* But as surely as God is faithful, our message to you is not "Yes" and "No" . . . but in Him it has always been "Yes." 2 Corinthians 1:18, 19b

Filling our cup of life with God's blessings received and opportunities to share those blessings with others requires saying no more often. Are you able to say no? In a world of e-mail and cell phones, people are busier than ever, find obligations pressing in on them, and often fill their lives with unimportant things. They live with the tyranny of the urgent. God's life mission for us and our life commitments often are neglected because we can't say no. Even church activities sometimes prevent us from living our faith as Christian witnesses.

St. Paul kept his focus on proclaiming Christ to the Gentiles. Sometimes his careful plans to visit churches had to be changed. He had to say no, even if he had earlier said yes. In Corinth, Paul's opponents tried to use his changed plans for a visit to discredit him as unreliable, saying yes and no out of the same mouth. For whatever reason, Paul had to say no to one of his visits. Yet he affirms his love for them and, more important, the never-changing yes of the Gospel of Christ whose promises never fail. "In Him it has always been 'Yes.'"

Resting in the Yes of salvation through faith in the crucified and risen Christ, we can say no when we must. Others will respect our focus on Christ and our desire to witness of His love. When they don't understand, we reach out in love but move on nevertheless. Christ also forgives our confessed sin when we say no incorrectly or in the wrong manner. His Yes enables us to say yes to Gospel opportunities and to say no when necessary. His love penetrates our anxiety and perplexity to make good decisions for the sake of Gospel outreach.

*Prayer:* Lord Jesus, think on me,
By anxious thoughts oppressed;
Let me your loving servant be
And taste your promised rest.

Lord Jesus, think on me,
Nor let me go astray;
Through darkness and perplexity
Point out your chosen way.
*LW* 231:2–3

# Colleagues to Make a Difference

## *Reading:* Acts 15:36–41

*Text:* But Paul chose Silas and left, commended by the brothers to the grace of the Lord. Acts 15:40

Bob Buford suggests that when you pursue the life mission given by God, you need the right people to help you and encourage you if you truly want to make a difference—colleagues who share your faith, your passion, and your mission direction. They probably have different gifts to complement your own competence and different perspectives to challenge you positively, but you are energized to be with them in the common task. All too often we expend four times as much energy trying to persuade unwilling and unmotivated people to join us.

Paul, ready to embark on his second missionary journey, came into sharp conflict with his partner, Barnabas, about whether Mark should accompany them. While Barnabas had helped Paul greatly to begin his ministry and to travel with him on his first journey, now they were no longer compatible. Barnabas took Mark and sailed to Cyprus, "but Paul chose Silas and left, commended by the brothers to the grace of the Lord." Later Paul added Timothy in Lystra (Acts 16:1–3) and probably the physician Luke (Acts 16:10ff) as colleagues. Certainly by the Spirit's power they made a major difference as the Gospel spread to Europe.

Who are your colleagues? Christian friends. Family members. Like-minded believers at work. Church members. Pray for the people who might join you, support you, encourage you, challenge you. Together, be honest; confess sins; pray for each other and the mission; rely on the Word of Christ for forgiveness, strength, and direction. The sending Christ, crucified and risen, will enable you to make a difference in people saved for eternity.

*Prayer:* Here our common faith unites us,
Closer than the closest twins,
Here the love of Christ ignites us,
Here our unity begins.
Bring back home the lost and scattered,
Bind up those whose lives are shattered,
Show the world what Christ has done,
To make us one.
*SP* 218:3

Copyright © 1988 Concordia Publishing House

# Independent? Dependent? Interdependent?

## *Reading:* 1 Corinthians 12:12–27

*Text:* Now you are the body of Christ, and each of you is a part of it. 1 Corinthians 12:27

You have identified God's life mission for you in your second half. Now the question arises, "How will I carry it out? Will I be independent, dependent, or interdependent?" At first blush, independent sounds good. Instead of being driven and controlled by others, I can act independently to carry out my life mission. But Bob Buford observes, "I cannot recall a single thing worth doing that I've accomplished by myself" (p.140). He goes on to say that the individualism rampant in our culture borders on selfishness with a focus on personal gain. Paul, in 1 Corinthians 12, describes the many parts of the one body designed to work together. When any single part tries to function independently, it doesn't work well. Therefore, we confess our sinful selfishness that lies at the heart of the drive for total independence.

Should we then embrace dependent living? Let others tell us what to do. Wait for someone else to lead us on our life mission. But dependent living based on conformity leads equally to sin. Paul writes, "Do not conform any longer to the pattern of this world, but be transformed by the renewing of your mind" (Romans 12:2). He further writes to Timothy, "For God did not give us a spirit of timidity, but a spirit of power, of love, and of self-discipline" (2 Timothy 1:6–7). We confess our sin of mindless dependence as weak followers of others.

Paul describes interdependence as God's design for Christ's body, the church: "Now you are the body of Christ, and each one of you is a part of it." All of us are dependent on Christ's atoning sacrifice for the world's sin and on God's Spirit to incorporate us into Christ's body through Baptism. Each of us is a new creation, uniquely gifted to serve, able to stand independently against a conforming world. But we serve and witness interdependently as a part of Christ's body. We need each other. We complement each other. Together we set the world ablaze with Christ!

*Prayer:* Lord Jesus, help us to work together as Your body to set the world ablaze with Your salvation. Amen.

June 22

# Learning Still

### *Reading:* Philippians 1:24–30

*Text:* And this is my Prayer: that your love may abound more and more in knowledge and depth of insight, so that you may be able to discern what is best. Philippians 1:9–10a

One of the important ingredients for achieving your life mission is a commitment to lifelong learning. As a student of adult and continuing education, I see the necessity of continuing to learn so God can make our life of service and witness more fruitful. We learn in many ways—formal courses, conferences, personal study, networking with experienced people, travel, and learning with others as we carry out our life mission. You will find great joy in learning as part of your second half adventure.

St. Paul prays for the Philippian Christians, "that your love may abound more and more in knowledge and in depth of insight, so that you may be able to discern what is best." He is thankful that God has brought them to faith in Jesus Christ and made them partners in the gospel (Philippians 1:3–6). But because of the temptations of a sinful world, the opposition and possible persecution from unbelievers, and the daily challenge of being faithful to God's mission for them, Paul prays for their ongoing growth in love, knowledge, and depth of insight. They will be learning still from God's Word in the school of experience within the fellowship of believers.

In what ways are you learning still? How is the study of God's Word deepening your insight? How does your regular involvement with God's people around Word and Sacrament help you to abound more and more in love? What other learning experiences are equipping you to carry out your life mission? Rest assured that God's Spirit will bring you Christ's forgiveness for confessed sin, comfort when you grow discouraged, joy in learning, and both strength and wisdom for your tasks. Learning still!

*Prayer:* Your living Word shine in our heart
And to a new life win us.
With seed of light implant the start
Of Christ-like deeds within us.
Help us uproot what is impure,
And while faith's fruits in us mature,
Prepare us for your harvest.
*LW* 336:2

# Respect for Externals

## *Reading:* Genesis 45:1–15

*Text:* "I am your brother Joseph, the one you sold into Egypt!" Genesis 45:4b

Bob Buford writes that in the second half of life, people come to have respect for externals, those things that we cannot change because they are beyond our control. In the first half we may have either attacked these externals or denied them. He suggests, "It is through respect that you begin to creatively find ways to turn those externals into opportunities" (p. 154).

In the Old Testament, Joseph provides a marvelous example of a believer who had respect for externals. When his brothers sold him into slavery, he had no choice in the matter. When sold to the official Potiphar, he simply became the best slave he could by God's grace and was put in charge of his master's household. When he resisted the advances of Potiphar's wife and became the victim of her slander, Joseph was thrown into prison, accepted that condition as a model prisoner, and was put in charge of those in the prison. When given an opportunity to interpret Pharaoh's dreams, he relied on God, gave God credit, and was made ruler of all Egypt under Pharaoh to manage the plentiful harvests and the years of famine. His respect for externals enabled him to carry out God's life mission for him of preserving Israel so the promised Messiah could come from Jacob's seed.

Evaluate the externals in your life. Are you attacking them futilely, denying them foolishly, or accepting and respecting them? Confessing the first two options as sin, we turn to our Lord as one who was obedient unto death and, through the binding decisions of religious leaders and a Roman governor, won the victory over sin, death, and the devil. He forgives us and helps us to see externals as opportunities for carrying out our life mission to His glory and for the salvation of many people worldwide. Respect for externals. The mission goes on!

*Prayer:* You fearful saints, fresh courage take;
The clouds you so much dread
Are big with mercy and will break
In blessing on your head.
*LW* 426:4

# The Freedom of Submitting

***Reading:*** **1 Peter 2:13–17**

*Text:* Submit yourselves for the Lord's sake to every authority instituted among men. 1 Peter 2:13

How do you deal with the role of authority in your life? Do you believe that rules are made to be broken? How has that belief affected your home life, your career under an employer, your relationship to government, including law enforcement officials and tax authorities? As sinners, we defy authority and struggle to be free. The more we break the rules, the more we fail to carry out God's life mission for us, and the more we are enslaved.

St. Peter urges his readers, "Submit yourselves for the Lord's sake to every authority instituted among men." You see, God has placed us under the authority of others at home, work, school, church, and in the government. They are His representatives on earth. And we are under God's authority directly and through these earthly rulers. Only within that authority, do we live, save, and witness. We bear witness to Christ through our submission. He set the example by His perfect obedience to the Father and His suffering and death on our behalf. More than an example, "He Himself bore our sins in His body on the tree, so that we might die to sins and live for righteousness; by His wounds you have been healed" (1 Peter 2:24).

Now comes the paradox that frees us to carry out our life mission under His authority. As Martin Luther writes in his *Freedom of the Christian Man*: "The Christian is free lord of all subject to none and the Christian is servant of all, subject to all." Saved by God's grace for Christ's sake through faith, we are free from the law of sin and death. That freedom leads us to submit to God's authority, also through earthly rulers, and to submit ourselves as servants to the needs of others. The freedom of submitting–to set the world ablaze with Christ!

*Prayer:* Earth, hear your Maker's voice;
Your great Redeemer own;
Believe, obey, rejoice,
And worship him alone.
*LW* 500:4

# The "Hidden Wholeness"

***Reading:*** **Romans 6:1–14**

*Text:* But present yourselves to God as those who have been brought from death to life, and your members to God as instruments of righteousness. Romans 6:13b (ESV)

Bob Buford uses Thomas Merton's phrase, the "hidden wholeness," to communicate that all you need is in your life already, that you do not need to chase after things outside of you to find fulfillment, such as money, fame, material possessions, and experiences. Buford summarizes his book in this way: "Whether you're in the first half of your life, in halftime, or playing the second half, God's desire is for you to serve Him just by being who you are, by using what He gave you to work with" (p. 160).

St. Paul in Romans 6 describes our baptismal life in Christ as the center of our relationship to God and our life of service: "We were buried therefore with Him by baptism into death, in order that, just as Christ was raised from the dead by the glory of the Father, we too might walk in newness of life" (v. 4). Our old self crucified with Christ, dead to sin and alive to God in Christ Jesus, we respond to Paul's admonition, "but present yourselves to God as those who have been brought from death to life, and your members to God as instruments of righteousness."

Paul describes our hidden wholeness–Christ *for* us on Calvary, Christ *in* us through our baptismal faith. We have everything we need for salvation and for our life mission to set the world ablaze with Christ. He gifted us in creation, redeemed us through Christ's death and resurrection, and sanctifies us through His Holy Spirit so we can work hand in hand with other believers to make a difference in the world. Repentant and reflective, we pursue God's personal mission for us as part of His worldwide mission.

*Prayer:* Remember what you once received
When called to faith and you believed:
What tested you, what strengthened you,
What Spirit's act made all things new.
Reborn, adopted child of God,
Set out with Him on paths untrod.
*SP* 248:2

Copyright © 2001 Concordia Publishing House

# Grace Place

### *Reading:* 2 Corinthians 12:7–10

*Text:* When anxiety was great within me, Your consolation brought joy to my soul. Psalm 94:19

A physician friend of mine has started a new ministry to Lutheran pastors and their spouses called Grace Place Lutheran Retreats. These retreats provide a "grace place" for "training in attitudes and skills to balance and integrate physical, spiritual, emotional, intellectual and relational health for the purpose of centering their public ministry and personal pilgrim journey in Christ. By God's grace through Christ, good health can encourage vibrancy and longevity in family and ministry life–abundant living." Couples returning to their congregation model integrated health to their members and community, thus energizing God's people in their Christian walk and witness.

The psalmist was sorely in need of such a grace place: "When anxiety was great within me, Your consolation brought joy to my soul." Aware of injustice in the world against the powerless, the psalmist finds his own anxieties, caused by both sin and adverse circumstances, brought before a gracious God who brings consolation in His promises. The result is joy and refreshment for ministry. Paul, suffering for his Gospel witness and burdened with a thorn in the flesh, receives an answer for anxiety from his Lord, "My grace is sufficient for you, for My power is made perfect in weakness" (2 Corinthians 12:9a). Forgiven and restored in God's grace place, Paul is reenergized for ministry to the Gentiles: "That is why, for Christ's sake, I delight in weakness, in insults, in hardships, in persecutions, in difficulties. For when I am weak, then I am strong" (2 Corinthians 12:10).

That's what outreach ministry is all about: providing a grace place in the arms of the crucified and risen Savior for hurting and powerless people worldwide. And our strength for this task requires a daily coming in our weakness and sin to God's grace place in our Baptism. We pray for and support Grace Place Lutheran Retreats that our shepherds may be shepherded to lead us with fresh energy in the great task of connecting people to Jesus.

*Prayer:* Tell of our Redeemer's grace,
Who, to save our human race. . . .
Gave himself as sacrifice.
*LW* 321:3

# Anniversary Memories

### *Reading:* Psalm 128

*Text:* Blessings and prosperity will be yours. Psalm 128:2b

Have you thought about your wedding anniversary as an opportunity to witness about your faith in Jesus Christ? When Gail and I celebrated our 40th anniversary, we invited many friends to our home for an open house. Our children and their spouses generously prepared the food and handled many arrangements. We invited our pastor to lead a brief worship service, including the renewal of our wedding vows. A close pastor friend gave a homily and encouraged comments from our children, and enlisted the guests in prayer for our marriage. My daughter, Amy, memorialized the event by preparing a special decorative photo album, featuring her summary comments about photographs taken by my son, Mark.

That day, those present joined us in thanking God for His years of blessing. Psalm 128 expresses the meaning and promise of that day: "Blessed are all who fear the LORD, who walk in His ways. You will eat the fruit of your labor; blessings and prosperity will be yours. Your wife will be like a fruitful vine within your house; your sons will be like olive shoots around your table. Thus is the man blessed who fears the LORD" (vv. 1–4).

Our celebration made it clear that God's love in Christ was totally responsible for our 40 years together. He brought us together as husband and wife, blessed us with three children, one now in heaven, and seven grandchildren. He sent His Son to die for us, incorporated our entire family into His church through the waters of Baptism, and honors us with the daily privilege of living for Him in witness and service.

We show others the anniversary book of memories and talk about Christ in our years of marriage. Think of your wedding anniversary as a time for witness! Pray for other homes that Christ may dwell there.

*Prayer:* Oh, blest the house whate'er befall,
Where Jesus Christ is all in all!
For if he were not dwelling there,
How dark and poor and void it were!
*LW* 467:1

# Where Generations Meet

***Reading:* Joshua 24:1–18**

*Text:* But as for me and my household, we will serve the LORD. Joshua 24:15

How do you witness of Christ across the generations in your family? Perhaps you might begin by reflecting on events or locations where the generations meet.

On several occasions, Gail and I have met our children and grandchildren at a pizza buffet. Abundant food. Fun. And a place to relate. Busch stadium, home of the St. Louis Cardinals, comes to mind. I took Mark, Amy, and Becky there when they were young. Now we repeat the experience with our grandchildren. There is much anticipation, conversation with nachos during the game, and memories afterward. A summer vacation together at Silver Dollar City in Branson, Missouri, provided much quality time during the trip, at meals, in the hotel, and at the amusement park. And going to church together in St. Louis; Washington, Missouri; or Minnesota focuses on the importance of Jesus Christ in our lives and witness.

The generations also came together at Shechem in the promised land of Canaan. Joshua, near the end of his life, recalls the generations and events of Israel's past–Abraham, Isaac and Jacob, the Egyptian years, freedom and the wilderness years under Moses and Aaron, the conquest of Jericho and settling this land of Canaan. Now he addresses the present generation and asks them to choose whom they will serve–idols of the nations or the true God. Joshua's witness across the generations is clear: "But as for me and my household, we will serve the LORD." The people replied, "We too will serve the LORD because He is our God" (Joshua 24:18).

Whether eating pizza, attending a ball game, vacationing, or worshiping in church, the generational witness is clear: We believe in Jesus as Savior by God's grace. As part of His church, we worship Him regularly and will serve Him every day so others may also believe and be saved.

*Prayer:* Oh, blest that house where faith is found
And all in charity abound
To trust their God and serve him still
And do in all his holy will!
*LW* 467:2

# Advancing the Gospel: In Chains

***Reading:* Philippians 1:1–12**

*Text:* What has happened to me has really served to advance the Gospel. Philippians 1:12b

By the power of God's Spirit, you may have a burning desire to help set the world ablaze with the Good News of Jesus Christ. You may see others going on servant events or mission trips. You may be praying for opportunities to witness of your faith.

But then you find the door clanging shut. You experience chains attached to your hands and feet–a sudden illness that puts you in the hospital, and drains your energy, a family crisis which consumes all your discretionary time, or a confining job where you feel trapped and can barely endure each hour of an endless week. Why is God thwarting your efforts to advance the Gospel worldwide?

Paul, that great missionary to the Gentiles, writes to the Philippian Christians from a very difficult situation. He finds himself in prison or as he describes it: "in chains" (Philippians 1:13). After worldwide travels and many missionary visits to establish new churches, Paul is probably spending time under house arrest in Rome. His future is uncertain. He may be put to death. He is not free to travel and set the world ablaze in new cities.

Yet Paul makes this startling statement: "Now I want you to know, brothers, that what has happened to me has really served to advance the Gospel." The next few devotions will unpack how Paul is able to advance the Gospel while "in chains." But for now, consider how a loving and forgiving God through Christ's death and resurrection might be using the prisons and chains of your life circumstances to "advance the Gospel" to His glory and for saving the lost around you.

*Prayer:* When I suffer pains and losses,
Lord, be near, let me hear
Comfort under crosses.
Point me, Father, to the heaven
Which your Son for me won
When his life was given.
*LW* 423:1

Copyright © 1982 Concordia Publishing House

# Advancing the Gospel: Palace Guard

## *Reading:* Acts 16:16–34

*Text:* It has become clear throughout the palace guard and to everyone else that I am in chains for Christ. Philippians 1:13

Paul, "in chains," advances the Gospel by making it clear to the whole palace guard that he is imprisoned because of his faith in Christ as his Savior from sin. The whole palace guard in Rome was a contingent of several thousand soldiers, many of whom would have had personal contact with Paul as his guard over the two years of his house arrest (Acts 28:16, 30). The word apparently spread among them that he both lived and proclaimed Christ-crucified and risen to his guards and the many other groups that visited him.

The Philippian Christians would no doubt have remembered the time when Paul and Silas had first visited their city, were dragged into the marketplace, stripped and beaten by the magistrates, thrown into prison in the inner cell with their feet in stocks, and carefully guarded by the jailer. They also would have recalled Paul and Silas praying and singing hymns to God at midnight with the other prisoners listening and the conversion of the jailer and his family after a jarring earthquake, when Paul kept all the prisoners from escaping. His actions and words about Jesus clearly advanced the Gospel.

Consider for a moment the prisons of your life–home, job, or other difficult circumstances. Your "guards" or fellow "prisoners" are watching and listening to you day by day. As you openly confess your sins and cling to Christ's cross for forgiveness through Word and Sacraments, as you live for Him humbly and faithfully in your daily calling, the Gospel is advanced "throughout the whole palace guard" because they see that you are "in chains for Christ."

*Prayer:* Dear Lord, thanks for the example of Saint Paul in prison. Help me to examine the "prisons of my life" and see them not as burdens but as opportunities for relying on the Spirit's power to live each day faithfully and compassionately so others may believe in Your salvation won for us on the cross. Amen.

# Advancing the Gospel: Brothers Encouraged

## Reading: Philippians 1:19–30

*Text:* Because of my chains, most of the brothers in the Lord have been encouraged to speak the word of God more courageously and fearlessly. Philippians 1:14

Paul "in chains" advances the Gospel in another powerful way. Many of those who visit him during his house arrest and many to whom he writes during his imprisonment are "encouraged to speak the word of God more courageously and fearlessly."

Paul is quite honest about his difficulties. He asks and thanks the Philippians for their prayers and credits "the help given by the Spirit of Jesus Christ" (Philippians 1:19). He trusts the Lord, that he will not be ashamed but "have sufficient courage so that now as always Christ will be exalted in [his] body, whether by life or by death" (Philippians 1:20).

His example of humility and courage emboldens the Philippians. He writes to them, "I will know that you stand firm in one spirit, contending as one man for the faith of the Gospel, without being frightened in any way by those who oppose you" (Philippians 1:27b–28a). The Gospel is advanced through Christians encouraged to speak and live boldly.

Have you considered how your example of speaking and living boldly for Christ while experiencing "prisons" and "chains" in your life might encourage other believers to do the same by the power of God's Spirit? Your candor about your own sin and weakness, your embrace of God's forgiveness through Christ, your reliance on the prayers of others and the help of the Spirit in Word and Sacraments will be used by God to embolden other Christians to speak and live boldly. The Gospel is advanced.

*Prayer:* For all your saints, O Lord, Who strove in you to live,
Who followed you, obeyed, adored, Our grateful hymn receive

For all your saints, O Lord, Who strove in you to die,
Who counted you their great reward, Accept our thankful cry.

They all in life and death, With you, their Lord, in view
Learned from your Holy Spirit's breath To suffer and to do.

For this your name we bless And humbly pray anew
That we like them in holiness May live and die in you.
*LW* 195:1–4

# Advancing the Gospel: Even out of Envy

## Reading: Philippians 1:15–18

*Text:* It is true that some preach Christ out of envy and rivalry, but others out of goodwill. Philippians 1:15

Amazingly, Paul recognizes that the Gospel is advanced even by his detractors who preach Christ out of envy and rivalry. What a generous and selfless spirit he demonstrates. While he suffers "in chains" for Christ, Paul knows that some "preach Christ out of selfish ambition, not sincerely, supposing that they can stir up trouble for me while I am in chains" (Philippians 1:17). These preachers preach a true, orthodox message but their motives are not pure. They see themselves in competition with Paul and want to make his imprisonment harder to bear.

Paul cares most about the spread of the Gospel so many will believe in Christ as their Savior. Therefore, despite being attacked and misrepresented by those who envy him, Paul is able to write: "But what does it matter? The important thing is that in every way, whether from false motives or true, Christ is preached. And because of this, I rejoice" (Philippians 1:18).

Do you find it difficult to deal with fellow Christians who seem to criticize or judge you in the "prisons" and "chains" of your life? In the midst of trials and suffering, you seek to advance the Gospel in your daily life of confession and absolution and your witness to Jesus as Savior. But some witness to Jesus with pure doctrine but with a lack of love and respect for you. How easy it would be to condemn them.

Paul's example moves us to repentance. He points us to priority number one–advancing the Gospel, no matter what the motives. That Gospel assures us, first of all, that God forgives our sins for Jesus' sake, our crucified and risen Savior. Then that Gospel moves us to a generous and unselfish spirit of rejoicing whenever the Gospel is proclaimed in its truth and purity so many are saved for time and for eternity.

*Prayer:* Oh, grant that nothing in my soul
May dwell but your pure love alone;
Oh, may your love possess me whole,
My joy, my treasure, and my crown!
All coldness from my heart remove;
My ev'ry act, word, thought be love.
*LW* 280

# No Idol Threat

## Reading: Psalm 115

*Text:* But their idols are silver and gold, made by the hands of men. Psalm 115:4

Have you ever been filled with fear by the chilling, authoritative word of someone with sinister intent–an armed thief, a fanatical terrorist, a cruel boss, or a vindictive teacher? You recognize that their words are no idle threat.

When you seek to set the world ablaze with the saving Good News of Jesus Christ, do you sometimes tremble with fear because someone may speak a challenging word of skepticism or atheism or loud allegiance to another religion or god? Do you hear their words as no idle threat?

The psalmist apparently faced criticism from the nations against the God of Israel. "Why do the nations say, 'Where is their God?'" (Psalm 115:2). Does he tremble because these words are no idle threat? To the contrary, the psalmist replies, "Our God is in heaven; He does whatever pleases Him. But their idols are silver and gold, made by the hands of men" (Psalm 115:3–4). The psalmist goes on to ridicule these idols as having mouths that cannot speak, eyes that cannot see, ears that cannot hear, noses that cannot smell, hands that cannot feel, and feet that cannot walk (Psalm 115: 3–7). He adds that those who make them will be just like them as will those who trust in them (Psalm 115:8). In effect, the psalmist is saying: Don't be afraid. There is no idol threat.

The psalmist's words to Israel are God's words to us as we witness boldly of salvation through faith in Jesus Christ: "You who fear Him, trust in the LORD–He is their help and their shield. The LORD remembers us and will bless us. . . . He will bless those who fear the LORD–small and great alike" (Psalm 115:11–13). Those who attack us bring an idle threat because there is no idol threat for those safe in the arms of Jesus.

*Prayer:* I am trusting you, Lord Jesus. Trusting only you;
Trusting you for full salvation. Free and true.

I am trusting you for power; You can never fail.
Words which you yourself shall give me Must prevail.
*LW* 408:1, 5

# America: Lost and Found

**Reading: Luke 15:1–10**

*Text:* "Rejoice with me; I have found my lost sheep." Luke 15:6b

The well-known parable about the lost sheep provides a different perspective on our country as we prepare to celebrate Independence Day. Where does America stand today?

Like the Pharisees and teachers of the law in the Bible reading, we often think we have arrived. We fancy our supremacy in the world and our high standard of living. We may even look down upon less fortunate peoples of the world. The Pharisees murmured that Jesus ate with tax collectors and sinners.

In reality America is lost whenever we attempt to succeed on our own power. We have chinks in our armor. We no longer control everything in world affairs. Other nations sometimes outstrip us in industrial productivity. We struggle with moral corruption and the breakdown of our families. Personally we fall short of God's glory. We often live selfishly instead of serving God. The Pharisees were lost but refused to admit their condition. Could we be more like the one lost sheep than the ninety-nine?

But God wants to find America. The Shepherd goes out of His way to seek us. He finds us confused and lost, bruised and bleeding, tired and forlorn. He takes us in His arms and brings us home. He has given His life for the sheep. America is found. God restores us to our heritage as a nation under Him. He forgives our arrogance and helps us share our bounty. He turns the Christians of America from self to His love. Once lost and now found, we rejoice in finding the lost. God bless America!

Where does America stand? Wrong question. We kneel before God in confession and let God find us in Jesus Christ.

*Prayer:* Dear Father, thank You for finding us lost sheep and restoring us to the fold. Help us to seek the lost at home and abroad, for Jesus' sake. Amen.

# A Culture Desperate for God

## Reading: Jonah 3:1–10

*Text:* "Let everyone call urgently on God. Let them give up their evil ways and their violence." Jonah 3:8b

Much has been written recently about institutional churches declining in America and Europe. Much has also been written about the evil in our world–declining moral standards, open hostility toward Christianity, and the proliferation of many religions and philosophies. Yet, at the same time, there are signs of an intense spiritual interest in our society. At times of crisis, whether the terrorist attacks of September 11, 2001, or shooting sprees in local schools, people flock to churches for spiritual comfort and direction. In some ways, we live in a culture desperate for God.

Based on a book by Reggie McNeal, entitled *The Present Future*, the next several devotions will describe the perspectives of this postmodern culture and use Scripture to explore ways to bring Christ to people as the only way to salvation and the only strength for daily living. Certainly our churches, gathered around Word and Sacraments, can send us forth as missionaries to reach a culture desperate for God. But we need discernment and the Spirit's power.

The people of Nineveh lived in wickedness and were headed for destruction. A reluctant prophet named Jonah left the comfort of Israel and went to them, after a detour in the belly of a great fish, to walk through the city and preach repentance. Amazingly, the whole city became desperate for God. The heathen king and his nobles wrote these words, "Let everyone call urgently on God. Let them give up their evil ways and their violence." The text simply records the grace-filled response of the Lord: "When God saw what they did and how they turned from their evil ways, He had compassion and did not bring upon them the destruction He had threatened" (Jonah 3:10).

However reluctant you might feel and estranged from our culture desperate for God, will you, by God's grace, join Jonah to walk through the cities and villages to listen and learn and to present Christ as Savior?

*Prayer:* Listen, listen God is calling<br>
Through the Word inviting,<br>
Offering forgiveness.<br>
Comfort and joy.<br>
*HS* 98 872, refrain

July 6

# Counting for Something

## Reading: Ephesians 2:6–10

*Text:* For we are God's workmanship, created in Christ Jesus to do good works, which God prepared in advance for us to do. Ephesians 2:10

One characteristic of the postmodern person is a desire to count for something as an individual. Reggie McNeal in *The Present Future* calls it "the Power of One." In our Internet society, an individual has broad access to information and can make a significant impact on society. Negatively, a teenage computer hacker can inflict millions of dollars of damage on corporations through a computer "virus." Positively, one individual can start a successful business from the home. Spiritually, many postmoderns want to make a difference in the world by participating in meaningful service.

The Christian message brings hope to such a person. Paul makes it clear that we are saved by grace through faith in Jesus Christ, not of ourselves, as the gift of God, not of works. But then he goes on to say in our text, "For we are God's workmanship, created in Christ Jesus to do good works, which God prepared in advance for us to do." Counted righteous for Christ's sake, each person also counts for something in daily life as a missionary of the Savior. Using God's gifts in service to others creates a hearing for the saving Gospel. God's Spirit gives each of us a unique mission in our places of influence to help set the world ablaze.

How can you relate to an unchurched friend who wants to count for something but is not looking to the church as a possible help? Might you listen to his hopes and dreams, frustrations and discouragements first? In what ways could you involve your friend in meaningful service with other Christians and in a simple study of Paul's words in Ephesians 2? What might be the right moment for you to talk about your relationship to Christ as Savior and how you find meaning in living as God's workmanship, created in Christ Jesus to do good works?

*Prayer:*

Teach us the lesson Jesus taught:
To feel for those his blood has bought,
That ev'ry deed and word and thought
May work a work for you.
*LW* 397:3

# Getting Connected

## Reading: Ephesians 2:11–22

*Text:* Consequently, you are no longer foreigners and aliens, but fellow citizens with God's people and members of God's household. Ephesians 2:19

A second characteristic of the postmodern person paradoxically is the importance of getting connected with others, while at the same time, desiring individual power. The Internet both empowers the individual and connects with others through websites and chatrooms. Cell phones abound to connect people. Large bookstores offer coffee bars and comfortable seating arrangements. Political, community, and charitable causes link people with the same interests, beliefs, and values.

Where does the Church fit in with the importance of getting connected? Unfortunately many postmoderns don't even consider church involvement, viewing churches as divisive, unwelcoming, or irrelevant to their needs. Try visiting restaurants or other gathering places on Sunday morning and observe people, many of whom don't give church attendance a passing thought.

Yet God's Church is the ultimate connecting and unifying factor in the world. Paul writes to the Ephesians about Christ's Church in glowing terms, "Consequently, you are no longer foreigners and aliens, but fellow citizens with God's people and members of Christ's household." Christ Himself is our peace, who has made Jews and Gentiles one new person and in this one body has reconciled both of them to God through the cross "by which He put to death our hostility" (Ephesians 2:16). Christ brings us together–moderns and postmoderns, all generations, ethnic groups, social classes, church people, and those who have no church background. We are "built on the foundation of the apostles and prophets, with Christ Jesus Himself as the chief cornerstone" (Ephesians 2:20).

Gathered around Word and Sacraments, we scatter to make connections in the neighborhood, community, workplace, and yes, on the Internet. Showing personal caring, we invite, include, and share Christ with postmodern friends so they, by God's grace, might believe in Jesus and join the fully connected family of all believers.

*Prayer:* Blest be the tie that binds Our hearts in Christian love;
The unity of heart and mind Is like to that above.
We share our mutual woes, Our mutual burdens bear,
And often for each other flows The sympathizing tear.
*LW* 295:1, 3

# Searching for Meaning

## Reading: Ephesians 1:3–14

*Text:* For He chose us in Him before the creation of the world to be holy and blameless in His sight. Ephesians 1:4

A third characteristic of the postmodern person is searching for meaning. "Why am I here? What is my purpose in life? There must be more to life than punching a time card, filling a slot, and living the rat race." That is why many postmoderns join a worldwide cause, engage in service projects, and experiment with all kinds of religions and philosophies which might provide meaning to their existence.

What an opportunity for Christian witness! St. Paul's letter to the Ephesians addresses this search in a powerful way: "For He chose us in Him before the creation of the world to be holy and blameless in His sight." Paul soars to unbelievable heights in verses 3–14 of chapter one, one sentence in the original Greek language, as he describes God's plan for the universe and for each believer. The God and Father of our Lord Jesus Christ blessed us with every spiritual blessing, chose us in Christ, predestined us to be adopted as His children through Christ, who redeemed us through His blood, the forgiveness of sins, and marked us in Christ with the seed of the promised Holy Spirit. All of this lavish grace is for a purpose: that we would live to the praise of His glory, holy and blameless in His sight as He brings all things in heaven and on earth together under one head, even Christ.

When our baptismal faith in Christ based on His purpose for us moves us into the community to serve Him in practical ways, we have opportunity to join postmoderns in their search for meaning and bear witness to God's eternal purpose for them to believe in Jesus as Savior, join the fellowship of believers, and live each day to the praise of His glory.

*Prayer:* This is a time to pause and ask:
"Why was I born, and for what task,
Why in a certain time and place,
And on which road to run life's race,
The calling on that New-Birthday
By Christ, the Life, the Truth, the Way?"
*SP* 248:1

Copyright © 2001 Concordia Publishing House

# Wildly Spiritual

### Reading: Colossians 2:8–23

*Text:* We have not stopped praying for you and asking God to fill you with the knowledge of His will, through all spiritual wisdom and understanding. Colossians 1:9b

A fourth characteristic of postmoderns is that they are "wildly spiritual." As Christians we spent most of the twentieth century defending against people with a scientific world view who denied the reality of anything you could not touch, see, or measure. We argued for the reality of the spiritual world ruled by God the Creator of the universe, both seen and unseen. Now postmoderns believe in the spiritual realm, accept miracles, explore gods and goddesses, as well as demons and witches. In their spiritual quest, they sample a smorgasbord of New Age religion, Eastern religions, and also Christian beliefs in Jesus Christ. Often they develop their own homemade religion from the above elements. But they are looking outside themselves to the spiritual world for help, recognizing how the scientific approach has failed to solve the world's problems.

St. Paul lived in a similar world that was "wildly spiritual." Each culture had its gods and goddesses. Sorcerers performed miracles. Into this world seeking help from outside, Paul proclaimed the true God who sent His only Son Jesus as a real human being to die on a cross for the sins of the world and to rise miraculously from the grave on the third day. His Spirit brought people to faith through the Word of Christ.

Against all secret religions with their "superior" spiritual wisdom, Paul arms the Colossian Christians by praying for "God to fill you with the knowledge of His will, through all spiritual wisdom and understanding." He prepares them for spiritual warfare against Satan and all false spiritual teachings.

What an opportunity for bringing our Savior to those on a spiritual quest! God is alive in today's world, exposing false religions and pointing to new life through faith in Christ and an ongoing spiritual growth in the company of God's people gathered around Word and Sacraments. He sends you, filled "with spiritual wisdom," into this "wildly spiritual" world to share Jesus as Savior.

*Prayer:* Holy Spirit, ground us in all spirtual wisdom through Your Word so we can reach the "wildly spiritual" with Christ. Amen.

# United by Brokenness

### Reading: 2 Corinthians 4:5–12

*Text:* But we have this treasure in jars of clay to show that this all-surpassing power is from God and not from us. 2 Corinthians 4:7

A fifth characteristic of postmoderns is that they see the world as united by brokenness. People are broken inside. Families and communities are broken and divided. Systems in society are broken. Disease, poverty, wars, natural calamities bring brokenness to people. Postmoderns desire to bring love and hope, to repair relationships so this brokenness may be healed.

What an important connecting point for our Christian witness! We know the reality of brokenness because of sin in the world and our own sin. As Paul writes to the Corinthians, "We have this treasure in jars of clay." One could also translate it, common clay pots or cracked-pots. Although an apostle, he knows his humanity. He has been hard-pressed, perplexed, persecuted, and struck down. He understands brokenness. We can identify with Paul and postmoderns because of our sin in a sinful world. We are united in brokenness.

But St. Paul almost rejoices in that brokenness because God has healed him. "But we do not preach ourselves, but Jesus Christ as Lord, and ourselves as your servants for Jesus' sake" (2 Corinthians 4:5). The cross is a symbol for brokenness. Jesus took our sin upon Himself on the cross and won the victory. His body was broken and His blood shed for us. As a result, Paul sees the light of Christ shining through his own "cracked pot" to show that the "surpassing power is from God and not from us." He adds, "We always carry around in our body the death of Jesus, so that the life of Jesus may also be revealed in our body" (2 Corinthians 4:10).

We let God reveal Jesus' death and life through our brokenness. Jesus is our priceless treasure. Then we invite postmoderns to find healing for their brokenness in Jesus so that together we might unite with them to bring Jesus' light and healing to a broken world.

*Prayer:* Come in sorrow and contrition,
Wounded, impotent, and blind,
Here the guilty, free remission,
Here the troubled, peace may find
Your true health it will restore,
So that you need thirst no more.
*LW* 96:2

# A World out of Whack

## Reading: Ephesians 2:1–5

*Text:* To bring all things in heaven and on earth together under one head even Christ. Ephesians 1:10b

A sixth characteristic of postmoderns is a sense of corporate guilt that the world is out of whack. They look around at their cities and find massive problems of poverty and decay or bureaucratic inefficiency. They criticize their nation for neglect of environmental issues or failure to deal with immigration problems. They look at the world in terms of terrorism, wars, racial hatred, rampant diseases such as AIDS, and conflict between the haves and the have-nots. In short, the world is not the loving place it is supposed to be. What can be done to make a difference short-term and long-term in a world out of whack?

St. Paul, writing to the Ephesians, has no idealistic views of the world because he knows the reality of sin, death, and the devil. He simply says, "You were dead in your trespasses and sins, in which you used to live when you followed the ways of this world and of the ruler of the kingdom of the air" (Ephesians 2:1–2). He further describes the world's behavior as "gratifying the cravings of our sinful nature and following its desires and thoughts" (Ephesians 2:3). A world out of whack!

But Paul also gives us reason to enter that world with faith in Christ and live with purpose to help put the world straight in matters of peace, compassion, and justice. He describes God's intent in Jesus Christ through His Church: "To bring all things in heaven and on earth together under one head, even Christ."

What a mission challenge! Sharing the postmodern concern for a world out of whack, we can join them in constructive efforts to make a better world and seize the opportunity in the process to point them to Jesus crucified and risen, as the only way to salvation.

*Prayer:* O God, whose will is life and good
For all of mortal breath,
Unite in bonds of servanthood
All those who strive with death.

Make strong their binds and hearts and wills
To drive disease afar,
To strive against the body's ills
And wage your healing war.
*LW* 396:1–2

July 12

# In Search of Sacred Space

## Reading: Acts 17:16–31

*Text:* "The God who made the world and everything in it is the Lord of heaven and earth and does not live in temples built by hands." Acts 17:24

A seventh characteristic of postmoderns is that they are in search of sacred space. Because they recognize the importance of spiritual things and are searching for meaning, they seek places for spiritual meditation. After September 11, 2001, they flocked to churches. They visit the Ground Zero shrine with towers of light beaming heavenward as symbols of hope. After the death of well-known people like Princess Diana or President Reagan, they place flowers and artifacts near the home or mourn other senseless deaths by violence with candlelight vigils. They are in search of sacred space.

Again, Christians have opportunity to use sacred space as a witness to the one true God–Father, Son, and Holy Spirit. Our churches can be open at special times of crisis or celebration to point to Jesus, the Savior. But we can also create sacred space out in the world in the name of Jesus, whether in malls, bookstores, schools, community centers or homes.

St. Paul, in his famous Mars Hill speech, moves right to the Areopagus in Athens and, pointing to a statue called "To an Unknown God," proclaims the true God who made the world as the Lord of heaven and earth and who does not live in temples built by hands. He then connects that God with the One He sent to an ignorant, sinful world to die on the cross and rise from the dead–Jesus Christ.

Worshiping that God around Word and Sacrament in the sacred space of our churches, we can move out into God's world and respect the search of postmoderns for sacred space by inviting them to join us and by proclaiming the Word of Christ where they are, thus creating sacred space in the heart of daily living.

*Prayer:* Gracious God, I come before thee;
Come thou also unto me;
Where we find thee and adore thee,
There a heav'n on earth must be.
To my heart, oh, enter thou,
Let it be thy temple now!
*LW* 198:2

# Expecting Miracles

## Reading: Acts 14:8–18

*Text:* "We are bringing you good news, telling you to turn from the worthless things to the living God." Acts 14:15b

An eighth characteristic of postmoderns is that they expect miracles to happen. What a far cry from the rational scientific view of modernism, denying any supernatural phenomena. Postmoderns look for signs in the stars. They see people healed and credit supernatural powers. Unfortunately, they don't usually look to the true God who sent His Son Jesus as the source of miracles.

The religious pagans of Paul's day also expected miracles. When Paul and Barnabas came to Lystra, they found a man crippled in his feet from birth. Paul looked directly at him, saw that he had faith to be healed and called out, "Stand up on your feet!" (Acts 14:10). The man jumped up and began to walk. The crowd's reaction is amazing. They shouted, "The gods have come down to us in human form!" (Acts 14:1). The local priest of Zeus came with bulls and wreaths so they could offer sacrifice to them. While very misguided, they obviously expected miracles to happen. Postmoderns can easily relate to this story.

But Barnabas and Paul tore their clothes and shouted to the crowd that they were merely human beings like the rest of the people. Then they used the miracle to give their clear witness: "We are bringing you good news, telling you to turn from these worthless things to the living God." Unfortunately, this crowd could not be persuaded and later stoned Paul and left him for dead. Nevertheless, some believed in Jesus as Savior.

We have opportunity, although sometimes not without risk, to walk in the midst of postmoderns with our confidence in the one true God to introduce people to salvation through faith in the crucified Christ. False gods, fascination with the supernatural, a "theology of glory" are "worthless things." The living God teaches a "theology of the cross" and presents Himself in the miraculous waters of Baptism and the bread and wine of the Sacrament. Miracles happen today, also for postmoderns, through our witness!

*Prayer:* Holy Spirit, use my witness to Jesus Christ as Savior to bring the miracle of rebirth to those expecting miracles. Amen.

# Divine Purpose in Everything

## Reading: Colossians 1:15–23

*Text:* He is before all things, and in Him all things hold together. Colossians 1:17

A ninth characteristic of postmoderns is their desire to find a divine purpose in everything. McNeal writes, "There are no coincidences. Everything is purposefully connected as proof of a loving God who wants people to love each other" (*The Present Future*, p. 58). This can be illustrated by Mark McGwire's breaking of Babe Ruth's and Roger Maris's home run records in 1998, with the Maris family in the stands and the karma emanating from Babe Ruth's bat in the Baseball Hall of Fame. It was *supposed* to happen that way (the later steroid controversy not withstanding).

Scripture clearly teaches that there is a divine purpose in everything, an excellent bridge to reaching postmoderns. In Colossians, Paul describes Christ in this fashion, "He is before all things, and in Him all things hold together." As the image of the invisible God, the firstborn over all creation, Christ is the head of the body, the Church. "For God was pleased to have all His fullness dwell in Him, and through Him to reconcile to Himself all things, whether things on earth or things in heaven, by making peace through His blood, shed on the cross" (Colossians 1:19–20). Once alienated from God and enemies in your minds because of your evil behavior, you have now been reconciled "by Christ's physical body, through death to present you holy in His sight, without blemish and free from accusation" (Colossians 1:22).

What a message to share with postmoderns about God's divine purpose in everything through Christ! Not a general, feel-good, superstitious sense of purposeful connection, but a solid, objective, life-transforming reality that leads us and postmoderns to the cross of Christ and a life of service in the world. Paul's endnote to this section speaks to us: "This is the gospel that you heard and that has been proclaimed to every creature under heaven, and of which, I, Paul, have become a servant" (Colossians 1:23b).

*Prayer:* New in outlook, new in hope,
Heightened vision, broadened scope;
In them glows a love divine,
Through them Jesus' virtues shine.
*HS 98* 835:8

Copyright © 1990 Concordia Publishing House

# Institutional-Brand Religion?

## Reading: Revelation 3:1–6

*Text:* "I know your deeds; you have a reputation of being alive, but you are dead." Revelation 3:1b

We have examined nine characteristics of postmoderns in an effort to understand their perspectives. In the next few devotions we will consider how today's church might best respond to a postmodern society with the Gospel of Jesus Christ. First, postmoderns often see churches like any other institution in society–retail businesses, corporations, government agencies, or even country clubs seeking memberships. They see competing denominations, each with its own brand, offering a certain product with expectations of attendance, voluntary participation, and financial contributions. No wonder they are reluctant to join a church.

God's Church, we know, is not like that characterization. But we would do well to start with an honest look at ourselves and our motives. In Revelation, the apostle John writes letters to seven churches in Asia Minor with words of both judgment and mercy. To the church in Sardis, he writes, "I know your deeds; you have a reputation of being alive, but you are dead." Strong words of judgment! Apparently in this city of great wealth and fame, the church was glorying in its reputation as a lively church but had departed from the message of Christ and a humble servant life for others. He says, "Remember, therefore, what you have received and heard; obey it, and repent" (Revelations 3:3).

Our church listens, remembers, and repents. Turning again to Christ as Savior, reflecting on His Word, reviewing our attitudes and approaches to the community, we receive God's forgiveness in the Sacraments and pray that we would present ourselves to postmoderns not as institutional-brand religion but as forgiven sinners, loving one another and available to serve others with the saving love of Jesus.

*Prayer:* Help us to serve you evermore
With hearts both pure and lowly;
And may your Word, that light divine,
Shine on in splendor holy
That we repentance show, In faith ever grow;
The pow'r of sin destroy And evil that annoy.
Oh, make us faithful Christians.
*LW* 293:3

# A Genuine Christian Movement

**Reading: Acts 2:42–47**

*Text:* They devoted themselves to the apostles' teaching and to the fellowship, to the breaking of bread and to prayer. . . . And the Lord added to their number daily those who were being saved. Acts 2:42, 47b

The best antidote to any charge of institutional-brand religion is letting God's Spirit work through the Church as a genuine Christian movement. The early Christians after Pentecost were seen as just such a movement. The Book of Acts describes their faithfulness to the apostles' teaching, their regular fellowship together around the Sacrament of Holy Communion and prayer. Furthermore, they experienced the reality of God's presence in wonders and miraculous signs, obvious love for one another, willingness to share possessions, and witness to the community around them. The result of their joyful worship and lives of thankful service, enjoying the favor of all the people, was a consistent missionary effort: "And the Lord added to their number daily those who were being saved." The world was being set ablaze with Christ through this genuine Christian movement.

In what ways can your church be used by God's Spirit to make a difference in this postmodern world? Faithfulness to Scripture and the Lutheran Confessions comes first. Regular fellowship together around Word and Sacraments is paramount. God, then, fills us with love and joy for one another and a burning desire to spread the Word of Christ in our communities and world. That faith in our Savior becomes contagious and touches many lives of postmoderns as we live out our relationship to Jesus through loving service. And the Lord will add daily those who are being saved. Repentant and forgiven, we join this genuine Christian movement that will indeed set the world ablaze!

*Prayer:* O mighty Rock, O Source of life,
Let your good Word in doubt and strife
Be in us strongly burning
That we be faithful unto death
And live in love and holy faith,
From you true wisdom learning.
Lord, your mercy on us shower,
By your power Christ-confessing,
We will cherish all your blessing.
*LW* 160:3

# Superior Reasoning?

## Reading: 1 Corinthians 1:18–25

*Text:* For the message of the cross is foolishness to those who are perishing, but to us who are being saved it is the power of God. 1 Corinthians 1:18

Is superior reasoning the best approach to postmoderns with the saving Gospel? In a modern world, everything needed to be logical and scientific in its approach. We learned to make well-reasoned arguments for the claims of Christianity. But postmoderns view their lives in a much more experiential way, valuing relationships and spirituality much more highly than reasoned discourse. They are accustomed to sound-bites and visual images and personal endorsements of friends or like-minded people.

Paul can teach us how to be missionaries in a culture that closely resembles his own in terms of spiritual landscape. He tried superior reasoning in his speech on Mars Hill as we observed previously. He argued eloquently that the true God was vastly superior to all other religions, but with little positive response. No wonder he stressed the importance of the Christian life to the new churches as a better way of engaging the culture.

To the Corinthians, he writes these words, "For the message of the cross is foolishness to those who are perishing, but to us who are being saved, it is the power of God." You see, God's Spirit works deep in our hearts to reveal the hopelessness of our human efforts and the need for God's salvation through the humiliating death of His Son on the cross in payment for the world's sin. Foolishness to the world's wisdom, but God's wisdom and power for us who believe.

We believe. We join to worship that saving God. We love one another. We live our faith out in the world. By God's Spirit, postmoderns notice the integrity of our faith and life. They want to know more about our God. And God brings them to faith in the cross of Christ. Not superior reasoning, but God's power through our humble witness to Christ-crucified!

*Prayer:* Your light to ev'ry sense impart,
And shed your love in ev'ry heart;
Your own unfailing might supply
To strengthen our infirmity.
*LW* 156:4

# Superior Living and Loving

## Reading: 2 Thessalonians 1:1–12

*Text:* With this in mind, we constantly pray for you that God may count you worthy of His calling. 2 Thessalonians 1:11

If not superior reasoning as the best approach to postmoderns, then what approach will be more effective? The simple answer: superior living and superior loving. In a world where words are cheap and voluminous, postmoderns look more to authentic lives, lived with love. If they can relate to you on a personal level and trust you, they are more likely to listen to your Christian witness.

St. Paul, for reasons of mission strategy, writes to all of the churches under his responsibility about the importance of their daily Christian lives in a decadent world. Yes, he is concerned about moral standards consistent with God's Law. But he knows that superior living and loving by the power of God's Spirit will bring many to a saving faith in Jesus Christ.

To the Thessalonians, he writes, "With this in mind, we constantly pray for you that God may count you worthy of His calling." They are suffering for their faith. They know Christ may return again soon. They are learning to love one another more and more as their faith grows. They are tempted to fall back into their old sinful lifestyles and to quit their jobs in view of Christ's coming again. But a forgiving God working through His Word and Sacraments is making them worthy of His calling and fulfilling His purpose in their lives of service, prompted by their faith. As a result, the name of their Lord Jesus is being glorified so many others will believe in Him.

Superior living and superior loving by God's grace for Christ's sake will make a powerful witness to postmoderns so they will believe in the name of Jesus as their Savior and join the community of the faithful, living and loving to His glory!

*Prayer:* Give me the strength to do With ready heart and willing
Whatever you command, My calling here fulfilling.
Help me do what I should With all my might, and bless
The outcome for my good For you must give success.
*LW* 371:2

# A Vibrant Relationship with Jesus

## Reading: Philippians 3:7–10

*Text:* What is more, I consider everything a loss compared to the surpassing greatness of knowing Christ Jesus my Lord, for whose sake I have lost all things. Philippians 3:8

Our devotions on the characteristics of postmoderns and effective ways to respond to them with the Gospel come to an end today. A vibrant relationship with Jesus, the gift of God's Spirit, serves as an attractive way to live and has the potential to intrigue postmoderns. This summarizes all of the responses we have considered.

St. Paul writes to the Philippians about God's grace in his life. He starts out by describing his former way of life—the right Hebrew pedigree, trained in the law as a Pharisee, zealous to the point of persecuting the church, faultless in legalistic righteousness. But now he has seen the light of Christ and everything else pales by comparison. "I consider everything a loss [human garbage or refuse] compared to the surpassing greatness of knowing Christ Jesus my Lord, for whose sake I have lost all things." He explains that none of this new relationship stems from his own righteousness that comes from the law but from "that which is through faith in Christ—the righteousness which comes from God and is by faith" (Philippians 3:9).

Those who know Paul see his vibrant relationship with Jesus. He confesses his sin regularly. He always points to Jesus Christ crucified. He lives that relationship through persecution and suffering. He is willing to give his life so others might believe in Jesus and experience a similar saving relationship. His faith and life influence prison guards, fiery opponents, government officials, hardened sailors, slaves, and successful business leaders.

Pray that God will use your vibrant relationship with Jesus to reach postmoderns desperately in need of salvation so your world will be set ablaze with Jesus Christ.

*Prayer:* Now carry out at any cost
A rescue mission for the lost
Before this time of grace runs out:
This is what life is all about.
God's loving plan is there for all
Who heed the Savior's urgent call.
*SP* 248:3

Copyright © 2001 Concordia Publishing House

# A Sunday on the Acropolis

## Reading: Acts 17:16–23

*Text:* "May we know what this new teaching is that you are presenting?" Acts 17:19b

On a recent trip, we visited Athens and toured the ancient Greek Acropolis with its Parthenon, Propylaia, Erechtheion, and Temple of Athena Nike. Our guide, Maria, talked almost reverently about the glory of ancient Greek ideas and ideals, embodied in this classical architecture. Later, as I climbed Mars Hill just west of the Acropolis where Paul was invited to join Epicurean and Stoic philosophers in the Council of the Areopagus, I sensed both the awe and the distress Paul must have felt amidst the grandeur, wisdom, and idolatry of ancient Athens.

Paul was preaching the good news about Jesus and the resurrection. He was greatly distressed to see the city full of idols. Day by day he reasoned in the synagogue with Jews and God-fearing Greeks and in the marketplace or Agora with the philosophers. They called him a babbler, advocating foreign gods, but were willing to give him a hearing on the Aesopagus: "May we know what this new teaching is that you are presenting?" The author of Acts adds that the Athenians and the foreigners who lived there did nothing but talk about and listen to the latest ideas.

In that context, Paul preached his famous sermon to the unknown God, calling for repentance from idolatry and clearly identifying Jesus, the man He appointed, as the risen Savior. A few men became followers of Jesus but some sneered at the resurrection of the dead and others were willing to debate further on an intellectual level. What courage and discernment Paul displayed in proclaiming the Gospel!

My Sunday visit to the Acropolis moved me to consider this twenty-first century world with its technological achievements, love of philosophical discussions, and pluralistic idolatry. Will I rely on God's Holy Spirit to proclaim Jesus as crucified and risen Savior each day and have the courage to join with unbelievers in discussing the only way to salvation?

*Prayer:* My gracious Master and my God,
Assist me to proclaim,
To spread through all the earth abroad
The honors of your name.
*LW* 276:2

# The Bema in Corinth: A Safe Place to Stand

**Reading: Acts 18:1–17**

*Text:* "Do not be afraid; keep on speaking, do not be silent. For I am with you, and no one is going to attack and harm you." Acts 18:9–10

From Athens, we visited the ruins of ancient Corinth. As we walked through the agora with its central shops, we saw a raised platform called the bema, originally built of white and blue marble. The bema served as a platform for public speaking. This is where Paul stood when he was brought "before the tribunal" in Corinth. Paul left Athens and went to Corinth, where he stayed and worked as a tentmaker with Aquila and Priscilla. Paul stayed in Corinth for a year and a half, teaching them the Word of God. During that time, the Jews made a united attack on Paul and brought him into court where he stood on the bema. What would happen to him?

Earlier the Lord had spoken to Paul in a vision: "Do not be afraid; keep on speaking, do not be silent. For I am with you, and no one is going to attack and harm you." What was Paul thinking as he stood on the bema? Was his life in danger and his ministry threatened? A man named Gallio was proconsul of the region, admired as a man of exceptional fairness and calmness. Before Paul could speak in his own defense, Gallio dismissed the charges of the Jews as no crime, but an internal dispute between Jewish groups. They were ejected from the court, and Paul was safe on the bema. He continued his ministry in Corinth for some time. God was faithful to His promise.

Before leaving the agora, we pastors in the group had our photo taken standing on the bema. I will not forget that moment. As all of us keep on speaking each day about Jesus crucified and risen as the only way to salvation, God will be with us and calm our fears. No matter what the outcome, we will be used to help set the world ablaze with Jesus. The bema is a safe place to stand.

*Prayer:* As true as God's own Word is true,
Not earth nor hell with all their crew
Against us shall prevail.
*TLH* 263:3

# Ephesus: An Urban Outreach Strategy

## Reading: Acts 19:8–20

*Text:* "This went on for two years, so that all the Jews and Greeks who lived in the province of Asia heard the word of the Lord." Acts 19:10

Our visit to first century Ephesus was the highlight of the trip for me. Because of extensive and painstaking work by the Austrian Archeological Institute over the past century, Ephesus has been uncovered as a major urban center of the Roman Empire. Its administrative center, marketplace, public baths, memorial temples, library, and great theater bring alive the events of Acts 19 regarding Paul's two- to three-year mission there. Our group listened to the reading of Acts 19 before walking into the theater seating 25,000 where Christians were dragged by the angry mob, provoked by Demetrius and the silversmiths. The archeologists have found the synagogue where Paul preached, the house of Tyrannus where he lectured, and reference to the silversmith, Demetrius.

Walking down the marble streets, I could visualize Paul's urban outreach strategy. Spending time in Ephesus, he not only reached many Jews and Greeks living there, but also impacted all the people who lived in the Roman province of Asia. Paul's circular letter to the Ephesians and John's letters to the seven churches of Asia Minor in Revelation, all in the vicinity of Ephesus, reveal the success of his urban strategy.

What urban outreach strategies are we using to spread the saving word of the Lord? Do we see centers of learning (libraries, universities), commerce (factories, financial institutions, retail stores, service and information companies), government, drama and the arts, and sports as places for bold witness to Jesus as Savior and humble service to meet human needs? Recognizing our own selfishness, fears, and lack of vision, we confess our sins, receive the forgiveness won by Christ on the cross, and make ourselves available for God's twenty-first century urban outreach strategy to set the world ablaze with Christ.

*Prayer:* And not alone to nations
In faraway retreats,
But ev'rywhere I broadcast
His love through crowded streets:
The lives that my life touches,
However great or small–
Let them through me see Jesus,
Who served and saved us all.
*LW* 320:4

Copyright © 1982 Concordia Publishing House

# Ephesus: A Baptistry in St. John's

**Reading: Revelation 2:1–7**

*Text:* "You have persevered and have endured hardships for My name and have not grown weary. Yet I hold this against you: You have forsaken your first love." Revelation 2:3–4

Our Ephesus tour included a visit to the ruins of St. John's Basilica where the apostle John is supposedly buried. Tradition says that John lived there for many years, along with Jesus' mother Mary. In the Basilica we saw a baptistry in the shape of a cross. The candidate for Baptism would walk down steps into the water and out the other end of the cross arm. Baptized into Christ's death and resurrection. Dead to sin. Alive to Christ.

In Revelation, John writes to Ephesus as one of the seven churches. He commends their endurance and perseverance as God's baptized children in the face of hardships. But then he adds a chilling rebuke: "You have forsaken your first love." Apparently that rebuke was heeded because the very ruins of St. John's Basilica and that cruciform baptistry bear testimony to God's Spirit at work in the Ephesian church, once in danger of falling away.

As we seek to set the world ablaze with the Gospel of Jesus Christ, the words of St. John ring in our ears. How easy it is to conform to the world and remain silent regarding our faith. How tempting to take God's grace for granted and try to live by our own strength until we forsake our first love. Confessing those sins, we remember our Baptism in the name of the Father and of the Son and of the Holy Spirit. Daily we die to sin and receive Christ's full forgiveness won on Calvary's cross. God makes us alive in Christ and restores Him as our first love. Then we live for Him, endure hardships for His name, and bear verbal witness of salvation through Christ alone.

That baptistry in St. John's Basilica will always remind me of the Savior whose cross has shaped my life and stir me to depend on His grace for a life of witness and service in this twenty-first century.

*Prayer:* Look to the Lord, who did atone
For sin, O fallen race.
Look and be saved through faith alone,
Be justified by grace.
*LW* 276:5

# Tulay: Our Turkish Guide

## Reading: Acts 18:24–28

*Text:* When Priscilla and Aquila heard him, they invited him to their house and explained to him the way of God more adequately. Acts 18:26b

When we toured Ephesus, our Turkish guide, a woman named Tulay, provided insightful background and commentary in clear and precise English. She also revealed information about herself and her beliefs. While a Muslim, her ideas about interpreting the Quran and the role of women fit the secular Turkish democratic state better than a strict adherence to Islam. Having studied Islam, Judaism, and Christianity, she expressed a preference for the humanity of Jesus over the other religions. Probably not yet a Christian because of no reference to Christ's atoning death on Calvary, she is at least searching for the true religion. While the group setting and time constraints did not permit going further with Tulay, she did at least hear the reading of Acts 19 before entering the theater in Ephesus.

I couldn't help but think about the role Priscilla and Aquila played in the spiritual and theological development of the great Christian orator Apollos, a recently converted Jew. While a learned man and a bold proclaimer of Jesus, he lacked a full understanding of Christian doctrine. "When Priscilla and Aquila heard him, they invited him to their house and explained to him the way of God more adequately." He then went on to a powerful ministry in Achaea as "a great help to those who by grace believed" (Acts 18:27), vigorously refuting the Jews in public debate, "proving from the Scriptures that Jesus was the Christ" (Acts 18:28).

I pray that some believing Christians might have opportunity to invite Tulay for personal conversation about Jesus, crucified and risen, as the only way to salvation for her and that she might be used to bear witness to Jesus as a tour guide, "a great help to those who by grace believed." Who do you know who is searching but not believing or uncertain about basic Christian doctrine that you might invite for Spirit-filled conversation?

*Prayer:* See all our sins on Jesus laid;
The Lamb has made us whole.
His soul was once an off'ring made
For ev'ry human soul.
*LW* 276:6

# The Dying Achilles

## Reading: 2 Corinthians 2:14–17

*Text:* For we are to God the aroma of Christ among those who are being saved and those who are perishing. 2 Corinthians 2:15

On the Greek island of Corfu, beautiful and fragrant in every way, stands an impressive palace called the Achilleion, built by the Austrian empress, Elizabeth, wife of Franz Joseph. The palace features a Carrara marble statue of the dying Achilles, that hero of Homer's *Iliad*, who had one fatal weakness—his heel. The statue conveys Achilles's agony as he attempts to pull out the fatal arrow in his heel. When Elizabeth tragically died at the hand of an anarchist assassin, the palace was bought by Kaiser Wilhelm II, who constructed a large, triumphant, and aesthetically ugly statue of Achilles because he could not countenance the thought of military defeat.

St. Paul describes his ministry as participating in God's triumphant procession in Christ and spreading everywhere the fragrance of the knowledge of Him, a sweet aroma to those who are being saved but the smell of death to those who are perishing. That triumph, though, is more like the dying Achilles than the conquering Achilles because Jesus gave Himself in death on the cross to pay for the sins of the world. In His atoning death comes victory, demonstrated by His resurrection from the grave.

The startling beauty and fragrance of Corfu remains. The palace with its sculpture impresses. But the aroma of Christ in His death and resurrection far surpasses the human efforts of Elizabeth and Wilhelm to create beauty. In our Baptism into Christ and His Church, we are able, confessing our human weakness and sin, to participate as forgiven children in God's triumphal procession to set the world ablaze with the aroma of Christ "among those who are being saved." What a privilege!

*Prayer:* Hence, all earthly treasure!
Jesus is my pleasure, Jesus is my choice.
Hence, all empty glory!
What to me your story
Told with tempting voice?
Pain or loss or shame or cross
Shall not from my Savior move me
Since he chose to love me.
*LW* 270:4

# God's Word and World

## Reading: Isaiah 55:8–13

*Text:* "For My thoughts are not your thoughts, neither are your ways My ways," declares the LORD. Isaiah 55:8

One of the more interesting paraphrases of the Bible in recent years is *The Message* by Eugene H. Peterson. In his introduction, he explains why he embarked on the project. In order to reach contemporary people adrift in a pluralistic world, Peterson felt the need to introduce both believers with little biblical background and inquirers to God's Word and God's world. The next several devotions will apply certain insights from Peterson's introduction to our task of helping set the world ablaze with Christ, using appropriate sections from Scripture.

Indeed we need to know God's Word, which introduces us to God's world. In Isaiah 55, that marvelous chapter of God's grace for the world, the Lord declares, "For My thoughts are not your thoughts, neither are your ways My ways." He offers the water of life, wine and milk, without money and without cost. If we listen to Him, our souls will delight in the richest of fares (Isaiah 55:1–2). Through David's Son, the Messiah, God will carry out His everlasting covenant with David and with us. Through our witness to the Messiah, we can summon nations and they will come to us for salvation (Isaiah 55:3–5). God's Word and world offer us sinners a saving promise.

But our sinful world and our sinful hearts do not understand God because His thoughts are not our thoughts and our ways are not His ways. Therefore, we need God's Spirit to open our hearts to God's Word and world. "Let the wicked forsake his way and the evil man his thoughts. Let him turn to the LORD, and He will have mercy on him, and to our God, for He will freely pardon" (Isaiah 55:7).

What a wonderful invitation to believe and to witness! We take God's Word into today's world so that many believe the Word of Christ and discover God's world of sin exposed and forgiveness freely offered. God's Word and world, first for us and then, through us, for others!

*Prayer:* It's light, descending from above,
Our gloomy world to cheer,
Displays our Savior's boundless love
And brings his glories near.
*LW* 332:3

# The Word Read and Lived

**Reading: Colossians 3:12–17**

*Text:* Let the word of Christ dwell in you richly. Colossians 3:16a

Eugene Peterson, in his introduction to *The Message*, describes the reader's interaction with God's Word not as coercion but as personal address where the reader has space and freedom to enter into the conversation between the Word read and the Word lived. We come into God's presence with what matters most to us–who we are, where we come from, where we are going. And God responds to our deepest longings with His saving Word for our daily lives and eternal future.

St. Paul captures this reality of the Word read and lived in Colossians 3:16: "Let the word of Christ dwell in you richly as you teach and admonish one another with all wisdom, and as you sing psalms, hymns and spiritual songs with gratitude in your hearts to God." God's Word is always the Word of Christ. It first convicts us of our sin and total inability to make ourselves righteous before God. Then it points us to Jesus Christ as the righteous One who paid for our sins on the cross. In our brokenness and despair, God's Word is always the Word of Christ for forgiveness of sins, life, and salvation.

That Word of Christ, then, is the Word lived. We worship around Word and Sacraments, singing "psalms, hymns and spiritual songs with gratitude" in our hearts to God. "As God's chosen people, holy and dearly loved," we live daily in the grace of our Baptism, clothing ourselves "with compassion, kindness, humility, gentleness, and patience" (Colossians 3:12). We forgive as the Lord forgave us, demonstrate love, and let the peace of Christ rule in our hearts (Colossians 3:13–15).

In short, whatever we do, whether in word or deed, we do it all in the name of the Lord Jesus, giving thanks to God the Father through Him (Colossians 3:17). And that life of word and deed becomes the Spirit's witness to the world of the Word of Christ. You see, the Word read is, in fact, the Word lived.

*Prayer:* For ev'ry thirsty, longing heart
Here streams of bounty flow
And life and health and bliss impart
To lavish mortal woe.
*LW* 350:2

# What Does This Mean?

**Reading: 1 Corinthians 2:6–16**

*Text:* But God has revealed it to us by His Spirit. 1 Corinthians 2:10

Dr. Martin Luther uses a very simple question in his *Small Catechism* to illumine the truths of God's Word: "What does this mean?" Generations of students have committed to memory Luther's answers to this question because they are clearly based on the sacred Scriptures. In a similar fashion, any exploration of God's Word and God's world so we may set the world ablaze with Christ starts with the same question: "What does this mean?"

St. Paul writes the Corinthians that we cannot have the understanding to answer that question on our own power. He affirms that he speaks a message of wisdom among the mature but quickly asserts that it is "not the wisdom of this age or of the rulers of this age, who are coming to nothing" (1 Corinthians 2:6). He adds that if the rulers of this age understood the message, they would not have crucified the Lord of glory (1 Corinthians 2:8). Then Paul uncovers the source of his message of wisdom: "But God has revealed it to us by His Spirit."

Every time we turn to the Scriptures and ask, "What does this mean?" we are praying for God's Spirit to break through the blindness of our sin and open our eyes to see Jesus as our Savior. In the process, we confess our sins, receive Christ's forgiveness, and begin to understand God's world better. We see the folly of human wisdom with its deception and embrace God's wisdom. We then speak the message of salvation through Christ to unbelievers by the Spirit's power. As Paul writes, "This is what we speak, not in words taught us by human wisdom but in words taught by the Spirit, expressing spiritual truths in spiritual words" (1 Corinthians 2:13).

The beauty of Dr. Luther's question, "What does this mean?" lies in its reliance on the Holy Spirit to bring understanding. For our own salvation and for our daily witness, Paul's final words in the chapter reassure us, "But we have the mind of Christ" (1 Corinthians 2:16b).

*Prayer:* Your Spirit send with light divine,
And let your truth within us shine.
*LW* 201:1

# How Is This Done?

**Reading: Psalm 119:9–16**

*Text:* I have hidden Your word in my heart that I might not sin against You. Psalm 119:11

Dr. Martin Luther employs a second question in his *Small Catechism*: "How is this done?" In the petitions of the Lord's Prayer, for example, Luther uses this question to highlight God at work in His church and in our everyday lives. In a similar fashion, our reading of God's Word moves us from Spirit-given understanding ("What does this mean?") to Spirit-led application of that understanding to our daily lives of service and witness ("How is this done?").

Psalm 119, a devotional on the Word of God, addresses the "How is this done?" question for the believer in God's promise. Each section is labeled with a different letter from the Hebrew alphabet. *Beth*, the second section, can serve as an example. The psalmist writes, "I have hidden Your word in my heart that I might not sin against You." Although eight different Hebrew words are used for "word" such as law, statutes, precepts, commands, laws or ordinances, decrees, word, and promise, the psalmist's use of "word" falls into two main categories: law and promise.

In our text ("I have hidden Your word in my heart"), *Pimrah*, the Hebrew word, means God's promise. First, aware of how often we fail to keep the word of God's Law, leading to flagrant and persistent sin, we, secondly, look in faith to God's greatest promise of sending the Messiah, Jesus Christ, to atone for our sins on the cross. Thirdly, we rely on God's promise to avoid sin against Him (v. 11) and to live according to His Word or directives (v. 9).

"How is this done?" Sin against God's Law confessed. Spirit-given trust in God's promise of salvation through Christ bestowed. In our baptismal life of confession and absolution, Spirit-led resistance to sin and obedience to God's Word for service and witness powerfully given. The Word lived each day! Fill in the specifics with your mouth, your hands, and your feet.

*Prayer:* Order my footsteps by your Word
And make my heart sincere;
Let sin have no dominion, Lord,
But keep my conscience clear.
*LW* 392:2

# The World of the Bible

## Reading: Psalm 106:1–11

*Text:* "When our fathers were in Egypt, . . . they did not remember Your many kindnesses, and they rebelled by the sea, the Red Sea." Psalm 106:7

Eugene Peterson's introduction to *The Message* urges regular study of the Scriptures because of contemporary neglect of God's Word and world. After devotions on God's Word, we move to devotions on understanding God's world. The world of the Bible seems far removed from computers, cell phones, Wall Street, and Hollywood. Yet that biblical world teaches us all we need to know for a dynamic witness to Christ in the twenty-first century. In the next five devotions we will study Psalm 106 to sample the world of the Bible for our times.

Psalm 106 is a confession of Israel's long history of rebellion against God. The psalmist begins with the rebellion in Egypt around the Red Sea events. God was faithful to His people in every age, including their time in Egypt. Yet we read, "When our fathers were in Egypt, . . . they did not remember Your many kindnesses, and they rebelled by the sea, the Red Sea," and with Pharoah's mighty chariots bearing down on them, they cried to Moses, "Was it because there were no graves in Egypt that you brought us to the desert to die?" (Exodus 14:11).

The world of the Bible is a world of rebellion. The twenty-first century world is also a world of rebellion against the true God. The psalmist speaks for us: "We have sinned, even as our fathers did; we have done wrong and acted wickedly" (Psalm 106:6).

The world of the Bible is also a world of God's deliverance. Moses stretched out his hand over the waters, and the waters parted. "God saved them from the hand of the foe; from the hand of the enemy He redeemed them" (Psalm 106:10). And God has redeemed us from our enemies (sin, death, and the devil) through the death and resurrection of His only Son Jesus Christ. In the next few devotions, a biblical view of today's world will help us witness of our Savior more boldly and effectively.

*Prayer:* Save us, O Lord our God, . . . that we may give thanks to Your holy name and glory in Your praise. Psalm 106:47

# Not a "Nicer" World

## Reading: Psalm 106:12–18

*Text:* But they soon forgot what He had done and did not wait for His counsel. Psalm 106:13

Our mission to set today's world ablaze with Christ will flounder if we think of our twenty-first century society as a "nicer" world. Travel posters describe clear waters, sandy beaches, and luxury resorts. Social planners assume the goodness of human nature to paint an idealistic future for this planet with a pristine environment, perfect acceptance of cultural diversity, and international peace based on nations loving each other.

The world of the Bible in Psalm 106 shatters all such illusions of a "nicer" world. Delivered from the Egyptians through the Red Sea parting, Israel praises God with song and dance while picturing a "nicer" world ahead with a quick trip through the wilderness to the Promised Land. But the psalmist sadly records those words, "They soon forgot what He had done and did not wait for His counsel." In rapid succession he tells how they gave into their craving in the wasteland, unhappy with inadequate water and food, and about Korah's rebellion against Moses. In the first instance, God sent a plague to consume many people. In the second instance, the earth opened up and consumed Korah, Dathan, and Abiram in a fiery death (Psalm 106:14–18). Sinful and rebellious hearts exploded any concept of a "nicer" world.

In our witness worldwide to the Savior, we do well to recognize first our own sinful and rebellious hearts and then the sin all around us in this old world. False optimism and utopian dreams of peace and universal love will not serve us well. As we remember God's mighty acts at the Red Sea, Jordan River Baptism, Maundy Thursday Passover Eucharist, Calvary crucifixion, and Joseph's empty garden tomb, we wait for His counsel. He convicts us of our sin, absolves us through His Word, encourages us through His body and blood, and sends us as ambassadors of His forgiveness, peace and love. God's new world based on God's unfailing promises!

*Prayer:* Jesus sinners will receive;
May they all this saying ponder
Who in sin's delusion live
And from God and heaven wander!
Here is hope for all who grieve:
Jesus sinners will receive.
*LW* 229:1

---

# Not a Neat and Tidy World

**Reading: Psalm 106:19–23**

*Text:* At Horeb they made a calf and worshiped an idol cast from metal. Psalm 106:19

Another enemy of setting the world ablaze with Christ is the effort to create a neat and tidy world. We don't like loose ends, unexpected twists to life, or events outside of our comfort zone.

Israel reacted against their uncertain life in the wilderness. God had summoned Moses to the holy mountain. He had not returned. Many grew impatient. They decided to take control, to create a neat and tidy world with something familiar and concrete. The psalmist describes their actions as follows: "At Horeb they made a calf and worshiped an idol cast from metal." The full story is recorded in Exodus 32. They ordered the making of a golden calf to represent the gods of Egypt and sacrificed burnt offerings. Aaron was their accomplice. The end result was not a neat and tidy world but disaster. Moses intervened with God, claiming God's own covenant promises, but then, angry at the people's willful sin, used the loyal Levite swords to kill 3,000 people.

Evil runs rampant in our world. When we forget God's covenant promises to create a neat and tidy world of our own making, chaos and destruction result from our sin. Only God can restore our world through His Son, the Sin-bearer, who brings a new creation from His crucifixion and resurrection. Repentant and forgiven, we rest in the liberating order of God's new creation and let Him direct our lives in a sinful, chaotic world as witnesses to salvation through Jesus Christ. Who needs a neat and tidy world of our own making when we live in the flow of God's love through Christ?

*Prayer:* My heart's delight,
My crown most bright,
Not wealth nor pride
Nor fortune's tide
Our bonds of love shall sever.
You are my Lord;
Your precious Word
Shall guide my way
And help me stay
Forever in your presence.
*LW* 358:4

# Not a Dream World

## Reading: Psalm 106:24–39

*Text:* They grumbled in their tents and did not obey the LORD. Psalm 106:25

An adolescent love song of the 1960s was entitled, "What a Wonderful World." Confessing that he didn't know much about chemistry, geography, algebra, or geometry, the vocalist crooned that if he could have the love of his girl, what a wonderful world it would be. All too many of us live in a dream world, wanting it to conform to our adolescent expectations. Whether 16, 36, or 70, we fret and complain when our dream world fails to materialize. Living in a dream world can never prepare us as witnesses of Jesus Christ.

In the ongoing saga of Psalm 106, the psalmist records these words from Israel's wilderness wanderings: "They grumbled in their tents and did not obey the LORD." He illustrates the dream world disappointments of their adolescent expectations in the wilderness years and even in the Promised Land of Canaan: They complained about insufficient water and inadequate food. They yoked themselves to the Baal of Peor when they engaged in sexual immorality and idolatry with Moabite women. At the waters of Meribah they angered the Lord by demanding water. In Canaan they mingled with the nation and adopted their customs, including idol worship and human sacrifice (Psalm 106:24–39). Because of sinful adolescent behavior, their dream world became a nightmare.

Again quoting the psalmist, "We have sinned, even as our fathers did; we have done wrong and acted wickedly" (Psalm 106:5). Whether adolescents in the 1960s or 2007, our peevish, irresponsible reaction to a shattered dream world leads us deep into sin and far removed from God's call on our lives. God's Son, in His Father's house at age 12, increasing in wisdom and stature and in favor with God and man, faced the real world under Satan's control and won the victory on Calvary. Repentant and forgiven, we draw strength from our Baptism, renounce adolescent expectations, and offer Christ's forgiveness to a world struggling with shattered dreams and destructive behaviors. In Christ, what a wonderful world it will be!

*Prayer:* All the vain things that charm me most,
I sacrifice them to his blood.
*LW* 114:2

# But a Real World

## Reading: Psalm 106:40–48

*Text:* Many times He delivered them, but they were bent on rebellion and wasted away in their sin. Psalm 106:43

To understand today's world so we can help set the world ablaze with Christ, we need first to understand the world of the Bible. A careful reading of that biblical world in Psalm 106 reveals that we do not live in a "nicer" world, a neat and tidy world, or a dream world, but a real world.

In the final verses of the psalm, the psalmist summarizes all that happened during forty years in the wilderness and during the entire history of Israel in the Promised Land from the judges to the Babylonian captivity with these words: "Many times He delivered them, but they were bent on rebellion and wasted away in their sin." Israel's real world was filled with their rebellion against a God who loved them and had set them apart as His special people. The unvarnished truth about their sin. The unvarnished truth about the consequences of their rebellion–namely oppression and subjection by many enemies. But Israel's real world also included the mercy and love of a faithful God who would not forsake them. "For their sake He remembered His covenant and out of His great love He relented" (Psalm 106:45).

Without fear, we face today's real world. The rebellion continues all around us in a culture that ignores or opposes the true God, but also in the sinful hearts of us all. Our world also suffers the consequences of that rebellion in terms of terrorism, injustice, oppression, and brokenness.

But, at the same time, God so loved the world that He gave His only begotten Son that whosoever believes in Him shall not perish but have everlasting life. God defeated all the rebellious forces of evil at the cross of Jesus Christ who paid the penalty in full for all our sins. God lives and rules through His church, His people gathered around Word and Sacraments and sent out as witnesses in His name. Real world. Real Savior. Real message of sin and salvation.

*Prayer:* Lord Jesus, think on me,
Nor let me go astray;
Through darkness and perplexity
Point out your chosen way
*LW* 231:3

# The Word of the Lord Grows

## Reading: Acts 5:29–42

*Text:* In this way the word of the Lord spread widely and grew in power. Acts 19:20

The Word of the Lord grows. Three times in the Book of Acts, these words sum up a period of the first church's history (Acts 6:7; 12:24; 19:20). This Word of God is God in action in history, ultimately through the death and resurrection of His Son, Jesus Christ, the Word made flesh (John 1:14).

God's Word introduces us to God's world so we can differentiate between false views of the world and the reality of the world from God's viewpoint. When we see both the world's rebellion and God's love for the world through Christ, we have a solid foundation for setting the world ablaze with the Gospel of Jesus Christ.

In Acts, the number of believers increased and their spiritual strength increased only because the Word of the Lord spread widely and grew in power. The Holy Spirit worked daily through the Word and Sacraments in the early Christian community. That is why the first disciples, despite threats and persecution, boldly proclaimed the Word: "Day after day in the temple courts and from house to house, they never stopped teaching and proclaiming the good news that Jesus is the Christ" (Acts 5:42). The Word of the Lord grows. We receive it for forgiveness and strength. We proclaim it to bring life and salvation to a real world in need of a Savior.

*Prayer:* Thy strong Word bespeaks us righteous;
Bright with thine own holiness,
Glorious now, we press toward glory,
And our lives our hopes confess.

Give us lips to sing thy glory,
Tongues thy mercy to proclaim,
Throats that shout the hope that fills us,
Mouths to speak thy holy name.

Alleluia, alleluia!
May the light which thou dost send
Fill our songs with alleluias,
Alleluias without end!
*LW* 328:3, 5

Copyright © 1969 Concordia Publishing House

# Jesus One on One: Centurion

**Reading: Matthew 8:5–13**

*Text:* "Go! It will be done just as you believed it would." Matthew 8:13

These daily devotions to set the world ablaze support the international One Mission Ablaze! effort to touch 100 million people with the saving Gospel of Jesus. But God's Spirit works "one on one" when there is a critical event—an opportunity to share Jesus with another person. The next eight devotions will explore Jesus reaching out one on one in His earthly ministry. Two such encounters have been chosen from each Gospel.

We begin with a text from Matthew that describes the encounter between Jesus and the centurion, whose servant "lies at home paralyzed and in terrible suffering" (Matthew 8:6). Here is a Gentile, not one of the house of Israel, seeking a miracle of healing from Jesus. How would our Lord respond? Who do you know with a need for help, standing outside of any relationship with the Lord and His church? How open and available are you to listen and respond?

Without hesitating, Jesus replies, "I will go and heal him." He has come for Jews and Gentiles alike as Matthew's Gospel makes clear. Now comes the surprising response from this military leader in charge of 100 Roman soldiers: "Lord, I do not deserve to have You come under my roof. But just say the word, and my servant will be healed" (Matthew 8:8). Humble, aware of his own sinfulness, he trusts Jesus to heal his servant by merely speaking a word. How often God's Spirit has already been preparing the hearts of those outside the church for a word of forgiveness and healing from the Savior.

Jesus is astonished at the centurion's evidence of great faith in God, for surpassing that of many within Israel. He simply replies, "Go! It will be done just as you believed it would." Matthew records, "And his servant was healed at that very hour" (Matthew 8:13b). This one on one encounter opens our eyes to see God's Spirit at work outside church walls, providing us countless opportunities to speak the word of Jesus for healing, life, and salvation.

*Prayer:* Lord, open our lips to speak Your Word of forgiveness and healing outside church walls. Amen.

# Jesus One on One: Canaanite Woman

### Reading: Matthew 15:21–28

*Text:* "Woman, you have great faith! Your request is granted." Matthew 15:28

Fresh from a sharp exchange with the Pharisees who insist on outer ritual cleanliness but are unclean on the inside, Jesus moves outside Israel into the region of Tyre and Sidon where He encounters a Canaanite woman pleading for her demon-possessed daughter's healing. He tests her faith severely. First, silence to her plea. Then, a discouraging reply, "I was sent only to the lost sheep of Israel" (Matthew 15:24). Finally, a demeaning remark, "It is not right to take the children's bread and toss it to their dogs" (Matthew 15:26).

What is Jesus doing here in His witness to the woman and to His disciples? What can we learn from Him for our own witnessing with those outside the church? He upholds faith in His atoning work as the only basis for a right relationship with God. God chose Israel as His special people through faith in His promises. They cannot depend upon the law for salvation, especially the ritual regulations. But this woman, a Gentile, cannot stand before God on her own merits either. She has no claim to receive the blessings of God's chosen people as an unbeliever in Israel's God.

But the woman demonstrates her sense of unworthiness and dependence upon Israel's God by humbly asserting, "Yes, Lord, but even the dogs eat the crumbs that fall from their masters' table" (Matthew 15:27). Then Jesus answers, "Woman, you have great faith. Your request is granted." And her daughter was healed immediately. Israel, saved only by faith in the promised Messiah. Gentiles, saved only by faith in the promised Messiah. Faith in a great God of grace, who sent His Son to die for the sins of the world.

From Jesus' encounter with the Canaanite woman, we learn the crucial role of faith. Sinners under God's Law, we live only through faith in Christ and recognize that everyone we encounter stands in need of that same saving faith in Christ, available freely by God's grace.

*Prayer:* Just as I am, thou wilt receive
Wilt welcome, pardon, cleanse, relieve;
Because thy promise I believe,
O Lamb of God, I come, I come. Amen.
*LW* 359:5

# Jesus One on One: Sick Woman

## Reading: Mark 5:24–34

*Text:* "Daughter, your faith has healed you. Go and be freed from your suffering." Mark 5:34

St. Mark, in his action-packed Gospel, also describes some powerful one on one events in Jesus' ministry. Jesus is on His way to help the daughter of a prominent synagogue ruler named Jairus. In the press of the large crowd, no one notices a desperate woman, subject to bleeding for twelve years. Mark tells us, "She had suffered a great deal under the care of many doctors and had spent all she had, yet instead of getting better she grew worse" (Mark 5:26).

Who do you know in desperate need? Perhaps that person goes unnoticed in the crowd but has been suffering physically, emotionally, or spiritually for years. You may be concentrating on an important task or mission for someone else. But that person may need your help. This woman decides to touch Jesus' cloak for healing, believing that He can meet her great need. Mark tells us that she was healed immediately and freed from her suffering.

Aware that power had gone from Him, Jesus asks, "Who touched My clothes?" (Mark 5:30). He looked around to see who had done it. Trembling with fear, the woman falls at His feet and tells Him the whole truth. Based on her testimony, Jesus says, "Daughter, your faith has healed you. Go in peace and be freed from your suffering."

In what ways can God use you to touch the lives of unnoticed people around you? You have the power of God's Word and His healing forgiveness at your disposal as a baptized child of God. As you listen with compassion, they can tell you the whole truth about their sin and need for a Savior. And you can announce the forgiveness of sins through faith in Christ one on one with the words, "Go in peace and be freed from your suffering."

*Prayer:* Your touch then, Lord, brought life and health,
Gave speech and strength and sight;
And youth renewed and frenzy calmed
Revealed you, Lord of light.
And now, O Lord, be near to bless,
Almighty as before,
In crowded street, by beds of pain,
As by Gennes'rets' shore.
*LW* 399:2

# Jesus One on One: Rich Young Ruler

**Reading: Mark 10:17–23**

*Text:* Jesus looked at him and loved him. Mark 10:21

St. Mark describes a dramatic but sad one on one meeting between Jesus and a rich young ruler. The young man runs to Jesus and falls on his knees with a genuine question, "Good Teacher," he asked, "what must I do to inherit eternal life?" (Mark 10:17). Jesus responds by quoting those commandments dealing with our relationships with others. With evident sincerity, the young man replies, "Teacher, all these I have kept since I was a boy" (Mark 10:20). He was thinking of external conformity to the law, not inner obedience.

How many people do you know who think of themselves as moral, ethical people, acceptable to God or society because of their sincerity and good conduct? How often are you tempted to claim the same ethical standing for yourself? How does Jesus view the young man's righteousness and ours?

Mark simply comments: "Jesus looked at him and loved him." He saw him as a special creation of the heavenly Father. He saw him as someone for whom He came to die. He also saw him as someone headed in the wrong direction, trusting his wealth more than God, trusting his own righteousness instead of God's righteousness through Christ.

As a result, Jesus demonstrated His love by asking him to sell everything and give to the poor and then to follow Jesus. Faced with this radical demand, the young man went away sad because he had great wealth. Jesus hoped he would forsake worldly wealth and receive God's free gift of eternal life (treasure in heaven) based on Christ's atoning sacrifice. Perhaps God's Spirit could still lead him to repentance and faith. Mark's Gospel doesn't tell us.

Jesus has looked at us and loved us. In our witnessing we need His look of love for others, whether they believe in Jesus or walk away sad. God's love at the right time can bring repentance and faith.

*Prayer:* Dear Savior, draw reluctant hearts;
To you let sinners fly
And take the bliss your love imparts,
Revive and never die.
*LW* 350:5

August 9

# Jesus One on One: Bent over Woman

## Reading: Luke 13:10–13

*Text:* "Woman, you are set free from your infirmity." Luke 13:12

St. Luke records a remarkable encounter in the synagogue between Jesus and a bent over woman. She had both spiritual and physical needs, crippled by a spirit for 18 years and bent over double. Can you identify with that woman? In what ways are you bent over—with troubles, problems, difficult relationships, the burden of debt, sickness, spiritual doubts, the guilt of sins past and present? Who do you know that is bent over and needing help—a family member, neighbor, friend, work associate?

Jesus wastes no time in reaching out: "When Jesus saw her, He called her forward and said to her, 'Woman, you are set free from your infirmity.' Then He put His hands on her, and immediately she straightened up and praised God" (Luke 13:12–13). Bent over, oppressed by Satan, feeling unworthy and self-conscious, the woman now is straightened up, freed from Satan's bondage, worthy because of faith in Jesus as her Savior, and praising God with her life of service and witness. What an encounter with Jesus!

Our one on one conversations spring from the fact that we have been straightened up and set free to praise God with our lives. Fresh from our healing encounter with Jesus, we seek those bent over like this woman and invite them into the presence of the forgiving and healing Christ. Through us, God's love flows to straighten them up and free them to praise God also. What a privilege to participate in such encounters with Jesus!

*Prayer:* Gather your children, dear Savior, in peace
And draw us to you with your passionate pleas;
Still seek us and call us to come and be blessed,
To find in your arms, Lord, safety, comfort, and rest.

Knowing you, loving you, naming you Lord,
We cluster around you and grow by your Word,
One day to remember those moments so rare,
Of caring and closeness, just because you are there.
*SP* 82:1–2

Copyright © 1983 Concordia Publishing House

# Jesus One on One: Zacchaeus

## Reading: Luke 19:1–9

*Text:* "Zacchaeus, come down immediately. I must stay at your house today." Luke 19:5

Jesus enters Jericho on His final journey to Jerusalem. He walks in the shadow of Gethsemane and the cross. Luke tells us that a man was there by the name of Zaccheus, a chief tax collector and a man of wealth. Immediately we know that he falls into the category of despised "sinner" from the viewpoint of the religious leaders. Zaccheus wants to see who Jesus is but, because he is short and blocked by the crowd, needs to run ahead and climb a sycamore-fig tree for a better view of Jesus. Will Jesus even notice?

Intent on Jerusalem and surrounded by a crowd, Jesus, nevertheless, stops by the tree, looks up, and speaks directly to the despised tax collector: "Zacchaeus, come down immediately. I must stay at your house today." Nothing at that moment is more important to Jesus than a one on one encounter with Zacchaeus. A brief conversation does not suffice. He desires to spend time with him as a guest in his home. He doesn't care how the crowd or religious authorities might react. He cares about the salvation of this man.

Zacchaeus comes down at once and welcomes Jesus gladly. He demonstrates his faith in Jesus by promising to give half of his possessions to the poor and to pay four times the amount to anyone whom he might have cheated. Jesus' response tells it all: "Today salvation has come to this house. . . . For the Son of Man came to seek and to save what was lost" (Luke 19:9–10).

Sinful and lost, like Zacchaeus, we welcome salvation from the Son of Man who has paid the full price for our sins. Like Jesus, we spend our days, crowded and purposeful as they might be, looking for the opportunity of the moment, that one person who wants to see Jesus through us and to receive salvation, free and life-changing by God's grace.

*Prayer:* Dear Lord, thank You for noticing me and bringing me to salvation. Open my eyes to see that person in need that I may invite them to You. Amen.

August 11

# Jesus One on One: Samaritan Woman

**Reading: John 4:4–30**

*Text:* "I who speak to you am He." John 4:26

John tells a compelling story of Jesus' meeting at a well in Sychor with a Samaritan woman of questionable moral character. The details of Jesus' compassion, witnessing skill, and bold truth-telling astound us at a natural setting for describing Himself as living water, Jacob's well. The unusual request for a drink of water from a Jewish man to a Samaritan woman. The conversation about "whoever drinks the water I give him will never thirst" (John 4:14). Her interest stirred, "Sir, give me this water so I won't get thirsty" (John 4:15), followed by Jesus' abrupt subject-changing imperative: "Go, call your husband, and come back" (John 4:16). The truth of her sinful life exposed: "The fact is you have had five husbands, and the one you have now is not your husband" (John 4:17–18). Her eyes opening: "Sir, I can see that You are a prophet" (John 4:19). "I know that Messiah (called Christ) is coming" (John 4:25). Then Jesus declared, "I who speak to you am He."

The woman, believing in Jesus as Messiah, is transformed by the Spirit to become a bold witness: "Then, leaving her water jar, the woman went back to the town and said to the people, 'Come, see a man who told me everything I ever did. Could this be the Christ?' They came out of the town and made their way toward Him" (John 4:29–30).

How simply and powerfully Jesus works in the natural settings of our daily lives to show us our sin and desperate spiritual thirst and then point us to Himself as the source of living water! How simply and powerfully Jesus can use us to tell the story one on one to others with the same thirst for that "spring of water welling up to eternal life" (John 4:14)!

*Prayer:* I heard the voice of Jesus say, "Behold I freely give
The living water, thirsty one; Stoop down and drink and live."
I came to Jesus, and I drank Of that life-giving stream;
My thirst was quenched, my soul revived,
And now I live in Him.
*LW* 348:2

# Jesus One on One: Blind Man

**Reading: John 9:1–11**

*Text:* "Go, wash in the pool of Siloam." John 9:7

What is the purpose for Jesus' one on one encounter with the blind man in John's Gospel? The story is simple and the healing literally very touching. He sees the blind man, spits on the ground, makes mud with the saliva, puts it on the man's eyes, and tells him, "Go, wash in the pool of Siloam." The man goes and washes and comes home seeing.

Jesus describes His purpose to the disciples before healing the blind man: "This happened so that the work of God might be displayed in his life" (John 9:3). With his sight, the blind man becomes a powerful witness to Jesus as the light of the world. His neighbors ask who healed him and how. The Pharisees attempt to discredit both Jesus and the blind man, even dragging his parents into the fray. The simple testimony of the man cannot be denied: "One thing I do know. I was blind but now I see" (John 9:25). After being thrown out by the Pharisees, he meets Jesus and discovers that He is the Son of Man. His response: "Lord, I believe," and he worshiped Him (John 9:38).

Jesus gave us our spiritual sight one on one in our Baptism so that the work of God might be displayed in our lives. He regularly strengthens us for witness through His body and blood in the Holy Sacrament. He opens our eyes again and again through His Word.

No matter how many people attempt to intimidate us or discredit our witness, God's purpose for our lives, to testify to Jesus as the Light of the world, continues to be fulfilled. In our daily interactions with others, we can powerfully and clearly say: "One thing I do know. I was blind but now I see." We believe and we worship Him.

*Prayer:* Amazing grace! How sweet the sound
That saved a wretch like me!
I once was lost but now am found,
Was blind but now I see!
*LW* 509:1

# Answering God's Call

## Reading: Acts 16:6–10

*Text:* During the night Paul had a vision of a man of Macedonia standing and begging him, "Come over to Macedonia and help us." Acts 16:9

Through a resettlement agency, a woman named Betty who belongs to a Lutheran church in St. Louis met the tribal leader of a community of 70 families from the African Somali Bantu people. The Bantu people were the slave class of the African country of Somalia. They were treated very poorly and through a terrible civil war had lived in refugee camps in another African country for ten years. Over 90% of these families are Muslims. Betty invited these Somali refugees to outdoor activities at her church, Christmas programs, and rummage sales; has built a strong relationship with them and; through her church, has helped meet their physical needs. What an unexpected mission opportunity in a Midwestern city!

How similar is Betty's experience to "the Macedonian call" Paul received on his second missionary journey. He had his plans made to enter Bithynia, but God's Spirit would not permit it. So they went down to Troas where at night Paul had a vision of a man from Macedonia begging him, "Come over to Macedonia and help us." God's call led Paul and his companions to a fruitful mission in Philippi, Thessalonika, Berea, Athens, and Corinth. The Gospel of Jesus Christ touched many lives in response to this unexpected call to Macedonia.

Could God be calling you to touch the lives of people in your city from different people groups around the world? In St. Louis an organization called Christian Friends of New Americans helps to coordinate such outreach efforts. In fact, Betty discovered CFNA to help her reach out. When the local church cares deeply, opportunities are created for the saving Gospel to be proclaimed. More on the Bantu people tomorrow.

*Prayer:* Hark, the voice of Jesus calling,
"Who will go and work today?
Fields are white and harvest waiting,
Who will bear the sheaves away?"
Loud and long the master calls you;
Rich reward he offers free.
Who will answer, gladly saying,
"Here am I. Send me, send me"?
*LW* 318:1

# An Amazing Discovery

## Reading: Acts 10:19–35

*Text:* Then Peter began to speak, "I now realize how true it is that God does not show favoritism but accepts men from every nation who fear Him and do what is right." Acts 10:34–35

Betty asked the Somali Bantu leader if the CFNA pastor could visit his critically ill wife in the hospital. His story is amazing. After seeing his father shot before his eyes, he was captured, only to be left for dead. He barely made it back home to find out that his wife had been raped by several men. They escaped to an African refugee camp and now live in St. Louis. As the pastor visited him at his wife's bedside, he was curious why the Muslim leader would allow a Lutheran pastor to pray with them.

He discovered that the man's father had sent him to a Mennonite missionary school to learn English. In his adolescence he was abused by his Muslim peers for not going to a Muslim or public school. Asked about the biggest difference between Islam and Christianity, he gave an answer that caused the pastor's eyes to widen and mouth to drop: "I believe that Jesus is like a bridge–like the bridge that takes us from the hospital parking garage to the lobby. You can't get from this life to the next without Him." Overwhelmed with this confession of Jesus, the pastor asked if he was a Christian. He quietly nodded and said that he was baptized as a teenager. He understands how much time it will take him to influence his peers and how dangerous it could become for him. What an amazing discovery!

Peter must have felt the same way when, after his vision of clean and unclean animals, men sent by the Gentile centurion, Cornelius, came to his house and took him to their master. Peter proclaimed the Gospel of salvation through Christ's death and resurrection and witnessed the conversion through Baptism of Cornelius' household. What an amazing discovery! No favoritism. Christ for all nations!

*Prayer:* Look to the Lord who did atone
For sin, O fallen race,
Look and be saved through faith alone
Be justified by grace.
*LW* 276:5

# Sergeant Kia

## Reading: Acts 10:1–8

*Text:* "Now we are all here in the presence of God to listen to everything the Lord has commanded you to tell us." Acts 10:33

The story of Cornelius has another parallel in this account from the headmaster of Highland Lutheran International School (HLIS) in Papua New Guinea: "Sergeant Kia is a reserve policeman from our village. He is committed to the school and did his best to provide a careful watch during the tribal fight. (In January, 2003, a conflict in close proximity to the school led to a fire that destroyed the schools' main buildings.) His own house was burnt down while looking after the school's security. Later, while on duty, his son was killed in the fight. Regardless of these experiences, Kia continued to secure the school from criminal activities–most often without pay.

"After his house burnt, I had him move in with me. When I discovered he was not baptized, I encouraged him to be baptized as soon as possible, especially at a time when his life was at risk. Sergeant Kia was baptized on Easter day."

Acts tells us that Cornelius, a Gentile, was a centurion in the Italian regiment at Caesarea. He and his family were devout and God-fearing, gave generously to people in need, and prayed to God regularly. But as a Gentile, he needed to know about Christ crucified and risen for his salvation. A vision called him to seek out Peter in Joppa who saw a vision of his own about the Gospel for Gentiles as well as Jews. When Peter arrived, Cornelius humbly listened to Peter's message that everyone who believes in Jesus receives forgiveness of sins. He and his household believed and were baptized. Who are your Cornelius and Sergeant Kia? Pray for them!

*Prayer:* O Christ, our light, O Radiance true,
Shine forth on those estranged from you,
And bring them to your home again,
Where their delight shall never end.

Lord, let your mercy's gentle ray
Shine down on others strayed away.
To those in conscience wounded sore
Show heaven's waiting, open door.
*LW* 314:1, 4

Copyright © 1978 *Lutheran Book of Worship*

# Helping to Set the World Ablaze

**Reading: Acts 6:1–7**

*Text:* So the word of God spread. The number of disciples in Jerusalem increased rapidly. Acts 6:7

Who sets the world ablaze with the saving Gospel of Jesus Christ? The apostles? Church leaders? Pastors? Missionaries? Answer: God sets the world ablaze through His Church. The apostles vigorously proclaimed the Word of Christ. Church leaders, pastors, and missionaries likewise play a significant role in the spread of the Good News. But every believer as part of Christ's Church helps to set the world ablaze.

In the Early Church after Pentecost, the Word of God worked powerfully through the believers as people were daily added to the fellowship. In Acts 6, the Twelve asked the community of believers to choose seven men to care for the needs of widows from the Hellenistic Greek part of the Church. This help supported the apostles in their ministry of the Word and contributed to the growth of the Church.

In the next several devotions, we will explore how God used various believers as part of the Church to set the world ablaze. Their names may be unfamiliar to you, but their contributions are significant. Ananias, Barnabas, James, Judas, Silas, and Lydia. The book of Acts is full of such Gospel helpers.

How might God's Spirit be working in your life right now? How might you best contribute to the spread of the Gospel? What opportunities is God giving you each day to witness personally or to help another Christian bear testimony? What needs around you are crying out to be met? Recognizing our sins and shortcomings, receiving Christ's forgiveness, won on Calvary's cross, living in the power of His resurrection, we make ourselves available to help set the world ablaze as the word of God spreads through His Church.

*Prayer:* Let none hear you idly saying,
"There is nothing I can do,"
While the multitudes are dying
And the master calls for you.
Take the task he gives you gladly;
Let his work your pleasure be.
Answer quickly when he calls you,
"Here am I. Send me, send me!"
*LW* 318:4

# Ananias: A World-Changing Errand

**Reading: Acts 9:10–19**

*Text:* "Go! This man is My chosen instrument to carry My name before the Gentiles." Acts 9:15

Who is Ananias and how did he help set the world ablaze? He is little known. His name could even be confused with the Ananias and Sapphira of the Jerusalem church who lied to God about their property and were carried out dead (Acts 5:1–11). But this Ananias is a faithful disciple in the Damascus church who is tapped for an important task. We know nothing else about him.

The Lord calls to him in a vision and asks him to go to the house of Judas on Straight Street and ask for a man from Tarsus named Saul. Saul has just been converted on the Damascus road from an aggressive persecutor of Christians to a believer in Jesus Christ as Savior. Blinded and fasting, he is awaiting further instructions from the Lord.

God has chosen this unknown Ananias for a world-changing errand: "Go! This man is My chosen instrument to carry My name before the Gentiles and their kings and before the people of Israel." Afraid for his life because of Saul's reputation and authority from the chief priests in Jerusalem, Ananias nevertheless goes to Saul, lays hands on him to restore his sight, baptizes him, and sends him on his worldwide mission. What a world-changing errand for this humble helper!

What might God be calling you to do? Whether you are little known or well-known, God says to you in your Baptism: "I have called you by name. You are Mine." Although you are not a Paul, God wants you to help set the world ablaze. What child might you teach or influence? What missionary might you encourage? Satan wants to raise doubts and discourage you. But the Savior of Saul and Ananias forgives, emboldens, and sends you on a world-changing errand.

*Prayer:* If you cannot speak like angels,
If you cannot preach like Paul,
You can tell the love of Jesus;
You can say he died for all.
If you cannot rouse the wicked
With the judgment's dread alarms,
You can lead the little children
To the Savior's waiting arms.
*LW* 318:2

# Barnabas: A Momentous Introduction

**Reading: Acts 9:26–30**

*Text:* But Barnabas took him and brought him to the apostles. Acts 9:27

Saul needed a great deal of help to be launched on his worldwide mission as apostle to the Gentiles. The unknown Ananias removed the scales of blindness. Now, filled with the Spirit and boldly proclaiming Christ, Saul needs the approval of the apostles in Jerusalem. The problem: They were all afraid of him, not believing he really was a disciple. The whole mission hangs in the balance.

Enter another background helper named Barnabas. First introduced as a believer in the Jerusalem church for selling his property and giving the proceeds to the apostles, he obviously has their respect because they call this Joseph, a Levite from Cyprus, Barnabas.

At the critical juncture where Saul wants to join the apostles and they suspect his motives, Barnabas steps forward with a momentous introduction: "But Barnabas took him and brought him to the apostles." He told them about Saul meeting the Lord on the Damascus road and about his fearless preaching in the name of Jesus while in Damascus. The apostles accepted the word of Barnabas, and Saul preached boldly in Jerusalem.

Like Barnabas, who might you endorse as a bold spokesman of the Lord Jesus? Who might you encourage to use their God-given gifts to set the world ablaze with the Good News of Jesus? How might God use you to encourage and authenticate a fellow believer for mission—a letter, an e-mail communication, a phone call, a personal meeting? Sometimes hesitant and unwilling to get involved, we lay our sins before the Lord and cling to His cross so the Spirit might use us for a momentous introduction in God's time.

*Prayer:* That everyone he chooses,
For reasons of his own,
Will find in Christ his calling
To live his love alone.
His presence always leads us
Till time no more shall be;
Christ's strength, his love, his comfort
Gives us his victory.
*LW* 320:5

Copyright © 1982 Concordia Publishing House

# Barnabas: A Discerning Choice

## Reading: Acts 11:19–26

*Text:* Then Barnabas went to Tarsus to look for Saul and . . . brought him to Antioch. Acts 11:25–26

Barnabas's contribution to the worldwide Gospel mission of St. Paul did not end with his introduction of him to the apostles in Jerusalem. Later, while serving the newly formed church in Antioch where the disciples were first called Christians, he saw the needs there and made a discerning choice.

You see, after Stephen's martyrdom, many persecuted believers scattered to distant cities like Antioch where they told the message of Jesus, crucified and risen, to Jews. Others from Cyprus and Cyrene came to Antioch and spoke to Greeks about the good news about the Lord Jesus. Luke tells us, "A great number of people believed and turned to the Lord" (Acts 11:21). The church at Jerusalem wanted to make certain that this new church was legitimate and sent Barnabas to check them out. Barnabas properly saw evidence of God's grace, encouraged them to faithfulness, and continued the work of evangelism.

But he sensed that this explosive growth and interaction of Jewish and Greek believers needed additional leadership. He went to Tarsus, found Saul, and brought him to Antioch. For a whole year the team of Barnabas and Saul carried out a powerful teaching ministry.

What a discerning choice! Another step in God's plan to set the world ablaze through Paul, His apostle to the Gentiles.

How might God be asking you for discernment to involve others in Christian outreach? Who might you choose to join you in witnessing or teaching or serving in some other way? How can you be a Barnabas in your church, neighborhood, or place of work?

*Prayer:* Come, Holy Ghost, God and Lord,
With all your graces now outpoured
On each believer's mind and heart;
Your fervent love to them impart.
Lord, by the brightness of your light
In holy faith your Church unite;
From every land and every tongue
This to your praise, O Lord, our God be sung,
Alleluia, alleluia!
*LW* 154:1

# James: A Mission-Freeing Speech

**Reading: Acts 15:13–21**

*Text:* When they finished, James spoke up: "Brothers, listen to me." Acts 15:13

Turmoil in the Church—many Gentiles coming to faith in Jesus as Savior brought with them a different cultural background. Jewish believers, holding to their traditions, especially circumcision, insisting on Gentile compliance. Result: An important council was held in Jerusalem to settle these issues. Believers from the party of the Pharisees spoke. Peter spoke. Barnabas and Paul reported on God's working in Gentile hearts. What would be the decision?

James, the brother of the Lord and recognized leader of the Jerusalem church, spoke. His answer assured the freedom of the Christian world mission while preserving unity in the Church. Basing his remarks on Scripture (Amos 9:11–12), James concludes, "It is my judgement, therefore, that we should not make it difficult for the Gentiles who are turning to God" (Acts 15:19).

While James did not himself go on a mission to the Gentiles, his timely, bold, and wise speech helped to set the world ablaze with the Gospel. Now the churches could get on with their outreach, Jews and Gentiles together in one body. A mission-freeing speech!

In today's world of sharp cultural differences, churches need an answer to questions about faithful Christian mission worldwide. Who will give the mission-freeing speech like James? Based on the clear testimony of Scripture, centered in the atonement of Jesus Christ, crucified and risen, relying on God's Spirit working through Word and Sacraments, this speech will not make it difficult for the Gentiles who are turning to God, but will respect the godly tradition of the Church. One mission, one message, one people to set the world ablaze!

*Prayer:* People and realms of ev'ry tongue
Dwell on his love with sweetest song;
And infant voices shall proclaim
Their early blessings on his name.

Blessings abound where'er he reigns:
The pris'ners leap to lose their chains,
The weary find eternal rest,
And all who suffer want are blest.
*LW* 312:3–4

# Judas and Silas: A Personal Confirmation

## Reading: Acts 15:22–33

*Text:* "Therefore we are sending Judas and Silas to confirm by word of mouth what we are writing." Acts 15:27

Ananias, Barnabas, and James, in uniquely different ways, helped set the world ablaze with the Gospel of Jesus Christ. In today's reading, two relatively unknown disciples help play another important role in the worldwide mission. The apostles in Jerusalem put the decisions of the Jerusalem Council in writing but feel the necessity for a personal confirmation of the written document through respected disciples from their midst. They choose Judas (called Barnabas) and Silas to accompany Paul and Barnabas to Antioch.

We are told that these men delivered the letter with the following result: "The people read it and were glad for its encouraging message" (Acts 15:31). Luke continues to describe the personal testimony of the Jerusalem messengers: "Judas and Silas, who themselves were prophets, said much to encourage and strengthen the brothers" (Acts 15:32). The power of their personal confirmation of the letter is evident after they had returned to Jerusalem. "But Paul and Barnabas remained in Antioch, where they and many others taught and preached the word of the Lord" (Acts 15:35).

Could you help set the world ablaze like Judas and Silas? When the mission needs to be confirmed, are you ready to provide confirmation and encouragement to those outreach efforts to the lost, no matter what their background or cultural experiences? Confessing our reluctance to stand up and be counted, we rely on God's forgiveness through Christ and speak the encouraging word so the Gospel will spread. In the process, God may also single us out like Silas to join the missionary outreach personally.

*Prayer:* Come, holy Fire, comfort true,
Grant us the will your work to do
And in your service to abide;
Let trials turn us not aside.
Lord, by your pow'r prepare each heart,
And to our weakness strength impart
That bravely here we may contend,
Through life and death to you, our Lord, ascend.
Alleluia, Alleluia!
*LW* 154:3

# Lydia: Opening Her Home

**Reading: Acts 16:11–15**

*Text:* When she and the members of her household were baptized, she invited us to her home. Acts 16:15

Paul responded to the Macedonian call in a vision and traveled to the city of Philippi, the first planting of the Gospel in Europe. What a significant outpost for setting the world ablaze! But how would he get started? Who would provide a home base for his mission operation? He goes to the river where the small number of Jews in this Roman colony assemble for worship.

There he meets a woman named Lydia, the very helper he needs. She is a prominent woman, a dealer in purple cloth. A Gentile but a worshiper of God, Lydia hears Paul's preaching of Jesus as Savior. We are told: "The Lord opened her heart to respond to Paul's message" (Acts 16:14b). She and her household are baptized. Then Luke records, "She invited us to her home. 'If you consider me a believer in the Lord, come and stay at my house.' And she preserved us" (Acts 16:15). Now Paul has his base of operations in the home of a respected business person and a faithful convert. Even after Paul leaves the city, her home becomes a center for the new church. As God opened her heart to understand the Scriptures, Lydia opened her home to the apostles.

Could the Lord be asking you to open your home for the spread of the Gospel? As a respected citizen, what is your circle of influence? Your neighbors? Business associates? Church friends? By opening your home, could you give other missionaries, pastoral or lay leaders, a home base for training and outreach? Whether in your home, office, or a favorite restaurant, you as a repentant sinner washed clean by the blood of Jesus can help connect people to Jesus and as a result set the world ablaze.

*Prayer:* Heirs together of the grace of life,
All baptized into the death of Christ
Born again, in love maturing,
From the altar free and cheerful,
Caring, winsome family of God.
Catch the vision! Share the glory!
Show the captives, tell them: Christ is here!
*SP* 58:3

Copyright © 1986 Concordia Publishing House

# A Servant and a Witness

## Reading: Acts 26:12–23

*Text:* "I have appeared to you to appoint you as a servant and as a witness of what you have seen of Me and what I will show you." Acts 26:16b

Paul stands as a prisoner in Caesarea before King Agrippa and Bernice. In his defense, he relates the story of his conversion on the Damascus road. Pulling no punches about his previous shameful life as a persecutor of Christians, he quotes the words of Jesus to him: "I have appeared to you to appoint you as a servant and as a witness of what you have seen of Me and what I will show you." A servant and a witness!

With his life on the line, Paul simply declares his faith in Jesus, crucified and risen, as the only way to salvation. He then describes his assigned servant task to Jew and Gentile alike, "to open their eyes and turn them from darkness to light, and from the power of Satan to God, so that they may receive forgiveness of sins and a place among those who are sanctified by faith in [Him]" (Acts 26:18).

Near the end of his life as missionary to the Gentiles, Paul recalls what Jesus revealed to him at his conversion and what He has shown him as he has carried out the Lord's commands as servant and witness. Festus thinks him mad. Agrippa asserts that he can't be persuaded to be a Christian in a short time. But Paul, as servant and witness, continues to pray for their salvation.

Persecutors of Christ by our active and passive sins, we have also come face to face with Jesus in our Baptism, in our daily confession of sin, in His life-changing Word, and at His Holy Meal. We have received the forgiveness of sins and "a place among those who are sanctified by faith" in Jesus. He commissions us as servant and witness. No matter how others respond to Christ's message, we continue to pray for "all who are listening" to join us in saving faith (Acts 26:29).

*Prayer:* Dear Lord, thank You for Paul's life as servant and witness. Give me a servant heart and a consistent witness of Your salvation to "all who are listening." Amen.

# The Witness of a Meal

## Reading: Acts 27:27–44

*Text:* After this he took some bread and gave thanks to God in front of them all. Then he broke it and began to eat. Acts 27:35

If you only read the above text without the full reading, you might think that the meal is Jesus' instituting the Lord's Supper or breaking bread in the home of the Emmaus disciples or the early Christians breaking bread together after Pentecost. Every such meal is a witness to the crucified and risen Christ and reminds us that He gives us His true body and blood in the Sacrament for the forgiveness of sins.

But the witness of this meal is dramatic because of the circumstances. Paul is aboard ship with 275 others, largely unbelievers, on his way to imprisonment and trial in Rome. Despite Paul's advice, they have sailed in late fall and run into hurricane force winds that batter them for fourteen days. Paul has assured them that they will all be spared even after a shipwreck. He urges them to eat so they can survive the shipwreck. Then comes the text, "After this he took some bread and gave thanks to God in front of them all. Then he broke it and began to eat." Luke tells us that they were all encouraged and ate some food themselves.

Paul thanks the God of creation who provides bread, controls the wind and waves, and will protect these 276 survivors. He thanks His Lord Jesus Christ who died for him and the others. The witness of this meal!

Have you thought about how God uses you in the meals you eat–when you faithfully worship and receive His Holy Meal, when you regularly thank God as you break bread together in your home and as you pray in restaurants. There is perhaps a special witness when you continue thanking God at meals when you are in crisis–facing serious illness and death, coping with the loss of a job or severe financial problems, or experiencing national or international tragedy. The triune God blesses us each day in front of all the other people in our lives. The witness of a meal!

*Prayer:* God is great. God is good. And we thank Him for our food. Amen.

# With Great Humility and with Tears

## Reading: Acts 20:17–21

*Text:* "I served the Lord with great humility and with tears, although I was severely tested by the plots of the Jews." Acts 20:19

The next few devotions will focus on Paul's farewell to the Ephesian elders in Miletus on his way to Jerusalem for arrest. What can we learn about how to set the world ablaze with the Gospel of Jesus Christ? Remember that Paul spent almost three years in Ephesus on his third missionary journey, developing close relationships with people in that new church. He summons the elders for a final meeting at Miletus.

Paul begins his farewell address with these words, "I served the Lord with great humility and with tears." He asks them to reflect on his ministry with them in the midst of severe testing by Jewish plots. "Humility" suggests his dependence upon God for strength and guidance when he first preached in the synagogue and then in the lecture hall of Tyrannus. He credited God's Holy Spirit for both the boldness of his preaching and the miracles he performed (Acts 19:8–12). "Tears" referred to his love for the Ephesians and the urgency with which he preached. Luke summarizes the impact of Paul's "humility and tears": "In this way the word of the Lord spread widely and grew in power" (Acts 19:20).

Where do "humility" and "tears" fit into your mission outreach? Faced with a world that increasingly opposes or ignores the message of salvation through faith in Jesus, do you ask God for humility to rest in His forgiving love and depend on His Spirit to empower you and guide you in bold, daily witness? Aware that Christ may come again soon, do you reach out with tears because of your love for those around you without Christ and because of the urgency to share Jesus with them as their only hope for eternal life? Listening in with the Ephesian elders, we discover Paul's repentant heart and find new zeal for witnessing "with humility and with tears."

*Prayer:* Chief of sinners though I be
Christ is all in all to me;
All my wants to him are known,
All my sorrows are his own.
He sustains the hidden life
Safe with him from earthly strife.
*LW* 285:4

# Compelled by the Spirit

**Reading: Acts 20:13–16, 22–24**

*Text:* "And now, compelled by the Spirit, I am going to Jerusalem, not knowing what will happen to me there." Acts 20:22

Setting the world ablaze happens only through the leading of God's Holy Spirit. Paul carried out his entire apostolic ministry with an awareness of the Spirit working through the Word of God. Now, near the end of his life, he fully believes that the Holy Spirit wants him in Jerusalem. He suspects that trouble and persecution await him there. Others warn him not to go. But he says to the Ephesian elders, "And now compelled by the Spirit, I am going to Jerusalem, not knowing what will happen to me there."

Already bearing in his body the marks of beatings, whippings, and imprisonment, Paul does not make decisions on the basis of external circumstances, but on his call to proclaim the Gospel to Jews and Gentiles alike. He is sensitive to the leading of God's Spirit, which in this case he finds "compelling." Later, when a prophet named Agabus symbolically takes Paul's belt and binds himself with it, Paul replies, "I am ready not only to be bound, but also to die in Jerusalem for the name of the Lord Jesus" (Acts 21:13).

What a splendid example for our witnessing! God's Spirit has brought us into God's family through our Baptism. He speaks through the Word of God and makes us "wise for salvation through faith in Christ Jesus" (2 Timothy 3:15). He comforts us each day. Why should we not depend on His leading in our lives of daily Christian witness? The external circumstances of suffering, reverses, opposition, even death, may only enhance our opportunities to be used for God's purposes. "Compelled by the Spirit," we confidently and joyfully participate in God's mission to set the world ablaze.

*Prayer:* Left to ourselves, we surely stray;
Oh, lead us on the narrow way,
With wisest counsel guide us;
And give us steadfastness that we
May follow you forever free,
No matter who divides us.
Gently heal those Hearts now broken;
Given some token You are near us,
Whom we trust to light and cheer us.
*LW* 160:2

# Finishing the Race

## Reading: 2 Timothy 4:6–8

*Text:* "If only I may finish the race and complete the task the Lord Jesus has given me—the task of testifying to the gospel of God's grace." Acts 20:24b

What perspective on life will best help you set the world ablaze with Jesus Christ? Paul's perspective on his way to a hostile confrontation in Jerusalem is that of a long distance runner, straining to finish the race. He describes his life's task given to him by the Lord Jesus as "the task of testifying to the gospel of God's grace." That's what his race is all about. The race started in the dust of the Damascus road, took him on three missionary journeys all over the Roman Empire, and now is headed to Jerusalem where he will begin his journey as a prisoner of Rome itself.

Throughout this marathon, which poses obstacle after obstacle and causes aching muscles and tortured breathing, Paul never loses sight of his task of testifying to Jews and Gentiles about God's saving grace through Christ Jesus. He considers his earthly life as worth nothing to him if he can finish the race and receive the free gift of eternal life in heaven as his crown. No wonder Paul sets the world ablaze with Christ!

Consider your life as a marathon race starting at your Baptism, nourished by the Word of God's grace and His forgiveness in the Sacrament alongside your brothers and sisters in the Church. Recognize the wear and tear of Satan's attacks on your body and spirit as he marshals the sinful world and your own flesh against you. Focus on Jesus' task for you—"the task of testifying to the gospel of God's grace." Live with abandon as you head for the finish line, joyful about additional opportunities to share your faith in Jesus. With that perspective, earthly life means little and the crown of eternal life by God's grace for Christ's sake through faith means everything. Imagine as you finish the race how God is setting the world ablaze through you!

*Prayer:* Run the straight race through God's good grace;
Lift up your eyes, and seek his face.
Life with its way before us lies;
Christ is the path, and Christ the prize.
*LW* 299:2

# The Whole Will of God

### Reading: Acts 20:25–31

*Text:* "For I have not hesitated to proclaim to you the whole will of God." Acts 20:27

What kind of church can set the world ablaze with Christ? Paul's answer as he addresses the Ephesian elders at Miletus is a church that understands "the whole will of God." He spent almost three years teaching them, based on the Old Testament Scriptures, the saving Gospel of Jesus Christ. He continued his instruction through a circular letter to the Ephesians and other nearby churches. He has called them together now for perhaps a final time to teach them some more as shepherds of the flock. Paul knows that the world will not know and believe in the saving Christ unless the church studies the Word, faithfully preaches and teaches the Word, and guards the Word against false teachers who come as savage wolves to threaten the flock.

With that conviction in his heart, Paul says, "For I have not hesitated to proclaim to you the whole will of God." He then admonishes these spiritual overseers to keep watch over themselves and over the flock as shepherds of the Church Christ bought with His own blood, guarding against distortion of the truth from without and from within.

God calls us to tell the world about salvation through faith in Jesus Christ, crucified and risen. In order to accomplish that great task, we heed the words of Paul to rely on God's Spirit working through Word and Sacraments to provide a solid foundation in the Church, based on understanding and proclaiming "the whole will of God"—law and Gospel, sin and grace, justification and sanctification, church and ministry, worship and witness. A Church committed to sound biblical theology has a clear outreach message to set the world ablaze with Christ. Thank God for faithful pastors and teachers! Thank God for faithful churches who proclaim the Good News.

*Prayer:* Preserve your Word, O Savior To us this latter day,
And let your kingdom flourish; Enlarge your Church we pray.
Oh, keep our faith from failing; Keep hope's bright star aglow.
Let nothing from truth turn us While living here below.
*LW* 337:1

# The Word of His Grace

## Reading: Acts 20:32–38

*Text:* "Now I commit you to God and to the word of His grace, which can build you up and give you an inheritance among all who are sanctified." Acts 20:32

Paul, the world missionary whose life's task was to testify to the gospel of God's grace, finishes his farewell address to the Ephesian elders with a word of encouragement. He wants them to be strong in the Lord, live in the assurances that their sins are forgiven, and regularly proclaim Christ's salvation to their flock so the world may believe through their witness.

Therefore, he concludes, "Now I commit you to God and to the word of His grace, which can build you up." He then knelt with them and prayed. They wept and embraced him before accompanying him to his ship. Paul's actions and his teaching had communicated to these spiritual leaders the word of God's grace. The whole will of God reveals both God's Law and His Gospel, our sin and His salvation. The Word of grace is pure Gospel–God's choosing us from eternity, the perfect sacrifice of Christ on our behalf, His glorious resurrection from the grave, the Spirit's bringing us to faith and keeping us in the faith through Word and Sacrament. These men are built up in their faith and ready to build up the Church for witness to the world by the Word of grace.

We stand back and reflect on our audience with the apostle Paul in Miletus. His ministry with humility and tears, his determination to travel to Jerusalem, compelled by the Spirit, his description of finishing the race at any cost, his faithful proclamation of the whole will of God, and now his emotional commendation of the Word of God's grace to build us up.

Our hearts overflow with God's grace and forgiveness in our lives. We rejoice to be part of the Christian community which builds us up. And God's Spirit gives us a burning desire to set the world ablaze with that Word of His grace.

*Prayer:* The Gospel shows the Father's grace,
Who sent his Son to save our race,
Proclaims how Jesus lived and died
That man might thus be justified.
*LW* 330:1

# Busch Stadium: The Old

## Reading: Psalm 105:1–5

*Text:* Remember the wonders He has done, His miracles, and the judgments He pronounced. Psalm 105:5

In this summer of 2005 Busch Stadium, the home of the St. Louis Cardinals since 1966, is in its final season. At the end of the season, the old stadium will be demolished to make way for the new one, which is currently being constructed in its shadow. Memories abound of exciting baseball games played in Busch Stadium and the exploits of Cardinal greats like Bob Gibson, Lou Brock, Ozzie Smith, Mark McGwire, and Albert Pujols. Fans from around the country are flocking to the old Busch Stadium to remember and to tell others about their poignant memories of times past.

The psalmist in Psalm 105 gives thanks to the Lord for His mighty acts in the past: "Remember the wonders He has done, His miracles, and the judgments He pronounced." Then he adds the missionary dimension of that remembering, "Make known among the nations what He has done. . . . Tell of all His wonderful acts" (Psalm 105:1b–2b). In this psalm, he concentrates only on God's saving acts in Canaan, Egypt, the Red Sea, the wilderness, and the Promised Land again. The people's many sins and rebellion, also part of this past, go unmentioned but only serve to intensify the memories of God's forgiveness, grace, and mercy to Israel.

One aspect of our mission to set the world ablaze with the Gospel of Jesus Christ involves remembering God's redeeming acts, centered in the death and resurrection of His Son and the outpouring of His Spirit upon the Church. Those memories intensify when we also remember our rebellious sin that led to strife, disunity, and a negative witness. Reminded again of God's forgiveness through Christ, we flock to worship around Word and Sacraments and tell others about salvation through faith in Christ.

*Prayer:* All honor, thanks, and praise to you,
O Father, God of heaven,
For mercies every morning new,
Which you have freely given.
Inscribe this on my memory:
My Lord has done great things for me;
To this day he has helped me.
*LW* 456:2

Copyright © 1982 Concordia Publishing House

# Busch Stadium: The New

## Reading: Isaiah 43:14–19

*Text:* "Forget the former things; do not dwell on the past. See I am doing a new thing!" Isaiah 43:18–19a

While fans pour into the old Busch Stadium to savor its rich memories, construction dust and detours remind them all that a new Busch Stadium will soon replace the old. For many, that change is uncomfortable: "What's wrong with old Busch Stadium? How can the new stadium, however luxurious, ever replace the old in our hearts?" Yet it rises toward completion and, when the old stadium is demolished in late fall, it will be ready for opening day, 2006.

Yesterday we heard the psalmist praise God for the memories of His mighty acts and encourage others to tell the nations. Unfortunately, Israel's history records other memories of the people's rebelling at every crucial moment. Their disobedience led them to a downward spiral of adultery, materialism, and military defeat leading to Babylonian captivity. They hung on to their memories of God's blessings in the past, but despaired of the future.

To them, Isaiah brings this message, "Forget the former things; do not dwell on the past. See I am doing a new thing!" From the wilderness of their sin, He would create a way in the desert with an endless supply of water. He would bring His repentant people home to rebuild and from them to raise up a Messiah who would pay for the world's sin with the once-for-all atoning sacrifice of His Son on the cross. This "new thing" would give them greater reason for praise and witness to the world than anything they had experienced in the past.

In our rebellion, we often cling to the old and resent the new in our homes, our churches, and our world. Yet God brings His new into our old world so we can bear bold testimony to Jesus in this twenty-first century. Forgetting the former things of our sinful existence, we look with hope and joy to embrace God's "new thing" in His Church through His Son to set the world ablaze with the Gospel.

*Prayer:* O Savior now my spirit raise,
Give new direction to my ways,
In all I view, in all I do,
To give you praise.
*SP* 254:6

Copyright © 1987 Concordia Publishing House

# My Pastor on the Mound

## Reading: 1 Timothy 4:12–16

*Text:* But set an example for the believers in speech, in life, in love, in faith, and in purity. 1 Timothy 4:12b

Last summer a special event occurred at Busch Stadium, in its final season, before a St. Louis Cardinal's game against Pittsburgh. Nearly 1,000 members and friends of Concordia Lutheran Church of Kirkwood gathered in the stands for Vern Gundermann Night. My pastor, who was once offered a contract as a pitcher for the Chicago White Sox, walked to the mound and threw the first pitch. As he and his family were introduced, our sizable group cheered and waved signs. Pastor Gundermann retired in December.

That event provided a powerful witness to those assembled of our appreciation of a humble man, God's ordained servant, who has always pointed us to Jesus Christ, our Savior. St. Paul's words to the young pastor, Timothy, applied to a youthful Vern Gundermann who turned down the baseball contract to devote himself to full-time pastoral ministry. Those words, by God's grace through faith in Jesus, have also characterized his 42-year ministry: ". . . but set an example for the believers in speech, in life, in love, in faith, and in purity." Paul then referred to the public reading of the Scripture, preaching and teaching. He concludes, "Watch your life and doctrine closely. Persevere in them, because if you do, you will save both yourself and your hearers" (1 Timothy 4:16).

Later that evening last summer, with a big smile on his face, Pastor Gundermann autographed the special program for children who came to him and for eager adults with developmental disabilities from the Bethesda Group Home. He also tried to position this special recognition night for all pastors who serve in the holy ministry. I believe that all who know Pastor Vern Gundermann and his dear wife Betty are better motivated and equipped to help set the world ablaze with Christ because of his servant heart and clear Christ-centered proclamation.

*Prayer:* Lord, thank You for the servant heart of my pastor and for his faithful proclamation of Your saving Gospel. Help me follow his example. Amen.

# A Race Like No Other

## Reading: 1 Corinthians 9:19–27

*Text:* Though I am free and belong to no man, I make myself a slave to everyone, to win as many as possible. 1 Corinthians 9:19

The Tour de France is a race like no other. As the crowning event of cycling, this race lasts more than three weeks in 23 stages, pitting the finest cyclists in the world against one another. The cyclists also belong to teams that help determine whether they can win the yellow jacket in Paris. The race requires intensive training, a strong team, speed and endurance, the ability to win both on flat land and in the mountains across Europe. The winner demonstrates skill, conditioning, and a clear focus on the goal.

St. Paul, as an apostle of Jesus Christ, runs a race like no other to win Jews and Gentiles to a saving faith in the Savior. He endures persecution, imprisonment, ridicule, and all manner of obstacles en route to his clear goal of knowing nothing among people except Jesus Christ and Him crucified. In our text he expresses his willingness to make himself a slave to everyone to win as many as possible—a Jew to the Jews, a Greek to the Greeks, all things to all men that he might save some. That disciplined self-sacrificing missionary outreach, Paul compares with runners in the famous Corinthian games. He recognizes his own sin and need for a Savior and depends upon God's power for his Gospel witness.

God calls us, forgiven sinners, washed clean in the blood of Jesus Christ, to embark upon a race like no other—setting the world ablaze with the Gospel of Jesus Christ. He leads us to people of many different backgrounds and needs. He points out the temptations and obstacles in the way. He trains us for the race through His Word and Sacraments among the assembled people of God, our team. Then He sends us forth, like Paul, to win as many as possible. What a thrill to ride in our spiritual Tour de France, a race like no other!

*Prayer:* Run the straight race through God's good grace;
Lift up your eyes, and seek his face.
Life with its way before us lies;
Christ is the path, and Christ the prize.
*LW* 299:2

# Modeling Mission

## Reading: 1 Thessalonians 3:6–13

*Text:* Therefore, brothers, in all our distress and persecution we were encouraged about you because of your faith. 1 Thessalonians 3:7

Recently my wife and I participated in a study of Paul's letters to the Thessalonians, written early in his ministry, around AD 51–52. With my eyes on setting the world ablaze for Christ, I noticed the interplay between Paul's ongoing mission in new cities and his relationship with the Thessalonian Christians. In a way, he was modeling mission for them. In another way, they were modeling mission for him and others. Always Paul and the Thessalonians, whether consciously or not, were modeling the mission of Christ, their Savior. The next several devotions will explore these modeling relationships to help us in our daily mission.

Paul came to Thessalonika on his second missionary journey as part of his response to the Macedonian vision. He was able to spend only three Sabbath days there with many converts before being forced to flee. In Berea, Athens, and Corinth, he opened new missions but continued to show concern for the fledgling believers in Thessalonika. He sends Timothy to visit and receives a very encouraging report about their faith and love under persecution. On one hand, he realized that they had followed his model of trusting Christ for salvation and living in love. On the other hand, he tells them how much their example means to him: "In all our distress and persecution we were encouraged about you because of your faith. For now we really live, since you are standing firm in the Lord" (1 Thessalonians 3:7–8).

Who are your models for mission? For whom might you be modeling mission? Remember: "To this you were called, because Christ suffered for you, leaving you an example, that you should follow in His steps" (1 Peter 2:21).

*Prayer:* For this time and place have we been born,
Gifted by the Spirit, trained and sent:
With the eyes of Jesus seeing,
With the hands of Jesus helping,
With the words of Jesus bringing life.
Catch the vision! Share the glory!
Show the captives, tell them: Christ is here!
*SP* 58:4

Copyright © 1986 Concordia Publishing House

September 4

# Modeling for Others

## Reading: 1 Thessalonians 1:2–10

*Text:* And so you became a model to all believers in Macedonia and Achaia. 1 Thessalonians 1:7

We don't always desire to serve as a model for others. Very much aware of our own faults and shortcomings, we would rather claim a false humility as Christians and reject the notion that we might be used by God to model mission for other individuals and churches.

The young and inexperienced group of Thessalonians certainly could have begged off from any mission modeling. Still learning from God's Word, still tempted by the sinful culture from which they had emerged, still struggling under persecution, they might have been content to live in the shadows.

Yet Paul writes about their "work produced by faith," their "labor prompted by love" and their "endurance inspired by hope in our Lord Jesus" (1 Thessalonians 1:3). As a result, he exclaims, "And so you became a model to all the believers in Macedonia and Achaia. The Lord's message rang out from you not only in Macedonia and Achaia—your faith in God has become known everywhere" (1 Thessalonians 1:7–8). You see, despite, or perhaps because of, their weakness, the Lord's message of salvation through faith in Christ alone spread widely. They modeled mission for others.

For whom do you model mission? How is the Lord's message of grace ringing out from you to others? In what ways is the Lord giving you His forgiveness, strength, and courage to serve as a mission model for others?

*Prayer:* Universal Body of the Lord,
Chosen, called, made just, and glorified:
Ours the faith, and ours the triumph,
Ours the peace the world is seeking;
Who on earth as privileged as we?
Heirs together of the grace of Life,
All baptized into the death of Christ
Born again, in love maturing,
From the altar free and cheerful,
Caring winsome family of God.
Catch the vision! Share the glory!
Show the captives, tell them: Christ is here!
*SP* 58:2–3

Copyright © 1986 Concordia Publishing House

# Modeling Other Churches

## Reading: 1 Thessalonians 2:13–16

*Text:* For you, brothers, became imitators of God's churches in Judea, which are in Christ Jesus: You suffered from your own countrymen the same things those churches suffered from the Jews. 1 Thessalonians 2:14

Who are your models for mission? Do other churches come to mind in your community, nationwide, or worldwide? If so, what behaviors, attitudes, and mission approaches have drawn your attention to them and helped you in your witness? Their prayer and worship life, their bold and creative outreach, their obvious love for one another, their persistence under trials? You probably find yourself modeling other churches in one way or another.

Paul calls the attention of the Thessalonians in the midst of persecution to the model of the churches in Judea: "For you, brothers, became imitators of God's churches in Judea, which are in Christ Jesus: You suffered from your own countrymen the same things those churches suffered from the Jews, who killed the Lord Jesus and the prophets and also drove us out" (1 Thessalonians 2:14–15). Apparently the Thessalonians drew comfort and courage from the faithful churches in Judea that had already experienced suffering for the faith. They kept proclaiming Jesus as Savior and reaching out to others, despite the risk to their lives. Now these Thessalonian Christians model Judean churches as they persevere in mission to reach "the Gentiles so they may be saved" (1 Thessalonians 2:16).

We need the modeling of other churches—persecuted African Christians in the Sudan; faithful churches reaching out to diverse ethnic groups in American cities; and creative, outreach-oriented churches in rural America with declining and aging populations. God's Spirit uses the ministry of Word and Sacraments to draw many to the Lord Jesus as Savior around the world. Thank God for these mission models!

*Prayer:* Blessed children, saints, elect of God,
Globe encircling cloud of witnesses:
We have heard the Christmas angels,
We have seen the Easter sunrise,
Cried with joy when Christ began his reign.
Catch the vision! Share the glory!
Show the captives, tell them: Christ is here!
*SP* 58:1

Copyright © 1986 Concordia Publishing House

# Modeling Our Spiritual Leaders

**Reading: 1 Corinthians 10:31–11:1**

*Text:* You became imitators of us. 1 Thessalonians 1:6a

The Church is only as strong as its spiritual leaders. They teach the Word of God in its truth and purity and administer the Sacraments faithfully according to the Gospel of Christ. They also serve as models of mission that enable churches to be models for others.

Paul writes to the Thessalonian Christians, "You became imitators of us." What did Paul and his associates model? They spoke "as men approved by God to be entrusted with the Gospel . . . not trying to please men but God, who tests their hearts" (1 Thessalonians 2:4). They not only shared the gospel of salvation through Christ but their very lives as well, "working night and day not to be a burden to anyone" (1 Thessalonians 2:9). They loved these Christians and rejoiced in their faith so much that Paul could write, "For what is our hope, our joy, or the crown in which we will glory in the presence of our Lord Jesus when He comes? Is it not you? Indeed, you are our glory and joy" (1 Thessalonians 2:19–20). In similar fashion, Paul wrote to the Corinthian Christians, "For I am not seeking my own good but the good of many, so that they may be saved. Follow my example as I follow the example of Christ" (1 Corinthians 10:33b–11:1). What a model of mission for these Christians!

Trust in Jesus Christ for salvation. Reliance on God's Holy Spirit working through the Word, humble self-giving and persistent love, priority to reaching the lost at any cost—Paul's modeling and the modeling of our spiritual leaders point to Christ and transform us into mission models for others.

*Prayer:* God of the prophets, bless the prophets' sons;
Elijah's mantle on Elisha cast.
Each age its solemn task may claim but once;
Make each one nobler, stronger than the last.

Make them apostles, heralds of your cross;
Forth let them go to tell all lands your grace.
By you inspired, they count all else but loss
And stand at last with joy before your face.
*LW* 258:1, 4

# Modeling Christ

## Reading: Ephesians 5:1–2

*Text:* You became imitators of us and of the Lord. 1 Thessalonians 1:6a

How do we model mission in today's world? For whom does God want us to be models? What mission churches and spiritual leaders serve as models for us? Everything comes down to one question: Who is the ultimate mission model–for the Macedonians, the Thessalonians, the Judeans, and the apostle Paul? Answer: Jesus Christ, our Lord!

Paul writes, "You became imitators of us and of the Lord." In 1 Corinthians, he says, "Follow my example as I follow the example of Christ" (1 Corinthians 11:1). To the Ephesians, he pens these words: "Be imitators of God, therefore, as dearly loved children and live a life of love, just as Christ loved us and gave Himself up for us as a fragrant offering and sacrifice to God" (Ephesians 5:1–2). As Jesus put it to His disciples who were intent on being first, "Whoever wants to become great among you must be your servant . . . just as the Son of Man did not come to be served, but to serve, and to give His life as a ransom for many" (Matthew 20:26, 28).

Jesus is the means, the example, and the message for our mission modeling. Because of our selfishness, rebellion, and disobedience, we need Jesus' ransom for our sins upon the cross. He is the only means to salvation. Because of our sinful flesh and the hostile world around us, we need Jesus' example of servanthood, forgiving love, and passion for the lost. Because of the confusing and false teachings in the world, we need the simple message of Jesus: "I am the Way, the Truth, and the Life. No one comes to the Father but by Me" (John 14:6).

Modeling Christ as the means, the example, and the message, we make ourselves available to model mission so the world will be set ablaze with His Gospel!

*Prayer:* See, from his head, his hands, his boast
Save in the death of Christ, my God;
All the vain things that charm me most,
I sacrifice them to his blood.
*LW* 115:3

# Bishop Pavel Uhorskai

## Reading: 2 Timothy 3:10–15

*Text:* But as for you, continue in what you have learned and have become convinced of, because you know those from whom you learned it. 2 Timothy 3:14

In early 1992, shortly after many countries of Eastern Europe had been liberated from Soviet control, I was privileged to travel to Slovakia. There I met the bishop of the Lutheran Church, Pavel Uhorskai. His steadfast faith in Jesus Christ and life of suffering inspired me then and continues to shape my witness.

As a young pastor with an evangelist's outreach to youth, he clashed with the Communist government because of his continuing proclamation of Christ as Savior. He spent time in prison and was then forced to work in construction for years, denied the opportunity to serve as a pastor. After the fall of Communism, he was chosen by the Lutheran Church in Slovakia to serve as their bishop. Now 70 years old, he serves with a clear focus on the Gospel, with a wisdom and kindness tempered by his years of suffering for his faith.

The time in his presence reminded me of Paul's witness to Timothy from prison based on his "teaching, way of life, purpose, faith, patience, love, endurance, persecutions, and sufferings" (2 Timothy 2:10). Paul's charge to Timothy reminds me of my meetings with Bishop Uhorskai and equally applies to you as you daily reach out in mission to those around you: "But as for you, continue in what you have learned . . . because you know those from whom you learned it, and how from infancy you have known the Holy Scriptures, which are able to make you wise for salvation through faith in Christ Jesus" (2 Timothy 3:14–15).

*Prayer:* And for your Gospel let us dare
To sacrifice all treasure;
Teach us to bear your blessed cross,
To find in you all pleasure.
Oh, grant us steadfastness
In joy and distress,
Lest we, Lord, you forsake.
Let us by grace partake
Of endless joy and gladness.
*LW* 293:4

# Unchained Word

## Reading: 2 Timothy 2:8–10

*Text:* But God's Word is not chained. 2 Timothy 2:9b

At the end of his long ministry, in chains and probably awaiting execution, St. Paul writes his friend and student, Timothy, a young pastor. His message is simple but powerful: "Remember Jesus Christ, raised from the dead, descended from David. This is my gospel, for which I am suffering even to the point of being chained like a criminal. But God's word is not chained" (2 Timothy 2:8–9).

Paul wants Timothy to trust and proclaim the saving Gospel—Jesus Christ true God ("raised from the dead") and true man ("descended from David") who paid the full price for our sins by His suffering and death. That Gospel has resulted in suffering and expected death for Paul. But his chains only lead him to tell Timothy that God's Word is not chained. Timothy is free to proclaim that Gospel that changes lives.

As we consider helping to set the world ablaze in this twenty-first century with the Gospel of Jesus Christ, Paul's message speaks to our hearts as well. No matter the cost to our personal lives (suffering, persecution, rejection, ridicule), we possess an unchained Word of salvation through the death and resurrection of Jesus, true God and true man. Entrusted to Christ's Church, this Gospel forgives our sins, strengthens us for witness, and changes lives around us by the Spirit's power. That unchained Word unchains people from their bondage to sin, death, and the devil.

*Prayer:* Grant, we implore you, almighty God, to your Church your Holy Spirit and the wisdom which comes down from above that your Word may not be bound but have free course and be preached to the joy and edifying of Christ's holy people, so that in steadfast faith we may serve you and in the confession of your name abide to the end; through Jesus Christ, your Son, our Lord, who lives and reigns with you and the Holy Spirit, one God, now and forever. Amen.
*LW* Divine Service 1, p. 156

Copyright © 1982 Concordia Publishing House

# An Instrument for Noble Purposes

**Reading: 2 Timothy 2:14–21**

*Text:* If a man cleanses himself from the latter, he will be an instrument for noble purposes, made holy, useful to the Master and prepared to do any good work. 2 Timothy 2:21

Our society takes great care to prepare people for effective leadership in the world. An intentional blend of formal education, on-the-job experience, workshops and seminars, and professional mentoring equips the individual for expanded responsibility and exceptional service.

St. Paul attempts to prepare Timothy for a lifetime ministry as a pastor in service to the Gospel. He refers to him as "an instrument for noble purposes." Earlier he urges Timothy to present himself to God "as one approved, a workman who does not need to be ashamed and who correctly handles the word of truth" (2 Timothy 2:15).

He counsels Timothy to look around and recognize the difference between what is noble and what is ignoble, between precious building materials like silver and gold and less usable materials like wood and clay, between godly qualities like righteousness, faith, love, peace, kindness, purity of heart and sinful worldly pursuits like godless chatter, evil desires of youth, and foolish and stupid arguments. As an instrument for noble purposes, Timothy can "gently instruct in the hope that God will grant them repentance leading them to a knowledge of the truth" (2 Timothy 2:25).

How important for our missionary work every day in a world full of ignoble pursuits and ungodly living: "Instruments for noble purposes"! Cleansed from our sins through Christ, focused on those who don't believe in Jesus, open to learn and grow through God's Word of truth, we seek God's wisdom to choose noble purposes as His instruments of Gospel witness.

*Prayer:* Give me the strength to do
With ready heart and willing
Whatever you command
My calling here fulfilling.
Help me do what I should
With all might, and bless
The outcome for my good,
For you must give success.
*LW* 371:2

# Reflections from the Mountains

## Reading: Psalm 36:5–6

*Text:* Your righteousness is like the mountains of God. Psalm 36:6a (ESV)

Recently my wife and I joined a group of Christian friends for a few days in the Rocky Mountains for planning, spiritual growth, and recreation. The next few devotions will comprise my "Reflections from the Mountains," based on the second half of Psalm 36. After exposing the transgressions of the wicked, the psalmist extols the greatness of God in these words, "Your righteousness is like the mountains of God."

Everywhere we saw mountains–from the Denver airport, through mountain passes in a steady rainfall, across the Continental Divide, and down the western side, through the windows of the spacious home where we gathered, on the patio early in the morning and at sunset. The mountains inspire awe and generate a spirit of humble thanksgiving in the presence of a majestic God. In humble praise, the psalmist compares God's righteousness with the mountains of Israel. In many psalms, God's righteousness and justice are linked with His steadfast love and faithfulness. You can count on God to be who He is and to act consistently just as you can count on the mountains.

We are unrighteous and unjust because of our sin, just like the wicked. All our righteousness is as filthy rags. But God sent His Son Jesus to be our righteousness through His sinless life and atoning death on the cross. God declares us righteous for Jesus' sake. We rest secure in His righteousness, just like the tall and sturdy mountains.

Our stay in the mountains filled us with the desire to tell others about the beauty, peace, and refreshment we experienced. God's righteousness through Christ in a similar way moves us to thank Him daily and to tell others about the forgiveness, new life, peace, and refreshment available to them by God's grace.

*Prayer:* There dwells the Lord our king,
The Lord our righteousness,
Triumphant o'er the world and sin,
The prince of Peace.
On Zion's sacred height
His kingdom he maintains
And glorious with his saints in light
Forever reigns.
*LW* 450:7

# Man and Beast You Save

**Reading: Psalm 50:10–15**

*Text:* Man and beast You save, O LORD. Psalm 36:6c (ESV)

Those days in the mountains provided some delightful views of wildlife. One morning, as I was reading my Bible, I looked out the front window and saw a doe walk right up to the wrought iron fence in front of the patio. She looked straight at me with her ears alert. She sensed no danger and walked in leisurely fashion through the side yard, followed closely by her fawn, and then moved up the mountainside. A few minutes later her yearling appeared, a little less sure of safety, and with a start, bounded up the mountainside at a sharper angle. I could not help but think of the psalmist's words, "Man and beast You save, O LORD."

Obviously, these words describe the physical preservation of humans and animals alike in God's creation. In Psalm 50, God speaks to His people about the sacrifices of thanksgiving for His salvation: "For every beast of the field is Mine, the cattle on a thousand hills" (Psalm 50:10). Then He applies that physical preservation to human beings, "Call upon Me in the day of trouble; I will deliver you, and you shall glorify Me" (Psalm 50:15).

But as I watched the trusting doe in a safe place, I thought of God's salvation through Jesus Christ. The doe was able to go about her daily life, caring for her fawn and releasing her yearling for independent living, just because she knew God's safe place for her. In the same way, God has brought me into the safe place of God's grace. Despite a cruel and wicked world, despite Satan's attacks, despite my own sinful nature, God sent His Son to bear my punishment on Calvary. Forgiven and set free in Christ through my Baptism, I have been incorporated into God's people and enjoy salvation and safety in the arms of my Savior.

From that safe place, I can go about my daily life in family, community, work activities, and world with thanksgiving to God for physical and spiritual deliverance and with a desire to share that salvation with others—"Man and beast You save, O LORD."

*Prayer:* All you beasts and cattle, bless the Lord;
All you children of mortals, bless the Lord—
Praise him and magnify him forever.
*LW* 9:16–17

Copyright © 1982 Concordia Publishing House

# The Abundance of Your House

## Reading: Psalm 36:7–10

*Text:* They feast on the abundance of Your house, and You give them drink from the river of Your delight. Psalm 36:8 (ESV)

As I reflect on my time in the mountains, the word "abundance" comes to mind—the mountain slopes carpeted in green, the colorful wildflowers, the clear, fast-flowing mountain streams, the picturesque villages of Vail and Beaver Creek, the comfortable mountain home where we stayed, the rich interactions personally and spiritually with our group of friends, the quiet reading of God's Word in that peaceful setting. This abundance made the words of the psalmist come alive for me: "How precious is Your steadfast love, O God! The children of mankind take refuge in the shadow of Your wings. They feast on the abundance of Your house, and You give them drink from the river of Your delight. For with You is the fountain of life; in Your light do we see light" (Psalm 36:7–9 ESV). His house refers to all creation from which flows the water of life. But I thought of the house where we gathered, from which we experienced the total blessings of the mountains. What abundance, a gift of God's hand!

Coming from the mountains back to our home on the Mississippi River bluffs of St. Louis, I am moved to share that abundance with others. Jesus says, "I came that they may have life and have it abundantly" (John 10:10 ESV). For Him, that meant laying down His life for the sheep as Good Shepherd. Post-resurrection, Jesus said to His disciples, "As the Father has sent Me, even so I am sending you" (John 20:21 ESV). Forgiven, restored, gifted with abundant life in Christ, we are sent to offer that abundant life to others, living in scarcity and want, physically and spiritually. Abundance of witness to Christ! God's promise by His grace in Proverbs: "Whoever brings blessing will be enriched, and one who waters will himself be watered" (Proverbs 11:25 ESV). Reflections from the mountains!

*Prayer:* From all that dwell below the skies
Let the creator's praise arise;
Alleluia, alleluia!
Let the redeemer's name be sung
Through ev'ry land by ev'ry tongue.
Alleluia, alleluia!
*LW* 440:1

# Town Haul Witness

## Reading: Acts 13:38–49

*Text:* When the Gentiles heard this; they were glad and honored the word of the Lord; and all who were appointed for eternal life believed. Acts 13:48

The Learning Channel (TLC) features a show called Town Haul. The hostess, skilled in interior design, and a builder, carpenter, and expert in landscape design chose a town somewhere in the United States with considerable charm and community spirit. The producers then help community leaders identify six families in need and enlist volunteers to help them bring joy to those worthy recipients in the form of gifts and home improvement projects.

Saturday evening we watched the first episode in Town Haul's new series because they had chosen Washington, Missouri, a quaint town on the banks of the Missouri River where our son-in-law serves as one of the pastors at Immanuel Lutheran Church. Two of the six families selected are members at Immanuel. As we viewed the outpouring of support for the Gant family, our eyes filled with tears because we observed how this Town Haul presentation was giving witness to Jesus Christ through the family's story and the outreach of Immanuel to them.

I was reminded of St. Paul's outreach in Pisidian Antioch on his first missionary journey. He went to the synagogue on the Sabbath and, by invitation, brought a message of encouragement to the people. He clearly proclaimed the forgiveness of sins through Jesus and justification through faith in Him. Invited back, they attracted almost the whole city to hear the word of the Lord. Although some Jewish leaders generated opposition to Paul's message, many Gentiles in the city "were glad and honored the Word of the Lord." In fact, we are told, "The word of the Lord spread through the whole region" (Acts 13:49).

In our twenty-first century, God's Spirit moves just as powerfully and can use your church and the witness of your home to proclaim Jesus Christ in actions and words. More on the Gant family and Immanuel in the next two devotions.

*Prayer:* And not alone to nations In far-away retreats,
But ev'rywhere I broadcast His love through crowded streets:
The lives that my life touches, However great or small—
Let them through me see Jesus, Who served and saved us all.
*LW* 320:4

Copyright © 1982 Concordia Publishing House

# Town Haul Family

## Reading: Psalm 102:1–12

*Text:* "You are the salt of the earth. But if the salt loses its saltiness, how can it be salty again?" Matthew 5:13

Town Haul in Washington, Missouri, tells the story of the Gant family. "Spider" Gant, owner of a small lawn care business, needed a kidney and pancreas transplant because of severe Type I diabetes. The procedure took place in Wisconsin. During the time of his surgery and recovery, he couldn't maintain his business on his own. His wife, Patty, a nurse, tried to pay the bills, and care for Spider and their adopted children, Jessica and Jonathan. While he recovered from his successful transplants, Patty developed a rare disease of the connective tissue and was hospitalized. Yet the family demonstrated a strong faith in the Lord and received support from their church.

As the project unfolds, we hear Spider saying that he is praying for Patty to be released from the hospital. They thank Immanuel Lutheran Church for their spiritual and tangible support and desire to provide the church school, through Town Haul's generosity, with musical instruments for their curriculum. When Patty enters a newly constructed solarium in their home, she comments, "God has a sense of humor. One year ago we didn't know if we could keep our house. Now, it is like paradise." In their life, the Gants are the salt of the earth, not losing their saltiness through adversity.

When Jesus in His Sermon on the Mount tells His disciples, "you are the salt of the earth," He means that God has made them salt to flavor and preserve their world, as part of God's kingdom on earth. Jesus, by His life, death, and resurrection, brought new life to the world and makes us "the salt of the earth" in our Baptism. The psalmist describes tremendous adversity through physical illness and although tempted to despair and lose his saltiness, he turns to the Lord, enthroned forever, who will have compassion on Zion and respond to the prayer of the destitute (Psalm 102). What a witness to Jesus the Savior through the attitudes, words, and perseverance of the Gant family, living as "the salt of the earth" by God's grace!

*Prayer:* That ev'ryone he chooses,
For reasons of his own,
Will find in Christ his calling
To live his love alone.
*LW* 320:5

Copyright © 1982 Concordia Publishing House

# Town Haul Church

## Reading: Matthew 5:14–16

*Text:* "You are the light of the world. A city on a hill cannot be hidden." Matthew 5:14

In the Town Haul episode on the Gant family, Immanuel Lutheran Church provides a witness to the television staff, the community, and the television viewers. You see the church at worship and their school as a setting for the presentation of musical instruments at the request of Patty and her daughter, Jessica, who attends the school. A Hollywood actor, Jack Wagner, is present to invite Jessica to appear on a television program. The Gants express their gratitude to Immanuel for taking care of their tuition during the difficult health days, providing meals, and helping to care for the children.

Jesus tells His disciples, "You are the light of the world. A city on a hill cannot be hidden." He describes a small clay lamp burning olive oil, not hidden, but placed on a stand to provide light for the house. Then Jesus adds, "In the same way let your light shine before men, that they may see your good deeds and praise your Father in heaven" (Matthew 5:16). Christ, the crucified and risen One, is the light of the world who shines through our lives to rescue people from the darkness of sin.

Washington, Missouri, is a city on the hill because of Town Haul's selection process. Immanuel Lutheran Church, simply by being God's people gathered around Word and Sacraments and serving people in need, like the Gants, is "the light of the world" bringing Christ as Savior to many. And the Gant family, relying on their Savior, is "the salt of the earth." How might God be positioning you and your church for a "salt and light" witness in your community and world? Town Haul opens our eyes to see new opportunities!

*Prayer:* Lord, gather all your children,
Wherever they may be,
And lead them on to heaven
To live eternally
With you, our loving Father,
And Christ, our brother dear,
Whose Spirit guards and gives us
The joy to persevere.
*LW* 320:6

Copyright © 1982 Concordia Publishing House

# Spirit Lifters

## Reading: Romans 8:14–17

*Text:* Having gifts that differ according to the grace given to us, let us use them . . . the one who does acts of mercy, with cheerfulness." Romans 12:6a, 8d (ESV)

Our daughter Amy recently returned with her pastor husband from a pastoral leadership conference. Inspired to identify her own personal mission at a time when she is rearing five sons under the age of ten (a significant mission in its own right), she embraced a passion for creating cards and decided to involve other women at Immanuel Lutheran Church in a Christian card ministry. The search for a name ended when the wife of a retired pastor, herself an avid card sender, suggested: Spirit Lifters. That name was enthusiastically adopted because it captures the purpose of these women–to lift the spirits of people in times of joy and sorrow: illness, grieving, anniversaries, baptisms, and professions of faith.

In Romans 12, Paul urges the body of believers, on the basis of God's mercies through the saving work of Christ, to recognize and use their God-given gifts in service to the world. One gift is described as "the one who does acts of mercy, with cheerfulness." Through cards, Spirit Lifters seems to fit this category. More important, as Paul writes in Romans 8, spirits are lifted by the Spirit of God pointing us to Christ: "The Spirit Himself bears witness with our spirit that we are children of God, and if children, then heirs–heirs of God and fellow heirs with Christ, provided we suffer with Him in order that we may also be glorified with Him" (Romans 8:16–17 ESV).

How might you be a spirit lifter, using God's gifts to encourage, comfort, and most of all point to Christ our Savior through whom we are His children and heirs? What a witness!

*Prayer:* In sickness, sorrow, want, or care,
Each others burdens help us share;
May we, where help is needed, there
Give help as though to you.

And may your Holy Spirit move
All those who live to live in love
Till you receive in heav'n above
Those who have lived to you.
*LW* 397:5–6

# Mori-Sensei

### Reading: 1 Timothy 1:12–17

*Text:* The grace of our Lord was poured out on me abundantly, along with the faith and the love that are in Christ Jesus. 1 Timothy 1:14

A missionary in Japan tells about his Japanese language instructor many years ago, a woman sensei, or teacher, named Mori. She was strict and formal, insisting on mastery of the language, but also loved as a teacher. However, she was not a believer in Jesus as Savior. When Mori-sensei died recently, the missionary was thrilled to hear that she had been baptized by a former missionary in October 2003.

When a memorial service was held in Tokyo, a letter was shared at her request: "In the midst of suffering, I finally got to the point where I was completely humbled. I began to sense that my former life was forgiven." The missionary concludes, "Our teacher, for so many years a symbol of the challenge to the Gospel, had finally been overwhelmed by the Holy Spirit quietly yet diligently at work in her heart. Now at her funeral, she was testifying to her Lord."

Mori's testimony reminds me of Paul's testimony to Timothy: "Even though I was once a blasphemer and a persecutor and a violent man, I was shown mercy because I acted in ignorance and unbelief. The grace of our Lord was poured out on me abundantly, along with the faith and the love that are in Christ Jesus. …Christ Jesus came into the world to save sinners—of whom I am the worst. But for that very reason I was shown mercy so that in me, the worst of sinners, Christ Jesus might display His unlimited patience as an example for those who would believe on Him and receive eternal life" (1 Timothy 1:13–16). Thank you, St. Paul and Mori-sensei for your witness to Jesus!

*Prayer:* Chief of sinners though I be, Christ is all in all to me;
All my wants to him are known, All my sorrows are his own.
He sustains the hidden life Safe with him from earthly strife.

Oh my Savior, help afford By your Spirit and your Word!
When my wayward heart would stray, Keep me in the narrow way;
Grace in time of need supply. While I live and when I die.
*LW* 285:4–5

# Christian Preschool in the Bush

## Reading: Deuteronomy 6:4–8

*Text:* "I praise You Father, Lord of heaven and earth, because You have hidden these things from the wise and learned, and revealed them to little children." Matthew 11:25

In Kenya, a missionary files this report about a Maasai Christian preschool in the African bush: "Education is Kenya's answer to getting a job and finding a way out of poverty. Even though this Christian Maasai community had talked about a Christian preschool, nothing had been done. They asked if I could help get them started. The help that I gave came in the form of a 3' x 4' blackboard that I made from a thin sheet of plywood and paint, a few school supplies, and encouragement from God's Word. They now have 37 children coming, from the ages of two to seven. The school day is from 8 a.m. to 12:30 p.m. Some children from distant areas must walk for one and a half hours to and from school. All this is made possible by one young woman who has agreed to be the teacher. We just pray that our Lord will continue to lead these little ones, and help them grow in the knowledge and admonition of our Lord Jesus Christ."

Reaching children–what a powerful way to set the world ablaze with Christ! In Deuteronomy Moses talks about the importance of passing on God's Word–commands and promises–to our families. Specifically, "Impress them on your children. Talk about them when you sit at home and when you walk along the road, when you lie down and when you get up" (Deuteronomy 6:7). And Jesus praises His Father "because He has hidden these things from the wise and learned, and revealed them to little children."

Preschool children of the Christian Maasai community in the bush. The children and the grandchildren in your family. The children in your church and community. Teach, impress upon them, let the Father reveal to them the story of Jesus and His love!

*Prayer:* Lord Jesus Christ, the children's friend,
To each of them your presence send;
Call them by name and keep them true
In loving faith, dear Lord, to you.
*LW* 470:1

Copyright © 1982 Concordia Publishing House

# Hurricane Katrina: The Reality

## Reading: Psalm 8:1–4

*Text:* What is man that You are mindful of him, and the Son of Man that You care for Him? Psalm 8:4 (ESV)

In the early morning hours of Monday, August 29, 2005, Hurricane Katrina struck the Gulf Coast of Louisiana, Mississippi, and Alabama with winds in excess of 140 miles per hour, causing a destructive sea surge near Gulfport and Biloxi and the eventual flooding of the city of New Orleans. The resultant communication breakdown, collapse of medical facilities, extensive loss of life, gathering of displaced residents under desperate living conditions, and total destruction of commercial and residential property made this killer storm one of the worst natural disasters in U.S. history.

The next several devotions will turn to God's Word for understanding and comfort in the immediate aftermath of Hurricane Katrina. How might the horrible reality of this storm and its effects anchor our faith in the God of our salvation and make us more effective in our witness to Jesus Christ? In Psalm 8, King David reflects on the majesty of God's creation–the heavens, moon, and stars in the night sky. He could have included the powerful forces of nature in the wind and the waves. In the face of God's almighty power, he sees how puny human beings are: "What is man that You are mindful of him?" Creatures, not the creator, and sinful human beings at that, we recognize with David our utter dependence on God's mercy for life and breath and salvation. The reality of Hurricane Katrina demonstrates the total inadequacy of our scientific achievement, our technology, and our national power and wealth. "What is man that You are mindful of him?"

How wonderful that the writer to the Hebrews applies these very verses to Jesus, our Savior: "But we see Jesus, who was made a little lower than the angels, now crowned with glory and honor because He suffered death, so that by the grace of God, He might taste death for everyone" (Hebrews 2:9). A real Savior in death for the ugly reality of Katrina–our comfort and our witness!

*Prayer:* In sorrow will he love you less?
For he who took for you a cross
Will bring you safe through ev'ry loss.
*LW* 420:2

Copyright © 1978 *Lutheran Book of Worship*

# Hurricane Katrina: Dominion

**Reading: Psalm 8:5–9**

*Text:* You have given him dominion over the work of Your hands; You have put all things under his feet. Psalm 8:6 (ESV)

The story of Hurricane Katrina moves far beyond the destructive reality. King David, although fully aware that sinful human beings are puny creatures under the Creator God, recognizes his own stewardship responsibility over the earth: "You have given him dominion over the work of Your hands; You have put all things under his feet." Reflecting God's own words in Genesis, "Let us make man in Our image, after Our likeness. And let them have dominion" (Genesis 1:26). David accepts his leadership role to manage God's affairs on earth.

Before the hurricane, weather forecasters gave scientific warning of the gathering storm and urged evacuation. Local, state, and federal governments tried to respond to the anticipated devastation through advance planning, orderly evacuation, and the placement of personnel and provisions for relief and rescue. They were exercising "dominion" as stewards. Their stewardship was imperfect due to the ferocity of the storm and unexpected problems. Much blame was directed at their response. Nevertheless, nationwide relief efforts were mounted in the wake of Katrina involving governmental agencies, the military, not-for-profit organizations like the Red Cross and church relief entities, plus a national outpouring of money, goods, and services. Human beings were exercising dominion. God worked through these stewardship efforts.

St. Paul applies these verses to Jesus, "And God placed all things under His feet and appointed Him to be head over everything for the church, which is His body" (Ephesians 1:22). Confessing the failure of our stewardship efforts as sin, we recognize the dominion of Christ through His death and resurrection. As part of His Church through Baptism, we participate in society to help exercise godly dominion by bringing relief, rescue, and rebuilding after natural disasters like Katrina. Our humble response ultimately brings witness through the Church to the crucified and risen Savior.

*Prayer:* Christ, by heav'nly hosts adored, Gracious, mighty, sov'reign Lord,
God of nations, King of kings, Head of all created things,
By the Church with joy confessed, God the Son forever blessed,
Pleading at your throne we stand, Save your people, bless our land.
*LW* 499:1

# Hurricane Katrina: Violence and Looting

## Reading: Psalm 10:1–14a

*Text:* In arrogance the wicked hotly pursue the poor; let them be caught in the schemes they have devised. Psalm 10:2 (ESV)

While the nation and world observed the devastation of Hurricane Katrina, they were shocked to see lawlessness threaten to overwhelm the city. How could cold and calculating thugs use this desperate situation for their own gain and go unpunished?

That wickedness is as old as our fallen world. The psalmist cries out to the Lord, "Why do You hide yourself in times of trouble? In arrogance the wicked hotly pursue the poor; let them be caught in the schemes that they have devised . . . the one greedy for gain curses and renounces the LORD" (Psalm 10:1–3). He refers to unscrupulous people in the land who boldly oppress the poor, commit theft and murder, and fear no reprisal from God or rulers. Then he adds, "But You do see, for You note mischief and vexation, that You may take it into Your hands" (Psalm 10:14a).

Why would we not expect a disaster to bring out the worst in people, the ugly reality of sinful and rebellious hearts—whether looters, snipers, price-gougers, or political gamesmanship? Hurricane Katrina exposed the reality of sin in our world. Order was restored. God stands in judgment of lawlessness. The wicked will pay the price. We recognize our own sinful hearts as well and our need for a Savior.

Nailed to a cross between two thieves, Jesus took upon Himself their sins and ours and prayed, "Father, forgive them for they know not what they do" (Luke 23:34 ESV). Criminals, soldiers, government authorities, religious leaders—all stand condemned for their sins but are offered forgiveness through Jesus' shed blood. Forgiven, we speak out for lawful justice in our society and point others to Jesus, the Savior.

*Prayer:* When men the offered help disdain
And willfully in sin remain,
Its terror in their ear resounds
And keeps their wickedness in bounds.

To Jesus we for refuge flee,
Who from the curse has set us free,
And humbly worship at his throne,
Saved by his grace through faith alone.
*LW* 329:4, 6

# Hurricane Katrina: Hope for the Needy

## Reading: Psalm 10:14b–18

*Text:* For the needy shall not always be forgotten, and the hope of the poor shall not perish forever. Psalm 9:18 (ESV)

Hurricane Katrina placed many people in great need—rich and poor alike, infants and children, senior adults, critically ill patients in evacuated hospitals, people with disabilities, those fleeing and those trapped in the cities, even rescue workers. Lives threatened and lost. Families separated. Homes and possessions destroyed. Places of work destroyed. Relocation to other parts of the country. Physical illness, mental stress, emotional exhaustion, spiritual emptiness. Where is hope for the needy?

The psalmist, oppressed by the wicked, sees a God who cares for those in need. He prays, "O LORD, You hear the desire of the afflicted; You will strengthen their heart; You will incline Your ear to do justice to the fatherless and the oppressed" (Psalm 10:17–18). God cares for the physical, mental, emotional, and spiritual needs of His created children.

In the hurricane disaster, God brought hope to the needy through military rescue helicopters, Red Cross emergency shelters, food and bottled water, volunteers, welcoming neighbors in another state, financial generosity worldwide, governmental benefits long term, and the comforting good news of salvation through Jesus Christ from the outstretched hands, open hearts, listening ears, and gentle healing words of the people of God.

Those in need continue to struggle and grieve their many losses. The future sometimes seems hopeless. The obstacles look overwhelming. But those very needs can point us to our own inability to solve problems by our own strength and wisdom. Confessing sins and admitting weakness, we look outside of ourselves to the One who created us and sent His only Son to the cross in payment of our sins. He longs to join us with the family of believers through Baptism where we find hope for the needy, now and eternally.

*Prayer:* Take heart, have hope, my spirit, And do not be afraid.
From any low depression, Where agonies are made.
God's grace will lift you upward On arms of saving might
Until the sun you hoped for Delights your eager sight.
*LW* 427:3

Copyright © 1982 Concordia Publishing House

September 24

# Hurricane Katrina: Witness from the Bog

## Reading: Psalm 40:1–5

*Text:* He drew me from the pit of destruction, out of the miry bog. Psalm 40:2 (ESV)

Yes, Hurricane Katrina left many people in need. But as God reached out to those in need, He also enabled many of His children in need to bear powerful witness to His salvation and deliverance. The psalmist, himself besieged by troubles including his own sin, brings witness in these words: "I waited patiently for the LORD; He inclined to me and heard my cry. He drew me out of the pit of destruction, out of the miry bog" (Psalm 40:1–2 ESV). His words sound almost like residents of the flooded city of New Orleans with contaminated water full of debris all around or the thick muck left on the Mississippi shore after the sea surge. David adds, "[He] set my feet upon a rock, making my steps secure. He put a new song in my mouth, a song of praise to our God" (Psalm 40:2b–3 ESV). David's witness is not about his circumstances but about his God: "You have multiplied, O LORD my God, Your wondrous deeds and Your thoughts toward us; none can compare with You! I will proclaim and tell of them, yet they are more than can be told" (Psalm 40:5).

Listen to the witness of people in need because of Katrina. Hear how God drew them from the pit and the miry bog. Notice that their circumstances may not be the best nor their struggles over. Don't miss their witness to the God who set their feet on a rock—Jesus Christ, the Rock of their salvation; and who made their steps secure in the midst of God's people gathered around Word and Sacraments. Observe their desire to reach out to others in need, even in the midst of their own real needs. Their witness from the bog will help to set the world ablaze with Christ. You may well find their witness contagious!

*Prayer:* His oath, his covenant, his blood
Sustain me in the raging flood;
When all supports are washed away,
He then is all my hope and stay.
On Christ, the solid rock I stand;
All other ground is sinking sand.
*LW* 368:3

# Hurricane Katrina: Response As Witness

**Reading: Matthew 25:31–46**

*Text:* "Truly, I say to you, as you did it to one of the least of these My brothers, you did it to Me." Matthew 25:40 (ESV)

A natural disaster like Hurricane Katrina in its harsh reality, which reveals both the best and the worst of humanity and leaves many people in need, also provides opportunity for Christian response as a witness to the Savior. That response flows from our faith in Jesus alongside other believers and joins the efforts of all others in the nation who are helping to rescue, relieve, and rebuild the affected area of the country. Our response may come in the form of financial contributions, provision of clothing and supplies, becoming a volunteer on location, or opening our homes and churches to displaced persons. When we respond best, we are unaware of how God is using us or why we serve.

In Jesus' famous description of the final judgment, He pictures the separation of the sheep from the goats. Those on the right, the believers in Him by God's grace through faith, He invites to inherit the kingdom prepared for them and commends them for their responses when He was hungry, thirsty, a stranger, naked, sick, and in prison. Totally surprised, these believers ask, "When?" He answers, "Truly, I say to you, as you did it to one of the least of these My brothers, you did it to Me."

In a similar fashion, we simply respond to those in need because of our faith relationship with Christ as Savior. We see Christ in their need, and they see Christ in our response. We have opportunity to tell them about our Savior and the free gift of eternal life through faith in Him. We give of ourselves with no strings attached. The rest is up to God's Spirit. Response as witness!

*Prayer:* But you have needy brothers here,
Partakers of your grace,
Whose names you will yourself confess
Before the Father's face.

Your face with rev'rence and with love
We in your poor would view,
And while we minister to them
Would do it as to you.
*LW* 395:2, 5

# Hurricane Katrina: Staying the Course

## Reading: Galatians 6:6–10

*Text:* And let us not grow weary of doing good, for in due season we will reap, if we do not give up. Galatians 6:9 (ESV)

Hurricane Katrina will not soon be forgotten. The severity of the storm. The extent of the damage. The difficulty and cost of the recovery. And the duration of its impact. This natural disaster demonstrates the importance of staying the course. The storm itself kept viewers glued to their television sets. The immediate aftermath likewise dominated all of the media. The initial response was a dramatic outpouring of contributions and volunteers from around the world. The ongoing question: Will relief efforts stay the course until the affected area is rebuilt and operational, until the people in need are back on their feet and functioning in society?

St. Paul registers a similar concern as he writes the Galatians about their love for each other within the Christian fellowship and in the community: "And let us not grow weary of doing good, for in due season we will reap, if we do not give up." He is referring to spiritual growth in the Christian life and Church. He knows that sowing to the sinful flesh will reap corruption. Remember the violence and looting after Katrina? He also knows that sowing to God's Spirit through immersion in the Word and Sacraments will result in reaping eternal life from the Spirit. Staying the course means staying connected to Christ as Savior and therefore consistently doing good to everyone and especially fellow believers. The harvest of believers will increase mightily.

God empowers believers to stay the course in helping victims of disasters like Hurricane Katrina. He also strengthens you, a forgiven sinner, through His Word to stay the course within your church and in your outreach to the community. We have learned many lessons from Hurricane Katrina to strengthen our reliance on Christ and to sharpen our witness to Christ in word and actions.

*Prayer:* Give me the strength to do
With ready heart and willing
Whatever you command,
My calling here fulfilling.
Help me do what I should
With all my might, and bless
The outcome for my good,
For you must give success.
*LW* 371:2

# Saturday Morning Reflections

## Reading: Psalm 119:25–32

*Text:* Make me understand the way of Your precepts, and I will meditate on Your wondrous works. Psalm 119:27 (ESV)

Sometimes I grow tired of the daily grind and need refreshment and a new perspective from the Lord for my life of service and witness. I share with you some Saturday morning reflections. Awaking naturally, I enjoyed the leisure of bringing in the newspaper, brewing a pot of coffee, and sitting in our seasonal room with a panoramic view of the green foliage in the woods behind our house. Joined by my wife, I ate breakfast, opened my Bible to the psalms for the day and reflected on God's world. Gail and I shared this special moment with some free-flowing conversation about God's abundant blessings, our callings in life, and the struggling, searching world in which we live.

The psalmist describes his own sorrow, suffering, and afflictions and then prays, "Make me understand the way of Your precepts, and I will meditate on Your wondrous works." In a way he was engaging in his own Saturday morning reflections. Looking to God's precepts (v. 27), word (v. 28), law (v. 29), rules (v. 30), testimonies (v. 31), and commandments (v. 32), he is no doubt led to understand his own sin and the sins of those who afflict him as well as the forgiveness that comes from God's promises, ultimately in the promised Messiah. He is then able to meditate on God's "wondrous works" (v. 27) that "enlarge his heart" (v. 32). Clinging to the Lord's testimonies, he is able to run in the way of God's commandments for another week of service and witness.

The psalm verses spoke to our hearts. Admitting our own sin and the effect of a sinful world upon our spirits, reminded of God's full and free forgiveness through Jesus' death and resurrection, we were able to meditate on God's "wondrous works" revealed in the view of God's green earth, the quiet time around a cup of coffee and meaningful conversation, and the insights from a portion of Scripture. Our Saturday morning reflections filled us with God's love in Christ!

*Prayer:* When all your mercies, O my God,
My waking soul surveys,
Transported with the view, I'm lost
In wonder, love, and praise.
*LW* 196:1

# Bible and Newspaper

## Reading: Psalm 119:41–48

*Text:* I will also speak of Your testimonies before kings and shall not be put to shame. Psalm 119:46 (ESV)

My Saturday morning reflections generated a thought-provoking insight for daily Christian witness. Remember, yesterday I mentioned bringing in the daily newspaper while brewing a pot of coffee. Have you ever felt guilty about putting off your daily Bible reading to read the newspaper first? I want both. Many times, the front page headlines, sports pages (especially news of the St. Louis Cardinals), and business section command my attention. Then comes my reading of Psalms and Proverbs. On this Saturday morning, I realized that Bible and newspaper belong side by side as resources for understanding God better and the world in which we witness of our faith in Jesus Christ.

The psalmist longs for reassurance of his salvation: "Let Your steadfast love come to me, O LORD, Your salvation according to Your promise" (Psalm 119:41). Why? "Then shall I have an answer for him who taunts me, for I trust in Your word" (Psalm 119:42). Later, he writes, "I will also speak of Your testimonies before kings and shall not be put to shame." God's Word for the world. Engaging the world with its taunts and daring to speak at the highest levels because of the Word of salvation.

Bible and newspaper: Both are needed in whatever order. We face the world squarely as chronicled in the newspaper (print or electronic). We see in it our own sin and need for a Savior and the desperate struggles of those without trust in Christ. We delight in God's Word that announces forgiveness through Christ's death and prepares us for witness to the world of that same forgiveness.

*Prayer:* Universal Body of the Lord,
Chosen, called, made just, and glorified:
Ours the faith, and ours the triumph,
Ours the peace the world is seeking;
Who on earth as privileged as we?
Catch the vision! Share the glory!
Show the captives, tell them: Christ is here!
*SP* 58:2

Copyright © 1986 Concordia Publishing House

# Blood-Red Vision of Life

## Reading: Hebrews 9:11–14

*Text:* "For the life of every creature is its blood: its blood is its life." Leviticus 17:14 (ESV)

Immanuel in the media. We find words, pictures, and examples in the daily newspaper that help us bear powerful testimony to salvation through Jesus Christ. During our Saturday morning reflections at the breakfast table, Gail called my attention to *Life, America's Weekend Magazine*, enclosed with that Saturday newspaper. The bright reds of the cover jumped out at me.

In the foreground of that cover is pictured the visionary digital photographer, Alexander Tsiares, with his penetrating dark eyes. Surrounding him, you see red and white blood cells magnified 31,000 times, as they swirl through an artery in one of his revolutionary images. The bold question in yellow block print: "Could This Man's Pictures Save Your Life?" Tsiares has embarked on a mission to depict the human body in all its glory and frailty so you will be inspired to get well–and stay well. Not necessarily based on a Christian vision or even a vision of God's creation, this article with its blood-red pictures provides talking points for our Christian witness.

In Leviticus, the Lord explains to Moses, "'For the life of every creature is its blood; its blood is its life.'" The life-giving nature of blood bears powerful witness to God's marvelous creation, and lies at the heart of the Old Testament sacrificial system. Most important, this passage points to our redemption through the blood of Christ: "He entered once for all into the holy places, not by means of the blood of goats and calves but by means of His own blood, thus securing an eternal redemption" (Hebrews 9:12 ESV).

That *Life* cover and article could help you open up conversation about a loving God who created life-giving blood for our bodies and forgiveness for our sin through the blood of Christ, a lamb without blemish or spot. This Man Can Save Your Life! That's a blood-red vision for life!

*Prayer:* Glory be to Jesus,
Who in bitter pains
Poured for me the lifeblood
From His sacred veins.
*LW* 98:1

September 30

# Bible in the Texas Foundation

## Reading: Matthew 16:13–20

*Text:* Built on the foundation of the apostles and prophets, Christ Jesus Himself being the cornerstone. Ephesians 2:20 (ESV)

During those same Saturday morning reflections, Gail and I discussed a unique article on the religion page: "Some Texas Homes Are Built around the Bible–Literally." Two different construction companies, one in Magnolia, Texas, and the other in the Dallas-Fort Worth area, place a Bible in the frame of the foundation before concrete is poured. Scripture verses, such as Psalm 127:1, are also printed on the wood framework of individual rooms. Reflective of the owners' Christian beliefs and ethical values, this practice is not intended to force their beliefs on anyone. The Dallas company says some customers bring their own Bibles to be placed in the foundations. Joyce Jones, a partner with her husband, says, "We are Christian, and our motto is: 'It all starts with a solid foundation.'"

Paul writes in Ephesians, "built on the foundation of the apostles and prophets, Christ Jesus Himself being the cornerstone." Both Jews and Greeks are incorporated into the Church and the whole structure grows into a holy temple in the Lord. The foundation is the apostolic witness to Christ, beginning with Peter's confession of faith at Caesarea Philippi. The Holy Scriptures consist of the written testimony of the apostles and prophets.

This article can provide you with a conversation starter. The construction owners witness their faith. Homeowners who believe in Christ can bring to others the biblical foundations of their home. Whether or not you like the idea, you can share your biblical faith in Christ, the importance of the apostolic witness through Word and Sacraments in your church, and point again to the chief cornerstone, Jesus Christ. What other newspaper events or articles might stimulate your Christian witness this week? Thank God for those Saturday morning reflections!

*Prayer:* The Church's one foundation is Jesus Christ her Lord;
She is his new creation By water and the Word.
From heaven he came and sought her To be his holy bride;
With his own blood he bought her, And for her life he died.
*LW* 289:1

# Woodland Beauty and Change

**Reading: Isaiah 5:1–4**

*Text:* My beloved had a vineyard on a very fertile hill. Isaiah 5:1b (ESV)

The next four devotions intend to challenge you to reflect upon your Christian witness through imagery from our backyard and God's Old Testament vineyard. Our backyard is a woodland with stately trees, saplings, and green foliage. We love the peaceful, beautiful view from our great room windows and cozy seasonal room. God's creation fills us with awe and thankfulness. But over the eight years of our residence here, we have observed the woodland changing. Some large trees have died and fallen into the hollow at the bottom of our sloping hillside. The growth of trees and proliferating foliage has shaded our yard so grass has difficulty growing and is being replaced by moss. The woodland is encroaching on our yard. Still beautiful, our woodland poses some problems.

The prophet Isaiah uses imagery of a vineyard to describe God's relationship to His people Israel: "My beloved had a vineyard on a very fertile hill." Isaiah describes how God dug up the hillside, cleared it of stones, and planted it with choice vines. He protected it with a watchtower and waited for the vines to produce grapes. It displayed the creative love of God for His people and witnessed of His love to other nations who saw Israel grow and prosper. But like my backyard, changes were taking place. Instead of good grapes, the vineyard was yielding wild grapes of rebellion and sin. God, the beloved, asks, "Why did it yield wild grapes?"

We are the planting of the Lord to witness to God's love in Christ our Savior. He intends our beauty and productive fruit to evoke awe and thankfulness in others as they turn to Him for salvation. But often, because of our sin, decay takes place and light is choked off by wild vines. We need to recognize the problems caused by our rebellion and turn to our Beloved for forgiveness so His vineyard and woodland continue to radiate His beauty for all to see.

*Prayer:* God, you made this world a garden,
Every harvest bearing seed.
Loving God, today as ever you anticipate our need;
you are ready with your answer long before we plead.
*SP* 110:1

Copyright © 1989 Concordia Publishing House

# Soil Erosion

## Reading: Isaiah 5:5–7

*Text:* For the vineyard of the LORD of hosts is the house of Israel. Isaiah 5:7a (ESV)

As our beautiful woodland changes it faces a serious problem in our sloping yard—soil erosion. The other day, I noticed that in two spots the ground had deep gouges and tree roots were exposed. Obviously the condition was deteriorating.

In Isaiah's Song of the Vineyard, he describes a similar deterioration in the condition of the vineyard of the Lord of hosts, which is the house of Israel. Like soil erosion, Israel's behavior and beliefs were destroying the fertile hillside—bloodshed instead of justice, an outcry instead of righteousness (Isaiah 5:7). Therefore, God declared that He would remove the hedge, break down the wall, and make the vineyard a waste, covered with briars and thorns (Isaiah 5:5–6). What was causing this soil erosion and what could be done?

Privileged and chosen to be the vineyard of the Lord of hosts, intended to bear beautiful fruit as a witness to God's love in Christ, do we see the gradual deterioration caused by our willful sin and our selfishness? What can we do about it so our witness might be beautiful and productive? Tomorrow's devotion will identify the problem and point to the One who alone can save us from this deterioration by His death on a tree. The hillside soil stabilized. Woodland beauty restored.

*Prayer:* From depths of woe I cry to you.
O Lord, my voice is trying
To reach your heart and, Lord, break through
With these my cries and sighing.
If you keep record of our sin
And hold against us what we've been,
Who then can stand before you?

Your grace and love alone avail
To blot out sin with pardon.
In your gaze our best efforts pale,
Develop pride and harden.
Before your throne no one can boast
That he escaped sin's deadly coast.
Our haven is your mercy.
*LW* 230:1–2

Copyright © 1978 Concordia Publishing House

# Drainage Problem

### Reading: Matthew 21:40–46

*Text:* When the LORD shall have washed away the filth of the daughters of Zion. Isaiah 4:4a (ESV)

On the advice of my son-in-law, I contacted a landscaping company to diagnose the problem of my soil erosion and to propose a workable solution so our beautiful backyard woodland might be preserved. That consultant concluded that there was a drainage problem. Rainwater was streaming down the stone path from our side yard and gouging troughs in the backyard soil on its way to the gully.

Isaiah's Song of the Vineyard exposes Israel's idolatry, adultery, greed, and injustice as the problem causing their deterioration as a nation. That rebellion caused God to lay waste to the vineyard at the hands of the Assyrian armies. Jesus, in Matthew's Gospel, builds on this song by telling the parable of the wicked husbandmen who exploit the master's vineyard for their own purposes, beat and kill his servants, and ultimately throw his son and heir out of the vineyard and kill him. Jesus then applies that parable to the chief priests' and Pharisees's rejection of Him as Messiah.

In other words, the drainage problem is no small problem. Unchecked, it will destroy the yard. That water is devastating. Isaiah uses these vivid words in chaper four, which we will study tomorrow, to describe the condition for restoration, "when the LORD shall have washed away the filth of the daughters of Zion and cleansed the bloodstains of Jerusalem from its midst" (Isaiah 4:4). The water needs to be drained away from the hillside so its destruction can cease. The flow of our sins is causing devastation in the woodland of our witness and must be stopped before any restoration can take place. Be looking tomorrow for the One who poured out His life in payment for our sins.

*Prayer:* His oath, his covenant, his blood
Sustain me in the raging flood;
When all supports are washed away,
He then is all my hope and stay.
On Christ, the solid rock I stand;
All other ground is sinking sand.
*LW* 368:3

# Woodland Witness

## Reading: Isaiah 4:2–6

*Text:* In that day the branch of the LORD shall be beautiful and glorious, and the fruit of the land shall be the pride and honor of the survivors of Israel. Isaiah 4:2 (ESV)

The landscape company representative, admiring the beautiful woodland setting, observed the soil erosion and identified improper water drainage as the problem. His solution was a drain trap at the end of the stone pathway, a pipe surrounded by rocks to take the water directly to the gully, fill dirt to cover the eroded soil, and the planting of hostas to anchor the hillside. Our woodland property has been restored as a witness to the beauty of God's creation.

Isaiah precedes the vineyard imagery of God's judgment upon Israel's sin with the promise imagery of the branch of the Lord: "In that day the branch of the LORD shall be beautiful and glorious." He points to the righteous branch of David, Jesus the Messiah who will hang on the tree of the cross to wash away the sins of Israel and the world. Then he describes how that saving branch will restore a new people of God: "The fruit of the land shall be the pride and honor of the survivors of Israel." God's forgiven and redeemed people take great pride in the fruit of the Lord's messianic reign evident in their lives of worship, service, and witness to the world.

And now, we welcome guests to see the beauty of our restored woodland, water drained appropriately, soil erosion stopped, and a new planting. That woodland witness symbolizes for me the joyful witness of God's people today, cleansed from their sins by the blood of Christ, restored to beauty, and taking pride in "the fruit of the land" evident in our lives of thankful worship and humble service to others in Jesus' name.

*Prayer:* Now a universal garden, seeded with your living Word,
grows with peace and love and beauty,
songs of freedom there are heard;
by your mercy, by your Spirit, thankful hearts are stirred.
*SP* 110:3

Copyright © 1989 Concordia Publishing House

# The Greatest Tension

## Reading: 1 John 2:15–17

*Text:* Do not love the world or the things in the world. 1 John 2:15 (ESV)

In his book, *Preaching to a Postmodern World*, Graham Johnston describes the greatest tension the contemporary church wrestles with—"how to reach the present age without selling out to it" (p. 10). In the next few devotions, we consider the postmodern world that God wants us to set ablaze with the saving Gospel of Jesus Christ. Gaining a hearing for the Gospel is difficult when many reject authority, absolute truth, and even rational thought. At the same time, postmodern people are more open to spiritual realities than those moderns only accepting the empirical evidence of a scientific world. But the tension remains—"how to reach the present age without selling out to it."

St. John's first epistle addresses a late first century world not totally unlike our own. An early form of gnosticism claimed that the spirit was good and body evil. Denying Jesus Christ as God in human flesh, they also practiced immorality without restraint—spiritual interests and carnal behavior. How similar to our present age! John clearly opposes selling out to his present age: "Do not love the world or the things in the world." He adds, "For all that is in the world—the desires of the flesh and the desires of the eyes and pride in possessions—is not from the Father but is from the world" (1 John 2:16).

At the same time, John desires to reach the world, "But if anyone does sin, we have an advocate with the Father, Jesus Christ the righteous. He is the propitiation for our sins, and not for ours only but also for the sins of the whole world" (John 2:1b–2). He is willing to live with the greatest tension so many may believe in Christ as Savior and Lord. How about you?

*Prayer:* What is the world to me!
With all its vaunted pleasure
When you, and you alone,
Lord Jesus, are my treasure!
You only, dearest Lord,
My soul's delight shall be;
You are my peace, my rest.
What is the world to me!
*LW* 418:1

# Risking Your Life

## Reading: 1 John 3:13–18

*Text:* Little children, let us not love in word or talk but in deed and in truth. 1 John 3:18 (ESV)

It is one thing to talk about the evils of the world today, postmodern to the core, and the pure Gospel of Jesus Christ, the Word made flesh. It is quite another thing to do something about reaching that world for Christ. In Graham Johnston's *Preaching to a Postmodern World*, he quotes Lesslie Newbigin saying that "the gospel is not heard but remains incomprehensible because the Church has sought security in its own past instead of risking its life in a deep involvement with the world" (p.10). Are you willing to risk your life by involving yourself in the lives of postmodern people?

John, who obviously opposes the world's sinful behavior, asks believers to get involved, "Little children, let us not love in word or talk but in deed and in truth." He pulls no punches about the risks, "Do not be surprised, brothers, that the world hates you" (1 John 3:13). Aware of the difficulty, John points to Christ's sacrifice as both power and example for our witness in the world: "By this we know love, that He laid down His life for us, and we ought to lay down our lives for the brothers" (1 John 3:16).

Jesus risked His life for us, still sinners, because He loved us. By His sacrificial death, He brings us life and fills us with His love for the world. "Let us not love in word or talk but in deed and in truth." Jesus can use that kind of love to bring many to a saving faith in Him. Are the risks worth it? The results will be eternal!

*Prayer:* Savior, thy dying love Thou gavest me;
Nor should I aught withhold, Dear Lord, from thee.
In love my soul would bow, My heart fulfill its vow
Some off'ring bring thee now, Something for thee.

Give me a faithful heart, Likeness to thee,
That each departing day Henceforth may see.
Some work of love begun, Some deed of kindness done,
Some wand'rer sought and won, Something for thee.
*LW* 374:1, 4

# Think Like a Missionary

## Reading: 1 John 4:1–6

*Text:* But test the spirits to see whether they are from God. 1 John 4:1b (ESV)

Let's suppose that you understand "the greatest tension" and are willing to "risk your life" to reach postmodern people in your world. To proceed, Graham Johnston suggests that you need to "think like a missionary" (p. 10). He adds, "biblical communication to a postmodern world should be approached in the same way that a missionary goes into a foreign culture. No missionary worth his or her salt would enter a field without first doing an exhaustive study of the culture he or she seeks to reach" (p. 10).

Who are you trying to reach? Where do they live and work? What influences shape their lives? What interests them, motivates them, troubles them? What friends do they choose? How do they spend their leisure time? What spiritual interests and questions do they have, if any? How does their culture differ from yours? These kinds of questions can help you think like a missionary.

John instructs his readers to explore the world for its spiritual influence. "Beloved, do not believe every spirit, but test the spirits to see whether they are from God." He distinguishes false prophets from those following the Spirit of God: "Every spirit that confesses that Jesus Christ has come in the flesh is from God, and every spirit that does not confess Jesus is not from God" (1 John 4:2b–3a). Before we can discern the spirits, we need to understand the culture and why people do what they do. Otherwise we may jump to faulty conclusions, either positive or negative.

Ultimately, the great divide becomes apparent: "They [false spirits] are from the world; therefore they speak from the world, and the world listens to them. We are from God. Whoever knows God listens to us" (1 John 4:5–6a). Thinking like a missionary leads us, with sensitivity, to the culture to proclaim Jesus Christ, crucified and risen, as the only way to salvation.

*Prayer:* Our own land's fairest breezes Bear sounds of steeple bells,
All nature's beauty pleases, Yet man builds countless hells.
In vain, with lavish kindness The gifts of God are strown;
Throngs turn from him in blindness To false gods of their own.
*LW* 322:2

October 8

# Two Burdens

**Reading: 1 John 4:7–21**

*Text:* Beloved, if God so loved us, we also ought to love one another. 1 John 4:11 (ESV)

As we face the postmodern world with all of its anti-biblical challenges and spiritual searching possibilities, two burdens, according to Graham Johnston, are thrust upon us: "Reach the listener, a fellow human being, with the message of Christ, and at the same time uphold the Word of God, faithfully and with integrity" (pp. 18–19). In other words, care deeply about our friend or acquaintance adrift in a confusing culture while at the same time clearly and truthfully offering Jesus to them according to God's Word. The burden of love and the burden of truth!

"Beloved, if God so loved us, we also ought to love one another." This is the burden of love that leads us to care no matter what because God loved us by sending His Son as the propitiation for our sins. It is also the burden of truth: "And we have seen and testify that the Father has sent His Son to be the Savior of the world" (1 John 4:14). Only through faith in Jesus, as revealed in God's Holy Word, can a person be saved. That knowledge of the truth about God's love in Christ moves us to love others in need of salvation: "By this is love perfected with us . . . because as He is so also are we in this world" (1 John 4:17).

Two burdens for our Christian witness. Two joyful burdens—love and truth—because Jesus, the great burden-bearer of our sins, first loved us.

*Prayer:* Jesus, your boundless love so true
No thought can reach, no tongue declare;
Unite my thankful heart to you,
And reign without a rival there.
Yours wholly, yours alone I am;
Be you alone my sacred flame.

Oh, grant that nothing in my soul
May dwell but your pure love alone;
Oh, may your love possess me whole,
My joy, my treasure, and my crown!
All coldness from my heart remove;
My every act, word, thought be love.
*LW* 280:1–2

# Balls and Strikes

## Reading: John 17:14–19

*Text:* "Sanctify them in the truth; Your word is truth." John 17:17 (ESV)

In *Preaching to a Postmodern World*, Graham Johnston quotes an illustration of Walter Truett Anderson about three home plate umpires explaining their philosophy: "One says, 'There's balls and there's strikes and I call 'em the way they are!' Another responds, 'There's balls and there's strikes and I call 'em the way I see 'em!' The third says, 'There's balls and there's strikes, and they ain't nothing until I call 'em!' " (p. 30). The first umpire, as a modernist, recognizes the reality of objective truth. The other two are postmoderns emphasizing the subjective and "truth is what we make it." When you next view a baseball game, think about the importance of objective truth to the integrity of the game.

In His high priestly prayer, Jesus doesn't pray about "balls and strikes" but He does pray for the disciples: "Sanctify them in the truth; Your word is truth." He wants them to continue believing the objective truth of God's Word as revealed to them so they will believe in Him, the crucified and risen Savior, as "the Way, the Truth, and the Life" (John 14:6). He then asks the Father to let them witness that truth to the world, "As You sent Me into the world, so I have sent them into the world" (John 17:18).

God sends us out with the good news, the truth of salvation through faith in Jesus as Savior as revealed in His Word to a world where many people see all truth claims as relative and pluralistic and their own truth as right for them. But God's Spirit will bring that saving truth home to confused and troubled hearts through our witness.

*Prayer:* To hope grown dim, to hearts turned cold
Speak tongues of fire and make us bold
To shine your Word of saving grace
Into each dark and loveless place.
Restrain, O Lord, the human pride
That seeks to thrust your truth aside
Or with some man-made thoughts or things
Would dim the words your Spirit sings.
*LW* 344:3, 5

Copyright © 1982 Concordia Publishing House

October 10

# The Blur of Morality

## Reading: Romans 1:18–32

*Text:* But they became futile in their thinking, and their foolish hearts were darkened. Romans 1:21b (ESV)

When truth goes, so does morality. In postmodern society, multiple standards of morality may apply and situational ethics prevail. Graham Johnston describes a morality of "what works for me." Lessons include: 1. Love yourself (everyone doing what is right in his or her own eyes). 2. Do unto others as you wish. Johnston quotes Gene Edward Veith, "Morality like religion is a matter of desire. What I want and what I choose is not only true (for me) but right (for me) . . . 'I have a right' to my desires. Conversely, 'no one has the right' to criticize my desire and my choices" (p. 41). 3. Do unto others . . . oh whatever (moral indifference–"So what's the big deal?") (pp. 39–43). This blur of morality leads to much chaos and despair.

How similar is today's postmodern world to St. Paul's description of human ungodliness and unrighteousness in the first chapter of Romans: "But they became futile in their thinking, and their foolish hearts were darkened." He further comments, "Therefore God gave them up in the lusts of their hearts to impurity, to the dishonoring of their bodies among themselves, because they exchanged the truth about God for a lie and worshiped and served the creature rather than the Creator" (Romans 1:24–25).

How do we bring the message of Christ to people with morality blurred? First, we confess our own sins of succumbing to our age. Is not our own morality sometimes blurred and our example tarnished by selfishness? Paul concludes that Jews and Gentiles alike fall short of God's glory. Second, forgiven through the blood of Christ, we uphold both the truth and the morality of God's Law revealed in the Holy Scriptures as curb and mirror in today's world. Third, we lift high the cross of Jesus Christ, who led a sinless life and died in payment for the sins of the world. He comes to those living in the chaos and despair of a blurred morality and offers new life.

*Prayer:* To Jesus we for refuge flee
Who from the curse has set us free,
And humbly worship at his throne
Saved by his grace through faith alone.
*LW* 329:6

# Not Ashamed

## Reading: Romans 3:21–26

*Text:* For I am not ashamed of the gospel, for it is the power of God for salvation to everyone who believes. Romans 1:16

A look at postmodernism—no absolute truth, the blur of morality, mix and match religion to taste, suspicion of all authority. What do we do about it? How do we witness of Jesus to postmoderns? These are urgent questions. Resolving the greatest tension—"how to reach the present age without selling out to it." Accepting the two burdens of love and truth. Graham Johnston, in his advice to preachers, also speaks to us as Christian witnesses: "Deal with the exclusive uniqueness of Christ" (p. 95).

St. Paul is compelling as "a servant of Christ Jesus, called to be an apostle, set apart for the Gospel of God" (Romans 1:1): "For I am not ashamed of the gospel, for it is the power of God for salvation to everyone who believes." Not ashamed! What a ringing testimony to the exclusive uniqueness of Christ! Later he writes about "the righteousness of God through faith in Jesus Christ for all who believe. . . for all have sinned and fall short of the glory of God, and are justified by His grace as a gift, through the redemption that is in Christ Jesus, whom God put forward as a propitiation by His blood, to be received by faith" (Romans 3:22–25a).

Not ashamed! No elastic Jesus, stretched to fit all sizes as a way to God. No pluralism of gods, pagan beliefs, home-cooked religion. But one God—the Father, the Son, and the Holy Spirit. One Savior, the God-man Jesus Christ, incarnate, crucified, risen, ascended, returning. One church, built on the foundation of the apostles and the prophets with Jesus Christ as the chief cornerstone. This is a clear witness to postmoderns: "I am not ashamed of the gospel, for it is the power of God for salvation to everyone who believes." Any other questions?

*Prayer:* Till then—nor is my boasting vain—
Till then I boast a Savior slain;
And oh, may this my glory be,
That Christ is not ashamed of me!
*LW* 393:6

October 12

# Good News for the Weak

## Reading: Romans 4:1–25

*Text:* He (Abraham) did not weaken in faith when he considered his own body, which was as good as dead (since he was about a hundred years old or when he considered the barrenness of Sarah's womb). Romans 4:19a (ESV)

Not ashamed of the Gospel! It can reach postmoderns even though they are sceptical of the biblical story of salvation as too sweeping. They are suspicious of any master plan with all the answers. They see it as a tool for exploitation and manipulation (Johnston, p. 107).

Far from being manipulative or elitist, the Gospel is good news for the weak. Jesus came as a helpless infant in Bethlehem, reached out to beggars, the lame, and the blind, opposed the religious authorities of His day, and as a humble servant went to death on a cross.

In Romans, St. Paul describes Abraham, given a wonderful promise by God, as weak in his body because of age. On their own He and Sarah were unable to bear a child who would fulfill the promise. But Abraham trusted God, and his faith was counted as righteousness. Isaac was born to them by God's grace. In the same way God comes to us in our weakness and sin, gives us faith, and counts it as righteousness to us, "who believe in Him who raised from the dead our Lord Jesus, who was delivered up for our trespasses and raised for our justification" (Romans 4:24–25).

When we witness to Jesus in humility as servants, when we admit our own weaknesses and need for a Savior, God can touch the hearts and lives of postmoderns where they need help and give them faith in the suffering Servant who died for them. Not ashamed of the Gospel! Good news for the weak!

*Prayer:* I trust, O Christ, in you alone;
No earthly hope avails me.
You will not see me overthrown
When Satan's host assails me.
No human strength, no earthly pow'r
Can see me through the evil hour,
For you alone my strength renew.
I cry to you! I trust, O Lord, your promise true.
*LW* 357:1

Copyright © 1978 *Lutheran Book of Worship*

# Good News for the Weary

**Reading: Romans 5:7–11**

*Text:* But God shows His love for us in that while we were still sinners, Christ died for us. Romans 5:8 (ESV)

Not ashamed of the Gospel! In his book, *Preaching to a Postmodern World*, Graham Johnston suggests an additional strategy for reaching postmoderns: The Gospel is "Good News for the weary." "For the person who has tried various options of life and found them wanting, who is weary of endless openness and possibilities, the Christian message provides a resolution," writes Peter Corney, quoted by Johnston (p. 109). To such weary searches, the clear Gospel with its straight answers touches their hearts and minds. Haddon Robinson observes, "Likewise, people want to listen to somebody who knows what the struggle is, but who has taken the Bible's message seriously" (Johnston, p. 109).

Paul effectively communicates that good news for the weary in Romans 5: "But God shows His love for us in that while we were still sinners, Christ died for us." Justified by faith, "We have peace with God through our Lord Jesus Christ. . . . More than that, we rejoice in our sufferings, knowing that suffering produces endurance, and endurance produces character, and character produces hope" (Romans 5:1, 3–4). Paul understands struggle, suffering, and searching but also God's salvation through Christ, because "we have gained access by faith into this grace in which we stand" (Romans 5:2a). "At just the right time, when we were still powerless, Christ died for the ungodly" (Romans 5:6).

Good news for the weary! What a privilege for us, forgiven sinners, at peace and rest from our weariness, to bring God's great good news to weary postmoderns bereft of human options and ready because of God's Spirit to receive peace with God through our Lord Jesus Christ.

*Prayer:* Seek where you may To find a way,
Restless, toward your salvation.
My heart is stilled, On Christ I build,
He is the one foundation.
His Word is sure, His works endure;
He overthrows All evil foes;
Through him I more than conquer.
*LW* 358:1

# Good News with a Personal Touch

## Reading: Romans 7:15–25

*Text:* Wretched man that I am! Who will deliver me from this body of death? Thanks be to God through Jesus Christ our Lord! Romans 7:24–25a (ESV)

Our final thought from Graham Johnston about how to reach postmoderns with Jesus Christ is this: Tell the good news with a personal touch! The Gospel stands on its own, the power of God unto salvation. God loved us from eternity, sent His Son to deal once for all with our sin by His death on the cross, and sent His Holy Spirit to bring us to faith in Christ through His Word and Sacraments. But that Gospel can reach postmoderns more effectively when presented as good news with a personal touch.

Johnston quotes Michael Green to demonstrate that telling a personal story is not a compromising alternative. Observing that the story of Paul's conversion plays a major role in the New Testament, Green writes, "Postmodernists will be open to hearing the stories of other persons because these stories give purpose and shape to social existence. . . . Postmodern people are not anti-religious but anti-ecclesiastical; therefore they may be open to the spiritual autobiography and personal testimony" (p. 110).

Paul clearly points to justification by God's grace for Christ's sake through faith in his letter to the Romans. Yet he connects that objective message to his own spiritual struggles with daily temptations to do the evil things and not do the good things. Concluding that because of his flesh sin dwells within him, he cries, "Wretched man that I am! Who will deliver me from this body of death?" He then looks outside of himself to proclaim the good news with a personal touch, "Thanks be to God through Jesus Christ our Lord!" Engaged in a similar spiritual struggle, can we not communicate the same good news to postmoderns with a personal touch?

*Prayer:* Your Son came to suffer for me,
Gave himself to rescue me,
Died to heal me and restore me,
Reconciled and set me free.
Jesus' cross alone can vanquish
These dark faces and soothe this anguish.
*LW* 233:3

# Autumn Ablaze

## Reading: Matthew 9:35–38

*Text:* You have filled my heart with greater joy than when their grain and new wine abound. Psalm 4:7

We sit on the broad veranda of the Abe Martin Inn at Brown County State Park nestled in the rolling hills of southern Indiana. Before us unfolds a panoramic view of autumn leaves ablaze with orange, red, and yellow colors against a brilliant blue sky. No matter what troubles, stress, or problems may have burdened us, our hearts are filled with greater joy at the wonders of God's creation ablaze before our eyes in autumn and harvest.

Our thoughts turn to the multitudes harassed and helpless like sheep without a shepherd with troubles, stress, and problems beyond our own. We remember the words of our Lord to His disciples, "'The harvest is plentiful but the workers are few. Ask the Lord of the harvest, therefore, to send out workers into His harvest field'" (Matthew 9:37–38).

Those vivid autumn colors remind us of God's undeserved favor coming into our drab, anxious, and sin-filled lives with the good news of the kingdom through the teaching, preaching, and healing of Jesus the Christ. His sacrificial suffering and death on a dark and gray Good Friday would be followed by a sunburst resurrection on Easter morning. Our hearts are filled with greater joy at the wonders of God's redemption ablaze.

Repentant, forgiven, eyes opened to the harvest, we recognize that God taps us to participate in His multicolored outreach to the lost worldwide. Our hearts are filled with greater joy at the wonders of God's one mission ablaze.

*Prayer:* Sing to the Lord of harvest, Sing songs of love and praise;
With joyful hearts and voices Your alleluias raise.
By Him the rolling seasons In fruitful order move;
Sing to the Lord of harvest A joyous song of love.

Bring to this sacred altar The gifts his goodness gave
The golden sheaves of harvest The souls Christ died to save.
Your hearts lay down before Him When at His feet you fall,
And with your lives adore Him Who gave His life for all.
*LW* 493:1, 3

October 16

# Falling Leaves

## Reading: 40:6–8

*Text:* The grass withers, the flower fades when the breath of the LORD blows on it. Isaiah 40:7 (ESV)

Autumn is indeed ablaze with the colors of God's creation, symbolic of His redemptive love in Christ, but then come the falling leaves. Right now the dried up, brown leaves are piling up in both my front yard and backyard woodland. As temperatures drop and chill winds blow, the leaves fall and will need to be raked or blown into our gully.

Isaiah describes human nature and a fallen world in similar terms, "The grass withers, the flower fades when the breath of the Lord blows on it." I could add to the falling leaves the browning of my hostas and the drying up of geraniums and even mums. Isaiah cries, "All flesh is grass" (Isaiah 40:6b). A disobedient Israel experiences the wrath first of the Assyrian and then the Babylonians bringing death, destruction, and exile. All seems hopeless, and they feel the breath of the Lord's judgment blowing upon them in their sin.

Falling leaves remind me of all the people in my neighborhood, community, and world who die in their sin without Christ. They cannot sustain life. They wither and fade. However, Isaiah is also sounding a word of hope: "But the Word of our God will stand forever" (Isaiah 40:8b). With the announcement of the Messiah's coming and a new day for a repentant Israel, he writes, "Comfort, comfort My people, says your God" (Isaiah 40:1). "He will tend His flock like a shepherd" (Isaiah 40:11a).

Falling leaves move me to help set the world ablaze with the good news ("the Word of our God will stand forever") of salvation through the death of Jesus Christ, our Good Shepherd, who "withered" and "faded" on the cross to pay for my sin. Needing His forgiveness of my own sin, I want others to receive that same forgiveness for eternal life where nothing withers or fades.

*Prayer:* Withered, without human might,
Its bloom cut off by frost and blight.
All flesh, like grass, wilts to the core,
But God's Word lives forevermore.
*LW* 21:5

Copyright © 1982 Concordia Publishing House

# A Splash of Light

**Reading: John 12:35–36**

*Text:* "I am the Light of the world. Whoever follows Me will never walk in darkness, but will have the light of life." John 8:12

Imagery can be powerful in helping us to understand how God works through us to reach others with the saving Gospel of Jesus Christ. Last Monday morning Gail and I were eating breakfast in our seasonal room. I glanced at the patterns of sunlight on the green leaves in the tops of the trees. Then I noticed a splash of light illuminating one leaf in the lower branches. That splash of light lasted for only a minute, and then the leaf returned to the shadows.

Remembering Jesus' words, "I am the Light of the world," I pictured Him as the sun of righteousness illuminating our dark world. Jesus also said to His disciple, "You are going to have the light just a little longer. Walk while you have the light, before darkness overtakes you" (John 12:35a). He would soon go to the cross on a dark Good Friday and defeat the powers of darkness by His perfect sacrifice. After a sunburst resurrection Jesus would return to the Father. In that sense, the splash of light on the leaf represents Jesus, incarnate, crucified, risen, and ascended for us and the world to see and believe.

Jesus continues, "Put your trust in the light while you have it, so that you may become sons of light" (John 12:36). And again, "Whoever follows Me will never walk in darkness but will have the light of life." In another sense, as children of His saving light, we have opportunities every day to let the splash of light illuminate a single leaf surrounded by leaves in dark shadows. For that moment, our touch of love–a listening ear, a voice of concern, a simple invitation to see Jesus as Savior–might bring the light of life to that person for eternity.

The morning splash of light on a single leaf transformed my breakfast into a holy moment of prayer that God might use me to bring moments of light to a dark world.

*Prayer:* The people that in darkness sat
A glorious light have seen;
The light has shined on them who long
In shades of death have been.
*LW* 77:1

October 18

# A Spray of Colors

## Reading: Genesis 12:1–3

*Text:* "I will also make you a light for the Gentiles that you may bring My salvation to the ends of the earth." Isaiah 49:6

Eating dinner in that same seasonal room a few days later, Gail called my attention to a spray of colors on the glass pane of a window leading into the kitchen—violet, blue, green, yellow, orange, and red. The western sun was shining through the beveled glass of our distant front door and projecting this prism of colors on the nearby window glass. We admired the rainbow colors as a gift of God's creation.

In the second of four servant songs, the Messiah speaks about God's call to a mission, not just for Israel's restoration, but far beyond: "I will also make you a light for the Gentiles that you may bring My salvation to the ends of the earth." Sometimes, this passage is called the "great commission of the Old Testament," along with Genesis 12:1–3 where Abraham is blessed to be a blessing to the nations of the world. The Bethel Bible Series pictures a kneeling Abraham holding a prism so God's light can refract the full spectrum of vivid colors throughout the world. Jesus Christ, the Light of the world, came as the suffering Servant to atone for the sins of Jews and Gentiles alike. Brought into His marvelous light through our Baptism, we join the servant people of God in a messianic mission to the ends of the earth. We hold the prism so God's saving light will explode into a spray of colors, bringing people of every language, nation, and tribe to faith in the Savior.

My hearts leaps at the thought of participating in such a great mission by God's grace for Christ's sake through faith. The spray of colors on a window pane at day's end moves me to serve as beveled glass for God's multicolored love to bring Christ's light to the world.

*Prayer:* The world's remotest races,
Upon whose weary faces
The sun looks from the sky,
Shall run with zeal untiring,
With joy your light desiring
That breaks upon them from on high.
*LW* 85:3

# From Iran to St. Louis: One Man's Story

## Reading: Acts 17:22–31

*Text:* God did this so that men would seek Him and perhaps reach out for Him and find Him, though He is not far from each one of us. Acts 17:27

In his famous sermon in Athens on Mars Hill, St. Paul points to an altar "To an Unknown God" and tells about the God of creation who made every nation of the earth in a certain time to live in a certain place "so that man would seek Him and find Him, though He is not far from each one of us." That God sent His Son Jesus to die for the world's sin and to rise from the grave. Today many are brought to faith in Jesus Christ as they travel around the world. Read the story of one Iranian man now living in St. Louis:

Ten years ago, in his mid-twenties, this man was living in Tehran, Iran, and like all Iranians, considered himself Muslim. Yet he felt like he was looking for God. The more he thought about it, the more he felt everything was wrong with Islam. He read the Koran and found that the more he read, the more questions he had. He wasn't happy. Life was dark; there was no harmony. Yet somewhere he felt a small light in his heart—a hope.

Afraid of possible persecution in Iran, he moved with his family to Germany, where a Christian aunt invited him to go to church with her. He felt for the first time that he could find the answers to his spiritual questions. Listening each week while his aunt held a Bible study in her home, he began to read the Bible with interest. He wanted a change in his life and believed in Jesus as God. In Christianity, he found the ultimate truth. Now in St. Louis, he wants to be a never-ending student of the Bible and a missionary to those that need to know Jesus, especially all of the people in Iran. He is very grateful to God for the gift of his Christian faith.

*Prayer:* "Come unto me, ye wand'rers,
And I will give you light."
O loving voice of Jesus,
Which comes to cheer the night!
Our hearts were filled with sadness,
And we had lost our way;
But thou hast brought us gladness
And songs at break of day.
*LW* 345:2

# Confirmation in Argentina

## Reading: Ephesians 2:19–22

*Text:* But now in Christ Jesus you who once were far away have been brought near through the blood of Christ. Ephesians 2:13

Paul's words in Ephesians about Gentiles as foreigners and aliens who once were far away "brought near through the blood of Christ" takes on fresh meaning in the testimony of Norma Campos who moved to Pampa Bolsa, Argentina, last year with her husband, Mario, and their four children. With no vehicle and little extra money for bus fares, they knew they would seldom see the family and friends they left behind. At her confirmation, Norma spoke these words:

"I didn't know anyone in this entire community when we came to live here last year. I lived in bitterness. The doors of my heart seemed to have been closed. One day, Mario and I decided to visit the Lutheran Church. We were welcomed by Liliana Castellano. She talked about Jesus and about the Church. From that day on, the doors of my heart opened to receive the Word of God and my life was changed. I said, 'Yes' when Pastor Victor invited people to join a confirmation class because I wanted to give my heart to God. To read the Bible is like having been given light for my soul. It seemed impossible to live life in this new place, but I am meeting the challenges. I seek to receive from the Holy Spirit strength to become a witness for Jesus Christ in the world."

We thank God for the Spirit-given faith of Norma, the personal witness of Liliana, and the Gospel teaching of Pastor Victor. The Ephesian Christians experienced the same reconciliation through the cross of Christ and the reality of a spiritual household. The missionary concludes, "May our hearts be set ablaze as we too share with others the Lord of life, Jesus Christ."

*Prayer:* Spirit of life, of love and peace,
Our hearts unite, our joy increase,
Your gracious help supply.
To each of us the blessing give
In Christian fellowship to live,
In joyful hope to die
*LW* 389:3

# Albanian Harvest in Philadelphia

**Reading: John 4:39–42**

*Text:* "I tell you open your eyes and look at the fields! They are ripe for harvest." John 4:35b

Jesus speaks to His disciples about a ripe harvest while the villagers came toward Him who have already heard about the Messiah from the Samaritan woman at the well. A similar harvest awaits in twenty-first century America. The following account describes a ministry to Albanians in Philadelphia:

"For the first time in Philadelphia, the city of brotherly love, The Lutheran Church–Missouri Synod has sponsored a summer school/camp and opened the doors to more than 56 Albanian children and their parents. The harvest is ready and the laborers came. As school let out for the summer, the children of northeast Philadelphia are left to babysit themselves as their first generation immigrant parents are all employed. The choice was simple: we either bring the Muslim children in and teach them about God's love in Jesus Christ, or we let them become latchkey kids in the hands of the social services courts. Albanian kids are being influenced by street culture. The time is now! Their souls are thirsty for Jesus; their hearts are opened to the truth that saves. This urgency brought about the creation of the summer camp.

"Grace Lutheran Summer Christian Camp was a glimpse of heaven as we saw inter-cultural families bring their children. We served Greek, Egyptian, Albanian, American, German, and British children. Their faces were bright with hope and joy when they sang, 'Jesus loves the little children, all the children of the world.' What was their favorite time? The Bible class. How often do you hear your neighborhood kids say, 'Tell us one more story of Jesus and His love, and one more story from the heroes of the Bible?'

"At the Closing Parent/Family Mission Festival, 36 families came to tell us they wanted to know Jesus and be baptized. Arrangements are being made to hold a baptismal service in September."

*Prayer:* Lord of harvest, great and kind,
Rouse to action heart and mind;
Let the gath'ring nations all
See your light and heed your call.
*LW* 321:6

Copyright © 1978 *Lutheran Book of Worship*

# Witness of a Name

## Reading: Genesis 17:1–27

*Text:* "No longer will you be called Abram; your name will be Abraham, for I have made you a father of many nations." Genesis 17:5

What's in a name? Have you ever thought of your name as a witness to your faith in Jesus Christ as Savior? My name, Stephen, means "crown" or "garland"—the crown of life given freely by Christ's death on the cross. The fact that Stephen in Acts was the first martyr for Christ adds to my witness. My family names are also significant: John, "God is good"; Amy, "beloved"; Ann, "grace"; Peter, "a rock."

In biblical times, names carried even a greater significance to describe the person or their mission in life. In Genesis 17, God reaffirms His covenant with Abram at age 99, including the promise of descendants from which the Messiah would come. Against all biological probabilities, He declares that Abram's wife, Sarai, will give birth to a son in her old age to be called Isaac. God also institutes the covenant of circumcision as a response to His covenant of promise. In the midst of this powerful chapter, God gives Abram a new name: "No longer will you be called Abram; your name will be Abraham, for I have made you a father of many nations."

Forever, that new name would be connected with God's gift of a son, Isaac, the blessing of many descendants into a great nation, the importance of the covenant of circumcision, and ultimately the birth of Jesus, who would save His people from their sins. What's in a name indeed?

Whatever the literal meaning of your name, you have been baptized in the name of the Father, and of the Son, and of the Holy Spirit. Because of this you bear the name Christian. And this name bears witness to the God of Abraham, Isaac, and Jacob and to the Savior born of Abraham's seed. Your baptismal name describes who you are—"child of God"—and why you live—"to show forth the praises of Him who has called you out of darkness into His marvelous light" (1 Peter 2:9b). What's in your name indeed?

*Prayer:* Baptized into your name most holy,
O Father, Son, and Holy Ghost,
I claim a place, though weak and lowly,
Among your seed, your chosen host.
*LW* 224:1

# Witness of a Birth

## Reading: Genesis 21:1–7

*Text:* Sarah became pregnant and bore a son to Abraham in his old age, at the very time God had promised him. Genesis 21:2

A promise is one thing, even sealed by a new name. The actual birth is another. How Abraham and Sarah must have rejoiced at the birth of little Isaac, arriving "at the very time God had promised him"! Earlier both Abraham (Genesis 17:17) and Sarah (Genesis 18:12) had laughed in disbelief that God could give them a child in their advanced age. Now, with that amazing and world-changing promise fulfilled, Sarah says, "God has brought me laughter, and everyone who hears about this will laugh with me" (Genesis 21:6). You see, Isaac means "he laughs." God's sense of humor was at work! He who laughs last laughs best. God's final laugh brings us resurrection joy at the victory of Jesus on the cross over sin, death, and Satan, culminating in His triumphant return at the Last Day.

Have you ever considered the witness possibilities of a birth—the natural or adopted birth of your own children or grandchildren, the birth of others in your circle of friends or family? Every birth is a blessing of God, reminding us of Isaac's and Jesus' promised birth. Because God has fulfilled His promises in Christ, we can say at the special birth in our life, "God has brought me laughter, and everyone who hears about this will laugh with me." Even when that birth is the result of an "unwanted" pregnancy or has serious complications, we can cling to the victory of the Babe of Bethlehem, Christ of Calvary, and the empty tomb.

Confessing our own disbelieving laughter, anxious thoughts, or indifference prior to a birth, we trust God's forgiveness in Christ, praise Him in each special birth, laugh with the new parents, encourage Baptism, and use the opportunity to witness of God's love in Christ. The witness of a birth!

*Prayer:* See this wonder in the making:
God Himself this child is taking
As a lamb safe in His keeping,
His to be, awake or sleeping.

Miracle each time it happens
As the door to heaven opens
And the Father beams, "Beloved,
Heir of gifts a king would covet!"
*HS 98* 842:1–2

Copyright © 1984 Concordia Publishing House

# Witness of a Sacrifice

### Reading: Genesis 22:1–19

*Text:* Then God said, "Take your son, your only son, Isaac, whom you love and go to the region of Moriah. Sacrifice him there as a burnt offering." Genesis 22:2

Abraham, with a new name and joyfully loving his only son, now is asked to bear the painful witness of sacrifice. God asked him to take Isaac and sacrifice him as a burnt offering on Mount Moriah. What a test of obedience! All of God's promises hinged on the life of this boy. The laughter at his miraculous birth would now be turned to tears of incalculable loss and his death.

Yet Abraham obeyed God as powerfully described in the lean narrative of Genesis 22. Donkey saddled. Wood cut. Three-day journey. Isaac the wood carrier. A heart-breaking conversation with the innocently curious Isaac. Altar built. Son bound and placed on the altar. Knife poised to slay his son. God's last-second intervention. "Now I know that you fear God, because you have not withheld from Me your son, your only son" (Genesis 22:12). Ram caught by its head in a thicket provided for the burnt offering. Abraham's earlier words to his son prophetic: "God Himself will provide the lamb for the burnt offering, my son" (Genesis 22:8a).

What witness is given by that sacrifice? We cannot help but think first of God's sacrifice of His only Son, Jesus, whom He loved, as the Lamb of God, who takes away the sin of the world. We also note Abraham's trust in the God of promise and his unquestioning though painful obedience. At times God calls us to give a witness of sacrifice, not precisely like Abraham, but in terms of painful suffering or the giving over of a loved one into the hands of the Lord. Sometimes the Lord provides a ram of healing or additional time together on this earth. Sometimes the Lord allows the pain to continue or the loved one to be taken from us. But always God has provided the Lamb of God for us. Our Spirit-given trust and sin-forgiven obedience may well provide a witness to His sacrifice.

*Prayer:* See all our sins on Jesus laid;
The Lamb has made us whole.
His soul was once an off'ring made
For ev'ry human soul.
*LW* 276:6

# Undeserved Promise for Witness

## Reading: Genesis 28:10–22

*Text:* "I am with you and will watch over you wherever you go, and I will bring you back to this land." Genesis 28:15

God's witness to His promises moves on from Abraham to Isaac to Jacob. Jacob seems so unworthy as a witness of the promised Messiah. Born the second of twins, grasping his brother Esau's heel, Jacob, "the grasper" grows up as a "deceiver." First, he talks Esau out of his birthright in exchange for lentil stew. Then, with the conniving of his mother, Rebekah, Jacob deceived his father, Isaac, by pretending to be Esau in order to receive his birthright blessing. Now he is forced to flee for his life from Esau's murderous rage. On his way to the home of his uncle, Laban, Jacob stops for the night with a stone for his pillow.

Despite Jacob's obvious unworthiness, the Lord appears to him in a dream of a stairway to heaven with angels ascending and descending. Having chosen Jacob even before his birth to receive the patriarchal blessing, the Lord speaks this undeserved but reassuring promise: "I am with you and will watch over you wherever you go." Alone, afraid, perhaps filled with guilt over his many sins, Jacob awakes to know the power, love, and forgiveness of his Lord: "Surely the LORD is in this place" (Genesis 28:16). In response to God's undeserved promise, he establishes a memorial to God at Bethel and vows to bear witness to Him when he returns to his father's house.

Might that same Lord be calling you to witness of His Son, Jesus, in the twenty-first century? Are we not equally undeserving of His promised salvation because of our self-serving and conniving deception? Does He bring us to Bethel—alone, afraid, and guilty, desperately needing forgiveness and refreshment for a witness task? In God's house, does He not point us to Jesus as our crucified and risen Savior coming to us through Word and Sacraments? Forgiven and empowered by God's undeserved promise, how will you respond as a witness to Jesus in your daily life?

*Prayer:* From your house when I return,
May my heart within me burn,
And at evening let me say,
"I have walked with God today."
*LW* 207:7

# A Limping Witness

## Reading: Genesis 32:22–32

*Text:* And he was limping because of his hip. Genesis 32:31b

Despite the blessing of God, Jacob struggles on. Desiring to marry Rachel, Jacob works seven years for her father, Laban, only to be deceived into marrying her older sister, Leah. He works seven more years for Rachel and then six additional years (Genesis 31:41) for livestock, countering Laban's trickery with his own. Despite Jacob's less than faithful witness to God, the Lord preserves and prospers his life for a return to his homeland.

Now, fearful of Esau's response to his homecoming, Jacob prepares to offer him lavish gifts in exchange for his family's safety. All alone at the Jabbok stream, Jacob wrestles all night with God in human form. At last, Jacob renounces his human striving and asks God for His blessing. With hip out of joint, a limping Jacob receives that blessing and the new name, Israel, "because you have wrestled with God" (Genesis 32:28). Now his limping witness reveals his own need for daily forgiveness and gives all glory to God, who leads him on to the fulfillment of God's promises through the Messiah, Jesus Christ.

Oh, how we struggle in the power of our sinful flesh—with ourselves, our family and friends, our opponents. We become weary, disheartened, and fearful—until we wrestle with God at Jabbok and experience our hip out of joint. Confessing sin and the futility of our fleshly struggle, we ask for and receive God's promised blessing of forgiveness and strength through His Son, Jesus, who wrestled sin, death, and Satan on Calvary, to overcome once and for all by His atoning death. Buried with Him by Baptism into death, we rise with Christ to a new life of service and witness in His Name. Our limping witness acknowledges our weakness and testifies to His saving strength!

*Prayer:* Lord, till we see the ending
Of all this life's distress,
Faith's hand, love's sinews strengthen,
With joy our spirits bless.
As yours, we have committed
Ourselves into your care
On ways made sure to bring us
To heav'n to praise you there.
*LW* 427:6

Copyright © 1982 Concordia Publishing House

# An Altar of Witness

## Reading: Genesis 35:1–15

*Text:* "Then come, let us go up to Bethel, where I will build an altar to God, who answered me in the day of my distress." Genesis 35:3

Jacob comes full circle. Fleeing Esau because of his own deception to gain a birthright, Jacob received God's promise at Bethel before moving on to his uncle, Laban. Struggling for years with the wily Laban, Jacob returns to his homeland after wrestling with God for a blessing. Now safely home, God instructs him to build an altar at Bethel. He first purifies himself and his family, renouncing all foreign gods. Then, at the very spot where his stone pillow became a memorial, Jacob builds an altar as witness to God. God again reveals Himself at Bethel and repeats His promise of land and descendants. Jacob and his household worshiped the Lord at this altar in Bethel. What a witness!

Have you thought about your regular worship in God's house as an altar of witness? There you purify yourself by confessing your sins and receiving God's absolution through your pastor. There you hear again and experience God's promises made long ago to Jacob at the baptismal font, the Lord's eucharistic table, and from the Word of Christ read and preached. There you witness to the world of God's love in Christ through your hymns of praise, offerings of love, prayers, and love for one another. Cleansed, empowered, and refreshed at your altar of witness, you take that saving message of Christ crucified and risen into your daily life. Like Jacob, you live God's promise in your family, neighborhood, community, and world so many bow the knee in worship before the throne of God's grace, saved by faith in Jesus.

Jacob's witness–undeserved promised from God, limping with God's blessing, at his altar of witness! How and where will others see your witness to Jesus?

*Prayer:* Thanks we give and adoration
For your Gospel's joyful sound.
May the fruits of your salvation
In our hearts and lives abound.
Ever faithful, ever faithful
To your truth may we be found.
*LW* 218:2

# Witness Problem: Gaining a Hearing

## Reading: Romans 10:8–17

*Text:* So faith comes from hearing, and hearing through the Word of Christ. Romans 10:17 (ESV)

What are some of the obstacles that stand in the way of our witness to Jesus Christ as Savior? How can we, with the Spirit's help, overcome them that others may be brought to saving faith in Jesus? The next few devotions surface some witness problems based on insights gained from *Culture Shift*, a book by David W. Henderson.

The first witness problem is gaining a hearing. We live in a world of talking heads, day in and day out deluging us with words—"pitching, selling, probing, persuading." Because of that reality, "how does the Christian gain a hearing for biblical truth?" God has spoken powerfully through His Son Jesus Christ, crucified and risen. His words convey life-giving power for salvation. But all too often "the world—distracted, bored, and restless—yawns" as the Word is spoken (pp. 20–21). Henderson adds, "In a world where everybody is talking, what happens to the person who really has something to say?" (p. 21).

Recognizing that only God's Word has power to bring people to faith, Henderson suggests three simple steps to gain a hearing in today's world: 1. Understand your world. 2. Enter your world. 3. Bring truth to bear from outside your world (pp. 37–44 ). St. Paul, in Romans 10, does just that as he recognizes the stubborn rejection of his own people, the Jews, and the alien world of the Gentiles hostile to Christian faith and life. "But how are they to call on whom they have not believed? And how are they to believe in Him of whom they have never heard?" (Romans 10:14).

With one ear attuned to God's saving Word and the other intent on the person we desire to reach in today's world, we trust God's Spirit to help us gain a hearing. Paul writes, "For everyone who calls on the name of the Lord will be saved" (Romans 10:13). Witness problem number one, gaining a hearing, is overcome as God works through you to bring Christ. "So faith comes from hearing, and hearing through the Word of Christ."

*Prayer:* Holy Spirit, give me ears to listen with respect and the right words to speak about Jesus. Amen.

# Witness Problem: Consumers

## Reading: John 15:1–17

*Text:* "You did not choose Me, but I chose you and appointed you that you should go and bear fruit and that your fruit should abide." John 15:16 (ESV)

A second witness problem is that we have developed a consumer mindset. Henderson writes, "Shoppers now through and through, we think about religion like we think about a new sweater. Does it fit? Is it in style? Will it meet my needs?" (*Culture Shift*, p. 48). He later lists some of the guiding principles in a consumer society that influence us and those we desire to reach with the Savior: mix and match (many stores, many brands); hunt for the bargain (high benefit, low cost); comparison shopping (no allegiances to any store); does it fit me? (not what is true but what fits me); return policy (take it back if it doesn't work or bores me) (p. 55). No wonder witness is difficult when the person without Christ has this consumer mindset regarding religion!

But Jesus, in John's Gospel, takes an entirely different approach with the disciples: "You did not choose Me, but I chose you and appointed you that you should go and bear fruit and that your fruit should abide." People who choose their own future will simply wither and die because of their sinful rebellion. God sent His Son as the life-giving vine through His sinless life and atoning death on the cross. He attaches us to the vine by grace through faith. Baptized in God's name, receiving forgiveness at His Table through His body and blood nourished by His Word, we are appointed to bear lasting fruit of service and witness.

As He chooses us for salvation, so He chooses those lost in a consumer mindset. Confessing our own consumerism, we bring the vine and branches message to those seeking a self-centered, low-cost, high benefit way of life so they may repent and receive the free gift of eternal life at the high cost of Jesus' death on the cross. Chosen by God's grace, they can join us in the high cost business of bearing fruit which abides.

*Prayer:* Lord, 'tis not that I did choose Thee;
That, I know, could never be;
For this heart would still refuse Thee
Had Thy grace not chosen me.
*TLH* 37:1

# Witness Problem: Spectators

## Reading: Luke 23:6–12

*Text:* When Herod saw Jesus, he was very glad . . . and he was hoping to see some signs done by Him. Luke 23:8 (ESV)

The third witness problem is a society reduced to being spectators. Because of routine jobs without much meaning, people moved from a rhythm of work and relaxation to a rhythm of boredom and escape. Modern media, including television and movies, provide that escape in the form of entertainment. We become spectators rather than participants, couch potatoes in our reclining chairs. In *Culture Shift*, Henderson puts it this way, "We plopped down and settled in, passive, alone, and wanting to be amused" (p. 75).

While our consumer mentality creates wrong thinking about choosing self-serving options, our life keeps us from thinking, as we passively expect to be entertained. Spectators present a serious witness problem for the message of a God, active in history, who saves us through Christ and incorporates us into a dynamic fellowship reaching out to the world. This requires thoughtful participation, not mindless entertainment!

In the story of Jesus' passion, St. Luke records an interlude with Jesus sent to King Herod: "When Herod saw Jesus, he was very glad . . . and he was hoping to see some signs done by Him." Not interested in confessing sins or facing the only One who could save him, Herod was hoping to be entertained as a spectator by Jesus' miracles. Disappointed with Jesus' silence, he created his own entertainment by having Jesus dressed in fine clothing, mocked by the soldiers, and treated with contempt before returning Him to Pilate.

How do we witness to spectators? Help them face reality—a world of suffering, rebellion, and evil from which there is no escape. Supply a singular focus in their distraction: God—who condemns sin but provides a Savior who entered a real world to pay for sin by His death. Call them to a community of Spirit-given faith in Christ where God's rhythm is worship and witness until He comes again.

*Prayer:* Cast afar this world's vain pleasure
And boldly strive for heav'nly treasure.
Be steadfast in the Savior's might.
Trust the Lord, who stands beside you,
For Jesus from all harm will hide you.
By faith you conquer in the fight.
*LW* 303:2

# Luther's Reformation Witness

## Reading: Romans 3:19–28

*Text:* I will speak of Your statutes before kings and will not be put to shame. Psalm 119:46

The film *Luther*, starring Joseph Fiennes, brings a fresh look at Martin Luther's bold witness to God's love in Jesus Christ. In Luther's words and actions, the viewer clearly sees that we are justified by God's grace for Christ's sake through faith. As St. Paul declares in Romans, "This righteousness from God comes through faith in Jesus Christ to all who believe . . . all have sinned and fall short of the glory of God, and are justified freely by His grace, through the redemption that came by Christ Jesus. God presented Him as a sacrifice of atonement through faith in His blood" (Romans 3:22–25).

Events in sixteenth-century Germany and Rome created a context for Luther's Gospel witness: Shocking abuses and false teaching in the Church, a changing political situation among regional princes in Germany, the threat of invasion from the infidel Turks. These combined with the emergence of young Charles V, the Holy Roman Emperor, give the learned and intense Augustinian monk an opportunity to speak against the practice of indulgences in his October 31, 1517, Ninety-five Theses, now celebrated as the birth of the Reformation. The recently invented printing press made it possible to spread copies around Europe. The resulting furor brought this humble churchman before Charles V at the Diet of Worms, where he was pressured to recant his "heretical" writings. His life was at stake. Simply and courageously, Luther refused to recant. As a result, he was made an outlaw of the empire. The words of the psalmist apply, "I will speak of Your statutes before kings and will not be put to shame."

God preserved Luther and his witness to Christ through years of writing, translating, preaching, and teaching so the Reformation message of "faith alone, grace alone, Scripture alone, Christ alone" continues in our day. The Ablaze! movement in the Lutheran Church intends to spread that Gospel message to 100 million people worldwide by the 500th anniversary of the Reformation, October 31, 2017. By God's grace, despite opposition, why not?

*Prayer:* Faith looks to Jesus Christ alone,
Who did for all the world atone;
He is our one redeemer.
*LW* 355:1

# The Witness of All Saints

## Reading: Revelation 7:13–17

*Text:* These are they who have come out of the great tribulation; they have washed their robes and made them white in the blood of the Lamb. Revelation 7:14

Today the Church celebrates All Saints Day and Commemoration of Martyrs. Many have gone before us believing in Jesus Christ as Savior, living lives of praise to God and service to those in need. Some have given their lives as martyrs for the sake of the Gospel. All stand before the throne and the Lamb, clothed in the robes of Christ's righteousness.

The words of Revelation, in response to the question, "Those in white robes, who are they and where do they come from?" (Revelation 7:13), make everything so clear: "These are they who have come out of the great tribulation; they have washed their robes and made them white in the blood of the Lamb." Their eternal life of service before the throne of God is joyfully focused on the Lamb: "For the Lamb at the center of the throne will be their shepherd; He will lead them to springs of living water" (Revelation 7:17). They enjoy this eternal praise by God's grace, for Christ's sake through faith.

Have you thought of their lives as a witness to you and an inspiration for your daily witness to the world in words and actions? Whether famous for their testimony in the midst of persecution and suffering, unknown in their martyrdom, or familiar to you as departed loved ones, these saints witness of their salvation through Christ alone, their eternal impact on the lives of others, and the glorious future freely given by a gracious God. What difference will they make in your life today, tomorrow, and as long as God gives you earthly breath? Whom is God leading you to touch with the Lamb whose blood makes our robes of righteousness white? When will you and those you touch with Christ join the witness of all saints before the throne?

*Prayer:* Apostles, prophets, martyrs,
And all the noble throng
Who wear the spotless raiment
And raise the ceaseless song–
For these, passed on before us,
We offer praises due
And, walking in their footsteps,
Would live our lives for you.
*LW* 193:4

# Capitol Hill

## Reading: Luke 21:10–19

*Text:* "And you will be brought before kings and governors for My name's sake. This will be your opportunity to bear witness." Luke 21:12b–13 (ESV)

Last week Gail and I joined about 300 other Easter Seals volunteers and staff to mount Capitol Hill in Washington, D.C., and speak to our senators and representatives about the needs of children and adults with disabilities and their families. We entered the seat of power with a quickened heartbeat and a dry mouth. We tried to advocate for people often hidden in society and without a voice of their own.

I was reminded of Jesus' words about the signs of the last times: "And you will be brought before kings and governors for My name's sake. This will be your opportunity to bear witness." Believers in Jesus may be brought before earthly powers because of their faith in Him and threatened with death or imprisonment unless they renounce their faith. Many Christians in our day worldwide have faced such persecution in Africa, Eastern Europe, China, and the Mideast.

Luke's key words apply to all of us: "This will be your opportunity to witness." Whether we face overt persecution or ridicule and disdain, God gives us opportunity to witness of our faith in Jesus Christ through our words and actions. On our own, we may keep silent or even avoid possible conflict situations. Remember, Jesus' disciples forsook Him and fled in His hour of greatest need.

But the same Christ who faced His accusers with dignity and truth went to the cross to pay for our sins and the sins of His accusers. That Christ, crucified and risen, emboldened Peter and John and the apostle Paul to bear witness to Jesus as Savior. Will God's Spirit, who gives us opportunity to witness, not also embolden us to testify of Jesus as Savior?

*Prayer:* His strength within my weakness
Will make me bold to say
How his redeeming power
Transforms my stubborn clay;
His touch of fire ignites me,
With courage I am sent,
My tongue-tied silence broken,
With grace made eloquent.
*LW* 320:3

Copyright © 1982 Concordia Publishing House

# Answering Machine Witness

**Reading: 1 Peter 1:22–25**

*Text:* "'But the word of the Lord endures forever.' And this word is the good news that was preached to you." 1 Peter 1:25 (ESV)

My daughter, Amy, who is married to a pastor and is helping me by keystroking the manuscript for this devotional book, called me yesterday with an idea. While trying to phone an elder of her church, she heard a Bible verse on his answering machine before the customary greeting. His wife confirmed the intent of using the answering machine as a witness to God's Word and added that the Bible verse is changed from time to time. Amy thought this unique concept was worth sharing.

St. Peter's first epistle underscores the power of God's Word for salvation. Quoting the prophet Isaiah, he communicates that while all flesh is like grass, which withers and fades, the Word of the Lord remains forever. Then Peter asserts, "And this word is the good news that was preached to you." He has already given hope to believers under persecution through the word of the prophets (1 Peter 1:10–12) and the apostolic proclamation (1 Peter 1:12) that "He has caused us to be born again to a living hope through the resurrection of Jesus Christ from the dead to an inheritance that is imperishable, undefiled, and unfading, kept in heaven for you, who by God's power are being guarded through faith for a salvation ready to be revealed in the last time" (1 Peter 1:3b–5).

Why not make God's saving Word available on answering machines, computer screens, wall hangings, refrigerators, bulletin boards, and bathroom mirrors? It is the power of God unto salvation for everyone who believes. Convicted of sin, pointed to Jesus as Savior, assured of forgiveness, life, and salvation through God's Word, how can we do less?

*Prayer:* God's Word is our great heritage
And shall be ours forever;
To spread its light from age to age
Shall be our chief endeavor.
Through life it guides our way,
In death it is our stay.
Lord, grant, while worlds endure,
We keep its teaching pure
Throughout all generations.
*LW* 333:1

# Makeup Prayers

**Reading: 1 Thessalonians 5:14–28**

*Text:* Pray without ceasing. 1 Thessalonians 5:17 (ESV)

My wife, Gail, also provided thoughts for the devotions in this book. When she recently led retreats for Christian women, she incorporated a practical idea for daily prayer and witness from a book by Patricia Lorenz, entitled, *Grab the Extinguisher, My Birthday Cake's on Fire*. The idea has the heading, "Makeup Prayers." The author, for her 49th birthday, received a makeup kit from her sister that included lipstick, eyeliner, blush, eye shadows, and little brushes to apply them. Not only did this makeup kit lead her to a daily habit of personal grooming, but it also helped her strengthen the habit of daily prayer. Her question: "What if I combined my prayer time with my makeup time?" (pp. 90–91).

As she daily applied makeup, she prayed prayers like this: "Lord, please let these eyes of mine see the needs of others and respond accordingly. Keep these cheeks smiling. Help me to see the good in others and to pass out smiles by the truckload. Lord, help me to use my mouth and the words that come out of it to Your glory. Help me to speak only with kindness" (p. 91). Makeup prayers. A daily habit and a godly motivation for witness.

Paul's words to the Thessalonians, "Pray without ceasing," often seem overwhelming to those who are accustomed to prayers at meal times and before bed but not "without ceasing." But these words in a section on final instructions simply intend to make prayer a regular part of the warp and woof of life as we relate to others–our spiritual leaders; those among us who are idle, faint-hearted, and weak; and those whom we serve (1 Thessalonians 5:12–18).

In other words, we keep God's salvation in mind throughout each day in our own need for His forgiveness through Jesus and in our opportunities for service and witness. Makeup prayers. Not a bad idea–in the same category with remembering our Baptism with a splash of water and pausing daily to read God's Word.

*Prayer:* Show me what I am to do;
Ev'ry hour my strength renew.
Let me live a life of faith;
Let me die your people's death.
*LW* 433:6

# Fruit-Bearing Required

## Reading: Luke 13:6–9

*Text:* "If it bears fruit next year, fine! If not, then cut it down." Luke 13:9

Jesus tells a harsh parable about required fruit-bearing. He reminds the people of His time that they have a mission to bear fruit with their lives. This particular fig tree had failed to bear fruit for three years so the owner ordered it cut down. Through this parable, Jesus warns the people that they have failed to live for God.

God made us beautiful fig trees in our Baptism, nurturing us to a growing faith in Jesus Christ as our Savior. He intends us to bear the fruit of Christ in our lives—by His grace. Yet often we, like Jesus' contemporaries, fail to produce fruit. We may have a poor credit rating, conduct ourselves poorly at sporting or social events, use foul language and unkind words, fail to care for others, neglect to attend church regularly, or decline to share our faith in Christ. Like the people to whom Jesus spoke, we need to repent.

In the parable, the owner gives the fig tree another chance, a year of grace to bear fruit. The gardener plans special nourishing care to give the tree every chance. God's grace and mercy pours forth to us as well. We have no need to despair. Because of Christ's death on the cross, God gives us another chance. He provides maximum nourishment. As we come humbly to Him. He forgives and restores us. His love alone can produce fruit in us. What the Church needs most is fig trees receiving nourishment and by God's grace continuing to bear fruit in word and deed. Fruit-bearing is required and supplied through Jesus Christ!

*Prayer:* He like a tree shall thrive,
With waters near the root;
Fresh as the leaf his name shall live,
His works are heav'nly fruit.
*LW* 388:3

# Earned, Not Given

**Reading: 1 Thessalonians 4:1–12**

*Text:* So that your daily life may win the respect of outsiders. 1 Thessalonians 4:12a

Large trucks on interstates often serve as billboards. Yesterday, as Gail and I were driving, she called my attention to the following message on a moving truck in large letters: "Earned, not given." One can only guess the intent—perhaps, "You should do business with us because we have earned it through our reliability, service, and timely delivery."

Whatever the intended meaning, that prominent truck message—earned, not given—provides a powerful thought for our Christian witness of faith in Jesus Christ. Words these days are cheap. We are bombarded with telephone and Internet sales pitches from unknown people and companies. Words alone generate scepticism, resistance, or even hostility. As we seek to set the world ablaze with the saving Gospel, we start by earning the respect of those we are trying to reach through our caring, our reliability, our lifestyle, and our daily life at home and at work. That right to speak the Gospel is earned, not given.

St. Paul makes a similar point to the Thessalonian Christians, bearing witness under persecution in 1 Thessalonians. He talks about them living in order to please God (4:1–2), avoiding sexual immorality (4:3–8), and showing love for one another more and more. Then he urges them, "Make it your ambition to lead a quiet life, to mind your own business and to work with your hands just as we told you, so that your daily life may win the respect of outsiders" (4:11–12a). Now they have a platform for sharing the Good News that salvation comes only through faith in Jesus Christ, crucified and risen, who will come again soon to take believers home to heaven (4:13–18).

Confessing our obvious sins in daily life, clinging to God's promised forgiveness through Christ each day, we ask for the power of His Spirit to use our lives for credible opportunities to witness—earned, not given!

*Prayer:* Forth in your name, O Lord, I go,
My daily labor to pursue,
You, only you, resolved to know
In all I think or speak or do.
*LW* 380:1

# Given, Not Earned

### Reading: Ephesians 2:1–10

*Text:* For the wages of sin is death, but the gift of God is eternal life through Christ Jesus our Lord. Romans 6:23

Yesterday's devotion focused on the words, earned, not given, seen on a truck with the message, "We desire to earn your business and do not expect it to be given to us without any reason." Those thoughts can help our witness by showing the importance of earning the right to witness through caring, faithful lives, guided by God's Spirit working through the Word of Christ.

Those truck billboards contain other messages as well. Sometimes they make reference to Bible verses and bear testimony to salvation through faith in Jesus Christ. Whether John 3:16 is used or Romans 6:23, their bold message could read: given, not earned.

Indeed, no one can earn salvation. Paul makes that very clear in his letter to the Romans. After carefully exposing the sin of Jews and Gentiles alike and declaring that no one can be declared righteous by observing the Law, he points to the righteousness from God that comes through faith in Jesus Christ. Christ's redemption makes all the difference (Romans 1–3). Paul summarizes it beautifully a few chapters later: "For the wages of sin is death, but the gift of God is eternal life through Christ Jesus our Lord." Christ, by His sinless life and atoning death on the cross, has earned salvation for us.

God then gives that salvation to us as a gift. Paul writes to the Ephesians, "For it is by grace you have been saved, through faith—and this not from yourselves, it is the gift of God—not by works, so that no one can boast" (Ephesians 2:8–9). Given, not earned! That is the message we earn the right to proclaim as "God's workmanship created in Christ Jesus to do good works which God prepared in advance for us to do" (Ephesians 2:10). Powerful witnessing lessons from truck billboards on how to participate in setting the world ablaze with Jesus Christ!

*Prayer:* By grace God's Son, our only Savior,
Came down to earth to bear our sin.
Was it because of your own merit
That Jesus died your soul to win?
No, it was grace, and grace alone,
That brought him from his heav'nly throne.
*LW* 351:2

# A Phone Call from Jan

**Reading: Isaiah 55**

*Text:* "So is My word that goes out from My mouth: It will not return to Me empty, but will accomplish what I desire and achieve the purpose for which I sent it." Isaiah 55:11

The Apple of His Eye is a mission society serving the Jewish community. Its New York City director, Gary, tells of a young man named Jan with whom he had many interactions over a year and a half, including weekly Bible study and discussion of books Jan was reading about different gods and religions. But Jan could not accept that Jesus is the Messiah and broke off contact. Letters and phone messages were ignored. But Gary kept praying for Jan.

Nine months later, on a Monday evening, Gary received a phone call from Jan: "I'd like to get together again." To the question, "Why is that?" he responded, "Well, I've kind of had a change of heart. I believe Jesus is the Messiah, and that without Him we're going to suffer in hell because of our sins." What an answer to prayer! What an encouragement to all of us for telling others about Jesus as Savior. We may never see the results of our witness, but God works through His Word.

That is exactly what God says in Isaiah 55: "As the rain and the snow come down from heaven, and do not return to it without watering the earth and making it bud and flourish, so that it yields seed for the sower and bread for the eater, so is My word that goes out from My mouth: It will not return to Me empty, but will accomplish what I desire and achieve the purpose for which I sent it" (Isaiah 55:10–11). John writes, "The Word became flesh and dwelt among us, and we beheld His glory, glory as of the only begotten of the Father, full of grace and truth" (John 1:14).

That phone call from Jan gives us added confidence in the Word of Christ and new impetus for persistent prayer and ongoing witness that Jesus is the Messiah.

*Prayer:* Enter, mighty Word, the field;
Ripe the promise of its yield.
But the reapers, oh, how few
For the work there is to do!
*LW* 321:5

Copyright © 1982 Concordia Publishing House

# Mission Helpers: Panama

## Reading: Acts 18:1–4

*Text:* And because he was a tentmaker, as they were, he stayed and worked with them. Acts 18:3

Matt, a short-term mission volunteer in Panama, writes these words: "My position here is that of Construction Coordinator. During the dry season, which is from January until April, many building projects take place. Five volunteer groups from the United States will come here to work on different projects. It is my responsibility to keep these groups of 13–20 people working together smoothly and also to provide continuity when one group leaves and the other arrives.

"When the work groups are here, I spend all of my time with them. We work, we talk, we eat together, but best of all we study God's Word and pray together every night. The mission field has opened my eyes wide to the work of missionaries. We all work long days and weeks. Yes, the work is exhausting, but time is short when it comes to spreading the Gospel to those who do not know its comfort yet. The reward of such important work is eternal and it is held with first priority here."

Matt's experience reminds me of Paul's helpers on his missionary journeys. In Corinth he met Aquila and Priscilla, who had come from Italy as tentmakers. He stayed and worked with them, and they supported his ministry, including further outreach in Ephesus to Apollos, a new convert with high missionary potential.

Believers in Jesus Christ seek one another out for Bible study, prayer, and fellowship. They lift up the hands of missionary pastors. They use their gifts to work side by side in the mission. And they reach out, as forgiven sinners, with the saving message of Christ-crucified worldwide with a sense of priority and urgency. Thanks, Matt, and all part-time volunteers around the world!

*Prayer:* Let none hear you idly saying,
"There is nothing I can do,"
While the multitudes are dying
And the master calls for you.
Take the task he gives you gladly;
Let his work your pleasure be.
Answer quickly when he calls you,
"Here am I. Send me, send me!"
*LW* 318:4

# Bearing Fruit to Win Souls

## Reading: Galatians 5:22–26

*Text:* The fruit of the righteous is a tree of life, and he who wins souls is wise. Proverbs 11:30

Wisdom became incarnate in Jesus, "in whom are hidden all the treasures of wisdom and knowledge" (Colossians 2:3), "for we preach Christ-crucified . . . to those whom God has called" (1 Corinthians 2:23–24). Proverbs 11 describes the believer in God's wisdom through the promised Messiah in these words: "The fruit of the righteous is a tree of life, and he who wins souls is wise."

Practical daily living because of Christ's righteousness on the cross is like the tree of life bearing fruit. That fruit witnesses to Christ, our tree of life, and wins souls to Him as the wisdom of God. Thus, the fruit of the Spirit described in Galatians 5 reveals the wisdom of God in Christ and wins souls to Christ, our righteousness. Bearing fruit, by God's grace, to win souls for Christ!

Helping to set the world ablaze with Christ comes from the wisdom of God revealed in His Word. First, He planted us by the rivers of life in our Baptism so that, connected to Christ, we might bear much fruit. Then, as we learn from His Word, God's Spirit makes us wise unto salvation through faith in Jesus Christ and teaches us the wisdom of daily living as a witness to Christ. The result is souls won as many are led to Christ's righteousness. What a joy to bear fruit and win souls as part of God's wisdom!

*Prayer:* Now a universal garden,
Seeded with your living Word,
Grows with peace and love and beauty,
Songs of freedom there are heard;
By your mercy, by your Spirit,
Thankful hearts are stirred.

In this corner of your garden,
Planted by a faithful few,
We have thrived by their endeavor;
As you blessed them, bless us too.
Find us, as you walk among us,
Bearing fruit for you.
*SP* 110:3–4

Copyright © 1989 Concordia Publishing House

# Sow the Seed Worldwide!

**Reading: Luke 10:1–18**

*Text:* "The harvest is plentiful, but the workers are few. Ask the Lord of the harvest, therefore, to send out workers into His harvest field." Luke 10:2

My wife and I planted tulip bulbs yesterday before the rain. The bulbs were of high quality. We followed the instructions carefully. Next spring we hope to enjoy some colorful tulips and share their beauty with others.

In Luke 10 Jesus describes a plentiful harvest before sending out the Seventy into the villages of Galilee. Sowing and harvesting both involve sharing God's love with others. When we sow the seed of God's Word, sometimes we are privileged to harvest a soul for Christ and sometimes someone else reaps the harvest. In either case, Christ asks us to sow the seed worldwide!

The harvest is plentiful. Seventy suggests the whole number of nations and, therefore, a worldwide mission. We start sharing the good news of salvation through faith in Jesus Christ at home, and we expand our vision to include people from many ethnic groups all over the world. God is preparing a bountiful harvest.

The laborers are few. Starting with 12 disciples, and now seventy, Jesus points to the seemingly impossible task. How precious He regards each worker who sows the seed and reaps the harvest!

We ask the Lord of the harvest to send forth laborers, and then make ourselves available for that task. He died to pay for our sins. He gives us new life and then sends us out on His mission.

How very much like planting tulips! We sow the seed. The powerful Word of God is of high quality. We follow the instructions carefully by praying and going. We place our planting in God's hands. Next spring we will rejoice to see everything in full bloom.

*Prayer:* So when the precious seed is sown,
Your quick'ning grace bestow
That all whose souls the truth receive
Its saving pow'r may know.
*LW* 342:4

# The Ripe Harvest before Us

**Reading: John 4:34–48**

*Text:* "The harvest is plentiful but the workers are few. Ask the Lord of the harvest, therefore, to send out workers into His harvest field." Matthew 9:37–38

Scripture uses many images to describe God's mission through the church to set the world ablaze with Christ. In the next several devotions we focus on "harvest" imagery so we can gain a harvest perspective of our task. Here, in the first of these devotions, we learn from Matthew and John about the ripe harvest before us.

In Matthew 9, Jesus compassionately surveys the crowds around Him looking, "harassed and helpless" (Matthew 9:36), and says to His disciples: "The harvest is plentiful but the workers are few. Ask the Lord of the harvest, therefore, to send out workers into His harvest field." He emphasizes the urgency of a ripe harvest and summons His disciples to prayer. Immediately thereafter, Jesus calls the Twelve and sends them out as workers into the harvest (Matthew 10:1–8).

In John 4, after supplying the Samaritan woman with Himself as living water for salvation and aware that many of the Samaritan villagers from her town would be coming to Him, Jesus says to His disciples: "I tell you, open your eyes and look at the fields! They are ripe for harvest" (John 4:35b). The physical fields in view were ripe for harvest, but so were the many people ripe for salvation. His words ring with urgency for His followers to work in the harvest fields immediately.

Are many in our twenty-first century world from every language, tribe, and people ripe for harvest? The seed has been sown and the plants are growing. Jesus wants us to open our eyes, to pray, and to go. He has brought us to the maturity of a saving faith, nurtured by His Word and Sacraments, Spirit-empowered to witness of Jesus. He sends us out into that ripe harvest before us.

*Prayer:* Hark, the voice of Jesus calling,
"Who will go and work today?
Fields are white and harvests waiting,
Who will bear the sheaves away?"
Loud and long the master calls you;
Rich reward he offers free.
Who will answer, gladly saying,
"Here am I. Send me, send me"?
*LW* 318:1

# The Harvest Within

## Reading: Galatians 6:7–10

*Text:* "But the one who received the seed that fell on good soil is the man who hears the word and understands it. He produces a crop, yielding a hundred, sixty, or thirty times what was sown." Matthew 13:23

Jesus' well-known parable of the sower in Matthew 13 provides a second harvest perspective. Various inadequate soils along the wayside, on rocky places, or among thorns prevent the seed that is the message about the kingdom from taking root and prospering. But, by God's grace, the seed falling on good soil brings salvation and a fruitful life at harvest time. The baptized child of God, trusting Christ for salvation, daily confessing sins and receiving forgiveness, seeking to witness and serve the Lord, is used by God to bear much fruit at harvest time.

St. Paul, in Galatians 6, recognizes our inner tension as saint and sinner by describing the harvest within: "A man reaps what he sows. The one who sows to please his sinful nature, from that nature will reap destruction; the one who sows to please the Spirit, from the Spirit will reap eternal life. Let us not become weary in doing good, for at the proper time we will reap a harvest if we do not give up" (Galatians 6:7b–9).

Boasting only in the cross of our Lord Jesus Christ, through which the world has been crucified to us and us to the world, we rely on the Holy Spirit working through Word and Sacraments to produce within us a fruitful harvest. Then God can send us as forgiven sinners into the ripe harvest before us, pointing only to Christ crucified for salvation. We hear the Word of Christ and understand. We renounce our old sinful nature. We live in our Baptism daily. God then produces fruit in our lives as a witness to His Son.

*Prayer:* Bring to the sacred altar
The gifts his goodness gave,
The golden sheaves of harvest,
The souls Christ died to save.
Your hearts lay down before him
When at his feet you fall,
And with your lives adore him
Who gave his life for all.
*LW* 493:3

# God's Seed and Harvest

**Reading: Mark 4:26–29**

*Text:* "As soon as the grain is ripe, he puts the sickle to it, because the harvest has come." Mark 4:29

Today's harvest perspective focuses on a brief parable found only in Mark's Gospel. While it is true that Satan works overtime to plant weeds in the world and our sinful flesh often sows seeds of destruction in our own lives, the great truth of God's plan of salvation is that God's seed is all powerful and His grace alone produces a harvest of salvation.

In Mark 4, Jesus says, "This is what the kingdom of God is like. A man scatters seed on the ground. Night and day, whether he sleeps or gets up, the seed sprouts and grows, though he does not know how. All by itself the soil produces grain–first the stalk, then the head, then the full kernel in the head. As soon as the grain is ripe, he puts the sickle to it, because the harvest has come."

Even as Jesus sends us as workers into the ripe harvest fields, we can stand in awe at the power of God's Word to transform lives, our own and those to whom we witness. We observe the seed of the saving Gospel germinating, sprouting, and developing to ripe grain. We can take no credit but only marvel at the love of God in Christ. We merely sow the seed through our scriptural witness. God's Spirit brings the results. And He also gathers in the harvest when it is ready.

Every time we gather with God's people around Word and Sacraments, we anticipate and experience the mysterious, powerful working of His seed in our midst and praise Him with our lips and in our lives. We take that same Word of Christ to others in our home, neighborhood, community, and place of work with the same anticipation of His Spirit at work to plant and bring a rich harvest. It is after all God's seed and harvest!

*Prayer:* On what has now been sown
Your blessing, Lord, bestow;
The pow'r is yours alone
To make it sprout and grow.
O Lord, in grace the harvest raise,
And yours alone shall be the praise!
*LW* 217:1

November 15

# Wheat and Weeds at Harvest Time

**Reading: Matthew 13:24–30; 36–43**

*Text:* "Let both grow together until the harvest." Matthew 13:30a

Today's harvest perspective addresses the reality of wheat and weeds growing side by side until harvest time. Jesus, in His Matthew 13 parable, describes good seed sowed by the Son of man, producing quality wheat, the sons of the kingdom, at harvest time, the end of the age. He also tells about the enemy, the devil, sowing weeds when everyone is sleeping that sprout at the same time as the good seed, looking deceptively like wheat. The weeds are the sons of the evil one. Ultimately, at the end of the age, God's angels will pull up the weeds and burn them in the fire. But in the meanwhile, lest an effort to pull the weeds might accidentally destroy the wheat, Jesus says, "Let both grow together until the harvest."

What does the reality of wheat and weeds side by side mean to our mission efforts to set the world ablaze with Christ? First, we rejoice that God has planted us as wheat for Jesus' sake and will keep us safe until the harvest. Second, children of the evil one exist all around us in our twenty-first century world, determined to choke off and destroy as much wheat as possible. The devil uses the world to seek destruction of Christ's Church.

Third, we cannot always distinguish the weeds from the wheat. Only God can judge the heart. Those who believe in Jesus Christ as the crucified and risen Savior are wheat. Those who reject Christ are weeds. Therefore, finally, we make ourselves available to plant the good seed of God's Word and Sacraments so the wheatfields will be ripe unto harvest worldwide. Aware of Satan and his poisonous weeds, we trust the divine Sower and Harvester to help us bear much fruit.

*Prayer:* All the world is God's own field,
Fruit unto his praise to yield.
Wheat and tares together sown,
Unto joy or sorrow grown.
First the blade and then the ear,
Then the full corn shall appear.
Lord of harvest, grant that we
Wholesome grain and pure may be.
*LW* 495:2

# The Final Harvest

## Reading: Revelation 14:14–20

*Text:* "The harvest is the end of the age, and the harvesters are angels." Matthew 13:39b

In the last several devotions, God has given us a harvest perspective from His Word to strengthen us for our task of setting the world ablaze with Christ. We see the ripe harvest before us, calling with urgency for workers in the kingdom. We recognize the struggle within us between God's Spirit and our sinful flesh and thank God for His harvest within, enabling us to bear much fruit. We credit only God at work in our world. It is, after all, God's seed and God's harvest. And we accept the reality of wheat and weeds growing side by side, believers by God's grace and unbelievers led astray by Satan.

In this last devotion on the subject, God's harvest perspective points us to the final harvest. Jesus concludes the parable of the wheat and the weeds with these words: "The harvest is the end of the age, and the harvesters are the angels." John, writing in Revelation, adds these thoughts: An angel speaks to the One sitting on the cloud, "Take your sickle and reap, because the time to reap has come, for the harvest of the earth is ripe" (Revelation 14:15). Yes, at the final harvest, the weeds of the unbelieving evildoers will be cast into the fiery furnace, and the wheat will be harvested as believers in Christ's atoning death, declared righteous, will shine like the sun in the kingdom of their Father (Matthew 13:40–43).

That final harvest calls for our rejoicing as God's thankful people, awaiting eternity with the Lord. That final harvest, with its judgment of sin and unbelief, summons us to work while it is day before the night comes when no one can work. Our work is worship, witness to Jesus, and service among the least, the last, and the lost so countless millions will stand, believing, as harvested wheat before the throne of the Lamb.

*Prayer:* Even so, Lord, quickly come To your final harvest home.
Gather all your people in, Free from sorrow, free from sin,
There, forever purified, In your garner to abide.
Come, with all your angels, come, Raise the glorious harvest home.
*LW* 495:4

November 17

# The Ultimate Deadline

## Reading: 2 Peter 3:7–10

*Text:* "Just as man is destined to die once, and after that to face judgment, so also Christ was sacrificed once to take away the sins of many people." Hebrews 9:27–28a

Deadlines loom constantly–bills, payments, projects at work, decisions major and minor. Sometimes deadlines stand in the way of our purpose for living and the relationships we value most highly. My wife recently read a novel in which one of the characters, who was quite ill, referred to her own death as "the ultimate deadline." It makes one pause in the middle of all the other deadlines.

Hebrews lays it on the line for each of us–"Man is destined to die once, and after that to face judgment." We will stand before God's judgment when we die, either to live with Him forever in heaven or to spend eternity in hell separated from Him. An ultimate deadline indeed. The epistle writer goes on to explain the only way not to fear that judgment as sinful human beings: "Christ was sacrificed once to take away the sins of many." By God's grace through faith in Christ, we can live with confidence and hope as that day approaches.

Perhaps for us the ultimate deadline refers to something else–preparing the world for Christ's second coming. Peter writes in his second letter, "The Lord is not slow in keeping His promise. . . . He is patient with you, not wanting anyone to perish, but everyone to come to repentance" (2 Peter 3:9). Then he adds, "But the Day of the Lord will come like a thief" (3:10).

Saved by Christ, we are here to bring others to repentance and the knowledge of the truth. We must work while it is day before the night comes when no one can work. What a wonderful purpose for living with priority attention to treasured relationships: helping others prepare for the ultimate deadline!

*Prayer:* O Christ, our light, O Radiance true,
Shine forth on those estranged from you,
And bring them to your home again,
Where their delight shall never end.

Make theirs with ours a single voice
Uplifted, ever to rejoice
With wond'ring gratitude and praise
To you, O Lord, for boundless grace.
*LW* 314:1, 5

Copyright © 1978 *Lutheran Book of Worship*

# End-of-the-Age Signs As Witness

**Reading: Matthew 24:1–14**

*Text:* "And this gospel of the kingdom will be preached in the whole world as a testimony to all nations, and then the end will come." Matthew 24:14

The Church Year is drawing to a close. Scripture readings focus on Judgment Day and the second coming of Christ. During His last days before the crucifixion, Jesus teaches about the signs that will precede the end of the age . . . false prophets, wars and rumors of war, famines and earthquakes, persecution of believers, and the increase of wickedness (Matthew 24:1–13). All of these signs to some extent are happening now, giving us an urgency to be prepared.

Then Jesus adds, "And this gospel of the kingdom will be preached in the whole world as a testimony to all nations, and then the end will come." In the face of growing evil and sinful rebellion, God wants the Gospel to be proclaimed throughout the world before the end of the age comes. In this sense, the end-of-the-age signs serve as a witness. The negative signs in nature and humanity lead us to repentance of our sins so we can receive forgiveness from Jesus coming to us in Word and Sacraments.

Then we look to the positive sign of the "gospel of the kingdom being preached in the whole world as a testimony to all nations." God opens our eyes to see that He wants us to help set the world ablaze with Christ through our prayers, our sacrificial giving, and our personal witness by word and deed so countless millions will bow the knee in faith to the Christ who brings salvation to all who believe.

*Prayer:* How will my heart endure
The terrors of that Day
When earth and heav'n before His face
Astonished shrink away?

Ye sinners, seek His grace
Whose wrath ye cannot bear;
Fly to the shelter of His cross
And find salvation there.
*TLH* 610:4, 6

# Day of the Lord Patience

## Reading: 2 Peter 3:3–13

*Text:* He is patient with you, not wanting anyone to perish, but everyone to come to repentance. 2 Peter 3:9b

Endtime living at the conclusion of another Church Year causes us to discern the times and to witness of salvation through faith in Christ with a sense of urgency. St. Peter asserts, "The Day of the Lord will come like a thief" (2 Peter 3:10). He exposes scoffers who follow their own evil desires and claim that the end will never come, forgetting about God's universal judgment through the flood (2 Peter 3:3–6).

Then Peter explains why the Day of the Lord has not yet come: "The Lord is not slow in keeping His promise, as some understand slowness. He is patient with you, not wanting anyone to perish, but everyone to come to repentance" (2 Peter 3:9). God loves the world so much that He exercises patience in bringing final judgment. Not wanting anyone to perish, He offers, through His Church on earth, opportunity for all people to repent of their sins and believe in Jesus Christ as their Savior before the Day of the Lord comes.

How will God's Spirit use you to reach scoffers, disobedient in their evil desires and oblivious to God's coming judgment? In what ways will your life reflect God's patience and persistence, exposing sin and offering forgiveness through Christ? What a joy to be part of a church that patiently offers Christ in Word and Sacraments in the rhythm of the Church Year until that final Day of the Lord! Urgency to reach the lost. Patience to let the Spirit work. Expectation of repentance and salvation before the Day of the Lord—through us!

*Prayer:* As surely as I live, God said,
I would not see the sinner dead.
I want him turned from error's ways,
Repentant, living endless days.

To us therefore Christ gave command:
"Go forth and preach in ev'ry land;
Bestow on all my pard'ning grace
Who will repent and mend their ways."
*LW* 235:1–2

# Compassion for the Lost

**Reading: Mark 6:30–34**

*Text:* When Jesus landed and saw a large crowd. He had compassion on them, because they were like sheep without a shepherd. Mark 6:34

In the abstract we can feel compassion for lost sinners the world over. In the concrete, however, compassion comes with much greater difficulty. We lead our daily lives to meet personal needs, earn a living, and keep family together. On occasion we may respond to a mission sermon and make calls for a new adult class. But normally we don't think much about the lost. If they intrude on our comfortable lives, we may even resent them.

How different the single-minded compassion of Jesus for the lost sheep. By example, He also challenged His disciples to a similar compassion. They had just returned from a successful preaching mission in the villages of Galilee. As they report to Jesus, there are so many people crowding around that they don't even have a chance to eat. Jesus, recognizing the need for rest, suggests that they go by boat to a quiet place. However, whey they arrive, they discover that multitudes have gone around the lake on foot to meet them. Does Jesus send them away until a more convenient time? No, He teaches them and later feeds the 5,000.

Compassion for the lost. Only God can fill us with it. Jesus sought us out as sheep needing a shepherd. He gave His life for us on the cross. He personally binds up our wounds and forgives our lack of compassion. He knows our need for rest with Him but He also places before us constantly, in the concrete, people who need His love and forgiveness–lost sheep. And He wants to use us to teach, feed, and heal them. How we need Jesus' compassion for the lost!

*Prayer:* Raise up, O Lord the Holy Ghost,
From this broad land a mighty host;
Their war cry, "We will seek the lost
Where you, O Christ, will come."
*LW* 316:6

# Inter-Ethnic Witness

## Reading: Acts 15:6–9

*Text:* And God, who knows the heart, bore witness to them by giving them the Holy Spirit just as He did to us. Acts 15:8 (ESV)

A suburban church near the Pentagon serving many military families has recently been led by God's Spirit to partner with other ethnic Christians to proclaim Christ. In their church building every weekend, one can hear Korean, Amharic, and Urdu being spoken along with English. A Korean church, Ethiopian immigrant ministry, and Pakistani/Afghan church meet to worship. The Anglo pastor and his people are learning from this inter-ethnic witness. They witness to Jesus by opening their facility for these other Lutheran ministries, but they also learn more about God's working in today's world from the fervent prayers, study of the Word, worship, and outreach efforts of the ethnic churches. They receive more than they give.

In the first century, the early Jewish believers in Christ were scattered by persecution. Soon God's Spirit began bringing Gentiles into the Church, first through Peter and then through Paul. As the Jerusalem Council convened to consider the realities of this inter-ethnic explosion in the Church, Peter reports about the new Gentile believers: "And God, who knows the heart, bore witness to them by giving them the Holy Spirit just as He did to us." He adds, "He made no distinction between us and them, having cleansed their hearts by faith" (Acts 15:9). Peter witnessed to Cornelius and his household, but he also learned from their Spirit-given faith in Jesus and their welcoming of Him into their home. Peter experienced inter-ethnic witness.

How is God working in your community? What believers have visited your church from other countries or from immigrant groups in your area? How might you witness to them of your faith in Jesus—hospitality, prayer, support, practical help? How might you learn from them about their new-found faith or their perseverance under persecution in other lands? God's Spirit may be moving mightily in North America through inter-ethnic witness!

*Prayer:* People and realms of ev'ry tongue
Dwell on his love with sweetest song
And infant voices shall proclaim
Their early blessings on his name.
*LW* 312:3

# Dinner at Levi's House

**Reading: Mark 2:13–17**

*Text:* While Jesus was having dinner at Levi's house, many tax collectors and "sinners" were eating with Him and His disciples. Mark 2:15

How will our church carry out One Mission Ablaze! to touch 100 million people with Jesus by the year 2017? The answer is one person at a time. How can we find and reach these people who need salvation through Jesus Christ. How about at the dinner table?

Jesus, at the beginning of His public ministry, was choosing His disciples. At the Lake of Galilee, Jesus spotted Levi at a tax collector's booth and asked him to follow. Levi, a controversial choice because of his hated profession, had many friends in the category of tax collectors and "sinners," friends in need of a Savior. Levi invited them for dinner with Jesus and His other disciples. What a great opportunity to introduce them to Jesus. The Pharisees, seeing Him eating with this highly suspect group, criticized Jesus for His actions. Jesus' reply: "It is not the healthy who need a doctor, but the sick. I have not come to call the righteous, but sinners" (Mark 2:17). Apparently the tax collectors and sinners were deeply appreciative of Jesus' presence and teaching because they recognized their spiritual sickness and need for forgiveness. They were no doubt thankful for Levi's dinner invitation.

Who are your friends and acquaintances who need an invitation to dinner at your house or some other special setting where they can be introduced to Jesus? Aware of your own sinfulness, salvation through Jesus, and call to follow Him, are you making a list and issuing some invitations? God's Spirit will guide you to the right people in the right setting at the right time for a special meeting with the Savior.

*Prayer:* "And whosoever cometh, I will not cast him out."
O patient love of Jesus Which draws away our doubt,
Which though we be unworthy Of love so great and free,
Invites us very sinners To come, dear Lord, to thee!
*LW* 345:4

# A Samaritan Thanksgiving

## Reading: Luke 17:11–19

*Text:* He threw himself at Jesus' feet and thanked Him—and he was a Samaritan. Luke 17:16

In this harvest season, we approach the national holiday of Thanksgiving. In many homes across the nation, family and friends gather at tables laden with turkey and all the trimmings, topped off with mouth-watering pies. We may or may not welcome these family dinners with thankful hearts. If circumstances prevent a family gathering because of living alone, illness, or recent tragedy, we may or may not take pause to thank God.

But the response of a Samaritan leper in Luke's gospel provides a powerful thanksgiving witness to lead us to repentance and then genuine thanksgiving because of God's grace in Jesus Christ. Ten lepers stand at a distance and cry out to Jesus for mercy. Sentenced to a slow painful death because of their incurable disease, outcasts and untouchables in society for the same reason, they desperately need help.

Jesus responds, "Go, show yourselves to the priests." We are told, "And as they went, they were cleansed" (Luke 17:14). A miracle happened. All were cleansed. The examination by the priests would confirm their healing. All had reason for thanksgiving, most of them Israelites. But only one returned, believing in Jesus as his Savior from sin as well as his healer of leprosy. "He threw himself at Jesus' feet and thanked Him—and he was a Samaritan." What a witness!

How will you give thanks this Thanksgiving and every succeeding day? What witness will God make to Jesus through your thanksgiving? Repentant, cleansed of sins, faith-filled by God's Spirit, we humbly and joyfully give thanks to Jesus. What a witness!

*Prayer:* All praise and thanks to God
The Father now be given,
The Son and him who reigns
With them in highest heaven,
The one eternal God,
Whom earth and heav'n adore;
For thus it was, is now,
And shall be evermore.
*LW* 443:3

# Elmer D.'s Heart Attack

**Reading: Psalm 118:5–21**

*Text:* I will not die but live, and will proclaim what the LORD has done. Psalm 118:17

My father-in-law, Elmer Dobberstein, who died in 1991, influenced the lives of countless people, including myself, through his humble Christian witness. After a major heart attack in 1979, he confided in me that his experience had given him a determination to reach out in love to at least one person every day. The amazing impact of that simple decision continued in an outreach begun many years before–greeting a toll booth operator on the interstate, a grocery clerk at the checkout line, a bowler in his weekly league, a church shut-in, a cancer patient traveling to a hospital in a neighboring town, an associate at the radio station where he did color commentary for sporting events, in addition to the more than 300 recipients yearly of his birthday cards and prize winners listed in the local newspaper who received his written congratulations and a *Portals of Prayer* devotional magazine.

My thoughts turn to the psalmist's words in Psalm 118: "I will not die but live, and will proclaim what the LORD has done." These words may well have been written by a Davidic king who had been surrounded by enemies determined to destroy him and the nation. Pushed back and about to fall, the psalmist was delivered by the Lord and exclaimed, "The LORD is my strength and my song; He has become my salvation" (Psalm 118:14). The whole people of God ended up using this psalm in its liturgy as a thanksgiving for national deliverance. Martin Luther, because of verse 17, counted Psalm 118 as his favorite psalm.

Spared from a near fatal heart attack, Elmer D. thanked his Lord and Savior Jesus Christ each day of his remaining 12 years by proclaiming what the Lord has done. In what ways can you proclaim the Lord's salvation in your daily life? What a joy to know that He is our strength, our song, and our salvation!

*Prayer:* Dear Lord, thank You for paying the full price for my salvation on Calvary. Help me to proclaim what You have done every day. Amen.

# The Witness of Thanksgiving

**Reading: 1 Corinthians 1:4–9**

*Text:* I will give thanks to the LORD with my whole heart, in the company of the upright, in the congregation. Psalm 111:1 (ESV)

In what ways can God use you to set the world ablaze with Christ? These devotions based on God's Word show you many ways. But Psalm 111 describes a reality you may not have considered: the witness of thanksgiving.

The psalmist writes, "I will give thanks to the LORD with my whole heart, in the company of the upright, in the congregation." Many people in today's world see only the problems of life, the evil surrounding them, the hopelessness of dealing with circumstances beyond their control. They struggle to find any reason for giving thanks. Without the Lord, we too would wallow in self-pity and despair without a peep of thanksgiving. As sinners, we still sometimes lose perspective.

But the psalmist cries out as one redeemed by the gracious, merciful, faithful, and just works of God who will send His own Son as the promised Messiah. And He has placed the psalmist in the congregation of the upright, justified by God's grace. Therefore, the psalmist can give thanks with a whole heart as he gathers with the people of God. That thanksgiving serves as a witness to the surrounding world. In that same spirit, Paul thanks God for the Corinthian Christians, who received the grace of God given in Christ Jesus, and gave testimony about Christ in their speech and knowledge (1 Corinthians 1:4–9). The witness of thanksgiving.

Forgiven for our thanklessness through the blood of Christ, we give daily thanks to our Lord with a whole heart and join with the fellowship of God's redeemed people around the eucharistic meal to touch today's desperate world with the witness of thanksgiving!

*Prayer:* We worship you, God of our fathers, we bless you;
Through trial and tempest our guide you have been.
When perils o'ertake us, you will not forsake us,
And with your help, O Lord, our struggles we win.

With voices united our praises we offer
And gladly our songs of thanksgiving we raise.
With you, Lord, beside us, your strong arm will guide us.
To you, our great Redeemer, forever be praise!
*LW* 494:2–3

# Studying His Works with Delight

**Reading: Psalm 111:2–9**

*Text:* Great are the works of the LORD, studied by all who delight in them. Psalm 111:2 (ESV)

What you study reveals a great deal about your heart—the *Wall Street Journal* or business page, the sports page or racing forms, the latest Internet prices for real estate, world travel, sports utility vehicles, or listings for movies, cable television shows, and pornography. What you study serves as a witness to what you believe.

The psalmist provides a powerful form of witness for believers: studying His works with delight! "Great are the works of the LORD, studied by all who delight in them." He then details and characterizes God's works, "full of splendor and majesty" . . . "righteousness endures forever". . . "provides food for those who fear Him" . . . "the power of His works" . . . "the works of His hands are faithful and just" . . . "He sent redemption to His people" (Psalm 111:2–9). Can't you just feel the psalmist's delight as he remembers and counts the Lord's wondrous works? What he studies bears eloquent witness to his faithful God.

What do you study with delight? Aware of the compulsive study flowing from a sinful heart, we confess our negative witness to those around us at home and at work. Clinging to the Lord's mighty works of creation and redemption through the blood of Christ, we receive His forgiveness in Word and Sacrament and let God's Spirit fill our hearts with delight as we daily study and recount His works in our lives and world—the fresh beauty of early morning, the Spirit speaking through quiet time of Word and prayer, the angelic protection through rush hour traffic, the wisdom for decision-making during a hectic work day, the spontaneous love of children and grandchildren freely given, the accepting touch of our spouse, the listening ear of a Christian friend, the joy of worship, which lifts up Christ as Savior, the coming to faith of a child, a teenager, or an adult by God's grace alone, the healing presence of God in a wicked world filled with terror and the abuse of political power. Studying His works with delight—what a witness!

*Prayer:* Ponder anew What the Almighty can do<br>
As with His love He befriends you.<br>
*LW* 444:3

# Responding to His Remembered Works

## Reading: Psalm 112

*Text:* The fear of the LORD is the beginning of wisdom; all those who practice it have a good understanding. Psalm 111:10 (ESV)

When we study God's works with delight, God's Spirit leads us to respond in service and witness. Psalm 111 and 112 belong together. Psalm 111 describes God's works. Psalm 112 describes the believer, saved by God's works and living the life of faith in God's promises. Psalm 111:10 sets the stage for our response to God's wondrous works: "The fear of the LORD is the beginning of wisdom; all those who practice it have a good understanding."

The psalmist had said, "He has caused His wondrous works to be remembered" (Psalm 111:4). God's Spirit helps us remember God's works, including the sending of His Son Jesus to die on the cross in payment for our sins. And Jesus would say after giving the disciples His body and blood in the Lord's Supper, "Do this in remembrance of Me" (Luke 22:19). In His works we remember that the Lord is gracious, merciful, righteous, and trustworthy (Psalm 111:3–7).

Therefore, Psalm 112 characterizes the believer, forgiven and restored, as "gracious, merciful, and righteous" (Psalm 112:4b). His heart is "firm, trusting in the LORD" and "steady," unafraid (Psalm 112:7–8). In response to God's works, the believer, who has remembered God's covenant, "will be remembered forever" (Psalm 112:6b). That's witness!

How will you respond to God's remembered works? How will you be remembered? He desires to work in you His own grace, mercy, righteousness, and trustworthiness. In your Baptism, He forgives you each day and helps you rise to a newness of life where you give generously, conduct your affairs with justice, and tell others of His work of redemption through Christ's death and resurrection. That's witness!

*Prayer:* O God of mercy, God of light, In love and mercy infinite,
Teach us, as ever in your sight, To live our lives in you.

Teach us the lesson Jesus taught: To feel for those his blood has bought,
That ev'ry deed and word and thought May work a work for you.
*LW* 397:1, 3

# Fishers of Men International

**Reading: Luke 5:1–11**

*Text:* "Don't be afraid; from now on you will catch men." Luke 5:10b

At the beginning of His public ministry, Jesus met the disciples at their own lake and then used fishing imagery to call them into His service.

Jesus unveils His fishing plan. Starting with a miracle on the lake, He calls the disciples to follow Him. For three years He trains them. Then He goes to the cross to pay for their sins, rises from the dead, and commissions them for a worldwide fishing trip. He calls us to a similar fishing trip. Made His own in Baptism, we learn from Him and we witness in family, community, nation, and world.

But we face obstacles to our fishing. The disciples struggled with catching men because they were provincially bound to Galilee and constantly worried about unfavorable fishing conditions as opposition to Jesus mounted. We often live provincial lives as well. How difficult we find it to picture Christ coming for people of every city, state, tribe, and nation! We become so preoccupied with daily unfavorable fishing conditions that we lose sight of God's international plan.

The Lord reveals His fishing method. He saturates us with His powerful, life-changing Word. Peter heard that Word from the pulpit of his boat before launching on that Galilee fishing adventure. And we hear that Word in worship and Bible study. Jesus applied that Word to the daily experience of the disciples. How could they ever forget the miraculous catch of fish, the mountaintop transfiguration, the footwashing, the holy Meal, the nail-pierced hands of the risen Lord? No wonder they responded to His call. We too respond to His ongoing call as fishers of men international.

*Prayer:* Raise up, O Lord the Holy Ghost,
From this broad land a mighty host;
Their war cry, "We will seek the lost
Where you, O Christ, will come."
*LW* 316:6

# Finding Faith During the College Years

## Reading: Acts 4:32–37

*Text:* Nevertheless, more and more men and women believed in the Lord and were added to their number. Acts 5:14

Do you think often about students going to college and pray that they keep their faith in Christ or find saving faith? A recent article in *Forest Magazine*, published by Concordia University, River Forest, Illinois, tells the moving story of a young woman named Melissa. Raised Roman Catholic, she wandered from the faith for several years, during which she experimented with non-traditional religions including the pagan Wicca.

On her way back to school from Christmas vacation in her sophomore year, Melissa saw a homeless man on the side of the street in freezing weather. Moved to pull over and give him a coat, some food, and a bottle of water, she heard him say, "God bless you" with a tear in his eye. She writes, "When I drove away, I started to cry. I started to wonder why it was that someone who had so little could have faith in God and I couldn't. Everyone around me supported my decision to become Lutheran, but I believe it was that man who forever changed my life and gave me all the encouragement I needed." Now graduated with a degree in Communications and Art and recently married, Melissa was confirmed during her time as a student at Concordia. She rejoices at God's daily presence in her life.

The early church provided a caring fellowship for new believers. Yet because of persecution and God's power at work in their midst, some were reluctant to identify themselves as believers. "Nevertheless, more and more men and women believed in the Lord and were added to their number."

Consider college as an important arena for Christian witness. With many obstacles to faith and many temptations to fall away from Christ, young people need the prayers and the support of Christian parents, friends, professors, and fellow students. Through our witness, many like Melissa will believe in the Lord and be added to our number.

*Prayer:* That caring parents, gracious Lord,
And faithful teachers find reward
In leading these, to whom you call,
To find in Christ their all in all.
*LW* 470:3

Copyright © 1982 Concordia Publishing House

# God's Language Or Ours?

## Reading: Genesis 11:1–9

*Text:* "Come, let us go down and confuse their language, so that they may not understand one another's speech." Genesis 11:7 (ESV)

Have you ever considered the power of language? A golden-tongued orator can hold audiences spellbound and influence them for good or evil. A demagogue like Hitler can lead the masses to destruction. Businesses can use language to sell their products, convince their investors, or use multiple languages to expand worldwide. Novelists, poets, and pamphleteers have attracted wide followings to shape opinion and values.

At a time when the whole earth had only one language, sinful human beings grasped the power of language to gain power and fame for themselves. They said, "Come, let us build ourselves a city and a tower with its tops in the heavens, and let us make a name for ourselves" (Genesis 11:4 ESV). Seeing their evil desire to become gods, the Creator God, Father, Son, and Holy Spirit, said, "Come, let us go down and confuse their language, so that they may not understand one another's speech." The Lord then dispersed them over the face of the earth. And the place was called Babel (confusion of tongues). Language, you see, belongs to God and not to us.

How do you use language? To confess God's glory or to curse Him? To communicate His love in Christ the Savior or to gain power and fame for yourself? To help people in need or to confuse and manipulate them for your own ends? As part of a sinful people dispersed over the face of the earth, we confess trying to make language our own for our own rebellious purposes.

Humble and repentant, we hear God's language of promise to Abraham in Genesis 12: "I will make of you a great nation, and I will bless you and make your name great so that you will be a blessing . . . and in you all the families of the earth shall be blessed" (Genesis 12:2–3 ESV). How might God's language, spoken by our lips, become a blessing to the families of the earth for salvation through Jesus Christ? That's tomorrow's devotion. God's language of promise, not ours!

*Prayer:* Father, forgive my wrong use of language. Speak Your language of promise to me and through me. Amen.

# Language As Witness

## Reading: Acts 2:1–13

*Text:* "And how is it that we hear, each of us in our own native language?" Acts 2:8 (ESV)

Language, perverted for power and fame, confused by God at Babel to disperse a sinful people! Language, employed in each native tongue, for witness to the crucified and risen Christ at Pentecost to unite a forgiven people!

Have you considered the power of language for witness? Not just the powerful Pentecost message in Acts 2. Not just the pastor's sermonic language on Sunday morning. Not just the eloquent and inspiring language of classical and contemporary Christian authors. But also the witness of your language each day to family, friends, associates at work, and contacts in the community.

You see, Jewish believers gathered from around the world on that first Pentecost. Still part of a sinful world, dispersed from the ancient tower of Babel, they had no knowledge of the recent death, resurrection, and ascension of Jesus of Nazareth. They were gathered for a Jewish festival called Pentecost. In addition to a rushing, mighty wind, tongues of fire, and a rousing sermon by Peter, the multitude heard testimony to the Savior from all of the disciples. From many nations and many languages, they asked, "And how is it that we hear, each of us in our own native language?" Language as witness to Jesus! Three thousand believed and were baptized that day.

God's language today through our lips sets the world ablaze with Christ . . . in Mandarin, Spanish, Arabic, Russian, Hmong, Bosnian, Japanese, and English. Confessing again our self-serving use of language and refusal to learn other languages, we hear in our own language the message of forgiveness through the shed blood of Jesus Christ and pray for His Spirit to use our language as witness each day. And He will use our words, based on His life-changing Word, to reach many for salvation. Language as witness!

*Prayer:* Let children hear the mighty deeds
Which God performed of old. . . .
Our lips shall tell them to our sons,
And they again to theirs
That generations yet unborn
May teach them to their heirs.
*LW* 472:1, 3

# Choice Land

## Reading: Genesis 13:1–18

*Text:* So Lot chose for himself the whole plain of the Jordan and set out toward the east. Genesis 13:11

Have you ever considered the mission implications of your choice of land? Where you choose to live makes a difference for your Christian witness–small town, urban changing neighborhood, suburban development, remote rural home, retirement community, downtown condominium, high-rise apartment. Each of these choices provides opportunities or threats to your Christian life.

When God called Abram to a new land, his nephew Lot traveled with him. They were both blessed with livestock and material possessions. Eventually they ran out of space and needed to separate into different land areas. Abram gave Lot the choice of land. What went into Lot's consideration? Did he consider who his neighbors would be and how their beliefs and moral values might influence him? Instead, it appears that Lot had an eye for the choice land, the best pasture land and water supply: "So Lot chose for himself the whole plain of the Jordan and set out toward the east." He moved his tents among the cities of the valley near Sodom. "Now the men of Sodom were wicked and were sinning greatly against the LORD" (Genesis 13:13). Later we learn how Lot barely escaped the Lord's destruction of that wicked city with its shameful and degrading rebellion against God.

We ask ourselves why we live where we live, by choice or circumstance. What temptations threaten to compromise our Christian confession of faith and lifestyle? What witness opportunities present themselves with our neighbors through word and example? Confessing our sins of poor choices or witness negligence, we turn to the God of Abraham who called him to witness in a new land so the nations would be blessed. We receive forgiveness through Jesus Christ, the seed of Abraham, who chose human flesh and a life in that same land of Canaan that would lead to His death on a cross. Through His resurrection, He offers us a pilgrim life of witness wherever we make our residence on our way to the choice land of heaven.

*Prayer:* Guide me ever, great Redeemer,
Pilgrim through this barren land.
I am weak, but you are mighty;
Hold me with your pow'rful hand.
*LW* 220:1

# Closed Door/Open Door

## Reading: 2 Kings 5:2

*Text:* Now bands from Aram had gone out and had taken captive a young girl from Israel, and she served Naaman's wife. 2 Kings 5:2

The other day we returned home in our van from shopping. Routinely, I pushed the garage door opener, but nothing happened. The door was closed and could not even be opened manually because the main spring was broken. This closed door created more than a little dissatisfaction. What would we do until an overhead door repair company could be summoned? Two days later, after the weekend, a reliable and experienced man came to replace the old spring with a new one and reattach the cable.

But the closed door led to an open door of another kind. The man, apologizing for not being available on the weekend, revealed his grief over three recent deaths of friends and family. We were able to sit at our kitchen table over glasses of cold water and talk about faith in Jesus as Savior for eternal life in heaven. I was privileged to give him a copy of my previous devotional book. Closed door/open door!

The young girl from Israel must have experienced a closed door when she was taken captive from her home in Israel to a strange country, Aram. There she was made a slave to the wife of a famous general named Naaman. But that closed door of slavery gave her an open door for witness. Naaman was diagnosed with leprosy, a dread incurable disease. The young girl took advantage of the open door and said to her mistress, "If only my master would see the prophet who is in Samaria! He would cure him of his leprosy" (2 Kings 5:3). As a result, Naaman visited Elisha and despite some angry skepticism about washing seven times in the Jordan, obeyed, was healed, and, more important, believed in the God of Israel. Closed door/open door!

What closed doors are you bemoaning that might be presenting you with an open door for witness?

*Prayer:* Blessings abound where'er he reigns:
The pris'ners leap to lose their chains,
The weary find eternal rest,
And all who suffer want are blest.
*LW* 312:4

# Herald of Good News

## Reading: Isaiah 40:1–11

*Text:* Get you up to a high mountain, O Zion, herald of good news. Isaiah 40:9a (ESV)

The Advent season focuses on God's promise to send salvation through the coming to earth of His Son Jesus Christ. That promise comes in the context of human sin. God's people Israel rebelled against God through idolatry and adultery. First, the northern kingdom was destroyed; then the southern kingdom was defeated, Jerusalem and the temple destroyed, and the people exiled for 70 years in Babylon. As Isaiah writes, "All flesh is grass, and all its beauty is like the flower of the field. The grass withers, the flower fades" (Isaiah 40:6b–7).

What place, then, does witness have in the Advent story? Isaiah describes God as coming to this very people, like a fading flower in their sin, with His forgiveness through the Word of God, which stands forever. Then He calls Zion, His people, to bring comfort that the Messiah is coming: "Get you up to a high mountain, O Zion, herald of good news." They are the witnesses, the heralds of good news. Their message: "He [God] will tend His flock like a shepherd; He will gather the lambs in His arms; He will carry them in His bosom, and gently lead those who are with young" (Isaiah 40:11).

What about us, modern day Zion as members of Christ's body, the Church? How do we fit into the Advent story? Because of our sin and rebellion, we are like withered grass and fading flowers. But the good news of Isaiah 40 has been fulfilled through the coming of Jesus as Babe of Bethlehem and Christ of Calvary. He chooses us as witnesses to the ends of the earth by telling us, "Get you up to a high mountain, O Zion, herald of good news." Until Jesus Christ comes again at the Last Day, we receive His daily forgiveness through Word and Sacraments and announce the kingdom of God to all who need the Good Shepherd to gather them in His arms for eternity.

*Prayer:* Witness, witness to the world
The glory of the Lord unfurled.
The hour now strikes, the dawn light breaks,
God keeps the promises he makes.
*LW* 21:4

Copyright © 1982 Concordia Publishing House

December 5

# A Mute Witness

### Reading: Luke 1:5–25

*Text:* When he came out, he could not speak to them. Luke 1:22a

There are lessons to be learned about witnessing from the Advent story about an aged priest named Zechariah in Luke 1. We know both Zechariah and Elizabeth as "upright in the sight of God, observing all the Lord's commandments and regulations blamelessly" (Luke 1:6). But they had no children. Zechariah is chosen to serve at the temple in the Most Holy Place. There the Lord's angel appears to him and announces that his aged wife will give birth to a son, named John, who will serve as messenger to prepare people's hearts for the Messiah.

Startled and unable to accept these words of promise, Zechariah ends up making a dramatic testimony not of his own choosing. Gabriel tells him, "And now you will be silent and not able to speak until the day this happens, because you did not believe my words" (Luke 1:20). The people were waiting and wondering why he stayed so long in the temple. "When he came out, he could not speak to them. They realized he had seen a vision, for he kept making signs to them but remained unable to speak" (Luke 1:22). His was a mute witness!

In what ways might God be using you to give a mute witness? Obviously the story of Zechariah is unique as God's saving plan unfolded in the fullness of time for the forerunner to announce Jesus as Messiah. Nevertheless, God's plan of salvation continues to unfold through His Church.

Are there times when you are filled with great joy to be chosen for service or with great sadness because of death or serious illness? Are you ever rendered speechless? At least, you cannot speak in public. Could our Savior be using your mute witness at such times, beyond your control, to demonstrate His great love, forgiveness, and comfort in your life? Might He be pointing others to Him through the witness of your Christian life?

*Prayer:* Upon your lips, then, lay your hand,
And trust his guiding love;
Then like a rock your peace shall stand
Here and in heav'n above.
*LW* 424:7

# Tongue Loosed for Witness

## Reading: Luke 1:57–66

*Text:* Immediately his mouth was opened and his tongue was loosed, and he began to speak, praising God. Luke 1:64

At times we cannot speak because we are overwhelmed with sorrow, grief, or unexpected joy. Ours is a mute witness. Others, like our pastor and Christian friends, may pray on our behalf and speak words of comfort and encouragement. God uses our endurance and humility to point to His love for us. But then comes the opportunity to speak as we reflect on God's salvation in our lives. The words of praise and witness seem all the more powerful because of our period of silence.

In the story of a priest named Zechariah, that is exactly what happened. He returned home from the temple in silence and remained mute during Elizabeth's nine month pregnancy until John, the forerunner of Christ, was born. Zechariah obediently wrote on a tablet, "His name is John" (Luke 1:63). "Immediately his mouth was opened and his tongue was loosed, and he began to speak, praising God." His verbal witness to God's plan of salvation after his months of silence gave powerful witness to his awe-filled neighbors and throughout the hill country of Judea. "Everyone who heard this wondered about it, asking, 'What then is this child going to be?' For the Lord's hand was with him" (Luke 1:66).

In what ways is the Lord loosing your tongue for witness? A teenager making it through a period of painful relationships, loneliness, or doubts about their future? A young mother adjusting to the reality of a newborn or several young children in the home? A young adult trying to find a career path after several false starts? A midlife crisis experience in job or home? Dealing with illness, death, and aging in the later years? As God reveals His love in Jesus in each of these situations, how will your tongue witness to the Savior? Your prayers, your praise, your simple testimony about Jesus your Savior will cause others to wonder and inquire about God's salvation for them. For the Lord's hand is with you.

*Prayer:* Hosanna! Blessed Jesus, Come in our hearts to dwell,
And let our lives and voices Your praise and glory tell.
*LW* 16:2

Copyright © 1982 Concordia Publishing House

# A Song of Witness

**Reading: Luke 1:67–80**

*Text:* To give His people the knowledge of salvation through the forgiveness of their sins. Luke 1:77

Zechariah, filled with the Holy Spirit, uses his unloosed tongue to sing a song to witness that has echoed in the Church through the centuries as the Benedictus. This marvelous song first praises the Lord God of Israel for His salvation in the past, through His covenant with Abraham and His deliverance from enemies, through the house of David. Then he looks to the future redemption that will be ushered in by his son, John, who will prepare the way for Jesus, whose perfect life of obedience and shedding of blood on the cross will lead us into the path of peace with God.

The heart of John's prophetic ministry will be "to give his people the knowledge of salvation through the forgiveness of their sins." He connects God's Old Testament salvation with the forgiveness of sins through Jesus' sacrificial death on the cross. The covenant with Abraham, the killing of the Passover lamb, the sacrificial system in tabernacle and temple–all involved the shedding of blood. God's new covenant centers in the forgiveness of sins: "For I will forgive their wickedness and will remember their sins no more" (Jeremiah 31:34a). John's preaching and Baptism lead to repentance and the forgiveness of sins. Jesus will seal the new covenant with His blood shed on Calvary and offered in the upper room eucharistic meal.

Every time we join in singing the Benedictus, so appropriate for the Advent season, we sing a song of witness to one another within the body of Christ and to the world for whom Christ died, "those living in darkness and in the shadow of death" (Luke 1:79). So sing fervently and joyfully with tongue unloosed to praise God!

*Prayer:* Come, O long expected Jesus Born to set our people free;
From our fears and sins release us By your death on Calvary.
Israel's strength and consolation, Hope to all the earth impart,
Dear desire of ev'ry nation, Joy of ev'ry longing heart.
*LW* 22:1

Copyright © 1978 *Lutheran Book of Worship*

# The Word for Witness

## Reading: Luke 3:1–18

*Text:* The word of God came to John, son of Zechariah in the desert. Luke 3:2b

Our Advent series on Zechariah culminates in the public ministry of his son, John, in the wilderness of Judea. The announcement of Gabriel and his response left Zechariah with a mute witness. The birth of John loosed his tongue to witness of God's plan of salvation in the famous song, the Benedictus. Now in the prophetic ministry of John we see the word for witness.

Luke begins his account of the forerunner of Christ: "The word of God came to John, son of Zechariah in the desert." John appears from the desert looking and sounding like the Old Testament prophets. Prepared for his significant ministry by extended time with the Lord, John is given "the word of God" for his proclamation. That word constitutes his clear, candid, life-changing witness– "preaching a baptism of repentance for the forgiveness of sins" (Luke 3:3b). He prepares people for the One whose sandals he is unworthy to untie (Luke 3:16). He relies totally on the Word of God for his proclamation, whether addressing complacent descendants of Abraham living as a brood of vipers, tax collectors, or soldiers. All need repentance so the way is prepared for the Lord and all mankind may see God's salvation.

Do you use the Word of God for witness? As you hear and read it during this season of Advent preparation, do you place yourself under John's call for repentance? Do you hear his good news that the kingdom of God is at hand in the life, death, and resurrection of Jesus of Nazareth? And will you, as a forgiven baptized child of God, use that same Word of God for witness to Jesus as Savior that all mankind may see God's salvation?

*Prayer:* On Jordan's bank the Baptist's cry
Announces that the Lord is nigh;
Awake and hearken, for he brings
Glad tidings of the King of kings!

Then cleansed be every life from sin;
Make straight the way for God within;
And let us all our hearts prepare
For Christ to come and enter there.
*LW* 14:1–2

# Spiritual Warfare

## Reading: Ephesians 6:10–13

*Text:* For our struggle is not against flesh and blood but against . . . the spiritual forces of evil in the heavenly realms. Ephesians 6:12

Never believe that a vibrant witness to Jesus as Savior will come without opposition. From within our sinful flesh and from the outside world will come unparalleled attacks against setting the world ablaze with the Gospel because we are engaged in spiritual warfare. The next several devotions, based on this reality, will help to equip us with God's never-failing resources so the mission can flourish.

St. Paul, that much tested warrior for the Lord, puts the anticipated attacks in these words: "For our struggle is not against flesh and blood but against the rulers, against the authorities, against the powers of this dark world and against the spiritual forces of evil in the heavenly realms." He minces no words. He hides nothing. He makes no slick advertising appeal for workers, promising great fringe benefits (at least not in this world).

Paul lays it on the line. As we step forward, saved by God's grace for Christ's sake through faith, and willingly begin to share with our family, friends, neighbors, work associates, and those in our community, nation, and world the truth that we are saved only through faith in Jesus Christ, who paid the full price for our sins on the cross and rose from the grave on the third day, we can literally expect all hell to break loose. The devil will marshall all his evil angels in the spiritual realm to use the sinful world around us and our own sinful flesh against our witness. No wonder we need the full armor of God. More on that tomorrow.

*Prayer:* Stand up, stand up for Jesus As soldiers of the cross.
Lift high his royal banner. It must not suffer loss.
From vict'ry unto vict'ry His army He shall lead.
Till ev'ry foe is vanquished And Christ is Lord indeed.

Stand up, stand up for Jesus; The trumpet call obey;
Stand forth in mighty conflict In this his glorious day.
Let all the faithful serve him Against unnumbered foes;
Let courage rise with danger And strength to strength oppose.
*LW* 305:1–2

# Full Armor of God

### Reading: Ephesians 6:10–13

*Text:* Put on the full armor of God so that you can take your stand against the devil's schemes. Ephesians 6:11

We can almost picture St. Paul in prison chained to a Roman soldier. Aware of Satan's spiritual warfare against his own mission to the Gentiles and against the faithful witness of the persecuted churches to whom he is writing, Paul looks at that soldier and finds powerful imagery to encourage struggling Christians. Pointing them to God's grace through Christ, he writes, "Put on the full armor of God so that you can take your stand against the devil's schemes."

Without question, spiritual warfare is reality. But God is stronger still. He sent His Son forth to war. With His sinless life, Jesus defeated Satan's temptations in the wilderness and at Gethsemane. His atoning death on the cross sounded the death knell for sin, death, and the devil. Risen from the grave and ascended to heaven, Jesus rules from His throne in heaven and will return to take us home. God's Spirit brings us to faith through our Baptism in that Son, the victorious warrior.

Our loving father equips us to do battle against Satan by providing us with His full armor. In the next several devotions we will consider both the defensive and offensive weapons He provides out of His love and grace. But we can count on His full armor that more than equips us to do battle, provide a clear Gospel witness, and win the victory. Weak and defenseless on our own, we will be fully armed in His strength.

Knowing the power of Rome's armies with well-equipped soldiers, I can picture Paul smiling as he brings hope to struggling Christians through the far more powerful full armor of God to fight spiritual warfare and bring many to faith in the Savior.

*Prayer:* Stand up, stand up for Jesus; Stand in his strength alone;
The arm of flesh will fail you. You dare not trust your own.
Put on the Gospel armor; Each piece put on with prayer.
Where duty calls or danger, Be never wanting there.
*LW* 305:3

# Defensive Weapons: Belt of Truth

## Reading: Isaiah 11:1–5

*Text:* Stand firm then, with the belt of truth buckled around your waist. Ephesians 6:14a

Many coaches in both basketball and baseball believe that the best offense is a good defense. By that, they mean that a strong defense will keep the game close and create opportunities for the offense to explode. When players on defense have taken the best the opposing offense has to give, they demoralize them and put them on the defensive.

In similar fashion, St. Paul uses the defensive armor of the Roman soldier to equip the Christian warrior to withstand the enemy attack and then powerfully go on the offensive. First, he describes the belt of truth. The belt gathered in the soldier's tunic and gave him freedom to operate. Also his sword hung from his belt.

For the Christian soldier, the belt of truth provides integrity, a faithfulness, that brings strength in the face of temptation. Jesus referred to Himself as "the truth" (John 14:6). In Isaiah 11:5, the Messiah is described as girded with truth: "Righteousness will be his belt and faithfulness the sash around his waist."

Because Jesus, the only Way to the Father, lived the truth, exposing Satan's lies, and died with full integrity for our sins, He girds us up with His truth to withstand Satan's attacks and to live with faithfulness as witnesses. We have freedom of action and can respond quickly. Truth means that we are honest with ourselves and quick to confess our sins. Truth means that we constantly point outside of ourselves to the One who is our Truth. That is why we gather in worship with God's people around Word and Sacraments. We confess the credal truth in His presence and then are sent out to confess Jesus as the Truth before the world.

*Prayer:* Preserve your Word, O Savior To us this latter day,
And let your kingdom flourish; Enlarge your Church, we pray.
Oh, keep our faith from failing; Keep hope's bright star aglow.
Let nothing from truth turn us While living here below.
*LW* 337:1

## Defensive Weapons: Breastplate of Righteousness

### Reading: Isaiah 59:12–20

*Text:* With the breastplate of righteousness in place. Ephesians 6:14b

When a soldier in biblical times went into battle, his vital organs needed to be protected. Otherwise he was vulnerable to the stray arrow or the well-aimed spear. Consequently, every soldier was equipped with a breastplate to provide armored protection.

As we go forth to witness of salvation through faith in Jesus, we need protection from the arrows and spears of Satan. He will spare no effort to destroy both our faith and our witness. His lies can ruin our reputation and our credibility to speak Christ's name. St. Paul recommends that we have "the breastplate of righteousness in place."

In the first place, as sinners we need the righteousness of Christ. Isaiah sees the many offenses and sins of the people, including his own–rebellion, treachery, lies, and injustice. (Isaiah 59:12–15). The Lord was displeased. "So His own arm worked salvation for him, and His own righteousness sustained him. He put on righteousness as His breastplate" (Isaiah 59:16b–17a). He sent His own righteous Son to pay for our sins on Calvary. We receive by God's grace the righteousness of God through faith in Jesus Christ (Romans 3:22) and with the forgiveness of our sins.

Second, God enables us to do right by God and by others. We stand for good against evil, working for what is just and right in God's eyes. Our breastplate of Christ's righteousness protects us in our spiritual warfare so many will know Him as Savior.

*Prayer:*

Jesus, your blood and righteousness
My beauty are, my glorious dress;
Mid flaming worlds, in these arrayed,
With joy shall I lift up my head.

Bold shall I stand in that great day,
Cleansed and redeemed, no debt to pay;
For by your cross absolved I am
From sin and guilt, from fear and shame.
*LW* 362:1–2

# Defensive Weapons: Shield of Faith

## Reading: Hebrews 11:32–12:3

*Text:* In addition to all this, take up the shield of faith with which you can extinguish all the flaming arrows of the evil one. Ephesians 6:16

The shield was a vital front line of defense for the Roman soldiers. The Greek word used here is not the word for a comparatively small round shield but for the great oblong shield worn by the heavily armored soldier, a shield made of two sections of wood glued together, covered with leather, and soaked in water. One of the most dangerous weapons in ancient warfare was a fiery dart with a point dipped in pitch and set ablaze. But the oblong shield could easily extinguish the fire.

Paul writes for the Christian warrior, "Take up the shield of faith with which you can extinguish the flaming arrows of the evil one." Satan attacks our witness with frightening intensity like fiery darts. Lies are told. Rumors fly about our church or character. Others may scoff at our words or seem indifferent. We may be distracted by problems at home or work. But God provides the shield of faith for the battle. Faith is a gift of God, not of works, lest anyone should boast. The object of faith is Jesus Christ, crucified and risen. Our baptismal faith, strengthened by regular study of the Word and worship with God's people around Word and Sacraments, is solid. Satan's fiery arrows are extinguished.

And that faith stands us in good stead when we are tried and tested. Like the great heroes of faith in Hebrews 11, God enables us to persevere in the most difficult circumstances, surrounded by a great cloud of witnesses, fixing "our eyes on Jesus, the author and perfecter of our faith who for the joy set before Him endured the cross, scorning its shame" (Hebrews 12:2). With the shield of faith we march forward to help set the world ablaze with the saving Gospel of our Lord.

*Prayer:* In you, Lord, I have put my trust;
Leave me not helpless in the dust,
Let me not be confounded.
Let in your Word my faith, O Lord,
Be always firmly grounded.
*LW* 406:1

# Defensive Weapons: Helmet of Salvation

## Reading: Ephesians 1:7–14

*Text:* Take the helmet of salvation. Ephesians 6:17a

Many an ancient soldier survived blow after blow to his body, protected by breastplate and shield, only to fall mortally wounded by an arrow, spear, or sword striking the unprotected head. For this reason, the helmet was provided as a vital part of the soldier's armor, worn also in victory marches through the conquered city.

St. Paul simply counsels the Ephesian Christians engaged in spiritual warfare, "Take the helmet of salvation." How Satan plays with our heads as we attempt to witness our faith! He raises doubts about our faith. He tells us we are inadequate to the task because we lack knowledge or the right words. He tries to make us wallow in guilt for sins already forgiven. He distracts our attention from Jesus and our task and nudges us toward worldly concerns and temptations. Even when we think we are protecting our actions from disobedience, Satan can still get inside our head.

How we need the helmet of salvation! Paul has already described God's salvation in an earlier chapter of Ephesians: "In Him we have redemption through His blood, the forgiveness of sins in accordance with the riches of God's grace" (Ephesians 1:7). To the Gentile believers he adds, "And you also were included in Christ when you heard the word of truth, the gospel of your salvation" (Ephesians 1:13a).

Our salvation in Christ as a helmet makes us confident to face spiritual warfare. We are motivated to serve the One who died for and rescued us. We want others to don the same helmet for their salvation and courage in the battle.

*Prayer:* Stand up, stand up for Jesus;
Stand in his strength alone;
The arm of flesh will fail you,
You dare not trust your own.
Put on the Gospel armor;
Each piece put on with prayer.
Where duty calls or danger,
Be never wanting there.
*LW* 305:3

# Offensive Weapons: Ready Sandals

## Reading: Romans 10:6–15

*Text:* And with your feet fitted with the gospel of peace. Ephesians 6:15

While defensive armor plays a very important role for soldiers and modern day Christians, offensive weapons are needed to carry the battle to the enemy and ultimately win the victory. No sports team can ever win a game without putting points or runs on the scoreboard. Since God calls us to witness our faith in Jesus Christ so unbelievers can be snatched from the jaws of hell by the power of God's Spirit, we also need God's offensive weapons.

St. Paul describes this armor, "and with your feet fitted with the gospel of peace." One could argue that the right kind of sandals or boots in modern armies could be considered defensive armor along with belts, breastplates, shields, and helmets. Certainly comfortable and protective footwear is basic to effective performance.

But Scripture talks about beautiful feet that run to bring good tidings of God's salvation. Isaiah 52:7 introduces the concept. The right sandals prepare us to share the good news. Peter writes, "But in your hearts set apart Christ as Lord. Always be prepared to give an answer to everyone who asks you to give the reason for the hope that you have" (1 Peter 3:15).

Most important, Paul, in his letter to the Romans, writes passionately about his desire for Israel and the Gentiles to be saved, "And how can they hear without someone preaching to them? And how can they preach unless they are sent? As it is written, 'How beautiful are the feet of those who bring good news'" (Romans 10:14c–15). Yes, sandals ready to bring the gospel of peace are God's offensive weapons. God provides the sandals. God prepares our hearts and our lips through His Son by His grace. What are we waiting for?

*Prayer:* Send now, O Lord, to ev'ry place
Swift messengers before your face,
The heralds of your wondrous grace,
Where you yourself will come.

To bring good news to souls in sin,
The bruised and broken hearts to win;
In ev'ry place to bring them in
Where you yourself will come.
*LW* 316:1, 3

# Offensive Weapons: Sword of the Spirit

## Reading: Ephesians 4:11–16

*Text:* Take . . . the sword of the Spirit which is the word of God. And pray in the Spirit on all occasions with all kinds of prayers and requests. Ephesians 6:17b–18

The sword is clearly an offensive weapon. Roman soldiers displayed offensive daring as they attacked the enemy and often won the victory. St. Paul identifies this weapon for Christians engaged in spiritual warfare as "the sword of the Spirit which is the word of God."

Picture first how Jesus wielded the sword of the Word as He faced Satan's temptation in the wilderness. Satan could not stand against that Word. Read Psalm 119, which is all about the words and commands of God. The psalmist writes, "I have hidden Your word in my heart that I might not sin" (Psalm 119:11). Paul writes to the Colossians, "Let the word of Christ dwell in you richly as you teach and admonish one another with all wisdom, and as you sing psalms, hymns, and spiritual songs with gratitude in your hearts to God" (Colossians 3:16).

This corporate use of the Word as the sword of the Spirit recalls Paul's earlier teaching in Ephesians about apostles, prophets, evangelists, pastors, and teachers preparing "God's people for works of service so that the body of Christ may be built up" (Ephesians 4:12). Together in one body, around the Word and Sacraments, we gain spiritual maturity, "no longer infants tossed back and forth by the waves, and blown here and there by every wind of teaching and by the cunning and craftiness of men in their deceitful schemery." Instead, speaking the truth in love, we will in all things grow up into Him who is the Head, that is Christ" (Ephesians 4:14–15).

Through the Word and prayer, the Spirit works to give us a mighty offensive weapon. The sword of the Spirit brings many to saving faith in Jesus the Christ. Thank God for His full armor–both defensive and offensive–to give us victory in spiritual warfare for the sake of Christ's mission to the world.

*Prayer:* Gird each one with the Spirit's sword,
The sword of your own deathless Word,
And make them conqu'rors, conqu'ring Lord,
Where you yourself will come.
*LW* 316:5

# Bearing Witness to the Light

**Reading: John 1:6–8, 19–28**

*Text:* He came as a witness to testify concerning that light. John 1:7a

The lights of Christmas—Advent candles, decorated street lamps, thousands of outdoor Christmas lights in dazzling colors, Christmas tree light strands, Bethlehem stars everywhere. These lights bring temporary joy and comfort in the darkness of our world. But do the lights of Christmas sometimes detract from the one Light shining forever to defeat the dreadful darkness of sin?

John came as a man sent from God into a dark world. He came bearing witness to that one Light, Jesus Christ. Many looked to John as the Light. They wanted to label him as the Messiah, or at least as Elijah or the prophet. John could have accepted the praise and pointed to himself as the shining Light, but he consistently refused to identify himself as more than a "voice . . . calling in the desert" (John 1:23). As John's gospel says, "He himself was not the light; he came only as a witness to the light" (John 1:8). And how well he served to point to Jesus as the Light of the world!

In the midst of Christmas lights and so many "stars" who draw attention to themselves as famous, important people, we are sorely tempted to seek recognition. We often secretly think that our own light shines rather brightly. But John's example serves to convict us of pride.

On our own, by nature, we live in darkness. We have no light. God's Son has shined brightly through His birth, life, death, and resurrection. He continues to bring light through His Word and Sacraments. By God's grace He has shined in our hearts with His light. We now recognize that whatever light we have is only reflected from Him. So we can joyfully bear witness to Jesus Christ, the Light of the world, at Christmas and all year long.

*Prayer:* The people that in darkness sat
A glorious light have seen;
The light has shined on them who long
In shades of death have been.
*LW* 77:1

# Christmas Witness of Home and Heart

**Reading: Luke 1:46–55**

*Text:* Unless the LORD builds the house, its builders labor in vain. Psalm 127:1

We love to prepare our house for Christmas and welcome family and friends into our home. A few years ago, after decorating and cleaning our house for a visit from our Minnesota family, we developed a major plumbing problem with a leak in the basement ceiling that resulted in plumbers spending four days taking out fixtures on all floors and cutting holes in walls and ceilings. Would our house be ready for the visit? No matter how beautiful our house looked on the outside, we needed to address the plumbing problems on the inside. I thought of the psalmist's words, "Unless the LORD builds the house, its builders labor in vain."

I found symbolism here for what God is doing in my life this Advent. My worship and witness may look good on the outside, but when my heart has major problems with selfishness or bitterness or indifference, I need confession of my sin and absolution from the God who sent His Son to Bethlehem and Calvary for me. Only God can tear down the walls of my heart, find the true problem, heal, and restore my soul. "Unless the LORD builds the house, its builders labor in vain."

That's the spirit of Mary's song, known as the Magnificat. "My soul magnifies the Lord, and my spirit rejoices in God my Savior, for He has been mindful of the humble state of His servant" (Luke 1:46–47). She goes on to describe how God scatters those who are proud in their inmost hearts and lifts up the humble.

By the way, the plumbers fixed the problem and restored our house just in time for a special family Christmas. And with hearts forgiven and restored, I pray that both your home and your heart will offer a joyful Christmas witness to the Savior.

*Prayer:* Ah, dearest Jesus, holy child
Make thee a bed, soft, undefiled
Within my heart that it may be
A quiet chamber kept for thee.
*LW* 38:5

Copyright © 1978 *Lutheran Book of Worship*

# Microwave Powerless

## Reading: 1 Corinthians 1:26–2:5

*Text:* "Not by might nor by power, but by My Spirit," says the LORD Almighty. Zechariah 4:6

Day after day our microwave provided cooking power—coffee heated, leftovers warmed up, bacon made crisp, popcorn popped. Last night, while watching a baseball game, I decided to pop some popcorn in the microwave during a commercial. I could hear the microwave timer ending the cycle. Opening the door, I was shocked at the limp package totally unpopped. I tried a different package with the same results. Dismayed, I realized that we were "microwave powerless."

When we undertake projects for the Lord and His Church—witnessing, serving in the community, ushering, teaching Sunday School, we may find some success and satisfaction in our own power. We might even come to expect the reliability of our own efforts. Then we come up short. What we always counted on doesn't work. We try harder and exhaust ourselves. We grow discouraged. Dismayed, we finally accept that we are powerless.

As God's exiled people in Babylon return home and attempt to rebuild the temple, their leader, Zerubbabel, realizes that he does not have the power of David or Solomon, that the temple will not have the same grandeur, and that the people are weak. But the angel of the Lord brings encouragement: "'Not by might nor by power but by my Spirit,' says the LORD Almighty."

In a similar fashion, God's New Testament people in Corinth faced a mighty Roman Empire and much hostility from Jews and Greeks alike. St. Paul encourages them, "God chose the weak things of the world to shame the strong" (1 Corinthians 1:27b). He points to Christ-crucified, the power of God. Perhaps it is not so bad to be "microwave powerless" when you have Christ as power for your witness!

*Prayer:* "Come unto me, ye fainting,
And I will give you life."
O cheering voice of Jesus,
Which comes to aid our strife!
The foe is stern and eager,
The fight is fierce and long;
But thou hast made us mighty
And stronger than the strong.
*LW* 345:3

# Power Restored

**Reading: Acts 1:6–11**

*Text:* "But you will receive power when the Holy Spirit comes on you." Acts 1:8a

"Microwave powerless!" No popcorn. That microwave joined today's trash pickup, and this morning we purchased a brand-new microwave, and power was restored. Already one of those popcorn packages has been popped and enjoyed. We have confidence in our new microwave's power.

Our power fails. We cannot generate our own power to save ourselves, believe, or live for God. Our old self needs the trash bin, dead and useless. But God restores power. His Son went to the cross in weakness and humility, but He won the victory over sin, death, and Satan, demonstrated by the power of His resurrection. God's Holy Spirit brings us to faith and gives power for a new life of service and witness.

To the still confused disciples, right before His ascension into heaven, Jesus promises, "But you will receive power when the Holy Spirit comes on you." For what purpose? "And you will be My witnesses in Jerusalem, and in all Judea and Samaria, and to the ends of the earth" (Acts 1:8). The early Church had full power restored and they boldly took the Gospel message to the ends of the earth.

Christ's resurrection power is ours through Baptism. We plug into His power source as we read His Word and receive His body and blood in Holy Communion. Power restored, we don't have to stop with popcorn, but literally explode with the dynamite of His Gospel in our daily witness and service. Are you trying to witness "microwave powerless" or are you witnessing with full power restored as a forgiven baptized child of God, clinging to the Savior's cross and empty tomb?

*Prayer:* His strength within my weakness
Will make me bold to say
How his redeeming power
Transforms my stubborn clay;
His touch of fire ignites me,
With courage I am sent,
My tongue-tied silence broken,
With grace made eloquent.
*LW* 320:3

Copyright © 1982 Concordia Publishing House

December 21

# Prayer Bench

## Reading: 1 Peter 3:8–16

*Text:* "For the eyes of the Lord are on the righteous and His ears are attentive to their prayers." 1 Peter 3:12

A large Midwestern church places major emphasis on involving individual Christians to reach the lost. They designate a particular place in their building where members go to meet invited guests. They call this area the "prayer bench." Waiting Christians are encouraged to pray for their invited friend that they would come and be open to the Spirit working through God's Word to bring them to saving faith in Jesus Christ. The "prayer bench" symbolizes the importance of prayer in Christian witness. Only God's grace can bring saving faith to people without Christ. Only God's grace can strengthen and equip us for outreach.

St. Peter emphasizes the importance of prayer in the Christian life for believers suffering because of their faith. He quotes Psalm 34, "For the eyes of the Lord are on the righteous and His ears are attentive to their prayers." Then he ties that prayer to their witness of word and deed: "But in your hearts set apart Christ as Lord. Always be prepared to give an answer to everyone who asks you to give the reason for the hope that you have. But do this with gentleness and respect, keeping a clear conscience, so that those who speak maliciously against your good behavior in Christ may be ashamed of their slander" (1 Peter 3:15–16). The Lord's ears are attentive to our prayers for courageous witness to Christ-crucified, the hope inside, by our words and our example.

Forgiven through Christ's death on the cross, refreshed and emboldened through Word and Sacraments, we go frequently to our "prayer bench" where we pray for witness opportunities, wisdom and courage to bear testimony to Jesus Christ as the only way to salvation, and the working of God's Spirit in the heart of the person we desire to reach with gentleness and respect.

*Prayer:* Christians, while on earth abiding,
Let us never cease to pray,
Firmly in the Lord confiding
As our parents in their day.
Be the children's voices raised
To the God their parents praised.
May his blessing, failing never,
Rest upon his people ever.
*LW* 434:1

# Learning to Acclaim Him

**Reading: Psalm 89:1–18**

*Text:* Blessed are those who have learned to acclaim You, who walk in the light of Your presence. Psalm 89:15

What does it take to bear bold witness to Christ in a world that regularly rejects and ridicules the only true God—Father, Son, and Holy Spirit? The psalmist, writing at the time of the destruction of Jerusalem and the impending Babylonian captivity, laments the apparent end of the Davidic dynasty and wonders if God has forgotten His covenant promises.

Yet he prefaces his lament with a wonderful song of praise to a faithful covenant God whose great love lasts forever. In that context, he writes, "Blessed are those who have learned to acclaim You, who walk in the light of Your presence." Learing to acclaim Him! That is our challenge as we desire to set the world ablaze with Christ.

You see, Israel forgot to acclaim God and went after other gods of wood and stone. Israel, rather than walking in the light of God's presence, walked in darkness. The result was the fall of Israel and then Judah, followed by a Babylonian captivity. We also forget to acclaim Him and often walk in the darkness of sin. No wonder the world seems to be winning and our feeble witness swallowed up by the loud voices of unbelief.

But God, whose love endures forever, never renounced His covenant nor abandoned His people. He would restore the land to His remnant people, and from David's seed send His only Son to victory on the cross, and from the empty tomb beam the light of His presence into a new creation. His Spirit in Word and Sacraments teaches us to acclaim Him and walk in the light of His presence. Learning to acclaim Him, we spread the light of Christ, and many will acclaim Him as Savior and Lord!

*Prayer:* Then raise to Christ a mighty song,
And shout his name, his glories tell!
Sing, heav'nly host, your praise prolong,
And all on earth, your anthem swell!
All hail, O Lamb for sinners slain!
Forever let the song ascend!
All hail, O Lamb enthroned to reign!
All hail, all hail! Amen, Amen.
*LW* 83:4

December 23

# Laughter As Witness

## Reading: Psalm 126

*Text:* Then our mouth was filled with laughter, and our tongues with shouts of joy. Psalm 126:2 (ESV)

A good friend and church leader has spent a lifetime encouraging laughter in the church. In a recent issue of *Encore Times*, a publication of the Association for Older Adults (ALOA), his address to an Arizona Lutherhostel is summarized. The healing qualities of laughter: "Laughter heals when it points to the cross and an empty tomb. . . . Laughter heals when it is seen as a gift of God; when it reminds us of our humanness. Laughter heals when it is focused on ourselves and not on others. Laughter heals when it relieves tension or removes barriers or when it affirms others." In this devotion, we see laughter as witness to others needing Christ.

The psalmist responds to the "great things" the Lord has done for us, especially the return from Babylonian captivity to Zion, with these words: "Then our mouth was filled with laughter, and our tongues with shouts of joy." That laughter was a witness to their captors and the people around them. Their tears of sorrow over their rebellion had been replaced with shouts of joy as witness: "Then they said among the nations, 'The LORD has done great things for them'" (Psalm 126:2b). Laughter and joy because of God's salvation through the promised Messiah!

Have you thought about laughter as witness–to your family, your church, your neighborhood, your co-workers? You can laugh at your own frailties, physical, mental, and emotional, because you have a caring Creator, a redeeming Savior, and a healing Spirit. You can rejoice, even in a sinful world filled with heavy burdens, because of God's healing love in Christ. And your laughter bears witness to Jesus Christ, who celebrated at the wedding of Cana and with His disciples in the post-resurrection upper room. You might just surprise many people as you set the world ablaze with your laughter in Christ!

*Prayer:* Blessed children, saints, elect of God,
Globe-encircling cloud of witnesses:
We have heard the Christmas angels,
We have seen the Easter sunrise,
Cried with joy when Christ began his reign.
Catch the vision! Share the glory!
Show the captives, tell them: Christ is here!
*SP* 58:1

Copyright © 1986 Concordia Publishing House

# Making Known Abroad

**Reading: Luke 2:15–20**

*Text:* And when they had seen it, they made known abroad the saying which was told them concerning this child. Luke 2:17 (KJV)

Everything important about setting the world ablaze with the Gospel of Jesus Christ can be found in the story of the shepherds on that first Christmas Eve. Simple folk, they tended their flocks by night, not suspecting the momentous Bethlehem birth. To them, solely by God's grace, came the angel of the Lord with a life-changing message: "Unto you is born this day in the city of David a Savior, which is Christ the Lord" (Luke 2:11 KJV). The angelic host praised God in the heavens. The same saving message comes to us this Christmas.

Their spontaneous and unanimous response to that message: "Let us now go even unto Bethlehem and see this thing which is come to pass." And they came with haste, and found Mary and Joseph, and the Babe lying in a manger" (Luke 2:15–16 KJV). Moved by the saving message, we come again and again to kneel at the manger, which prefigured the wood of His cross. We see Him with our own eyes at the baptismal font, the lectern, and the altar table of His body and blood.

The shepherds rose from their worship at the manger to witness: "And when they had seen it, they made known abroad the saying which was told them concerning this child." Good tidings of great joy, which shall be to all people. A Savior born with swaddling clothes and a manger as a sign. Glory to God in the highest and on earth peace, good will toward men. The response by the Spirit's power: "And all they that heard it wondered at those things which were told them by the shepherds" (Luke 2:18 KJV).

We see. We make known abroad. The message of Christ, the Savior, carries its own saving power to all people walking in the darkness of sin. The Spirit brings the response in many hearts through our testimony. A world ablaze with the Gospel of Jesus Christ!

*Prayer:* Look, look, dear friends, look over there!
What lies within that manger bare?
Who is that lovely little one?
The baby Jesus, God's dear Son.
*LW* 37:7

Copyright © 1978 *Lutheran Book of Worship*

December 25

# Christmas in Togo

## Reading: Luke 2:8–20

*Text:* Suddenly a great company of the heavenly host appeared with the angel, praising God. Luke 2:13

Missionaries in Togo, Africa describe how the Togolese celebrate Christmas. After starting with an all night service of praise, prayer, and dancing under a moonlit sky, waiting for the glory of Christmas morning, a gathering of Lutheran congregations in the village of Sissick settle themselves on wood benches in the circle of a huge mango tree's shade, after having refreshed themselves with tchak pa (a locally made millet drink) and a meal with African peanut sauce. Their account continues:

"Drums were out and ready, and the sun was already getting high in the sky. Quietly the drums began, but as soon as the dancers formed their ring around the mango tree, the beats picked up and the real dancing began. And they danced and danced. We read the Christmas story, sang songs of praise, and heard the pastor's message as well, but nothing seemed to shout praises to God so loudly as the dancing. As is the custom here, the next day (Sunday) was spent celebrating baptisms, confirmations, and the burning of fetishes. Fetishes are items that are used in protection from evil spirits in the traditional religion. Burning them is truly a sign of seeking a right relationship with God. At the service, 20 people (babies and adults) were brought into God's family through Baptism."

Think of your fellow believers in Togo as you celebrate the Savior's birth this Christmas Day. Like the angel choirs singing praises of "Glory to God in the highest," they join you in praises to God for the gift of His Son as our only Savior from sin. Their singing and dancing of joyful celebration are backed by their renunciation of their former pagan customs and their bold affirmation of their baptismal faith. Like them, we celebrate, receive God's gracious forgiveness, and share our faith in the Christ Child with others.

*Prayer:* My heart for very joy now leaps;
My voice no longer silence keeps;
I too must join the angel throng
To sing with joy his cradlesong.
*LW* 38:6

Copyright © 1978 *Lutheran Book of Worship*

# Christmas Ablaze

## Reading: Luke 2:1–8

*Text:* And she gave birth to her firstborn, a son. She wrapped Him in cloths and placed Him in a manger, because there was no room for them in the inn. Luke 2:7

A missionary in Krygystan writes this account about a Christmastime visit to a small village where nineteen people gathered and eight were baptized, one of whom desires to study God's Word to be a missionary:

"Visiting this group, we sat in a tiny, cold, and dark room. It had no tree, no open gifts strewn about, no Christmas candles, or nativity sets. The smell was not of pine but rather of unwashed bodies. And yet hope was there–hope, light, and grace. As I listened to fathers tell of their faith in Jesus and ask that they and their children be baptized, as I heard them bravely say that Christ was more important than their traditions and their relationships with family or friends, my heart melted within me. Here was Christmas. Here was life.

"I began to think about the first Christmas. God came down to us in a place very much like that room in Lesnoye. It was cold, smelly, and dark. Mary and Joseph were probably not very clean, and certainly the shepherds and animals were filthy. None of that mattered at all, did it? Not then and not now."

As we gather in our festively decorated homes and candlelit churches to celebrate the Savior's birth, this account from a missionary may give us pause for reflection. The familiar Christmas story of that Bethlehem birth in a manger centuries ago takes on new meaning. The Son of God is born as a real human being–in very humble circumstances–to begin His journey to a cruel cross where He will die between two common criminals for our salvation.

That saving message sets the whole world ablaze, extending to a tiny, cold, and dark room in a remote village. Perhaps their joy and desire for Baptism will also help us this year to celebrate a Christmas ablaze with missionary zeal.

*Prayer:* The Light Eternal breaking through,
Made the world to gleam anew;
His beams have pierced the core of night,
He makes us children of the light. Alleluia!
*LW* 35:4

Copyright © 1978 Concordia Publishing House

December 27

# Shelter

## Reading: Psalm 91

*Text:* He who dwells in the shelter of the Most High will rest in the shadow of the Almighty. Psalm 91:1

Summer sizzles in St. Louis. The combination of heat, humidity, and a blazing sun often makes us scurry for any kind of shelter—a tree, an overhanging roof to provide shadow from the sun, or an air-conditioned haven in car or house. How refreshing and welcoming is that shelter!

Psalm 91, which is filled with God's promises and will provide the basis for the next few devotions, begins with the welcome promise of shelter. The psalmist faces an unbelievable combination of perils—attacks from enemies, physical disease and plagues, the fears of night and day. Exhausted physically, mentally, emotionally, and spiritually, he points to God's unfailing promise: "He who dwells in the shelter of the Most High will rest in the shadow of the Almighty." How refreshing and welcoming is that shelter!

When we go on God's mission of setting the world ablaze with Christ, we can expect every sort of peril, far worse than heat and humidity. Our sins press in on us as burdens. Our physical energy is depleted, sometimes by illness, often by exhaustion. Our relationships with others sometimes sour or become adversarial, leaving us alone. Our mental and emotional stability is upset by Satan's attacks and the sense of overwhelming responsibilities. We scurry for shelter of any kind from the blazing sun of adversity. None is adequate or lasting until we find rest as repentant sinners in God's unfailing promise through the death and resurrection of Jesus Christ: "He who dwells in the shelter of the Most High will rest in the shadow of the Almighty." Forgiveness. Rest. Renewal. Energy for witness. How refreshing and welcoming is that shelter!

*Prayer:* Lord Jesus, since you love me,
Now spread your wings above me
And shield me from alarm.
Let angel guards sing o'er me:
The child of God shall meet no harm.
*LW* 485:4

# Refuge

## Reading: Psalm 91:2–8

*Text:* I will say of the LORD, "He is my refuge and my fortress, my God, in whom I trust." Psalm 91:2

The last few hurricane seasons have produced multiple deadly storms striking the Atlantic and Gulf coasts of the southern United States. Reeling from devastation, weary residents have learned to brace themselves for powerful hurricanes. In each case, many people evacuate their homes and seek refuge somewhere with sturdy walls and at a safe distance. How they need refuge!

The psalmist continues his rehearsal of the promises of God in Psalm 91. In so many devious ways, enemies attack and leave God's people reeling with physical and mental exhaustion, yet still needing to brace themselves for the next onslaught. How they need refuge! And the psalmist responds with life-giving words: "I will say of the LORD, 'He is my refuge and my fortress, my God in whom I trust.'" Always there for His people. Always a completely safe refuge, offering forgiveness and protection. Always a mighty, impregnable fortress.

In today's world filled with international terrorism, self-seeking, power-hungry greed, and open attacks against the Church of Jesus Christ, we find ourselves reeling and exhausted from our daily lives of service and witness. We brace ourselves for the next attack and grow discouraged. How we need a refuge!

And our loving God responds with Himself as mighty fortress and refuge, sending His Son, Jesus Christ, the valiant one, to fight for us and defeat the old evil foe through His death on the cross. Trusting Him for salvation, we seek refuge in His forgiveness and offer that same refuge to all those battered by the storms of life in a sinful world. How they need a refuge, our refuge, which is Christ!

*Prayer:* Who trusts in God a strong abode
In heav'n and earth possesses;
Who looks in love to Christ above,
No fear that heart oppresses.
In you alone, dear Lord, we own
Sweet hope and consolation,
Our shield from foes, our balm for woes,
Our great and sure salvation.
*LW* 414:1

December 29

# Rescue

## Reading: Psalm 91:9–16

*Text:* "Because he loves Me," says the LORD, "I will rescue him." Psalm 91:14

When we go on mission for our Lord, we find great comfort in knowing that He provides both shelter from the blazing sun of adversity and refuge from the attacks of Satan. However, that very mission takes us right out into the danger-filled world in which we live. Sometimes, unable to find shelter or retreat to a refuge, we simply need rescue like a medical corpsman coming to the aid of a soldier fallen in battle or a lifeguard coming to save a swimmer caught in a deadly undertow.

The psalmist once again brings an unfailing promise to God's people, who sometimes find themselves caught like a bird in a trap or struck by an arrow on the battlefield: " 'Because he loves Me,' says the LORD, 'I will rescue him.' " Wounded, helpless, vulnerable, God's people receive their rescuer with thanksgiving and seek to recover so they can rejoin the battle and rescue someone else in need. The psalmist describes God's continuous rescue for the believer: "He will call upon Me, and I will answer him; I will be with him in trouble, I will deliver him and honor him. With long life will I satisfy him and show him My salvation" (Psalm 91:15–16).

As we witness and when we fall wounded, whether because of our sin, the enemy's attack, or the depletion of our own resources, we look to the Rescuer, Jesus Christ. Like a medical corpsman or a lifeguard, He put His own life at risk to rescue us and, in reality, gave His life on the cross in payment for our sin in order to rescue us from sin, death, and the devil. Rescued and thankful, we join His rescue team, the Church, on a mission to bring salvation to the world through our witness and service. He will answer our prayers, be with us in trouble, and bring us deliverance as long as we live until we experience His salvation eternally.

*Prayer:* See all our sins on Jesus laid;
The Lamb has made us whole.
His soul was once an off'ring made
For ev'ry human soul.
*LW* 276:6

# Joy to the World

## Reading: Psalm 100

*Text:* But the angel said to them, "Do not be afraid. I bring you good news of great joy that will be for all the people." Luke 2:10

A few years ago I was privileged to ride on the Lutheran Hour float in the Tournament of Roses Parade in Pasadena, California. The theme of the float was "Joy to the World, the Lord Has Come." The float covered with flowers, seeds, and grasses featured candles, with inset pictures of the Nativity, trumpets, and a music scroll with notes. While the float made its way along the parade route, a contemporary musical version of "Joy to the World" played for all to hear.

The crowds in every set of bleachers and curbside viewing area included many people who joined in the singing of the familiar carol . . . people from "every nation and tribe"—football fans from Nebraska, African Americans, Hispanics, and Asians, a young woman in a wheelchair singing her heart out. As the only religious float in the parade during the months after the tragic terrorist attacks of September 11, 2001, amidst renewed patriotism, the float's theme and song seemed to strike a deep spiritual chord in people's hearts, causing them to sing from memory the powerful words of "Joy to the World."

I felt the Spirit of God touching my heart as I sang and directed the crowds over and over again as the parade route unfolded. It symbolized how God wants us to reach out to the multitudes of all nations with the "good news of great joy" in a freedom of expression springing from the spontaneity of a New Year's Day parade.

In a world scarred by terrorist violence, open blasphemy of the Christian faith, and rampant rebellion against God's Law, the angel's message of a Savior, humbly born in Bethlehem's manger to save the world from its sin, reaches our hearts in need of forgiveness and fills our lips with a song of joy for the world—The Lord has come as your Savior too.

*Prayer:* Joy to the world, the Lord is come!
Let earth receive its King;
Let ev'ry heart prepare him room
And heav'n and nature sing; And heav'n and nature sing.
And heav'n and heav'n and nature sing.
*LW* 53:1

# New Year's Eve Witness

**Reading: John 21:20–25**

*Text:* This is the disciple who is bearing witness about these things, . . . and we know that his testimony is true. John 21:24 (ESV)

Another year is coming to a close, and are you preparing to celebrate on New Year's Eve? What kind of witness to Jesus Christ do you bring? I am not referring to your manner of celebrating or where you celebrate (although a distinct positive or negative impression is given by your behavior). Rather, these Ablaze! devotions have focused on God's light shining in our repentant hearts and through us to others with the saving Gospel of Jesus Christ. The Scripture texts have shaped our attitudes, our perspectives, our words, and our actions toward a daily, persistent, joyful witness to Jesus in our twenty-first century world alongside other Christians worldwide.

John writes about himself in the closing verses of his gospel, "This is the disciple who is bearing witness about these things, . . . and we know that his testimony is true." John, in his old age, remembers standing forgiven with Peter and the other disciples in the presence of the risen Christ, having just eaten a breakfast of fresh fish miraculously caught at Jesus' command and cooked on a charcoal fire. By the Spirit's power, he has written the marvelous account of the Word-made-flesh, the Light of the world, the resurrection and the life—Jesus, the Lamb of God, who takes away the sin of the world. John has much to celebrate, and his witness is true.

His witness continues through us as we prepare to enter a new year of God's grace. The world is not big enough to contain the books that could be written about Jesus' actions on our behalf, but there is room for our stories about God's faithfulness in our lives. And the true testimony flowing from God's Word and Sacraments in the fellowship of believers will set the world ablaze with Jesus Christ as the only way to salvation. With John, we have much to celebrate this New Year's Eve as our witness to Jesus continues.

*Prayer:* We gather up in this brief hour
The mem'ry of your mercies:
Your wondrous goodness, love, and pow'r
Our grateful song rehearses.
*LW* 181:3

## Bibliography

Buford, Bob. *Half Time*. Grand Rapids: Zondervan Publishing House, 1994. Copyright Robert P. Buford, 1994. (Devotions June 3–25)

Henderson, David W. *Culture Shift*. Grand Rapids: Baker Books, 1998. (Devotions October 28–30)

Johnston, Graham. *Preaching to a Postmodern World*. Grand Rapids: Baker Books, 2001. (Devotions October 4–14)

McNeal, Reggie. *The Present Future*. San Francisco: Jossey-Bass, A Wiley Imprint, 2003. (Devotions July 5–19)

Peterson, Eugene. *The Message*, Introduction pp. 9–11. Colorado Springs: Nav Press, 2002. (Devotions July 26–August 3)